OCEAN TO OCEAN

———•———

Sandford Fleming's Expedition
Through
CANADA IN 1872.

———•———

BEING A DIARY KEPT DURING A JOURNEY FROM

THE ATLANTIC TO THE PACIFIC

*With the Expedition of the Engineer-in-Chief of the
Canadian Pacific and Intercolonial Railways.*

———

BY

THE Revd. GEORGE M. GRANT,
OF HALIFAX, N. S.,
SECRETARY TO THE EXPEDITION.

———•———

WITH SIXTY ILLUSTRATIONS.

———•———

PROSPERO

CANADIAN COLLECTION

**TORONTO
2000**

Ocean to Ocean:
Sanford Fleming's Expedition
Through Canada in 1872

This edition first published by
Prospero Books in 2000
from the 1873 James Campbell & Son edition

Canadian Cataloguing in Publication Data

Grant, George M. (George Monro), 1835-1902
Ocean to Ocean:
Sanford Fleming's expedition through Canada in 1872...

(Prospero Canadian Collection)
Facsim. reprint.
Originally published: Toronto: J. Campbell, 1873.
ISBN 1-55267-138-0

1. Canada - Description and travel.
2. Overland journeys to the Pacific.
3. Fleming, Sanford, Sir, 1827-1915.
I. Title. II. Series.
FC73.G72 2000   917.10451   C00-931940-9
F1015.G72 2000

Prospero Books
90 Ronson Drive, Toronto, Ontario, Canada
M9W 1C1

Printed on acid free paper

Printed in Canada by Webcom Ltd.

SALMON COVE, NASSE RIVER, BRITISH COLUMBIA

TO THE PUBLIC.

Our preface consists of an apology to you, and of thanks to friends.

The book, except the first chapter and the last, is simply a Diary written as we journeyed. It is a round unvarnish'd tale, and we hope that its truthfulness may compensate for its defects.

We know that it has many literary mistakes. You will attribute them all to the circumstances under which it was written, and to the fact that the writer, living a thousand miles away from the printer, had no sufficient opportunities to correct the proofs.

The illustrations are mainly from photographs and on this account may be considered of special interest.

Our maps of the country, east of the Rocky Mountains, are mainly from Captain Palliser's; those of the Pacific slope from Governor Trutch's map of British Columbia. For a number of the plates illustrating the Dawson route we are indebted to Mr. Desbarats and his artists; to the latter and to a kind lady in Ottawa, for making pictures out of our own rude but, we believe, faithful outlines.

Our best thanks are due to Professor Daniel Wilson for his sketches of Nepigon Bay and River, and to Mrs. Hopkins for permitting the publisher to copy her wonderful painting of " Running a Rapid;" unfortunately, the beauty of the picture has been marred in reducing it to so small a scale. Finally, we thank those who made the sketches of Bute Inlet and the Hamathco River ; and all and sundry who kindly assisted us in one way or another.

CONTENTS.

....

CHAPTER I.

CHAPTER II.

FROM HALIFAX, NOVA SCOTIA, TO THUNDER BAY, LAKE SUPERIOR.

CHAPTER III.

FROM THUNDER BAY TO FORT GARRY.

CHAPTER IV.

PROVINCE OF MANITOBA.

CONTENTS.

CHAPTER XI.

FROM KAMLOOPS TO THE SEA.

CHAPTER XII.

THE COAST, AND VANCOUVER'S ISLAND.

CHAPTER XIII.

CONCLUSION.

LIST OF ILLUSTRATIONS.

Illustrations marked thus * are from Photographs.

OCEAN TO OCEAN.

SANDFORD FLEMING'S PACIFIC EXPEDITION.

The Members:

The Chief, ... Sandford Fleming, C. E., Ottawa.
 " Doctor, ... Arthur Moren, M. D., Halifax.
 " Botanist, ... John Macoun, M. A., Belleville.
 " Photograoher, etc., . Charles Horetzky, ex-H. B. Officer.
Frank, ... Son of the Chief, (a lad of 16).
Terry, the Cook, ... (Sergeant) Terrance McWilliams.
The Secretary, ... Rev. Geo. M. Grant, Halifax.

Fellow Travellers:

The Colonel, (from Toronto to Fort Garry) Col. Robertson Ross, Adjutant-General.

Hugh, son of Col. Robertson Ross, (a lad of 16).

Mr. McDougal, (from Fort Garry to Edmonton), Superintendent of Wesleyan Missions on the Saskatchewan.

Mr. Macaulay, (from Carlton to Edmonton), Hudson Bay Co. Officer.

Mr. King,   do   do

Mr. Adams, (from Edmonton to St. Ann's),   do

Guides, Voyageurs, Packers, etc.

Ignace, Louis, Baptiste, Toma, etc., (from Shebandowan to the North-west Angle.)

Emilien, Jerome, Marchand, Friedrich, Willie, (from Fort Garry to Fort Carlton.)

Maxime, (from Fort Garry to Lake St. Albert.)

Souzie, (from White Horse Plains to Edmonton.)

Haroosh, Legrace, The Little Bird, (from Carlton to Fort Pitt.)

Kisanis, Cheeman, (from Fort Pitt to Edmonton.)

Brown, Beaupré, (from Edmonton to Forks of Fraser River.)

Valad, (from Lake St. Ann's to Forks of Fraser River.)

Jack, Joe, (from Forks of Fraser River to Kamloops.)

OCEAN TO OCEAN

THROUGH CANADA IN 1872.

CHAPTER I.

Introductory.

TRAVEL a thousand miles up a great river; more than another thousand along great lakes and a succession of smaller lakes; a thousand miles across rolling prairies; and another thousand through woods and over three great ranges of mountains, and you have travelled from Ocean to Ocean through Canada. All this Country is a single Colony of the British Empire; and this Colony is dreaming magnificent dreams of a future when it shall be the "Greater Britain," and the highway across which the fabrics and products of Asia shall be carried, to the Eastern as well as to the Western sides of the Atlantic. Mountains were once thought to be effectual barriers against railways, but that day has gone by; and, now that trains run between San Francisco and New York, over summits of eight thousand two hundred feet, it is not strange that they should be expected soon to run between Victoria and Halifax, over a height of three thousand seven hundred feet. At any rate, a Canadian Pacific Railway has been undertaken by the Dominion; and, as this book consists of notes made in connection with the survey, an introductory chapter may be given to a brief history of the project.

For more than a quarter of a century before the Atlantic was connected by rail with the Pacific public attention had been frequently called, especially in the great cities of the United States,

A

to the commercial advantage and the political necessity of such connection ; but it was not till 1853 that the Secretary of War was authorized by the President to employ topographical engineers and others "to make explorations and surveys, and to ascertain the most practicable and economical route for a railroad from the Mississippi River to the Pacific Ocean." From that time the United States Government sent a succession of well-equipped parties to explore the western half of the Continent. The reports and surveys of these expeditions fill thirteen large quarto volumes, richly embellished, stored with valuable information concerning the country, and honestly pointing out that, west of the Mississippi Valley, there were vast extents of desert or semi-desert, and other difficulties so formidable as to render the construction of a railroad well nigh impracticable. Her Majesty's Government aware of this result, and aware, also, that there was a " fertile belt," of undefined size, in the same longitude as the Great American Desert, but north of the forty-ninth degree of latitude, organized an expedition, under Captain Palliser, in 1857, to explore the country between the west of Lake Superior and the Rocky Mountains ; and also "to ascertain whether any practicable pass or passes, available for horses, existed across the Rocky Mountains within British Territory, and south of that known to exist between Mount Brown and Mount Hooker," known as the " Boat Encampment Pass." It was unfortunate that the limitation expressed in this last clause, was imposed on Captain Palliser, for it prevented him from exploring to the north of Boat Encampment, and reporting upon the "Yellow Head Pass," which has since been found so favourable for the Railway and may soon be used as the "gateway" through the mountains to British Columbia and the Pacific. The difficulties presented by passes further south, and by the Selkirk Mountains, led Palliser to express an opinion upon the passage across the Mountains as hasty

and inaccurate as his opinion, about the possibility of connecting Ontario or Quebec with the Red River and Saskatchewan Country is now found to be. After stating that his
expedition had made connection between the Saskatchewan
Plains and British Columbia, without passing through United
States Territory, he added,—" Still the knowledge of the
country, on the whole, would never lead me to advise a line of
communication from Canada, across the Continent to the
Pacific. exclusively through British Territory. The time has
forever gone by for effecting such an object; and the unfortunate choice of an astronomical boundary line has completely
isolated the Central ·American possessions of Great Britain
from Canada in the east, and also almost debarred them from
any eligible access from the Pacific Coast on the west." The best
answer to this sweeping opinion, is the "Progress Report" on the
Canadian Pacific Railway exploratory survey, presented to
the House of Commons, in Ottawa, in the Session 1872, in which
the advantages of the Yellow Head Pass over every other
approach to the Pacific are shown ; and as complete an answer
to the second part will be furnished in the Report to be
presented in the spring of 1873. The journals of Captain
Palliser's explorations, extending over a period of four years,
from 1857 to 1860, were printed *in extenso* by Her Majesty's
Government in a large " Blue Book," and shared the fate of all
blue books. There are, probably, not more than half a dozen
copies in the Dominion. A copy in the Legislative Library at
Ottawa is the only one known to the writer. They deserved a
better fate, for his own notes and the reports of his associates,
Lieutenant Blakiston, Dr. Hector, M. Bourgeau and Mr.
Sullivan, are replete with useful and interesting facts about the
soil, the flora, the fauna, and the climate of the plains and the
mountains. M. Bourgeau was the botanist of the expedition.
On Mr. Sullivan, an accomplished mathematician and astro-

nomical observer and surveyor, devolved the principal labors of
computation.   Dr. Hector, to whose exertions the success of the
expedition was chiefly owing, had the charge of making the
maps, both geographical and geological ; and, whenever a side
journey promised any result, no matter how arduous or dangerous it might be, Dr. Hector was always ready.   His name is
still revered in our North-west, on account of his medical skill
and his kindness to the Indians, and most astonishing tales are
still told of his travelling feats in mid-winter among the mountains.

After printing Captain Palliser's journal, Her Majesty's
Government took no step to connect the East of British America
with the Centre and the West, or to open up the North-west to
emigration, although it had been clearly established that we had
a country there, extending over many degrees of latitude and
longitude, with a climate and soil equal to that of Ontario.   In
the meantime, the people of the United States, with characteristic energy, took up the work that was too formidable for their
government.   Public-spirited men, in Sacramento and other parts
of California, embarked their all in a project which would make
their own rich State the link between the old farthest East and the
Western World on both sides of the Atlantic.   The work was
commenced on the east and west of the Rocky Mountains.
Congress granted extraordinarily liberal subsidies in lands and
money, though in a half sceptical spirit, and as much under the
influence of " Rings " as of patriotism.   When the member for
California was urging the scheme with a zeal that showed that
he honestly believed in it, Mr. Lovejoy, of Illinois, could not
help interjecting, " Does the honorable member really mean to
tell me he believes that that road will ever be built ?"   " Pass
the Bill, and it will be constructed in ten years," was the answer.
In much less than the time asked for it was constructed, and it
is at this day as remarkable a monument to the energy of our

neighbours as the triumphant conclusion of their civil war, or the re-building of Chicago. Three great ranges of mountains had to be crossed, at altitudes of eight thousand two hundred and forty, seven thousand one hundred and fifty, and seven thousand feet ; snow-sheds and fences to be built along exposed parts, for miles, at enormous expense ; the work, for more than a thousand miles, to be carried on in a desert, which yielded neither wood, water, nor food of any kind. No wonder that the scheme was denounced as impracticable and a swindle. But its success has vindicated the wisdom of its projectors ; and now no fewer than four different lines are organized to connect the Atlantic States with the Pacific, and to divide with the Union and Central Pacific Railways, the enormous and increasing traffic they are carrying.

While man was thus triumphing over all the obstacles of nature in the Territory of the United States, how was it that nothing was attempted farther north in British America, where a " fertile belt" stretches west to the base of the Rocky Mountains, and where the mountains themselves are pierced by river-passes that seem to offer natural highways through to the Ocean ? The North American Colonies were isolated from each other ; the North-west was kept under lock and key by the Hudson Bay Company ; and though some ambitious speeches were made, some spirited pamphlets written, and Bulwer Lytton, in introducing the Bill for the formation of British Columbia as a Province, saw, in vision, a line of loyal Provinces, from the Atlantic to the Pacific, the time had not come for "a consummation so devoutly to be wished." Had the old political state of things continued in British America, nothing would have been done to this day. But, in 1867, the separate Colonies of Canada, New Brunswick and Nova Scotia, became the Dominion of Canada ; in 1869 the Hudson Bay Company's rights to the North-west were bought up ; and, in 1871, British Columbia united itself

to the new Dominion ; and thus the whole mainland of British
America became one political State under the ægis of the
Empire. One of the terms on which British Columbia joined the
Dominion was, that a railway should be constructed within ten
years from the Pacific to a point of junction with the existing
railway systems in the Provinces of Ontario and Quebec, and
surveys with this object in view were at once instituted.

What did this preparatory survey-work in our case mean ? It
meant that we must do, in one or two years, what had been
done in the United States in fifty. To us the ground was all
new. None of our public men had ever looked much beyond
the confines of their particular Provinces; our North-west, in some
parts of it, was less an unknown land to the people of the States
along the boundary line than to the people of the Dominion ;
and, in other parts, it was unknown to the whole world. No
white man is known to have crossed from the Upper
Ottawa to Lake Superior or Lake Winnipeg. There were
maps of the country, dotted with lakes and lacustrine
rivers here and there; but these had been made up largely from
sketches, on bits of birch-bark or paper, and the verbal descriptions of Indians ; and, as the Indian has little or no conception
of scale or bearings ; as in drawing the picture of a lake, for
instance, when his sheet of paper was too narrow, he would,
without warning, continue the lake up or down the side; an
utterly erroneous idea of the surface of the country was given.
A lake was set down right in the path of what otherwise was an
eligible line, and, after great expense had been incurred, it was
found that there was no lake within thirty miles of the point.
In a word, the country between Old Canada and Red River
was utterly unknown, except along the canoe routes travelled by
the Hudson Bay men north-west of Lake Superior. Only five or
six years since, a lecturer had to inform a Toronto audience that
he had discovered a great lake, called Nepigon, a few miles to the

north of Lake Superior. When so litttle was known, the task was no light one. Engineers were sent out into trackless, inhospitable regions, obliged to carry their provisions on their backs over swamps, rocks, and barriers, when the Indians failed them, to do their best to find out all they could, in as short a time as possible.

Far different was it with our neighbours. They could afford to spend, and they did spend, half a century on the preparatory work. Their special surveys were aided and supplemented by reports and maps extending back over a long course of years, drawn up, as part of their duty, by the highly educated officers of their regular army stationed at different posts in their Territories. These reports, as well as the unofficial narratives of missionaries, hunters, and traders, were studied, both before and after being pigeon-holed in Washington. The whole country had thus been gradually examined from every possible point of view ; and, among other things, this thorough knowledge explains the success of the United States' Government in all its treaty-making with Great Britain, *when territory was concerned.* The history of every such treaty between the two Powers is the history of a contest between knowledge and ignorance. The one Power always knew what it wanted. It therefore presented, from the first step in the negotiation to the last, a firm and apparently consistent front. The other had only a dim notion that right was on its side, and a notion, equally dim, that the object in dispute was not worth contending for.

Was it wise, then, for the Dominion to undertake so gigantic a public work at so early a stage in its history ? It was wise, because it was necessary. By uniting together, the British Provinces had declared that their destiny was—not to ripen and drop, one by one, into the arms of the Republic—but to work out their own future as an integral and important part of the grandest Empire in the world. They had reason for making such an election. They believed that it was better for themselves and for their neighbours ; better for the cause of human liberty and true progress, that it should be so. But it is not necessary to discuss the reasons. No outside power has a right to pronounce upon them. The fact is enough, that, on this central point, the mind of British America, from the Atlantic to the Pacific, is fixed. But, to be united politically and disunited physically, as the different parts of Prussia were for many a long year, is an anomaly only to be endured so long as it could not be helped; and when, as in our case, the remedy is in our own hands, it is wise to secure the material union as soon as possible.

On the twentieth of July, 1871, British Columbia entered the Dominion. On the same day surveying parties left Victoria for various points of the Rocky Mountains, and from the Upper Ottawa westward, and all along the line surveys were commenced. Their reports were laid before the Canadian House of Commons in April, 1872. In the summer of the same year, Sandford Fleming, the Engineer in Chief, considered it necessary to travel overland, to see the main features of the country with his own eyes, and the writer of these pages accompanied him, as Secretary. The expedition started from Toronto on July 16th, and on October 14th, it left Victoria, Vancouver's Island "on the home stretch." During those three months a diary was kept of the chief things we saw or heard, and of the impressions which we formed respecting the country, as we journeyed from day to day and conversed with each other on the subject. The diary was not written for publication, or, if printed at all, was to have been for private circulation only. This will explain the little personal details that occur through it; for allusions and incidents that the public rightly consider trivial, are the most interesting items to the private circle. But those who had a right to speak in the matter said that the notes contained information that would be of interest to the general public, and of value to intending immigrants. They are therefore presented to the public, and they are given just as they were written so that others might see, as far as possible, a photograph of what we saw and thought from day to day.. A more readable book could have been made by omitting some things, coloring others, and grouping the whole; but, as already explained, the object was not to make a book. The expedition had special services to perform in connection with one of the most gigantic public works ever undertaken in any country by any people; it was organized and conducted in a business-like way, in order to get through without disaster or serious difficulty; it did not turn aside in search of adventures or of sport; and therefore an exciting narrative of hair-breadth escapes and thrilling descriptions of "men whose heads do grow beneath their shoulders" need scarcely be expected.

CHAPTER II.

From Halifax, Nova Scotia, to Thunder Bay, Lake Superior.

Halifax.—Intercolonial Railway. —Moncton.—Miramichi. —Restigouche.—Matapedia.—
Cacouna.—Lord Dufferin—Rivière du Loup.—Quebec.—Montreal.—Toronto.—Colling-
wood.—A man overboard.—Owen Sound.—Steamer *Frances Smith.*—Provoking delays.
—Killarney.—Indians. — Bruce Mines.—Sault Ste. Marie. — Lake Superior.—Sun-
set.—Full Moon.—Harbor of Gargantua.—The Botanist.—Michipicoten Island.—
Nepigon Bay.— Grand Scenery. —Sunday on Board.—Silver Islet.—Prince Arthur's
Landing.

1st July, 1872.—To-day, three friends met in Halifax, and
agreed to travel together through the Dominion from the Atlantic to the Pacific. All three had personal and business matters to
arrange, requiring them to leave on different days, and reach the
Upper Provinces by different routes. In these circumstances
it was decided that Toronto should be the point of rendez-vous
for the main journey to the Far West, and that the day of
meeting should be the 15th of July. One proposed to take the
steamer from Halifax to Portland, and go thence by the Grand
Trunk Railway *via* Montreal; another, to sail up the Gulf of
St. Lawrence from Pictou to Quebec, (the most charming voyage
in America for wretched half-baked mortals, escaping from the
fierce heat of summer in inland cities) ; and it was the
duty of the third—the chief of the party—to travel along the
line of the Intercolonial Railway, now under construction,
through Nova Scotia and New Brunswick to its junction with
the Grand Trunk in the Province of Quebec. This narrative
follows the footsteps of the Chief, when more than one path is
taken. But, though it was his duty to make a professional
examination of all the engineering works in progress on the
Intercolonial,—the Eastern link of that great arterial highway
which is to connect, entirely through Canadian Territory, a

(10)

Canadian Atlantic port with a Canadian Pacific port,—the reader would scarcely be interested in a dry account of the culverts and bridges, built and building, the comparative merits of wooden and iron work, the pile-driving, the dredging, the excavating, the banking and blasting by over 10,000 workmen, scattered along 500 miles of road. The Intercolonial is to link, with rails of steel, the Provinces of Nova Scotia and New Brunswick with the Province of Quebec; the Grand Trunk unites Quebec and Ontario ; and the Canadian Pacific Railway is to connect the latter with Manitoba and British Columbia, as well as with the various unborn Provinces which, in the rapid progress of events, shall spring up in the intervening region. But the work of actual railway-construction is an old story ; and, if told at all, must be served up at some other time in some other way. The object of the present narrative is to give an account of what was observed and experienced in out-of-the-way places, over a vast extent of Canada little known even to Canadians. It will be sufficient for our purpose, therefore, to begin at Toronto, passing over all that may at any time be seen on the line from Halifax to Truro, and northerly across the Cobequid Mountains to Moncton. From Moncton, westward, there is much along the line worthy of description, but thousands of Railway tourists will see it all with their own eyes in a year or two ;—the deep forests of New Brunswick, the noble Miramichi river with its Railway bridging on a somewhat gigantic scale, the magnificent highland scenery of the Baie des Chaleurs, the Restigouche, and the wild mountain gorges of the Matapedia. But, without delaying even to catch a forty or fifty-pound salmon in the Restigouche, we hasten on with the Chief up the shores of the great St. Lawrence, hearing, as we pass Cacouna in the second week of July, a cheer of welcome to Lord Dufferin, the new Governor General, who had just landed with his family, escaping from the dust and heat of cities and the Niagara Volunteer Camp, to enjoy the saline atmosphere and sea bathing, which so many thousands of Her Majesty's subjects seek along the lower St. Lawrence at this season. At Rivière du Loup a Pullman Car receives us. Passing the cliffs of historic Quebec, we cross the broad St. Lawrence by that magnificent monument of early Canadian enterprise, that triumph of engineering skill, "The Victoria Bridge," opposite Montreal. Two days are necessarily spent at Ottawa in making final arrangements, and Toronto is reached at the time appointed for the rendez-vous.

July 15th.—To-day, the various members of the overland expedition met at the Queen's Hotel the Chief, the Adjutant General, the boys, Frank and Hugh, the Doctor and the Secretary, and arranged to leave by the first train to-morrow morning. On the Chief devolved all the labor of preparation. The rest of us had little to do except to get ourselves photographed in travelling costume.

July 16th.—Took train for Collingwood, which is about a hundred miles due north from Toronto. The first half of the journey, or as far as Lake Simcoe, is through a fair and fertile land; too flat to be picturesque, but sufficiently rolling for farming purposes. Clumps of stately elms, with noble stems, shooting high before their fan shape commences, relieve the monotony of the scene. Here and there a field, dotted with huge pine stumps, shows the character of the old crop. The forty or fifty miles nearest Georgian Bay have been settled more recently, but give as good promise to the settlers. Collingwood is an instance of what a railway terminus does for a place. Nineteen years ago, before the Northern Railway was built, an unbroken forest occupied its site, and the red deer came down through the woods to drink at the shore. Now, there is a thriving town of two or three thousand people, with steam saw-mills, and huge rafts from the North that almost fill up its little harbor, with a grain elevator which lifts out of steam barges the corn from Chicago, weighs it, and pours it into railway freight-waggons to be hurried down to Toronto, and there turned into bread or whiskey, without a hand touching it in all its transportations or transformation, Around the town the country is being opened up, and the forest is giving way to pasture and corn-fields. West of the town is a range of hills, about one thousand feet high, originally thickly wooded to their summits, but now seamed with roads and interspersed with clearings. Probably none of us would have noticed them, though their beauty is enough to attract passing attention, had they not been pointed out as the highest " Mountains" in the great Province of Ontario !

We reached Collingwood at midday, and were informed that the steamer *Frances Smith* would start for Fort William, at two P.M. Great was the bustle, accordingly, in getting the baggage on board. In the hurry, the gangway was shoved out of its place, and when one of the porters rushed on it with a box, down it tilted, pitching him, head first, into the water between the pier and the steamer. We heard the splash, and ran, with half a dozen others, just in time to see his boots kicking frantically as they disappeared. " Oh it's that fool S——," laughed a bystander, " this is the second time he's tumbled in." " He can't swim," yelled two or three, clutching at ropes that were tied, trunks and other impossible life-preservers. In the meantime S—— rose, but, in rising, struck his head against a heavy float that almost filled the narrow space, and at once sank again, like a stone. He would have been drowned within six feet of the wharf, but for a tall, strong fellow, who rushed through the crowd, jumped in, and caught him as he rose a second time. S——, like the fool he was said to be, returned the kindness by half throttling his would-be deliverer ; but other bystanders, springing on the float, got the two out. The rescuer swung lightly on to the wharf, shook himself as if he had been a Newfoundland dog, and walked off ; nobody.

seemed to notice him or to think that he deserved a word of praise. On inquiring, we learned that he was a fisherman,—by name, Alick Clark—on his way to the Upper Lakes, who, last summer also had jumped from the steamer's deck into Lake Superior, to save a child that had fallen overboard. Knowing that Canada had no Humane Society's medal to bestow, one of our party ran to thank him and quietly to offer a slight gratuity; but the plucky fellow refused to take anything, on the plea that he was a good swimmer and that his clothes hadn't been hurt.

At two o'clock, it being officially announced that the steamer would not start until six, we strolled up to the town to buy suits of duck, which were said to be the only sure defence against mosquitoes of portentous size and power beyond Fort William. Meeting the Rector or Rural Dean, our Chief, learning that he would be a fellow-passenger, introduced the Doctor to him. The Doctor has not usually a positively funereal aspect, but the Rector assumed that he was the clergyman of the party and a D.D., and cottoned to him at once. When we returned to the steamer, and gathered round the tea table, the Rector nodded significantly in his direction: he, in dumb show, declined the honor; the Rector pantomimed again, and with more decision of manner; the Doctor blushed furiously, and looked so very much as if an " aith would relieve him," that the Chief, in compassion, passed round the cold beef without " a grace." We were very angry with him, as the whole party, doubtless, suffered in the Rector's estimation through his lack of resources. The doctor, however, was sensitive on the subject and threatened the secretary with a deprivation of sundry medical comforts, if he didn't in future attend to his own work.

At six o'clock it was officially announced that the steamer would not start till midnight. Frank and Hugh got a boat and went trawling; the rest of us were too disgusted to do even that, and so did nothing.

July 17th.—The *Frances Smith* left Collingwood at 5.30 A.M. "We're all right now," exclaimed Hugh, and so the passengers thought, but they counted without their host or—captain. We steamed slowly round the Peninsula to Owen Sound, reaching it about eleven o'clock. The baggage here, could have been put on board in an hour, but five hours passed without sign of even getting up steam. In despair, we went in a body to the captain to remonstrate. He frankly agreed that it was "too bad," but disclaimed all responsibility, as the Government Inspector, on a number of trifling pleas, would not let him start, nor give him his certificate,—the real reason being that he was too virtuous ever to bribe inspectors. The deputation at once hunted up the Inspector, and heard the other side. He had ordered a safety-valve for the boilers and new sails a month before, but the captain had " humbugged," and done nothing. The valve was now being fitted on, the sails were being bent, and the steamer would be ready to start in half an hour. Clearly, the Inspector, in the interest of the travelling public, had only done his duty, and the captain was responsible for the provoking delays. We told him so, without phrases, when he promised to hurry up and get off quickly to and from Leith,—a port six miles from Owen Sound, where he had to take in wood.

Leith was reached at 6.30, and we walked round the beach and had a swim, while two or three men set to work leisurely to carry on board a few sticks of wood from eight or ten cords piled on the wharf. At ten P.M., there being no signs of a start, some of us asked the reason and were told that the whole pile had to be put on board. The two or three laborers were lounging on the wharf with arms a-kimbo, and the captain was dancing in the cabin with some of the passengers, male and female, as unconcernedly as if all were out for a pic-nic. He looked somewhat taken aback when the Chief called him aside, and asked if he commanded the boat, or if there was anybody in command ;

but, quickly rallying, he declared that everything was going on splendidly. The Chief looked so thundery, however, that he hurried down stairs and ordered the men to " look alive ;" but as it would take the two or three laborers all night to stow the wood, half a dozen of the passengers volunteered to help, and the Royal Mail steamer got off two hours after midnight.

An inauspicious beginning to our journey this ! Aided all the way by steam, we were not much more than one hundred miles in a direct line from Toronto, forty-four hours after starting. At this rate, when would we reach the Rocky Mountains ? To make matters worse, the subordinates seemed to have learned from their leader the trick of "how not to do it."

Last night a thunder storm soured the milk on the boat, and though at the wharf, and within a few hundred yards of scores of dairies, it did not occur to the steward that he could send one of his boys for a fresh supply. To-day, after dinner, an enterprising passenger asked for cheese with his beer, and of course did not get it, as nobody knew where it had been stowed. In a word the *Frances Smith* wanted a head, and, as the Scotch old maid lamented, "its an unco' thing to gang through the warld withoot a heid."

June 18th.—To-day, our course was northerly through the Georgian Bay towards the Great Manitoulin Island. This island and some smaller ones stretching in an almost continuous line, westward, in the direction of Lake Superior, form, in connection with the Saugeen Peninsula, the barrier of land that separates the Georgian Bay from the mighty Lake Huron. These two great inland waters were one, long ago, when the earth was younger, but the water subsided, or Peninsula and Islands rose, and the one sea became two. Successive terraces on both sides of Owen Sound and on the different islands showed the old lake beaches, each now fringed with a firmer, darker, escarpment than the stony or sandy flats beneath, and

Pl. 1.

THE BRUCE MINES, STEAMBOAT LANDING.

marked the different levels to which the waters had gradually subsided.

The day passed pleasantly, for, as progress was being made in the right direction, all the passengers willingly enjoyed themselves, while on the two previous days they had only enjoyed the Briton's privilege of grumbling. Crossing the calm breadth of the Bay, past Lonely Island, we soon entered the Strait that extends for fifty miles between the North shore and Manitoulin. The contrast between the soft and rounded outlines of the Lower Silurian of Manitoulin and the rugged Laurentian hills, with their contorted sides and scarred foreheads, on the mainland opposite, was striking enough to evoke from a Yankee fellow-passenger the exclamation, "Why, there's quite a scenery here!" The entrance to the Strait has been called Killarney, according to our absurd custom of discarding the musical, expressive, Indian names for ridiculously inappropriate, European ones. Killarney is a little Indian settlement, with one or two Irish families to whom the place appears to owe very little more than its name. On the wharf is an unshingled shanty—"the store"—the entrepôt for dry goods, hardware, groceries, "Indian work," and everything else that the heart of man in Killarney can desire. As you look in at the door, a placard catches your attention, with

LOOK HERE GENTS.

ENGLISH AND IRISH VOCUBULARY,

for sale here;

and, further in, another placard hangs on the wall with the Killarney *Carpe Diem* motto of

TO-DAY FOR CASH AND

TOM-MORROW FOR NOTHING.

The Indians possessed, until lately, the whole of the Island of Manitoulin as well as the adjoining Peninsula; but, at a grand

B

pow wow, held with their Chiefs by Sir Edmund Head, while Governor of Old Canada, it was agreed that they should, for certain annuities and other considerations, surrender all except tracts specially reserved for their permanent use. Some two thousand are settled around those shores. They are of the great Ojibbeway or Chippewa nation,—the nation that extends from the St. Lawrence to the Red River, where sections of them are called Salteaux and other names. West from the Red River to the Rocky Mountains, extend the next great nation of the Algonquin family,—the Crees. The languages of these two nations are so much alike, that Indians of the one nation can understand much of the speech of the other. The structure is simple, there being about a hundred and fifty mono-syllabic radical roots, the greater number of which are common to Ojibbeway and Cree, and on these roots the language has grown up. Most of the Ojibbeways on Manitoulin are Christianized. At one point on the Island, where the steamer called, we met Mr. Hurlburt, a Methodist Missionary,—a thoughtful, scholarly man—who has prepared, with infinite pains, a grammar of the language, and who gave us much interesting information. He honestly confessed that there was little, if any, difference in morals between the Christianized Indians around him and the two or three hundred who remain pagan; that, in fact, the pagans considered themselves quite superior, and made the immorality of their Christian countrymen their great plea against changing from the old religion.

July 19th.—This morning we entered a beautiful island-studded bay, on the north shore of which is the settlement round the Bruce and Wellington Copper Mines. The mines have been very productive, and give employment now to three or four hundred men and boys, whose habitations are, as is usually the case at mines, mere shanties. One, a little larger than the others, in which the "Gaffer" lives, is dignified with the title

Pl. 2.

SAULT STE. MARIE (from the South Side).

BK

of "Apsley House." From the Bruce Mines we sailed westerly through a channel almost as beautiful as where the St. Lawrence runs through the "thousand islands." A "silver streak of sea," glittering in the warm sun, filled with rounded islets of old Huronian rock, that sloped gently into the water at one point, or more abruptly at another, and offered every variety and convenience at the heart of bather could desire ; low, rugged, pine clad shores ; soft bays, here and there, with sandy beaches : all that is required to make the scene one of perfect beauty is a back-ground of high hills. Everywhere, through Ontario, we miss the mountain forms, without which all scenery is tame in the eyes of those who have once learned to see the perpetual beauty that clothes the everlasting hills.

St. Joseph, Sugar, and Neebish Islands, now take the place of Manitoulin ; then we come to the Ste. Marie River, which leads up to Lake Superior, and forms the boundary line between the Dominion and the United States. At the Sault, or rapids of the river, there is a village on each side ; but, as the canal is on the United States side, the steamer crosses, to go through it to the great Lake. The canal has two locks, each three hundred and fifty feet long, seventy feet wide, twelve deep, and with a lift of nine feet. It is well and solidly built. The Federal Government has commenced the excavations for the channel of another. Though the necessity for two canals, on the same side, is not very apparent, still the United States Government, with its usual forethought, sees that the time will soon come when they shall be needed. The commerce on Lake Superior is increasing every year ; and it is desirable to have a canal, large enough for men-of-war and the largest steamers. We walked along the bank, and found, among the men engaged on the work, two or three Indians handling pick and shovel as if "to the manner born," and probably earning the ordinary wages of $2.25 per day. The rock is loose and friable calciferous sandstone, red-

dish-colored, and easily excavated. Hence the reason why
the Sault Ste. Marie, instead of being a leap, flows down
its eighteen feet of descent in a continuous rapid, wonderfully
little broken except over loose boulders. The water is wear-
ing away the rock every year. As it would be much easier to
make a canal on the British side of the river, one ought to
be commenced without delay. The most ordinary self-respect
forbids that the entrance to our North-west should be wholly in
the hands of another Power, a Power that, during the Riel disturbances at Red River, shut the entrance against even our
merchant ships. In travelling from Ocean to Ocean through
the Dominion, more than four thousand miles were all our own.
Across this one mile, half-way on the great journey, every
Canadian must pass on sufferance. The cost of a canal on our
side is estimated, by the Canal Commissioners in a blue-book,
dated February 2nd, 1871, at only $550,000. Such a canal, and
a Railway from Nepigon or Thunder Bay to Fort Garry, would
give immediate and direct steam communication to our North
West, within our own Territory.

At the western terminus of the canal, the Ste. Marie River
is again entered. Keeping to the north, or British side, we come
to the Point aux Pins, covered with scrub pine (*Pinus Banksiana*)
which extends away to the north from this latitude. Rounding
the Point aux Pins, the river is two or three miles wide; and, a
few miles farther west, Capes Gros and Iroquois tower up
on each side. These bold warders, called by Agassiz "the
portals of Lake Superior," are over a thousand feet high;
and rugged, primeval Laurentian ranges stretch away from
them as far back as the eye can reach. The sun is setting when
we enter "the portals," and the scene well worthy the approach
to the grandest lake on the globe. Overhead the sky is clear,
and blue, but the sun has just emerged from huge clouds which
are emptying their buckets in the west. Immediately around is

Pl. 3.

MOOSE MOUNTAIN, NEPIGON BAY.

a placid sea, with half a dozen steamers and three-masted schooners at different points. And now the clouds, massed into one, rush to meet us, as if in response to our rapid movement towards them, and envelope us in a squall and fierce driving rain, through which we see the sun setting, and lighting up, now with deep yellow and then with crimson glory, the fragments of clouds left behind in the west. In ten minutes the storm passes over us to the east, our sky clears as if by magic, and wind and rain are at an end. The sun sets, as if sinking into an ocean ; at the same moment the full moon rises behind us, and, under her mellow light, Lake Superior is entered.

Those who have never seen Superior get an inadequate, even inaccurate idea, by hearing it spoken of as a 'lake,' and to those who have sailed over its vast extent the word sounds positively ludicrous. Though its waters are fresh and crystal, Superior is a sea. It breeds storms, and rain and fogs, like the sea. It is cold in mid-summer as the Atlantic. It is wild, masterful, and dreaded as the Black Sea.

July 20th.—Sailed all night along the N. E. coast of the great Lake, and in the morning entered the land-locked harbour of Gargantua.

Two or three days previously the Chief had noticed, among the passengers, a gentleman, out for his holidays on a botanical excursion to Thunder Bay, and, won by his enthusiasm, had engaged him to accompany the expedition. At whatever point the steamer touched, the first man on shore was the Botanist, scrambling over the rocks or diving into the woods, vasculum in hand, stuffing it full of mosses, ferns, lichens, liverworts, sedges, grasses, and flowers, till recalled by the whistle that the captain always obligingly sounded for him. Of course such an enthusiast became known to all on board, especially to the sailors, who designated him as 'the man that gathers grass' or, more briefly, 'the hay picker' or 'haymaker.' They regarded him, because of his scientific failing, with the respectful tolerance with which all fools in the East are regarded, and would wait an extra minute for him or help him on board, if the steamer were cast loose from the pier before he could scramble up the side.

This morning the first object that met our eyes, on looking out of the window of the state-room, was our Botanist, on the highest peak of the rugged hills that enclose the harbour of Gargantua. Here was proof that we, too, had time to go ashore, and most of us hurried off for a ramble along the beach, or for a swim, or to climb one of the wooded rocky heights. Every day since leaving Toronto we had enjoyed our dip ; for the captain was not a man to be hurried at any place of call, and, annoyed though our party were at the needlessly long delays, there was no reason to punish ourselves by not taking advantage of them occasionally.

Half a dozen fishermen, Alick Clark among them, had come from Collingwood to fish in Superior for white fish and salmon trout, and having fixed on Gargantua for sum- mer head-quarters, they were now getting out their luggage, nets, salt, barrels, boats, &c. We went ashore in one of their boats, and could not help congratulating them heartily on the beauty of the site they had chosen. The harbour is a perfect oblong, land-locked by hills three or four hundred feet high on every side except the entrance and the upper end, where a beautiful beach slopes gradually back into a level of considerable extent. The beach was covered with the maritime vetch or wild pea in flower, and beach grasses of various kinds. When the Botanist came down to the shore, he was in raptures over sundry rare mosses, and beautiful specimens of Aspidium fragrans, Woodsia hyperborea, Cystopteris montana, and other rare ferns, that he had gathered. The view from the summit away to the north, he described as a sea of rugged Laurentian hills covered with thick woods.

L KTSAGEGAN NEPIGON RIVER.

From Gargantua, the captain, who now seemed slightly conscious that time had been lost, steered direct for Michipicoten Island. In the cozy harbour of this Island, the S.S *Manitoba* lay beached, having run aground two or three days before, and a little tug was doing its best to haul her off the rock or out of the mud. For three hours the *Frances Smith* added her efforts to those of the tug, but without success, and had to give it up, and leave her consort stranded. In the meantime some of the passengers went off with the Botanist to collect ferns and mosses. He led them a rare chase over rocks and through woods, being always on the look out for the places that promised the rarest kinds, quite indifferent to the toil or danger. The sight of a perpendicular face of rock, either dry or dripping with moisture, drew him like a magnet, and, with yells of triumph, he would summon the others to come and behold the treasure he had lit upon. Scrambling, puffing, rubbing their shins against the rocks, and half breaking their necks, they toiled painfully after him, only to find him on his knees before some "thing of beauty" that seemed to them little different from what they had passed by with indifference thousands of times. But if they could not honestly admire the moss, or believe that it was worth going through so much to get so little, they admired the enthusiasm, and it proved so infectious that, before many days, almost every one of the passengers was bitten with 'the grass mania,' or 'hay fever,' and had begun to form "collections."

July 21st.—Sunday morning dawned calm and clear. The Rural Dean read a short service and preached. After dinner we entered Nepigon Bay, probably the largest, deepest, safest, and certainly the most beautiful harbour on Lake Superior. It is shut off from the Lake by half a dozen Islands, of which the largest is St. Ignace,—that seem to have been placed there on purpose to act as break-waters against the mighty waves of the

Lake, and form a safe harbour; while, inside, other Islands
are set here and there, as if for defence or to break the force
of the waves of the Bay itself; for it is a stretch of more
than thirty miles from the entrance to the point where Nepigon
River discharges into the Bay, in a fast flowing current, the
waters of Nepigon Lake which lies forty miles to the north. The
country between the Bay and the Lake having been found
extremely unfavourable for Railway construction, it will probably
be necessary to carry the Canadian Pacific Railway farther
inland, but there must be a branch line to Nepigon Bay, which
will then be the summer terminus for the traffic from the West,
(unless Thunder Bay gets the start of it) just as Duluth is the
terminus of the "Northern Pacific."

The scenery of Nepigon Bay is of the grandest description;
there is nothing like it in Ontario. Entering from the east
we pass up a broad strait, and can soon take our choice
of deep and capacious channels, formed by the bold ridges
of the Islands that stud the Bay. Bluffs, from three hundred
to one thousand feet high, rise up from the waters, some of
them bare from lake to summit, others clad with graceful
balsams. On the mainland, sloping and broken hills stretch
far away, and the deep shadows that rest on them bring
out the most distant in clear and full relief. The time will come
when the wealthy men of our great North-west will have their
summer residences on these hills and shores; nor could the
heart of man desire more lovely sites. At the river is an old
Hudson Bay station, and the head-quarters of several surveying
parties for the Canadian Pacific Railway. The Chief, therefore,
has business here, and the Doctor also finds some ready to
his hand, for one of the engineers in charge is seriously ill;
but the captain can spare only an hour, as he wishes to be out
of the Bay by the western Channel, which is much narrower than
the eastern, before dark. We leave at 5.30, and are in Lake

NEPIGON RIVER *(looking towards the Bay.)*

Pl. 5.

Superior again at 8.30. The passengers, being anxious for an evening informal service, the captain and the Rural Dean requested our secretary to conduct it. He consented, and used, on the occasion, a form compiled last year specially for surveying parties. The scene was unusual, and perhaps, therefore, all the more impressive. Our Secretary, dressed in grey homespun, read a service compiled by clergymen of the Churches of Rome, England and Scotland; no one could tell which part was Roman, which Anglican or which Scottish, and yet it was all Christian. The responses were led by the Dean and the Doctor, and joined in heartily by Romanists, Episcopalians, Baptists, Methodists and Presbyterians; for there were sixty or seventy passengers present, and all those denominations were included in the number. The hymns were,—"Rock of Ages" and "Sun of my Soul;" these, with the "*Gloria Patri*," were accompanied on a piano by a young lady who had acted for years as the leader of a choir in a small Episcopal Chapel, and she was supported, right and left, by a Presbyterian and a Baptist. The sermon was short, but, according to the Doctor, would "have been better, if it had been shorter;" but all listened attentively, and no one could tell from it to what particular Church the preacher belonged. The effect of the whole was excellent; when the service was over, many remained in the saloon to sing, converse, or join in sacred music, and the evening passed delightfully away. The ice was broken; ladies and gentlemen, who had kept aloof all the week, addressed each other freely, without waiting to be introduced, and all began now to express sorrow that they were to part so soon. It was near the "wee sma' hour" before the pleasant groups in the saloon separated for the night.

At one, A. M., we arrived at "Silver Island,"—a little bit of rock in a Bay studded with islets. The most wonderful vein of silver in the world has been struck here. Last year, thirty men took out from it $1,200,000; and competent judges say that, in all probability, the mine is worth hundreds of millions. The original $50 shares now sell for $25,000. The company that works it is chiefly a New York one, though it was held originally by Montreal men, and was offered for sale in London for a trifle. Such a marvellous "find" as this has stimulated search in every other direction around Lake Superior. Other veins have been discovered, some of them paying well, and, of course, the probability is that there are many more undiscovered; for not one hundredth part of the mineral region of Lake Superior has been examined yet, and it would be strange indeed if all the minerals had been stumbled on at the outset. Those rocky shores are, perhaps, the richest part of the whole Dominion.

During the halt at Silver Island we went to bed, knowing that the steamer would arrive at Thunder Bay early in the morning. So ended the first half of our journey from Toronto to Fort Garry, by rail ninety-four miles, by steamboat five hundred and thirty miles. The second half would be by waggons and canoes;—waggons at the beginning and end; and, in the middle, canoes paddled by Indians or tugged by steam launches over a chain of lakes, extending like a net work in all directions along the watershed that separates the basin of the great Lakes and St. Lawrence from the vast Northern basin of Hudson's Bay. The unnecessary delays of the *Frances Smith* on this first part of our journey had been provoking; but the real *amari aliquid* was the Sault Ste. Marie Canal. The United States own the southern shores of Superior, and have therefore only done their duty in constructing a canal on their side of the Ste. Marie River. The Dominion not only owns the northern shores, but the easier access to its great North-west is by this route; a canal on its side is thus doubly necessary. The eastern key to two-thirds of the Dominion is meanwhile in the hands of another Power; and yet, if there ought to be only one gateway into Lake Superior, nature has declared that it should be on our side. So

SILVER ISLET.

long ago as the end of the last century, a rude canal, capable of floating large loaded canoes without breaking bulk, existed on our side of the river.* The report of a N. W. Navigation Company in 1858 gives the length of a ship canal around the Ste. Marie rapids on the Canadian side as only 838 yards, while on the opposite side the length is a mile and one-seventh. In the interests of peace and commerce, and because it would be a convenience to trade now and may be ere long an absolute national necessity, let us have our own roadway across that short half mile. Canada can already boast of the finest ship canal system in the world; this trifling addition would be the crowning work, and complete her inland water communication from the Ocean, westerly, across thirty degrees of longitude to the far end of Lake Superior.

(*) May 30th (1800) Friday, Sault Ste. Marie. Here the North-West Company have another establishment on the North side of the Rapid. * * * Here the North-West Company have built locks, in order to take up loaded canoes, that they may not be under the necessity of carrying them by land, to the head of the Rapid, for the current is too strong to be stemmed by any craft.—*Harmon's Journal.*

CHAPTER III.

From Thunder Bay to Fort Garry.

Shebandowan Road.—Rich Vegetation.—Rivers Kaministiquia and Matawan.—Sheban-
dowan Lake.—Luggage.—Emigrants.—Canoe train.—Iroquois Indians.—Sir George
Simpson's guide.—Lake Kashaboiwe.—The Height of Land.—Lac des Mille Lacs.—
Baril portage and Lake.—First night under canvas.—Lake Windigostigwan.—Indian
encampment.—Chief Blackstone's wives.—The Medicine-man.—Lake Kaogassikok.—
Shooting Maligne rapids. — Lake Nequaquon. — Loon portage. — Mud portage. —
American portage.—Lake Namoukan.—Rainy Lake.—Fort Francis.—Rainy River.—
Hungry Hall.—Slap-jacks.—Lake of the Woods.—The North West Angle.—A tough
night.—Oak point.—First glimpse of the prairies.—Floral treasures.—The Dawson
route.—Red River.

July 22nd.—At 5 A. M., arrived at Prince Arthur's Landing,
Thunder Bay, about four miles from the Kaministiquia river,
a fine open harbour, with dark cliffs of basaltic rock and
island scenery second only to Nepigon. Population is flowing
rapidly to these shores of Lake Superior. Already more than a
hundred stores, shanties, or houses are scattered about 'the
Landing.' The chief business is silver mining, and prospecting
for silver, copper, galena, and other valuable minerals known to
exist in the neighbourhood.

The engineer of the surveying parties between Ottawa and
Red River, and the assistant superintendent of the Dawson
Route to Fort Garry met us at the Landing and invited us to
breakfast in their shanty. After breakfast, our baggage was
packed on a heavy waggon, and instructions were given to the
driver to keep moving till he reached Shebandowan Lake, the
first of the chain to be traversed in canoes.

Shebandowan is forty-five miles from Lake Superior, about 800
feet higher, and near the summit or watershed of the district. At
10.30 A. M., we started for that point, the Chief and the Doctor in
a buggy, the others in a light waggon. Drove in three hours to

(28)

THUNDER CAPE, ENTRANCE TO THUNDER BAY

"fifteen-mile shanty" through a rolling country with a steady upward incline, lightly wooded for the first half and more heavily for the latter half of the distance. The flora is much the same as in our Eastern Provinces ; the soil light, with a surface covering of peaty or sandy loam, and a subsoil of clay, fairly fertile and capable of being easily cleared. The vegetation is varied, wild fruits being especially abundant,—raspberries, currants, gooseberries, and tomatoes ; flowers like the convolvulus, roses, a great profusion of asters, wild kallas, water-lilies on the ponds, wild chives on the rocks in the streams, and generally a rich vegetation. It is a good country for emigrants of the farmer class. The road, too, is first rate, a great point for the settler ; and a market is near. Whatever a settler raises he can easily transport to the ready market that there always is near mines. Miners are not particular about their lodging, but good food and plenty of it they must have.

At the "fifteen-mile shanty," we stopped for an hour and a half to feed the horses, and to dine. A Scotchman from Alloa, Robert Bowie, was "boss of the shanty," and gave us the best dinner we had eaten since leaving Toronto ;—broth, beaf-steak, bread, and tea. The bread, light and sweet as Paris rolls, was baked in Dutch ovens, buried in the hot embers of a huge fire outside, near the door, and Robert accepted the shower of compliments on its quality with the canny admission that there were " waur bakers in the warld than himsel'."

We walked on for the next three or four miles till the waggon overtook us. The soil became richer, the timber heavier, and the whole vegetation more luxuriant. Six miles from the fifteen-mile shanty we crossed the Kaministiquia—a broad and rapid river,—which, at this point, is, by its own course, forty-five miles distant from where it falls into Lake Superior. The valley of the river is acknowledged to be a splendid farming country. A squatter, who had pitched camp at the bridge end last year, on his way

to Red River, and had remained instead of going on because
everything was so favourable, came up to have a talk with us, and
to grumble, like a true Briton, that the Government wasn't doing
more for him. Timothy was growing to the height of four and five
feet, on every vacant spot, from chance seeds. A bushel and
a-half of barley, which seemed to be all that he had sown, was
looking as if it could take the prize at an Ontario Exhibition.

The soil, for the next five miles, was covered luxuriantly with
the vetch, or wild pea. The road led to the Matawan,—a
stream that runs out of Lake Shebandowan into the Kaministiquia. Both rivers are crossed by capital bridges. The
station at the Matawan was in charge of a Mr. Aitken and
his family, from Glengarry. He had arrived exactly two months
ago, on the 22nd of May, and he had now oats and barley up,
potatoes in blossom, turnips, lettuce, parsnips, cucumbers, etc.,
all looking healthy, and all growing on land that, sixty days
before, had been in part covered with undergrowth, stumps,
and tall trees, through which fires had run the year previous.
Mr. Aitken was in love with the country, and, what was of
more consequence, so was Mrs. Aitken, though she confessed to
a longing for some "neighbours." They intended to make it
their future home, and said that they had never seen land so
well suited for farming. Everything was prospering with them.
The very hens seemed to do better here than elsewhere. One
was pointed out with a brood of twenty strong healthy chickens
around her ; Guinea hens and turkeys looked thriving.

Everything about this part of country, so far, has astonished us.
Our former ideas concerning it had been that it was a barren
desert ; that there was only a horse trail, and not always that, to
travel by ; that the mosquitoes were as big as grasshoppers, and
bit through everything. Whereas, it is. a fair and fertile land,
undulating from the intervales of the rivers up to hills and
rocks eight hundred feet high. The road through it is good

Pl. 8

SCALE OF MILES

THUNDER BAY TO FORT FRANCIS.

enough for a king's highway, and the mosquitoes are not more vicious than in the woods and by the streams of the Lower Provinces; yet this fine land is wholly untaken up. Not half a dozen settlers are on the road for the first twenty-six miles; and for the next twenty, not half that number. How many cottars, small farmers, and plough boys in Britain, would rejoice to know that they could get a hundred acres of such land for one dollar an acre, money down; or at twenty cents per acre after five years settlement on it! They could settle along the high road, take their produce to a good market, and be independent landholders in five years. This was the information about the price of land that the settlers gave us. Why "free" grants are not offered, as in other parts of Ontario or in Manitoba, it is impossible to say.

From the Matawan to Shebandowan lake was the next stage, twenty miles long. We passed over most of it in the dark, but could see, from the poor timber and other indications, that the latter half was not at all as good as the first. The road was heavy, varying between corduroy, deep sand, and rutty and rooty stretches, over which the waggon jolted frightfully. Though the colonel beguiled the way with many a story of the wars, all were tired and ready for bed by the time the Lake was reached.

So passed the first day of our expedition, for we counted that the journey only began at Thunder Bay. We had been twelve hours on the road; but, as the day had been cool and showery, did we not feel over-fatigued on arriving at Shebandowan. An old-countryman, Morris, was in charge of the shanty. He had given up his kitchen to half a dozen emigrants who were going on in the morning to Red River, and had reserved beds for us in little nooks upstairs.

July 23rd.—Rose at sunrise, and found, much to our disgust, that the baggage waggon had not arrived. An hour after, however, it came in, and, along with it, two young gentlemen, M.... and L.... with a canoe and Indians on their way to Red River. They were travelling for pleasure, and, as they had been on the road all night, and were tired, seedy and, mosquito-bitten, they represented very fairly, in their own persons, the Anglo-Saxon idea of pleasure.

At Shebandowan all our luggage was now gathered on the wharf, to be stowed in the canoes which were to carry us westerly for the next three hundred and eighty miles, along the chain of lakes. The Chief looked hard at the united heap, and then proposed that Morris should take charge or possession of all that could be dispensed with ; and that, before we left Fort Garry, only a certain number of pounds-weight should be allowed to each. Much luggage is a nuisance, even where there are railways, especially if extra weight has to be paid for ; but it is simply intolerable where frequent portages intervene, over which everything has to be carried on men's backs. Morris made no objection to the Chief's proposal, and it was carried *nem. con.*

At 8 A. M., the baggage having been stowed in the canoes, the Indians paddled out, and hooked on to a little steam tug, kept on the lake for towing purposes : a line was formed, the word given, and, after a few preliminary puffings, the start was made and we proceeded along the lake. The mode of locomotion was, to us, altogether new, and as charming as it was picturesque. The tug led the way at the rate of seven knots, towing, first a large barge with immigrants, second a five-fathom canoe with three of our party and seven Indians, third a four-fathom canoe with two of us and six Indians, fourth same as number three, fifth M.... and L....'s canoe. We glided along with a delightful motion, sitting on our baggage in the bottoms of the canoes. The morning was dull and grey, and the shores of the lake looked sterile and fire-swept, with abundant indications of mineral wealth. Gold and silver have been found at Sheban-

THUNDER BAY *(from Prince Arthur's Landing)*

Pl. 9

dowan, and prospecting parties are now searching all accessible spots.

Our Indians were Iroquois, from Caughnawaga, near Montreal, and a few native Ojibbeways. Their leader was Ignace Mentour, who had been Sir George Simpson's guide for fifteen years; and the steersman of his canoe was Louis, who had been cook to Sir George on his expeditions, and looked every inch the butler of a respectable English family; we fell in love with him and Ignace from the first; another of the Iroquois had been one of the party which sought for Franklin by going down the McKenzie River to the Arctic Sea. Two old pupils of Ignace, named respectively Baptiste and Toma, were the captains of the two smaller canoes; they were all sinewy, active, good looking men. Ignace's hair was grey, but he was still as strong as any of the young men; he paddled in the bow of the big canoe, leading the way, and quietly chewed tobacco the whole time. In his young days he had been a famous runner, and had won foot races in every town on both sides of the St. Lawrence. These Iroquois, and most of the Ojibbeways we have met, are men above the medium size, broad shouldered, with straight features, intelligent faces, and graceful, because natural, bearing.

At the west end of the lake we came to a camp of seventy or eighty Ojibbeways—two-thirds of them children;—they had been there for three weeks, of course doing nothing for a living; more were expected, and, when all would have assembled, a grand pow-wow would be held, at which a Treaty was to be made between them and the Indian Commissioner of the Dominion, by which they were to cede, for a consideration, all their rights to the land, that would hinder settlers from coming in. Poor creatures! not much use have they ever made of the land; but yet, in admitting the settler, they sign their own death warrants. Who, but they, have a right to the country; and if "a man may do what he

C

likes with his own," would they not be justified in refusing to
admit one of us to their lakes and woods, and fighting us to the
death on that issue ?   But it is too late to argue the question ;
the red man, with his virtues and his vices,—lauded by some as
so dignified, abused by others as so dirty—is being civilised off
the ground.   In the United States they have, as a rule, dealt
with him more summarily than in British America, but it comes
to pretty much the same in the end, whether he is " improved
off," or shot down at once as a nuisance.   His wild, wandering
life is inconsistent with modern requirements : these vast
regions were surely meant to maintain more than a few thousand
Ojibbeways.

Three hours steaming brought our flotilla to the west end of
the lake.   A portage of three quarters of a mile intervenes
between it and Lake Kashaboiwe.   The Indians emptied the
canoes in a trice ; two shouldered a canoe, weighing probably
three hundred pounds, and made off at a rapid trot across the
portage.   The others loaded the waggon of the station with the
luggage, and carried on their backs, by a strap passed over their
foreheads, what the waggon could not take.   This portage-strap
is three or four inches broad in the middle, where it is adjusted
to the forehead : its great advantage to the voyageur is that
it leaves him the free use of his arms in going through the woods.
A tug had been placed on Kashaboiwe, but, as the machinery
was out of gear, the Indians paddled over the lake, doing the
ten miles of its length in two hours.   The wood on this lake is
heavier than on Shebandowan : poplars, white birch, red, white
and scrub pine, all shew well.   The second portage is between
Kashaboiwe and Lac des Mille Lacs, and is called " Height of
Land," as the water here begins to run north and west instead of
east and south.   The lakes, after this, empty at their west ends•
At the east end of Lac des Mille Lacs, a little stream three
yards wide, that flows in a tortuous channel with gentle current

OSKONDAGEE, (on the road to Shebandowra.)

BK

into the lake, eventually finds its way to Hudson's Bay. The "Height of Land" is about a thousand feet above Lake Superior.

We now entered a lovely lake, twenty-two miles long; its name explains its characteristic. As the steam launch, stationed on it, happened, unfortunately, to be at the west end, the Indians again paddled the canoes for about four miles, when we met the launch coming back; it at once turned about and took us in tow. After a smart shower the sky cleared, and the sun shone on innumerable bays, creeks, channels, headlands and islets, which are simply larger or smaller rocks of granite covered with moss and wooded to the water's brink. Through these labyrinths we threaded our way, often wondering that the wrong passage was never taken, where there were so many exactly alike. Fortunately, the fire-demon has not devasted these shores. The timber, in some places, is heavy; pine, aspen, and birch being the prevailing varieties. Every islet in the lake is wooded down to the water's edge. Our Botanist, though finding few new species, exulted in his holiday and looked forward, with eager hope, to the flora of the plains. "This expedition," he said, "is going to give me a lift that will put me at the head of the whole brigade;" but, as we drew near our third portage for the day, his face clouded. "Look at the ground, burnt again." One asked if it was the great waste of wood he referred to. "It's not that, but, they have burned the very spot for botanizing over." What is a site for shanty and clearing, compared to Botany! At the end of Lac des Mille Lacs is Baril Portage, less than a quarter of a mile long. M—— and L—— resolved to camp here, as they had had no sleep the previous night and their Indians were tired; but, though the sun was only an hour high, we resolved to complete our programme, by doing the next lake, Baril. No steamer has been put on this lake; but the Indians paddled over its eight miles of length in an hour and forty minutes. The bluffs around Baril are bolder than those rising from the' previous lakes, and the vegetation very similar. We hurried over the next portage, and, at the other end met the station-keeper, who had a comfortable tent pitched for the emigrants, strewn with fragrant pine and spruce branches.

It was impossible to avoid admiring the activity and cheerfulness with which our Indians worked. Their canoes were attended to, as well as the baggage, in half the time that ordinary servants would have taken. They would carry as heavy a load as a Constantinople porter, at a rapid trot across the portage, run back for another load without a minute's halt, and so on till all the luggage was portaged, and everything in readiness for starting on the next lake.

A fire was quickly kindled, and search made for the eatables, blankets and everything needed for the night, when the discovery was made that, though the colonel had his blankets and the botanist his pair, a big package with the main supply had been left behind, very probably as far back as the " Height of Land." The frizzling of the ham in the frying pan, and the delicious fragrance of the tea, made us forget the loss for the time. We all sat around the fire, gipsy-like, enjoying our first gipsy meal, and very soon after threw ourselves down on the water-proof, that covered the sweet-smelling floor of the tent, and slept the sleep of the just.

July 20th.—The Chief awoke us in the grey misty dawn. It took more than a little shaking to awaken the boys; but the botanist had gone off, no one knew when, in search of new species. As we emerged from our tent, Louis and Baptiste appeared from theirs, and kindled the fire. They next unrolled a lump of scented soap, brush and comb; went down to the stream, washed and made their toilettes, and then set to work to prepare for breakfast, ham, beefsteak, bread and tea. It never seemed to occur to our Ojibbeways to wash, crop, or

HEAD OF LAKE SHEBANDOWAN.

dress their hair. They let it grow, at its own sweet will, all
around their faces and down their necks, lank, straight and stiff,
helping the growth with fish oil ; whereas, every one of the
Iroquois had "a good head of hair," thick, well cropped, and,
though always black, quite like the hair of a civilized man
instead of a savage. Our Ojibbeways had silver rings on their
fingers, broad gaudy sashes and bedraggled feathers bound
round their felt hats. The Iroquois dressed as simply and neatly
as " blue jackets."

It had been chilly through the night, and the cold mist clung
heavily to the ground in the morning. The air is colder than
the water from evening till morning. Hence the evening and
morning mists, which disappear an hour or two after sunrise,
rise and form into clouds, which, sooner or later, empty themselves back again on the land or lakes.

After breakfast we embarked on the mist-covered river that
runs into Lake Windegoostigwan. The sun soon cleared away the
mists and we glided on pleasantly, down long reaches of lake,
and through narrow, winding, reedy passages, past curved
shores, hidden by rank vegetation, and naked bluffs and islets
covered with clumps of pines. Not a word fell from the Indians'
lips, as they paddled with all the ease and regularity of machinery. The air was delightful, and all felt as if out on a holiday.
In three hours the fifteen miles of Windegoostigwan were
crossed, and we came to a portage nearly two miles long. This
detained us three hours, as the waggon had to make two
trips from lake to lake, over a new road, with our luggage.

A man from Glengarry, Ontario, was in charge of the portage;
he had lived here all winter, and said that he far preferred the
winter weather to that of the Eastern Provinces. Great as
is the summer rain-fall, it is quite different in winter; then
the days are clear and cloudless, and so sunny and pleasant
that he was accustomed to go about in his summer clothing,

except in the mornings and evenings. Three feet of snow fell in
the woods after Christmas, and continued dry and powdery till
April, when it commenced to melt, and soon after the middle of
May it was all gone, and vegetation began to show itself at
once.

At the west end of the portage is a small encampment of
Ojibbeways, around the wigwam of Blackstone, said to be
their most eloquent chief, and accordingly set down as " a great
rascal " by those who cannot conceive of Indians as having rights,
or tribal or patriotic feelings. He was absent, but we saw one
of his three wives sitting on a log, with two or three papooses
hanging round her neck, and his oldest son, a stout young
fellow, who could not speak a word of English or French, but who
managed to let us know that he was sick. The Doctor was
called, and he made out that the lad had a pain in his back, but,
not being able to diagnose more particularly, was at a loss what
to do for him. Our Chief suggested a bit of tobacco, but the
Doctor took no notice of the profane proposal ; luckily enough,
or the whole tribe would have been sick when the next " Medicine-man " passed their way. Blackstone's wife was not more
comely than any of the other Indian women ; that is, she was
dirty, joyless-looking and prematurely old. All the hard work
falls to the lot of the women : the husband hunts, fishes,
paddles, or does any other work that a "gentleman" feels he
can do without degradation ; his wife is something better than
his dog, and faithfully will he share with her his last morsel;
but it's only a dog's life that she has.

Our next lake was Kaogassikok, sixteen miles long. The
shores of this, too, were lined with good-sized pine, white, red,
and scrub. To-day more larch and cedar shewed among the
birch and pine than yesterday. When the country is opened up,
all this timber will be very valuable, as sleepers and ties for the
Pacific Railway, and lumber, for building purposes, can be

obtained here in abundance, if nowhere nearer the plains. The trees can be cut down at the water's edge, rafted, and sent by water to Winnipeg. Numbers of fine trees are now growing in the water; for, by damming up the outflow of the lakes to make the landing places, the water level has been raised and the shore trees have thus been submerged several feet. They will rot, in consequence, and fall into the lakes sooner or later, and perhaps obstruct the narrow channels. The timber gets heavier as we go on; at the west of Kaogassikok are scrub pines, three feet in diameter; but, unfortunately, about one-third of them are punky or hollow. Here are two portages, Pine and Deux Rivières, separated by only two miles of water; consequently much detention owing to our magnificent quantities of baggage. Two Indians, suffering from dysentery, applied for relief at Pine Portage, and received it at the hands of the Doctor: he has already had about a dozen "cases," either of white or red men, since we left Owen Sound. The first two were at Nepigon, one the engineer, and the other a dying man, carried on board the steamer there, to be taken home, and who was also kindly ministered to by the captain and one or two of the lady passengers. Our party have, thus far, received little at the Doctor's hands, sundry "medical comforts" always excepted.

After paddling over four miles of the next lake the Indians advised camping, though the sun was more than an hour high. As we had experienced the discomforts of camping in the dark the night before, and as the men were evidently tired, we landed and pitched the tents on a rocky promontory at the foot of a wooded hill. Scarcely were our fires lighted, when M——'s canoe came up, and then another with a stray Indian, his wife, papooses, dog—that looked half wolf—and all their traps. After a good swim, we sat down to our evening meal, which Louis had spread on a clean table-cloth on the sward. In front

of us was the smooth lake ; on the other side of it, two miles off,
the sun was going down in the woods.   The country ahead
broke into knolls, looking in many parts like cultivated
parks ; around us the white tents and the ruddy fires, with
Indians flitting between, or busy about the canoes, gave anima-
tion to the scene and made up a picture that will long live in the
memory of many of us.

The Indians never halt without, at once, turning their canoes
upside down, and examining them.   The seams and crevices in
the birch bark yield at any extra strain, and scratches are made
by submerged brushwood in some of the channels or the shallow
parts of the lakes.   These crevices they carefully daub over with
resin, which is obtained from the red pine, till the bottom of an
old canoe becomes almost covered with a black resinous coat.

The stray Indian pitched camp an hundred yards off from
us ; and, with true Indian dignity, did not come near to ask for
anything, though quite equal to take anything that was offered
or left behind.

July 25th.—Up before four A. M., and, after a cup of hot tea,
started in excellent spirits.   Our three canoes had tried a race
the night before, over the last four miles of the day's journey,
and they renewed it this morning.   The best crew was in
the five-fathom boat, of which Ignace was captain and Louis
steersman.   The captains of the other two, Baptiste and Toma,
pushed their old master hard to-day ; as one or the other stole
ahead, not a glance did Ignace give to either.   Doggedly, and
with averted head, he dug his paddle deeper in the water,
and pegged away with his sure steady stroke, and though the
others, by spurting, forced themselves half-a-canoe-length ahead
at times, they had not the stay of the older men, and every race
ended with Ignace leading.   Then he would look up and with
sunshine on his broad, handsome face throw a good humoured
joke back, which the others would catch up with great glee

These races often broke the monotony of the day. "Up, up," or "hi, hi," would break suddenly from one of the canoes that had fallen behind. Everyone answered with quickened stroke that sent it abreast of the others. Then came the tug of war. The graceful, gondola-shaped canoes cut through the water as though impelled by steam. The *Buffalo*, or Ignace's canoe,—so called from the figure of an Indian with a gun, standing before a buffalo, that he had painted on the bow—always led at the first; but often the *Sun*, Baptiste's lighter craft, would shoot ahead, and sometimes Toma's, the *Beaver*, under the frantic efforts of her crew, seconded by one or two of us snatching up a paddle, would lead for a few minutes. The chivalry of our Indians, in the heat of the contests, contrasted favourably with that of "professionals," no "foul" ever took place, though the course often lay through narrow, winding, reedy, channels. Once, when Baptiste at such a place might have forced ahead by a spurt, he slacked speed gracefully, let Ignace take the curve and win. Another time, when neck and neck, he saw a heavy line dragging at the stern and called Louis' attention to it. No one ever charged the other with being unfair and no angry word was ever heard ; in fact, the Indians grow on us day by day. It is easy to understand how an Englishman, travelling for weeks together with an Indian guide, so often contracts a strong friendship for him ; for the Indian qualities of patience, endurance, dignity and self-control, are the very ones to evoke friendship.

The sun rose bright but was soon clouded. Ten good miles were made and then the halt called for breakfast, at a beautiful headland, just as it commenced to rain. Now we got some idea of what a rainy day in these regions means. After breakfast we put on our water-proofs, covered up our baggage and moved ahead, under a deluge of rain that knew no intermission for four hours. Most of the water-proofs proved to be delusions ; they had not been made for these latitudes. The canoes would have filled, had we not kept bailing, but, without a word of complaint, the Indians stick to their paddles.

From the lake we passed into the Maligne River, and there the current aided us. In this short, but broad and rapid stream, are six or seven rapids, which must be "shot" or portaged round; we preferred the "shooting" wherever it was practicable for such large and deeply-laden canoes as ours.

To shoot rapids in a canoe is a pleasure that comparatively few Englishmen have ever enjoyed, and no picture can give an idea of what it is. There is a fascination in the motion, as of poetry or music, which must be experienced to be understood : the excitement is greater than when on board a steamer, because you are so much nearer the seething water, and the canoe seems such a fragile thing to contend with the mad forces, into the very thick of which it has to be steered. Where the stream begins to descend, the water is an inclined plane, smooth as a billiard table ; beyond, it breaks into curling, gleaming rolls which end off in white, boiling caldrons, where the water has broken on the rocks beneath. On the brink of the inclined plane, the canoe seems to pause for an instant. The captain is at the bow,—a broader, stronger paddle than usual in his hand— his eye kindling with enthusiasm, and every nerve and fibre in his body at its utmost tension. The steersman is at his post, and every man is ready. They know that a false stroke, or too weak a turn of the captain's wrist, at the critical moment, means death. A push with the paddles, and, straight and swift as an arrow, the canoe shoots right down into the mad vortex ; now into a cross current that would twist her broadside round, but that every man fights against it ; then she steers right for a rock, to which she is being resistlessly sucked, and on which it seems as if she would be dashed to pieces ; but a rapid turn of the captain's paddle at the right moment, and she rushes past the black mass, riding gallantly as a 'race horse. The waves boil up at the side

SHOOTING A RAPID.

threatening to engulf her, but, except a dash of spray or the cap of a wave, nothing gets in, and, as she speeds into the calm reach beyond, all draw long breaths and hope that another rapid is near.

At eleven o'clock we reached Island Portage, having paddled thirty-two miles,—the best forenoon's work since taking to the canoes—in spite of the weather. Here a steam launch is stationed; and, though the engineer thought it a frightful day to travel in, he got ready at our request, but said that he could not go four miles an hour as the rain would keep the boiler wet the whole time. We dined with M——'s party, under the shelter of their upturned canoe, on tea and the fattest of fat pork, which all ate with delight unspeakable, for there was the right kind of sauce. The day, and our soaked condition, suggested a little brandy as a specific; but their bottle was exhausted, and, an hour before, they had passed round the cork for each to have a "smell" at, in lieu of a " drain." Such a case of " potatoes and point" moved our pity, and the chief did what he could for them. The Indians excited our admiration;—soaked through, and over-worked as they had been, the only word that we heard, indicating that they were conscious of anything unusual, was an exclamation from Baptiste, as he gave himself a shake,—" Boys, wish I was in a tavern now, I'd get drunk in less than tree hours, I guess."

At two o'clock, the steam launch was ready, and, about the same time, the sky cleared a little; a favorable wind, too, sprang up, and, though there were nowers or heavy mists all the time, the launch towed us the twenty-four miles of Lake Nequaquon in three and a quarter hours. The scenery was often very fine, but being of the same kind as that for more than a hundred miles back, it began to be monotonous, and we craved for a few mountains.

Next came Loon portage; then paddling for five miles; then

Mud portage, worthy of its name; another short paddle; and then American portage, at which we camped for the night—the sun having at last come out and this being the best place for pitching tents and the freest from mosquitoes. Tired enough all hands were, and ready for sleep, for these portages are killing work. After taking a swim, we rigged lines before huge fires, and hung up our wet things to dry, so that it was eleven o'clock before anyone could lie down. "Our wet things," with some, mean all. The doctor and the secretary had stowed theirs in water-proof bags, kindly lent them by the Colonel; but, alas, the bags proved as fallacious as our "water-proofs!" Part of the Botanist's valise was reduced to pulp, but he was too eager in search of specimens to think of such a trifle, and, while all the rest of us were busy washing and hanging out to dry, he hunted through woods and marshes, and, though he got little for his pains, was happy as a king.

Our camping ground had been selected by the Indians with their usual good taste. A rocky eminence, round two sides of which a river poured in a roaring linn; on the hill sombre pines, underneath which the tents were pitched; and lower down a forest of white birch. More than one of the party dreamed that he was in Scotland, as he was lulled to sleep by the thunder of the waterfall.

July 26th.—Up again about three, A. M., and off within an hour, down a sedgy river, with low swampy shores, into Lake Nameukan. The sun rose bright, and continued to shine all day; but a pleasant breeze tempered its rays. At mid-day, the thermometer stood at 80° in the shade, the hottest since leaving Owen Sound. One day on Lake Superior it was down to 48°, and the average at mid-day since we landed at Thunder Bay was from 55° to 60°.

After twelve miles paddling, halted at a pretty spot on an islet for breakfast. Frank caught a large pickerel and M—— shot a few pigeons, giving us a variety of courses at dinner. M——'s Indians tried a race with us to-day, and after a hard struggle, got ahead of Toma and Baptiste, but Ignace proudly held his own and wouldn't be beaten. However, among the many turns of the river, Toma, followed by Baptiste, circumvented their old master, by dashing through a passage overgrown with weeds and reeds instead of taking the usual channel. When Ignace turned the corner he saw the two young fellows coolly waiting for him a hundred and fifty yards ahead. They gave a sly laugh as he came up, but Ignace was too dignified to take the slightest notice; Baptiste was so pleased that he sang us two Iroquois canoe songs.

Eighteen miles, broken by two short portages, (for we took a short cut instead of the public route), brought us about mid-day to Rainy Lake; here we were told, but, as it turned out, incorrectly, was the last steam launch that could be used on our journey, as the two on Rainy River and Lake of the Woods had something wrong with them.

The engineer promised to be ready in two hours, and to land us at Fort Francis, at the west end of Rainy Lake, forty-five miles on, by sundown. But in half an hour the prospect did not look so bright, as, across the portage, by the public route, came a band of eighteen emigrants, men, women and children, who had left Thunder Bay five days before us, and whom we had passed this forenoon, when we took our short cut. They had a great deal of baggage, and were terribly tired. One old woman, eighty-five years of age, complained of being sick, and the doctor attended to her. As we had soup for dinner, he sent some over to her, and the prescription had a good effect. While waiting here we took our half dried clothes out of the bags, and, by hanging them on lines under the warm sun, got them pretty well dried before starting.

At three, P. M., at the cry of " All aboard," our flotilla formed

at once,—the steam launch towing two large barges with the
emigrants and their luggage, and the four canoes. The afternoon
was warm and sunny, and there was a pleasant breeze on the
Lake. In half an hour every Indian was asleep in the bottom
of his canoe.

The shores of Rainy Lake are low, especially on the northern
side, and the timber is small; the shores rocky, with here and there
sandy beaches that have formed round little bays; scenery tame
and monotonous, though the islets, in some parts, are numerous
and beautiful.

By nine o'clock, we had made only thirty miles. Our steamer
was small, the flotilla stretched out far and the wind was ahead.
We therefore determined to camp; and, by the advice of the
engineer, steered for the north shore to what is called the
Fifteen Mile House from Fort Francis, said house being two
deserted log huts. In a little bay here, on the sandy beach, we
pitched our tents and made rousing fires, though the air was
warm and balmy, as if we were getting into a more southern
region. The botanist, learning that we would leave before day-
break, lighted an old pine branch and roamed about with his
torch to investigate the flora of the place. The others visited the
emigrants to whom the log-huts had been assigned, or sat round
the fires smoking, or gathered bracken and fragrant artemisia
for our beds.

July 27th.—Had our breakfast before four A. M., and in less
than half an hour after, were *en route* for Fort Francis. Two
miles above the Fort the Lake ends and pours itself into Rainy
River, over a rapid which the emigrant's barges had not oars to
shoot. They were cast off, and we went on to the Fort and
sent men up to bring them down. The Fort is simply a Hudson's
Bay Company's trading post;—the shop and the cottages of the
agent and employés in the form of a square, surrounded by
stockades about ten feet high. From the Fort is a beautiful view

Pl. 12.

FORT FRANCIS.

of the Chaudière Falls which have to be portaged round. These are formed by the river, here nearly two hundred yards wide, pouring over a granite ridge in magnificent roaring cascades. A sandy plain of several acres, covered with rich grass, extends around the Fort, and wheat, barley, and potatoes are raised ; but, beyond this plain, is marsh and then rock. A few fine cattle, in splendid condition, were grazing upon the level. On the potato leaves we found the "Colorado Bug," that frightful pest which seems to be moving further east every year.

Half a dozen wigwams were tenanted in the vicinity of the Fort, and there were scores of roofless poles, where, a fortnight ago, had been high feasting for a few days. A thousand or twelve hundred Ojibbeways had assembled to confer with Mr. Simpson, the Dominion Indian Commissioner, as to the terms on which they would allow free passage through, and settlement in, the country. No agreement had been come to, as their terms were considered extravagant.

Justice, both to the Indians and to the emigrants who are invited to make their home in this newly opened country, demands that a settlement of the difficulty be made as soon as possible. It may be, and very probably is, true that some of them are vain, lazy, dirty, and improvident. The few about Fort Francis did not impress us favourably. They contrasted strikingly with our noble Iroquois. The men were lounging about, lolling in their wigwams, playing cards in the shade, or lying on their faces in the sun ; and, though not one of them was doing a hand's turn, it was a matter of some difficulty to get four or five to go with us to the North-west Angle, to replace those who had come from Shebandowan and whose engagement ended here. There were some attempts at tawdry finery about them all. The men wore their hair plaited into two or more long queues, which, when rolled up on the head, looked well enough, but which usually hung down the sides of the face, giving them an effeminate look, and all the more so because bits of silver or brass were twisted in or ringed round with the plaits. One young fellow that consented to paddle, had long streamers of bright ribbon flying from his felt hat. Another poor looking creature had his face streaked over with red ochre—of course to show how brave and blood-thirsty he was. Some wore blankets, folded loosely and gracefully about them, instead of coats and trousers; but one thing we remarked was that every one of them had some good clothes; the construction of the road being the cause of this, for all who wish can get employment in one way or another in connection with it. At Fort Francis the hulls of two steamers, to be over a hundred feet in length, for use on Rainy river and Lake of the Woods, are now being built; and Indians who cannot work at bringing in timber or at ship carpentering, can be employed as voyageurs, or to improve the portages, or to fish or hunt, or in many other ways. But whatever the benefits that have been conferred on them, or whatever their natural defects, they surely have rights to this country, though they have never divided it up into separate personal holdings. They did not do so, simply because their idea was that the land was free to all. Each tribe had its own ground, which extended over hundreds of miles, and every man had a full right to all of that as far as he could occupy it. Wherever he could walk, ride, or canoe, there the land and the water were his. If he went to the land of another tribe, the same rule held good; he might be scalped as an enemy, but he ran no risk of being punished as a trespasser.

And now a foreign race is swarming over the country, to mark out lines, to erect fences, and to say "this is mine and not yours," till not an inch shall be left the original owner. All this may be inevitable. But in the name of justice, of doing as we would be done by, of the "sacred rights" of property, is not the Indian entitled to liberal, and, if possible, permanent compen-

Pl. 14.

FORT FRANCIS TO FORT GARRY.

sation ? What makes it difficult to arrange a settlement with the Ojibbeways is, that they have no chiefs who are authorized to treat for them. This results from their scattered and dispersed state as a nation. The country they live in is poorly supplied with game, and produces but little of itself, and the Indian does not farm. It is thus impossible for them to live in large bodies. They wander in groups and families from place to place, often suffering the extreme of hunger, and sometimes starved outright. Each group has generally one or more men of greater moral or physical power than the rest, and these are its chiefs, chiefs who have no hereditary rank, who have never been formally elected, and who are quietly deposed when greater men than they rise up. Their influence is indirect, undefined, wholly personal, and confined to the particular group they live with. They can scarcely speak for the group, and not at all for the nation. When anything has to be done for the nation as a whole, there is then no other way but for the nation to meet *en masse.* Even then they elect no representative men, unless specially requested. Those of greatest age, eloquence, or personal weight, speak for the others; but decisions can be come to only by the crowd. Of course they could not have existed, thus loosely bound together, had they lived in large bodies, or been pressed by powerful enemies. But they are merely families and groups, and their lands have no special attraction for other Indian tribes. Neither can they be formidable as enemies to settlers on this same account, should the worst come to the worst; but their feebleness makes it the more incumbent on the Government of a Christian people to treat them not only justly but generously.

After breakfast we resolved to paddle down the river, till overtaken by the steam launch with the emigrants. The day was very warm; when we landed, about twelve miles on, to dine, the thermometer stood at 87 ° in the shade. Our secretary left the thermometer at this halt, hanging on the shady

D

side of a tree ; but, fortunately, the Chief was able to produce another from the bag.

Rainy River is broad and beautiful; and flows with an easy current through a low-lying and evidently fertile country. For the first twenty-five miles, twenty or thirty feet above the present beach or intervale, rises, in terrace form, another, evidently the old shore of the river, which extends far back, like a prairie. The richness of the soil is evident, from the luxuriance and variety of the wild flowers. Much of the land could be cleared almost as easily as the prairie ; other parts are covered with trees, pines, elms, maples, but chiefly aspens.

Thirty-five miles from Fort Francis we ran the Manitou rapids and, five miles further on, the Sault, neither of them formidable. A moderately powerful steamer could easily run up as well as shoot them. Beyond the Sault we landed to take in wood for the tug, and tea for ourselves. The Botanist came up to us in a few minutes with wild pea and vetch vines eight feet high, which grew so thickly, not far off, that it was almost impossible to pass through them. The land is a heavy loam,—once the bed of the river,—and is called " Muskeg" here, though, as that is the name usually given to ancient peat-bogs or tamarack swamps abounding in springs, it is not very appropriate. The time will come when every acre of these banks of Rainy river will be waving with grain, or producing rich heavy grass, for countless herds of cattle.

It was now sunset, and the captain of the tug said that it would take six hours yet to reach " Hungry Hall." We resolved, in accordance with our programme, to go on; but the Colonel preferred to camp and, perhaps, overtake us next day. So it was decided, but the Iroquois did not like the arrangement at all, as it was a break-up of their party; Louis tried to get with us by exchanging places with Baptiste, but Baptiste couldn't see it. We were sorry to part with Ignace and Louis, even for twenty-

HUNGRY HALL.

four hours, and perhaps altogether; but as the night was pleasant, and we wished to rest the next day, and stick to our programme on all occasions if possible, we had to say "good-ye." M——'s party came with us, and so did the barges withthe emigrants.

On we swept, down the broad, pleasant river, with its long reaches, beautiful at night as they had been in the bright sunshine. At times a high wall of luxuriant wood rose on each side, and stretched far ahead in curves that looked, in the gloaming, like cultivated parks. Occasionally an islet divided the river; and, at such places, a small Indian camp was usually pitched. Of the seventy-five miles of Rainy River, down which we sailed to-day, every mile seemed well adapted for cultivation and the dwellings of men. At eleven o'clock the moon rose; at half-past twelve we reached Hungry Hall, a post of the H. B. Company and a village of wigwams, out of which all the natives rushed, some of them clothed scantily and others less than scantily, to greet the new comers, with "Ho! Ho!" or "B'jou, B'jou." Baptiste urged us not to stop here, as the Indians of the place were such thieves that they would "steal the socks off us," and spoke of good camping ground a mile and a half further on. We took his advice, after getting a supply of flour, pork, and tea from the store, and, after asking the captain of the steamer to delay starting on the morrow as long as he possibly could, paddled ahead. We soon reached Baptiste's point, pitched our tents over luxuriant masses of wild flowers heavy with dew, and, in a few minutes, were all sound asleep.

July 28th.—This morning, for the first time since leaving Lake Superior, we enjoyed the luxury of a long sleep, and the still greater luxury of an hour's dozing, that condition between sleeping and waking in which you are just enough awake to know that you are not asleep. There was no hurry to-day, it was the day of rest; and we hoped that the steamer wouldn't come till the afternoon or the morrow.

At 8.30 A. M., as breakfast was getting ready, a distinguished
visitor appeared, an old stately looking Indian, a chief, we were
informed, and the father of Blackstone.   He came with only one
attendant ; but two or three canoes made their appearance about
the same time, with other Indians, squaws, and papooses who
squatted in groups on the banks at respectful distances. The old
Indian came up with a "B'jou, B'jou," shook hands all round, and
then drawing himself up,—knife in one hand, big pipe in the
other, the emblems of war and peace—commenced a long
harangue.   We didn't understand a word ; but one of the men
roughly interpreted, and the speaker's gestures were so expressive that the drift of his meaning could be easily followed.
Pointing, with outstretched arms, north, south, east and west,
he told us that all the land had been his people's, and that he
now, in their name, asked for some return for our passage through
it.   The aim of all the eloquence was simply a breakfast ; but
the bearing and speech were those of a born orator.   He had
good straight features, a large Roman nose, square chin, and, as
he stood over six feet in his moccasins, his presence was most
commanding.   One great secret of impressive gesticulation—the
free play of the arm from the shoulder, instead of the cramped
motion from the elbow—he certainly knew.   It was astonishing
with what dignity and force, long, rolling, musical sentences
poured from the lips of one who would be carelessly classed by
most people as a Savage, to whose views no regard should be
paid.   When ended, he took a seat on a hillock with the dignity
natural to every real Indian, and began to smoke in perfect
silence. He had said his say, and it was our turn now.   Without
answering his speech, which we could only have done in
a style far inferior to his, the Chief proposed that he should have
some breakfast. To show due respect to so great an O-ghe-mah, a
newspaper was spread before him as a table-cloth, and a plate of
fried pork placed on it, with a huge " slapjack " or thick pancake

made of flour and fat, one-sixth of which was as much as any white man's stomach could digest. A large pannikin of tea, a beverage the Indians are immoderately fond of, was also brought, and, by signs, he was invited to "fall to." For some moments he made no movement, either from offended pride or expectation that we would join him, or, more likely, only to show a gentlemanly indifference to the food. But the fat pork and the fragrant tea were irresistible. Many a great man's dignity has been overcome by less. After he had eaten about half, he summoned his attendant to sit beside him and eat, and to him, too, a pannikin of tea was brought. We then told the old man that we had heard his words ; that we were travellers carrying only enough food for ourselves, but that we would bring his views to the notice of the Government, and that his tribe would certainly receive justice, as it was the desire of our Great Mother the Queen, that all her children—red as well as white—should be well cared for. He at once assented, though whether he would have done so with equal blandness had we given him no breakfast is questionable.

At 10 o'clock, the steamer came along to our great disappointment, but there was nothing for it but to 'hook on.' A few miles through long reaches of wide expanding sedge and marsh brought us to the Lake of the Woods. An unbroken sheet of water, ten miles square, called "The Traverse," is the first part of this Lake that has to be crossed ; but, as a thunder storm seemed brewing behind us, the captain steered to the north behind a group of islets that fringe the shore. In half an hour an inky belt of cloud stretched over us from north to south, and, when it burst, the torrent was as if the lake had turned upside down. The storm moved with us, as in a circle, flashes of lightning coming simultaneously from opposite quarters of the heavens. First we had the wind and rain on our backs, then on the left, then in our faces, and then on the right. The captain made for a little bay in an islet near at hand, and, though the weather cleared, it looked threatening enough to make him decide to put the steamer's fire out and wait. The islet was merely a sand dune, covered with coarse grasses and small willows, though in a storm these sand hills might be mistaken for formidable rocks. As there was not enough wood on it for both parties, we gave it up to the crew and the emigrants, and paddled to another a mile ahead. This islet was of gneissoid rock and had a bold headland covered with good wood. The botanist found the ash-leaved maple, the nettle tree, and an abundance of wild flowers; twenty-four kinds that he had not seen since joining the expedition, and, of these, eight with which he was unacquainted.

Scarcely were our canoes hauled up, when the Colonel came along. His men had been so anxious to have all their party together that they had paddled steadily at their hardest for seven hours. Louis at once set to work to get dinner; and, it being Sunday, several delicacies were brought out in addition to the standing dishes of pork, biscuit, and tea. From the Colonel's stores came Mullagatawny soup, Bologna sausage, French mustard, Marmalade, and, as every one carried with him an abundant supply of the famous ' black sauce,' we had a great feast.

After dinner, all the party, except the pagan Ojibbeways, assembled for divine service. The form compiled for the surveying parties was read; the '*Veni Creator*' sung in Iroquois by the Indians; and a short sermon preached. Although the Iroquois understood but few words of English, they listened most devoutly, and we listened with as much attention to their singing. To hear those children of the forest, on a lonely isle in a lake that Indian tradition says is ever haunted by their old deities, chanting the hymn that for centuries has been sung at the great Councils and in the high Cathedrals of Christendom, moved us deeply.

After tea, candles were lit in the tents, as this evening we were not too tired to read. Our candlestick was a simple and effective Indian contrivance. A stick of any length you desired was slit at the top and then stuck in the ground. A bit of birch-bark or paper was doubled; in the fold the candle was placed, and the ends were then inserted in the slit. The stick thus held the ends tight, and the candle upright. We spent a quiet pleasant evening and about 10 o'clock "turned in."

July 29th.—Rose fresh and eager for the journey, and had a dip in the lake; there was a heavy sea on the *traverse*, and, as the little steamer was not very sea-worthy, it was doubtful if she would attempt the passage. But, while we were at breakfast, she was announced as making in our direction. Orders were at once given to take down the tents and embark the stores, but the Indians showed some reluctance to move. They said that it would be safer to trust to the paddles; that the waves in the middle of the *traverse* would be heavy, and that, if the canoes were forced through them, the bow or side would be broken in. We overruled their doubts, with a show of confidence, and started at 7.30 A.M.

Instead of the long single line of canoes that had been formed on previous days, they were now formed two abreast, and the connecting lines of the first two were shortened, and tied to the middle bench of the big barge which contained the emigrants' luggage. This worked admirably, as the barge broke the waves, and, in the comparatively smooth water immediately behind her, the two canoes rode easily, the five-fathom one to windward and a smaller one under her lee; close after these came the other two canoes. The passage was made safely, and the water for the rest of the day was only rippled slightly, as we took a circuitous route through innumerable islets, instead of the short and direct one over the unbroken part of the lake. The forenoon was cold and cloudy, but occasionally the sun shone cheerily out. Every one was thankful for the clouds and coolness, as they could note and enjoy the changing scenery, whereas the day before yesterday, in coming down Rainy River, they had suffered from the rays of the sun beating down fiercely, and reflected on every side from the water. To sit still in the canoes and suffer headache and drowsiness was a heavy price to pay for the pleasure of a glowing sun. The Indians, who seemed able to do without sleep, if necessary, but willing to take any quantity when they could get it, now slept soundly in the bottom of the canoes.

At mid-day we landed for dinner in a bay on a fire-swept islet. The Doctor and L—— baked and fried some very superior slap-jacks, which were a welcome addition to the invariable *menu* of tea, pork, and biscuits. The Colonel and the boys made the circuit of the islet with their guns ; but saw nothing worth shooting at except a solitary duck, which they didn't get. The Botanist was disappointed in his explorations, and took to collecting beetles as he couldn't get flowers.

Lake of the Woods has been shorn of much of its beauty by the fires which have swept over many of its islets; and, the character of its beauty being the same as that with which we had been already almost surfeited, it did not strike us as it certainly would one coming from the west. The fires have also revealed the nakedness, as far as soil is concerned, of its shores and islets which are low, hard, gneissoid rocks, covered with but poor timber even where it has been spared.

In the afternoon a favorable wind helped us on ; the barge hoisted a sail, and between wind and steam we made seven or eight miles an hour. The tug stopped twice for wood ; but such despatch was shown that though there was neither wharf nor platform, and the tug had to be held by boat hooks to the rocks, and at the same time kept from dashing against them, the whole thing was done at each place in ten minutes. Captain Bell's style of wooding up contrasted favorably with that of the captain of the *Frances Smith.*

The last eight or nine miles of the Lake, which were to be the last of our journey by water, led up a long bay to what is called the "North-west Angle," a point from which a road has been made to Fort Garry, so that travellers by this route now escape the terrible portages of the Winnipeg river and the roundabout way by Lake Winnipeg. The breeze chased us up finely, and we congratulated ourselves on having started in the morning, as the passage across "The Traverse" would have been an impossibility with the afternoon's wind. The land became lower as we sailed west. We were approaching the Eastern boundary of the great prairies, that extend to the west for the next thousand miles. A vast expanse of reeds lined both sides of the channel, and beyond these the wood looked poor and scrubby. The Indians, however, assured us that the land was good,—indeed, that it was the only lake of all that we had seen that had any land about it at all.

At sunset, the "North-west Angle," the end of this side of the Lake of the Woods, was reached. It seems that this point, though far North of the 49th degree, or the boundary line between the Dominion and the United States, is claimed by the Republic, and that their claim is sustained by an evident verbal mistake in the Treaty that defines the boundary. "North-west" has been inserted instead of "South-west." If so, it is only another instance in which the diplomatists of the Empire have been outwitted by the superior knowledge and unscrupulousness of our neighbours.

As we rounded out of the Bay into a little creek, the "Angle" seemed to be a place of some importance to the eyes of travellers who had not seen anything like a crowd in their last four hundred miles of travel. Fifty or sixty people, chiefly Indians, crowded about the landing place, and the babble and bustle was to us like a return to the world; but, after having satisfied themselves with a good look at us, and a joyous boisterous greeting to our Ojibbeways, whom they carried off to an Indian and half-breed "ball" in the neighborhood, we were left alone in the dirtiest, most desolate-looking, mosquito-haunted of all our camping grounds. In such circumstances it was indispensable to be jolly; so Louis was summoned and instructed to prepare for supper everything good that our stores contained. The result was a grand success, and the looks of the place improved materially.

The chief received two letters at this point; one from Governor Archibald inviting us to come direct to Government House at Fort Garry: another from the District Superintendent of the road, putting some few things of his at our disposal and also his half-breed cook. As cook had taken advantage of his master's absence to treat and be treated up to the hilarious point, his services, much to his amazement, were quietly dispensed with. At 11 o'clock we turned in under our canvas, having arranged that the waggons to take us on should be ready at 4 A. M.

July 30th.—Waked at 4.30, by the arrival of the waggons and the sound of heavy rain. Drank a cup of tea and were off in an hour on the hardest day's journey that we had yet had. It was two o'clock the following morning when we got out of the waggons for the night's rest, having travelled eighty miles in the twenty hours.

Those eighty miles, between the North-west Angle and Oak Point, were through a country monotonous and utterly uninteresting in appearance, but with resources that are sure to be developed as the country farther west is opened up. The first twenty miles are across a flat country, much of it marshy, with a dense forest of scrub pine, spruce, tamarack, and, here and there, aspens and white birch. On both sides of the road, and in the more open parts of the country, all kinds of wild fruit grow luxuriantly ; strawberries, raspberries, black and red currants, etc., etc., and, as a consequence, flocks of wild pigeons and prairie hens are numerous.   The pigeons rest calmly on the branches of dead trees by the roadside, as if no shot had ever been fired in their hearing.   Great difficulties must have been overcome in making this part of the road, and advantage has been skilfully taken of dry spots and ridges of gravel or sand that occur here and there, running in the same general direction as the road. All this part of road has been corduroyed and then covered-over with clay and sand, or gravel, where they could be got.   The land here is heavy black loam with clay underneath, just like prairie land ; with the prairie so near it is not likely to be soon cultivated ; but the wood on it will be in immediate demand both for railway purposes and scantling.

The next section of the country is of a totally different character.   It is light and sandy, getting more and more so, every ten miles or so further west.   This total change in the character of the soil afforded a rich feast to our Botanist.   In the course of the day he came on two or three distinct floras ; and, although not many of the species were new, and, in general features, the productions of the heavy and the light soils were similar to those of like land farther east in Ontario and the Lower Provinces, yet the luxuriance and variety were amazing.   He counted over four hundred different species in this one day's ride.   Great was the astonishment of our teamsters, when they saw him make a bound from his seat on the waggon to the ground, and rush to the plain, wood, or marsh.   At first, they all hauled up to see what was the matter.   It must be gold or silver he had found ; but when he came back triumphantly waving a flower or bunch of grass, and exclaiming : " Did you ever see the like of that ?" " No, I never," was the general response from every disgusted teamster.   The internal cachinnation of a braw Scotch

lad, from the kingdom of Fife, over the phenomenon, was so
violent, that he would have exploded had he not relieved
himself by occasional witticisms; "Jock," he cried to the teamster
who had the honor of driving our Botanist, " tell yon man if he
wants a load o' graiss, no' to fill the buggy noo, an' a'll show him
a fine place where we feed the horse." But when one of us
explained to the Scot that all this was done in the interests of
science, and would end in something good for schools, he ceased
to jibe, though he could not altogether suppress a deep hoarse
rumbling far down in his throat—like that of a distant
volcano,—when the Professor, as we now called him, would come
back with an unusually large armful of spoil. The bonny Scot
was an emigrant who had been a farm servant in Fife five
years ago. He had come to the "Angle" this spring, and was
getting thirty dollars a month and his board, as a common
teamster. He was saving four-fifths of his wages, and intended
in a few months to buy a good farm on the Red River among
his countrymen, and settle down as a Laird for the rest of his
life. How many ten thousands more of Scotch lads would
follow his example if they only knew how easy it would be for
them !

At our first station, White Birch river, thirty miles from the
angle, we had a lunch of Bologna sausage, and bread baked by
the keeper of the Station, a very intelligent man, a Scotchman like the rest, who had once been a soldier. He was
studying hard at the Cree and Ojibbeway languages, and gave
us much interesting information about the country and the
Indians. He attributed the failure of Mr. Simpson, to make a
treaty with the Indians at Fort Francis, in great measure to the
fact that Indians from the United States had been instigated by
parties interested in the Northern Pacific Railway to come across
and inflame their countrymen on our side to make preposterous
demands. The story does not sound improbable to those who

BIRCH CREEK STATION, ON THE ROAD TO FORT GARRY.

know the extremes which Railway Kings and companies in New York, and elsewhere in the Republic, have gone in pushing their own line and doing everything *per fas atque nefas* to crush opposition ; and the promoters of the N. P. Railroad are not in the best of humor at present because of the failure to float their bonds in London or Frankfort, and because of the promising out-look for the Canadian Pacific Railway. It is a little remarkable that the Indians all over the Dominion are anxious to make Treaties, and are easily dealt with, except in the neighbourhood of the boundary line. Mr. Simpson, in his Report dated November, 1871, states that he had no difficulty with the Indians in Manitoba Province, except near Pembina ; and there he says, " I found that the Indians had either misunderstood the advice given them by parties in the settlement, well disposed towards the Treaty, or, as I have some reason to believe, had become unsettled by the representations made by persons in the vicinity of Pembina whose interests lay elsewhere than in the Province of Manitoba ; for, on my announcing my readiness to pay them, they demurred at receiving their money until some further concession had been made by me."

Seventeen miles further on—at White Mud river—we dined ; S—— making some capital tomato-soup, and Mrs. McLeod, of the Station, giving us some blueberry jam and good bread. Had we known what was before us, some at least would have voted for remaining here all night.

The next stage was to Oak Point, thirty-three miles distant. The first half was over an abominable road, and, as we had to take on the same horses, they lagged sadly. The sun had set before we arrived at Broken Head creek, only half-way to Oak Point. Somewhere hereabouts is the eastern boundary of Manitoba, and we are not likely to forget soon the rough greeting the new Province gave us. Clouds gathered, and, as the jaded horses toiled heavily on, the rain poured down

furiously and made the roads worse.   It was so dark that the
teamsters couldn't see the horses ; and, as it unfortunately
happened that neither of them had been over this part of the
road before, they had to give the horses free rein to go where
they pleased, and—as they were dead beat—at the rate they
pleased.   The black flies worried us to madness, and we were
all heavy with sleep.   The hours dragged miserably on, and the
night seemed endless ; but, at length emerging from the wooded
country into the prairie, we saw the light of the station two
miles ahead.   Arriving there wearied and soaked through, we
came to what appeared to be the only building—a half-finished
store of the Hudson Bay Company;—entering the open door,
barricaded with paint pots, blocks of wood, tools, etc., we climbed
up a shaky ladder to the second story, threw ourselves down
on the floor, and slept heavily beside a crowd of teamsters
whom no amount of kicking could awake.   That night-drive
to Oak Point we "made a note of."

July 31st.—Awakened at 8 A. M., by hearing a voice exclaiming, "thirty-two new species already ; it's a perfect floral garden."
Of course it was our Botanist, with his arms full of the treasures
of the prairie.   We looked out and beheld a sea of green
sprinkled with yellow, red, lilac, and white.   None of us had
ever seen a prairie before, and, behold, the half had not been
told us !   As you cannot know what the Ocean is without seeing
it, neither can you in imagination picture the prairie.

Oak Point is thirty miles east from Fort Garry, and a straight
furrow could be run the whole distance, or north all the
way up to Lake Winnipeg.   A little stream—the Seine—runs
from Oak Point into the Red River.   The land along it in
sections extending two miles into the prairie is taken up by the
French half-breeds ; all beyond is waiting for settlers.

After a good breakfast of mutton chops and tea, prepared by
the half-breed cook at the Station, we started in our waggons

for Fort Garry across the prairie. Tall, bright yellow, French marigolds, scattered in clumps over the vast expanse, gave a golden hue to the scene; and red, pink, and white roses, tansy, asters, blue-bells, golden rods, and an immense variety of compositæ, thickly bedded among the green grass, made up a bright and beautiful carpet. Farther on, the flowers were fewer; but everywhere the herbage was luxuriant, admirable for pasturage, and, in the hollows, tall enough for hay. Even where the marshes intervened, the grass was all the thicker, taller and coarser, so that an acre of marsh is counted as valuable to the settler as an acre of prairie.

The road strikes right across the prairie, and, though simply a trail made by the ordinary traffic, is an excellent carriage road. Whenever the ruts get deep, carts and waggons strike off a few feet, and make another trail alongside; and the old one, if not used, is soon covered with new grasses. There is no sward; all the grasses are bunch. Immense numbers of fat plover and snipe are in the marshes, and prairie hens on the meadow land.

At 3 P.M., we reached the Red River, which flows northward, at a point below its junction with the Assiniboine, and crossed in a scow; drove across the tongue of land, formed by it and the Assiniboine coming from the west, into the village of Winnipeg, and from there to the Fort, where the Government House is at present.

Thus we finished our journey, from Lake Superior to Red River, by that Dawson road, of which all had previously heard much, either in terms of praise or disparagement. The total distance is about five hundred and thirty miles; forty-five at the beginning and a hundred and ten at the end by land; and three hundred and eighty miles between, made up of a chain of some twenty lakes, lakelets and lacustrine rivers, separated from each other by spits, ridges, or short traverses of land or granite rocks, that have to be portaged across. For those three hundred and

eighty miles the only land suitable for agriculture is along Rainy
River, and, perhaps, around the Lake of the Woods. North and
south the country is a wilderness of lakes, or rather tarns on a
large scale, filling huge holes scooped out of primitive rock. The
route is all that the tourist could desire ; the scenery picturesque, though rather monotonous owing to the absence of
mountains; the mode of travelling, whether the canoes are
paddled or tugged, novel and luxurious ; and, if a tourist can
afford a crew of Indians and three or four weeks' time, he is certain to enjoy himself, the necessity of having to rough it a good
deal only adding zest to the pleasure.

The road has been proved already on two occasions to be
a military necessity for the Dominion, until a railway is built
farther back from the boundary line. If Canada is to open up her
North-west to all the world for colonisation, there must be a
road for troops, from the first: there are sufficient elements
of disorder to make preparedness a necessity. As long as
we have a road of our own, the United States would perhaps
raise no objection to Canadian volunteers passing through Minnesota ; were we absolutely dependent, it might be otherwise.

In speaking of this " Dawson road " it is only fair to give full
credit for all that has been accomplished.   Immense difficulties
have been overcome, insomuch that, whereas it took Colonel
Wolsley's force nearly three months, or from early in June to
August 24th, to reach Fort Garry from Thunder Bay, a similar
expedition could now do the journey in two or three weeks.

But, as a route for trade, for ordinary travel or for emigrants to
go west, the Dawson road, as it now exists, is far from satis-
factory.   Only by building a hundred and fifty-five miles or so
of railway at the beginning and the end, and by overcoming the
intervening portages in such a way that bulk would not
have to be broken, could it be made to compete even with the
present route by Duluth and the railway thence to Pembina.

The question, then, is simply whether or not it is wise to do this, at an expenditure of some millions on a road the greater part of which runs along the boundary line, after the Dominion has already decided to build a direct line of railway to the North-west. This year about seventy emigrants have gone by the road in the six weeks between June 20th and August 1st. The station-masters and other agents on the road, as a rule, do their very utmost; they have been well selected, and are spirited and intelligent men ; but the task given them to do is greater than the means given will permit. The road is composed of fifteen or twenty independent pieces; is it any wonder if these often do not fit, especially as there cannot be unity of understanding and of plan, for there is no telegraph along the route and it would be extremely difficult to construct one?

CHAPTER IV.

Province of Manitoba.

August 1st.—Fort Garry.—The Province of Manitoba, in which we now are, is the smallest Province in the Dominion, being only three degrees of longitude, or one hundred and thirty-five miles long, by one and a-half degrees of latitude, or a hundred and five miles broad ; but, as it is watered by two magnificent rivers, and includes the southern ends of the two great lakes, Winnipeg and Manitoba, which open up an immense extent of inland navigation, and as almost every acre of its soil is prairie, before many years it may equal some of the larger Provinces in population. At present the population numbers about fifteen thousand, of whom not more than two thousand are pure whites. One-fifth of the number are Indians, either living in houses or wanderers, one-third English or Scotch half-breeds, and rather more than a third French half-breeds. "Order reigns in Manitoba," though wise ruling is still required to keep the conflicting elements in their proper places. By the legislation that made Manitoba a Province, nearly one-sixth of the land was reserved for the half-breeds ; owing to some delay in carrying out this stipulation, the Metis, last year, got suspicious and restless, and the Fenians counted on this when they invaded the Province from Pembina and plundered the Hudson's Bay Company's post near the line. As the half-breeds live along

(66)

the Red River from Pembina north, the situation was full of danger ; had they joined the Fenians, the frontier would have been at once moved up to Fort Garry. Everyone can understand the serious consequences that would have followed the slightest success on their part. Happily the danger was averted by prompt action on the part of the Governor. The whole population rallied around him, and the Fenians, not being able to advance into the country, were dispersed by a company of United States regulars, after being compelled to disgorge their plunder. A Battalion of Canadian militia, stationed at different points along Red River, now keeps the peace and guarantees its permanence. The land difficulty has been settled by faith being kept with the half-breeds ; a treaty has been made with the Indians that extinguishes their claims to the land ; and, as the whole of the Province has been surveyed, divided off into townships, sections, and sub-sections, emigrants, as they come in, can either get accurate information in the Winnipeg Land-office as to where it would be best for them to settle, or they can visit and then describe the piece of land they wish to occupy. There is room and to spare for all, after doing the fullest justice to the old settlers. Even the one-sixth reserved for them cannot, in the nature of things, be permanently held by those among whom it may now be divided. There is no Jewish law preserving to each family its inheritance forever. The French half-breeds do not like farming, and they therefore make but poor farmers ; and, as enterprising settlers with a little capital come in, much of the land is sure to change hands. The fact that land can be bought from others, as well as from the Government, will quicken instead of retarding its sale.

After breakfast this morning, we had an opportunity of conversing with several gentlemen who called at Government House : the United States Consul, the Land Commissioner, Officers of the Battalion, Dr. Schultz, and others. All spoke in the highest terms of the climate, the land, and the prospects of the Province and of the North-west.   Nothing shows more conclusively the wonderful progress of Manitoba and the settled condition into which it has emerged from the chaos of two or three years ago, than the fact that the Hudson's Bay Company sold at auction, the other day, in building lots, thirteen acres of the five hundred of their Reserve around Fort Garry, at the rate of $7000 per acre. At half the rate, for the rest, the Hudson's Bay Company will receive for this small reserve more than the money payment of £300,000 stg., which Canada gave for the whole territory ; and, if a few acres favorably situated bring so much, what must be the value of the many million of acres transferred to the Dominion ?   The policy of the Company now is exactly the opposite of what it used to be; formerly all their efforts were directed to keep the country a close preserve ; now they are doing all in their power to open it up.   The times have changed and they have changed with them.   And, regarding them merely as a Company whose sole object has been and is to look after their own interests and pay good dividends to the shareholders, their present policy is as sagacious for to-day as the former was for yesterday.   While a fur trading Company with sovereign rights, they did not look beyond their own proper work ; they attended to that, and, as a duty merely incidental to it, governed half a continent in a paternal or semi-patriarchal way, admirably suited to the tribes that roamed over its vast expanses.   But, as they can no longer be supreme, it is their interest that the country should be opened up ; and they are taking their place among new competitors, and preparing to reap a large share of the fruits of the development.   For many a year to come they must be a great power in our North-west.

To-day was spent in seeing men and things, the land and the rivers, in and around Fort Garry. The Chief drove twenty miles down the Red River, to the Stone Fort, the Governor and the rest of the party accompanying him five miles to Kildonan, where they called on the Rev. Mr. Black. The farms have a frontage of eight chains on the river, and run two miles back, with the privilege of cutting hay on two miles more in the rear. The people are Highlanders from Sutherland shire, and, though they knew but little about scientific farming when they settled, the excellence of the land and their own thrifty habits have stood them in good stead. They have all saved money, though there was no market for produce, except what the Hudson's Bay Company required, till within the last two or three years. Mr. Black has been their minister for twenty years. He mentioned the curious fact that all the original emigrants were Presbyterians, but that, as no minister was sent to them from the Church of Scotland, the missionaries of the Church of England attracted great numbers to their communion, by wisely adapting their service to Scottish tastes. Till recently, the Scottish version of the psalms was sung in the Cathedral, and the afternoon service was altogether on the Presbyterian model. The Missionaries, Archdeacons, and Bishops have been earnest evangelical men, several of them Scotchmen too. It is, therefore, no wonder if even Scottish dislike of prelacy gave way before such a combination. There are now Methodist and Presbyterian clergymen in the Province, as well as Roman Catholic and Episcopal. They all have missions to the Indians, and report that, while the great majority of the Crees and other tribes to the north-west are Christianized, the majority of the Ojibbeways around Fort Garry and to the east are still pagans. The Ojibbeway seems to have more of the gipsy in him than any of the other tribes, and to cling more tenaciously to the customs, traditions, and habits of life of his ancestors. It may be that the rivalry of the Churches that he sees at Red River, and the vices of the white men that he finds it easy to pick up—

drunkenness especially—have something to do with the obstinacy of his paganism. The drunkenness of Winnipeg is notorious ; the clergy do all in their power, by precept and example, to check it, but they accomplish little. The Roman Catholic Bishop and his priests, all the Presbyterian and Methodist Ministers, the Episcopal Archdeacon and several of his clergy are teetotallers ; but the " saloons " of Winnipeg are stronger than the Churches.

In conversation with the Archdeacon and Mr. Black, we learned that the various denominations were building or preparing to build " Colleges." A common school system of unsectarian education has been established by the Local Government, one-twentieth of the land reserved as a school endowment, and power given to the townships to assess themselves ; but, strange to say, nothing has been done to establish a common centre of higher education. The little Province with its fifteen thousand inhabitants will therefore soon rejoice in three or four denominational " Colleges."

We called on Archdeacon McLean, who declared his intention of spending the next twelve months in England, and giving lectures there on the North-west, as a field for emigrants. He is the right kind of man for such duty, and will do more to make Manitoba known than a dozen ordinary emigration agents. We also called on the Wesleyan Minister and Archbishop Taché ; but, unfortunately, both were from home, so at 3 P.M. we went to the camp and saw the battalion reviewed. After the review, the Adjutant General complimented the men, and most deservedly, on the admirable order and cleanliness of the camp, the excellence of the " galley," and their good conduct in their relations with the citizens. The men were smart, stout, clean-looking soldiers, and went through various movements with steadiness and activity. Many of them settle in the country as their term of service expires, free grants of land being given to all who have served for a year.

August 2nd.—Having arranged to leave Fort Garry to-day, we did so, but with extreme reluctance, so great was the kindness of the Governor, his private Secretary, and indeed of all classes. Archbishop Taché called this morning, and delighted us with his polished manners and extensive knowledge of the country. He does not think very highly of the Saskatchewan valley as a future grain-producing country, differing in this respect from every other authority; but he speaks in glowing terms of the Red-deer Lake and River which runs into the Athabaska, sometimes called Lac la Biche, a better name because there are innumerable ' Red deer' lakes. In that far away country, extending to the north of the North Saskatchewan, the wheat crops of the mission have never suffered from summer frosts but once. It certainly is one of the anomalies of the North-west, that the way to avoid frosts is to go farther north. To hear on the same day the U S. Consul and the Archbishop speak about 'the fertile belt' is almost like hearing counsel for and against it. The Consul believes that the world without the Saskatchewan would be but a poor affair ; the Archbishop that the 'fertile belt' must have been so called because it is *not* fertile. But how explain the Archbishop's opinions ? The evidence he adduced in support of them suggests the explanation ; he confined himself to facts that had been brought before him ; but his induction of facts was too limited. It, doubtless, is true that at Lac la Biche wheat is raised easily, and that at the R. C. Missions, near the Saskatchewan, it suffers from summer frosts ; but the only two R. C. settlements that we heard of in the Saskatchewan country, viz. those at St. Albert's and Lake St. Ann's, we visited, and could easily understand why they suffered. They are on the extreme north-west of the ' belt,' at an altitude above sea-level of from 2000 to 2500 feet, and were selected by the half-breeds not with a view to farming, for the French half-breed is no farmer, but because of the abundance of white fish in the lake, and sturgeon in the river, and because they were convenient for buffalo hunting and trapping, as well as for other reasons. The substance of the disputed matter seems to be this : every one else believes in 'the fertile belt' of the Saskatchewan ; the Archbishop believes that there is a belt farther north much more fertile.

At Fort Garry, farewell greetings had to be exchanged with the colonel and his son. Military duties required his presence in the Province for ten days, and we could not wait. M—— and L—— also parted with us here ; and Horetski, who had been sent on ahead to make the necessary arrangements for the journey westward, joined us ; so that our party from this date numbered six. A French half-breed, named Emilien, had been engaged to conduct us across the plains, as far as Fort Carleton, after the approved style of prairie travel. Emilien's cavalcade for this purpose was, in our ignorant eyes, unnecessarily large and imposing ; but before many days we found that everything was or might be needed. The caravan is not more needed in the East, across the deserts, than it is in the West, across the fertile but uninhabited prairies. Provisions for the whole party and for the return journey of the men must be carried,—unless you make frequent delays to hunt,—your tents and theirs, in other words, house and furniture ; kitchen, larder, and pantry ; tool-chest and spare axle-trees ; clothes, blankets, water-proofs, arms and ammunition, medicine-chest, books, paper-boxes for specimens to be collected on the way, and things you never think of till you miss them.

Our caravan consisted of six Red River wooden carts, in which were stowed the tents, baggage, and provisions ; a horse to each cart, and three drivers, one of them the cook for the six carts ; two buckboards, or light, four-wheeled waggonettes, for any of us to use when tired of the saddle ; saddle horses for the party, and two young fellows with Emilien to drive along a pack of eighteen horses, as a change of horses is required once or twice a day

Pl. 17.

FORT GARRY TO FORT ELLICE.

SCALE OF MILES

20 15 10 5 0   20

when it is intended to travel steadily at the rate of two hundred and fifty miles a week. The native horses are small, except those that have been crossed with Yankee or Ontarian breeds ; but, though small and often mean-looking, it is doubtful if the best stall-fed horses could keep up with them on a long-journey.

Emilien started from the Fort with his carts and band of horses at 10 A.M. We followed at mid-day, the Governor accompanying us to "Silver Heights," six miles up the Assiniboine. This had been his own country residence, but is now owned by D. A. Smith, Esq., M. P., the head of the H. B. Company in America. We met here Mr. Christie, late chief factor at Edmonton, Mr. Hamilton, of Norway House, Mr. McTavish and others from different parts of the great North-west; and received from Mr. Smith assistance and highland hospitality, of the same kind that every traveller has experienced, in crossing the continent, wherever there is an H. B. post.

A few words about this Hudson's Bay Company may be allowed here, not only because of the interest attaching to it as the last of the great English monopolies, but because, to this day, it is all but impossible for a party to cross the country from Fort Garry to the Pacific without its co-operation. Its forts are the only stations on that long route where horses can be exchanged, provisions bought, and information or guides obtained. The Company received its charter in the year 1670. The objects declared in that charter were fur-trading and the Christianising of the Indians. The two objects may be considered incongruous in these days; but history must testify that the Company as a rule sought to benefit the Indians as well as to look after its own interests. At first, and for more than a century, it displayed but little activity, though its profits were enormous. Its operations were chiefly confined to the shores of Hudson's Bay; but in 1783, a rival Company called "the North West"—consisting chiefly of Canadians—disputed their claims, entered the

field, and pushed operations so vigorously, that the old Company
was stirred into life and activity.   A golden age for the red man
followed.   Rival traders sought him out by lake and river side;
planted posts to suit every tribe; coaxed and bribed him to
have nothing to do with the opposition shop; assured him that
Thomas Codlin and not Short had always been the friend of
the Indian; gave him his own price for furs, and—what he liked
much better—paid the price in rum. Over a great part of North
America the conflict raged hotly for years, for the Territory
over which the Hudson's Bay Company claimed jurisdiction
was the whole of British America,—outside of the settled Eastern
Provinces of Upper and Lower Canada, New Brunswick and Nova
Scotia,—a territory twenty-six hundred miles long and fourteen
hundred broad.   The rival Companies armed their agents,
servants, and half-breed voyageurs, and many a time the quarrel
was fought out in the old-fashioned way, in remote wildernesses,
where there were no Courts to interfere and no laws to appeal to.

In 1821 the two Companies, tired of this expensive contest,
agreed to coalesce, and the present Hudson's Bay Company was
incorporated Some details as to its constitution may be gleaned
from a work published in 1849, entitled "Twenty-five years in
the Hudson's Bay Territory," by John McLean. The shareholders
elected a Governor and Committee to sit in London and represent
them.   This body sent out a Governor to the Territory, whose
authority was absolute.   He held a Council at York Factory in
Hudson's Bay, of such chief factors and chief traders as could
be present; but these gentlemen had the right only to advise,
they could not veto any measure of the Governor.   The vast
territory of the Company was divided into four departments, and
those departments into districts.   At the head of each department and district a chief factor or chief trader generally presided,
to whom all officials within its bounds were amenable.   The
discipline and etiquette maintained were of the strictest kind,

and an *esprit de corps* existed between the 3,000 officers,—commissioned and non-commissioned, voyageurs, and servants,—such as is only to be found in the army or in connection with an ancient and honorable service. The Company wisely identified the interests of its agents with its own, by paying them not in fixed salaries, but with a certain share of the profits ; and the agents served it with a devotion and pride honorable to all parties. The stock of the Company was divided into an hundred shares, sixty of these belonging to the capitalists, and forty being divided among the chief factors and chief traders.

The first territory lost by the Company was two-thirds of that lying between the Rocky Mountains and the Pacific. Oregon was lost to them when yielded in 1846 to the United States, after the ten years' joint occupancy ; and Vancouver's Island and British Columbia, when they were formed into Provinces. The fertile plains along the Red River, the Assiniboine, and the two Saskatchewans ought to have been opened up by the Empire and formed into Colonies long ago : but their real value was not known. It was not the business of the Company to call attention to them as fitted for any other purpose than to feed buffalo : for those plains were their hunting grounds, and their posts on them were kept up chiefly for the purpose of supplying their far northern posts with pemmican, or preserved buffalo-meat. The Company did what every other corporation would have done, attended simply to its own business. The more sagacious of its leading men knew that the end was coming, as the country could not be kept under lock and key much longer. They could not enforce their monopoly ; for they had no authority to enlist soldiers, they were not sure of their legal rights, and the tide of emigration was advancing nearer every day. Eight or nine years ago, when Governor Dallas was shown some gold washed from the sand-bars of the Saskatchewan, his remark was, " the beginning of the end has come." Gold would bring miners, merchants, farmers, and free-trade, so that fur-bearing animals and monopolies would need to fall back to the frozen north; still, the end would have been longer delayed had the British Provinces not united. But, in 1869, the Company's rights to all its remaining territories were bought up, under Imperial authority, by the Dominion of Canada, and, as a monopoly and a semi-sovereign power, the Company ceased to exist.

To return to our diary. A walk in the garden at Silver Heights was sufficient to prove to us the wonderful richness of the soil of the Assiniboine valley. The wealth of vegetation and the size of the root crops astonished us, especially when informed that no manure had been used and very little care taken. The soil all along the Assiniboine is either a dark or light-coloured loam, the vegetable or sandy loam that our gardeners are anxious to fill their pots with; a soil capable of raising anything. After dinner, we said 'good-bye' to the Governor, a statesman of whom even opponents will hereafter record that he deserved well of the country, because, on all great occasions, he preferred country to self or party, and of whose work in Manitoba we ought to say and would say much more, were it not for the fact that we had partaken of his hospitality. Driving rapidly on for five or six miles, Mr. Jones of the Railway Commissariat accompanying us, we overtook our cavalcade, which had made but indifferent progress on account of sundry leave-takings by the way. The country along the road is partly settled, but, with few exceptions, the farmers evidently do not farm. Till lately they had not much inducement, for there was no market : but they have neither the knowledge nor the inclination to farm systematically ; and, in a few years, most of the present occupants will be bought out and go west.

As specimens of what may be done here, the farm of one Morgan was pointed out. He had bought it some years ago,

for £50; and this year, he had already been offered £450 for
the potatoes growing on it. A Wesleyan Missionary told us
that, last year, he had taken the average of ten good farmers near
Portage la Prairie, and found that their returns of wheat were
" seventeen bushels to one,"—and that on land which had been
yielding wheat for ten years back, and which would continue to
yield it, on the same terms, for the next thirty or forty.

We drove on in the quiet, sunny afternoon, at a pleasant rate,
over a fine farming but unfarmed, country, to the " White Horse
Plains," and rested at " Lane's Post," about twenty-five miles
from Fort Garry. Lane is a North of Ireland man, a good
farmer, and, like all such, enthusiastic in praise of the country.
" What about wood and water ?" we asked. "Plenty of both
everywhere," was his answer. Wherever wells had been dug on
the prairie near to his place, water had been found. On the
Assiniboine and the creeks running into it, or north into
Lake Manitoba, there was abundance of good timber; and,
where none existed, if aspens were planted, they grew, in five
years, big enough for fence poles.

Our first evening on the prairie was like many another which
followed it. The sky was a clear, soft unflecked blue, save all
around the horizon, where pure white clouds of many shapes
and masses bordered it, like a great shield of which only the rim
is embossed. The air was singularly exhilarating, yet sweet and
warm, as in more southern latitudes. The road was only the
trail made by the ordinary traffic, but it formed nevertheless an
excellent carriage road. Far away stretched the level prairie,
dotted with islets of aspens; and the sun, in his going down,
dipped beneath it as he does beneath the sea. Soon after
sunset, we reached our camping place for the night, an open
spot on the banks of the river, thirty-three miles from Fort
Garry, on the east side of Long Lake, with plenty of dry wood
for our fires, and good feed for the horses near at hand. Scarcely

were our fires lighted when another traveller drove up, the Rev. Mr. McDougal, Wesleyan Missionary at Fort Victoria near Edmonton. We cordially welcomed him to our camp, and asked him to join our party. He was well known to us by reputation as a faithful Minister, and an intelligent observer of Indian character. He had been nine times over the plains, and evidently knew the country better than our guides. On this occasion, he was accompanied only by his Cree servant Joseph, or, as it is pronounced in Cree, " Souzie."

August 3rd.—We found this morning that it was not so easy to make an early start with a pack of horses as when canoes only were in question. Two or three of the pack were sure to give trouble, and the young fellows in charge had at least half an hour's galloping about,—which they didn't seem to regret much,—before all were brought together. Watering, harnessing, saddling, and such like, all took time. To-day the Chief and Secretary drove on ahead twenty-seven miles with Mr. Jones to Portage la Prairie, to write letters that the latter was to take back to Fort Garry. The rest followed more slowly, and the whole party did not reunite for the second start of the day till four P. M.

The road and the country were much the same as yesterday. We were crossing the comparatively narrow strip of land between the Assiniboine and Lake Manitoba, along which the Railway must run. Long Lake, or a creek that is part of it, is near the road for the greater part of the distance. It is difficult to get at the water of the lake, because of the deep mire around the shores ; and so we took the word of one of the settlers for it, that it is good though warm. Water, from a well by the roadside, that we drank, was good, and cold as ice. All the land along this part of the Assiniboine, north to what is called the " Ridge," for eight miles back has been taken up, but a great part is in the hands of men who do not understand the treasures they could take out

INDIAN ENCAMPMENT ON THE PRAIRIE.

of it; and there is abundance of the same kind of land farther back, for new settlers. As we drove past in the early morning, prairie hens and chickens rose out of the deep grass and ran across the road, within a few feet of us; while, on mounds of hay in a field lately mown, sat hawks, looking heavy and sated, as if they had eaten too many chickens for breakfast. On the branches of oaks and aspens sat scores of pigeons, so unmoved at our approach that they evidently had not been much shot at. We asked a farmer who had recently settled, and was making his fortune at ten times the rate he had done in Ontario, if he ever shot any of the birds. "No," he contemptuously answered, "he was too busy; the half-breeds did that sort of thing, and did little else." Day after day, he would have for dinner fried pork or bacon, and tea, when he could easily have had the most delicious and wholesome varieties of food. He told us that, in the spring, wild geese, wavies, and ducks could be shot in great number; but he had eaten only one goose in Manitoba. Surely it was a fellow feeling that made him so "wondrous kind."

Portage la Prairie is the centre of what will soon be a thriving settlement, and, when the railway is built, a large town must spring up. On the way to the little village, we passed, in less than ten miles, three camps of Sioux— each with about twenty wigwams,—ranged in oval or circular form. The three camps probably numbered three hundred souls. The men were handsome fellows, and a few of the women were pretty. We did not see many of the women, however, as they kept to the camps doing all the dirty work, while the men marched about along the road, every one of them with a gun on his shoulder. The Indian would carry his gun for a month, though there was not the slightest chance of getting a shot at anything. These Sioux fled here nine or ten years ago, after the terrible Minnesota massacre, and here they have lived ever since. One amiable-looking old woman

was pointed out as having roasted and eaten ten or twelve
children.   No demand was made for their extradition, probably
because they had been more sinned against than sinning.
Frightful stories are told of the treatment of Indians by miners ;
and there are comparatively few tales of Indian atrocities to
balance them.   When the Sioux entered British territory they
had with them old George III medals, and they declared that
their fathers had always considered themselves British subjects
and that they would not submit to the rule of the " long knives."
They are and always have been intensely loyal to their " great
mother," and, during Riel's rebellion, were ready and anxious to
fight for the Queen.   We were told that the United States
authorities had offered pardon if they would return to their own
lands · for the Government at Washington is desirous now to
do justice to the Indians, though its best efforts are defeated by
the cupidity and knavery of its agents ; but the Sioux would
not be charmed back.   The settlers all around the Portage speak
favorably of the Sioux.   They are honest and harmless, willing
to do a day's work for a little food or powder, and giving little
or no trouble to anybody.

The doctor at the portage entertained us hospitably.   He
spoke highly of the healthiness of the climate, showing himself
as an example.   There seems nothing lacking in this country
but good industrious settlers.

At four P.M. we started for the next post, " Rat Creek," ten
miles off.   The sky was threatening, but, as we always disregarded appearances, no one proposed a halt.   On the open
prairie, when just well away from the Hudson's Bay Company's
store, we saw that we were in for a storm.   Every form of beauty
was combined in the sky at this time.   To the south it was such
blue as Titian loved to paint : blue, that those who have seen
only dull English skies say is nowhere to be seen but on canvas
or in heaven; and the blue was bordered to the west with vast

billowy mountains of the softest, fleeciest white. Next to that, and right ahead of us, and overhead, was a swollen black cloud, along the under surface of which greyer masses were eddying at a terrific rate. Extending from this, and all around the north and east, the expanse was a dun-coloured mass livid with lightning, and there, to the right, and behind us, torrents of rain were pouring, and nearing us every moment. The atmosphere was charged with electricity on all sides, lightning rushed towards the earth in straight and zigzag currents, and the thunder varied from the sharp rattle of musketry to the roar of artillery; still there was no rain and but little wind. We pressed on for a house, not far away; but there was to be no escape. With the suddenness of a tornado the wind struck us,—at first without rain —but so fierce that the horses were forced again and again off the track. And now, with the wind came rain,—thick and furious; and then hail,—hail mixed with angular lumps of ice from half an inch to an inch across, a blow on the head from one of which was stunning. Our long line of horses and carts was broken, Some of the poor creatures clung to the road, fighting desperately. others were driven into the prairie, and, turning their backs to the storm, stood still or moved sideways with cowering heads, their manes and long tails floating wildly like those of Highland shelties. It was a picture for Rosa Bonheur; the storm driving over the vast treeless prairie, and the men and horses yielding to or fighting against it. In half an hour we got under the shelter of the log-house a mile distant; but the fury of the storm was past, and in less than an hour the sun burst forth again, scattering the clouds, till not a blot was left in the sky, save fragments of mist to the south and east. Three miles farther on was the camping place. The houses of several settlers were to be seen on different parts of the creek. One of them was pointed out as the big house of Grant, a Nova Scotian, and now the farthest west settler. We were on the confines of the " Great Lone Land."

F

August 4th.—Enjoyed a long sleep this morning and breakfasted at 8 A. M. Had intended to rest all day, but Emilien
refused. He had contracted to do the journey in so many days,
and would do it in his own way; and his way was to travel on
all days alike. He agreed, however, to make a short journey so
that we might be able to overtake him, though not starting till
late in the afternoon.

At 10 A. M., we went over to Grant's house to service. Mr.
McDougall and a resident Wesleyan Missionary officiated. About
fifty people were present, and in the afternoon a Sunday School
of thirty children was held in the same room. Some of us
dined at Grant's, and the rest with one of his neighbours—
McKenzie. Both these men seem to be model settlers. They
had done well in Ontario, but the spirit of enterprise had
brought them to the new Province. One had come three years
ago, and the other only last year; and now one had a hundred
and twenty acres under wheat, barley and potatoes, and the
other fifty. In five years both will have probably three or four
hundred acres under the plough. There is no limit to the amount
they may break up except the limit imposed by the lack of
capital or their own moderation. This prairie land is the place
for steam ploughs, reaping, mowing, and threshing machines.
With such machinery one family can do the work of a dozen
men. It is no wonder that these settlers speak enthusiastically
of the country. The great difficulties a farmer encounters
elsewhere are non-existent here. To begin with, he does not
need to buy land, for a hundred and sixty acres are given away
gratuitously by the Government to every *bonâ fide* settler;
and one third of the quantity is a farm large enough for any
one who would devote himself to a specialty, such as the raising
of beets, potatoes, or wheat. He does not need to use manure, for,
so worthless is it considered, that the Legislature has had to pass
a law prohibiting people from throwing it into the rivers. He

has not to buy guano, nor to make compost heaps. The land, if it has any fault, is naturally too rich. Hay is so abundant that when threshing the grain at one end of the yard, they burn the straw at the other end to get rid of it. He does not need to clear the land of trees, stumps or rocks,—for there are none. Very little fencing is required, for he can enclose all his arable land at once with one fence,—and pasture is common and illimitable. There is a good market all over Manitoba for stock or produce of any kind, and, if a settler is discontented he can sell his stock and implements for their full value to new comers.

And what of the Indians, the mosquitoes, and the locusts? Myths, as far as we could learn, with as little foundation as myths generally have. Neither Crees nor Sioux have given those settlers the slightest trouble. The Sioux ask only for protection, and even before Governor Archibald made the Treaty with the Sauteaux and Crees by which they received a hundred and sixty acres of land per family of five, and three dollars per head every year for their rights to the country, they molested no one. "Poor whites," were they about in equal numbers, would give ten times as much trouble as the poor Indians, though some of the braves still paint ferociously and all carry guns. And the mosquitoes, and the grasshoppers or locusts, no one ever spoke of, probably because the former are no greater nuisance in Manitoba than in Minnesota or Nova Scotia, and the latter have proved a plague only two or three times in half a century. Every country has its own drawbacks. The question must always be, do the advantages more than counterbalance the drawbacks? Thus, in returning home through California we found that the wheat crop, this year, amounted to twenty millions of bushels. The farmers told us that, for the two preceding years, it had been a failure owing to long continued drought, and that, on an average, they could only count on a good crop every

second year, but, so enormous was the yield then, that it
paid them well to sow wheat.   Take, too, the case of the great
wheat-raising State of what, as distinguished from the Pacific,
may be called the Eastern States. The wheat crop of Minnesota
this year amounts to twenty millions of bushels.   But, up to
1857, enough wheat was not raised in the State to supply the
wants of the few thousands of lumbermen who first settled
Minnesota.   Flour had to be sent up the Mississippi from St.
Louis, and the impression then was very general that one half
of Minnesota consisted of lakes, sandhills, sandy prairies, and
wilderness, and that the winters were so long and so cold in the
other half that farming could never be carried on profitably ;
and, doubtless, severe remarks could be made with truth against
Minnesota, but it is also the truth that twenty years ago its
population was five thousand, and that now it is five hundred
thousand.   The soil of Minnesota is not equal in quality to
the soil of Manitoba. Calcareous soils are usually fertile.   And
Manitoba has not only abundant limestone everywhere, but
every other element required to make soil unusually productive.
Whereas, when you sail up the Red River into Minnesota, the
limestone disappears, and the valley contracts to a narrow
trough, only two or three miles wide, beyond which the soil is
thin and poor.   But, notwithstanding all difficulties, most of the
emigrants to Minnesota are prospering.   Hundreds of thousands
of hardy Welshmen and Scandinavians poured into the new
State, secured land under the Homestead Acts or bought it
from Railway Companies, lived frugally—chiefly on a bread
and milk fare—for the first few years, and they are now well-to-do
farmers. Seeing that all the conditions for prosperous settlement
are more favourable in Manitoba, is it not easy to foresee a similarly rapid development, if those entrusted with its destinies and
with the destinies of our great North-west act with the energy and
public spirit of which our neighbours show so shining an example ?

It is not hard to trace the sources of all those alarming rumours, that we heard so much of at a distance, concerning the climate and soil of Manitoba. Our friends on Rat Creek gave us an inkling of them. On their way from St. Paul's, Minnesota, with their teams and cattle, at every post they heard those rumours in their most alarming shapes, all of course duly authenticated. They were repeatedly warned not to impoverish their families by going to a cold, locust-devoured, barren land, where there was no market and no freedom, but to settle in Minnesota. Agents offered them "the best land in the world," and when, with British stupidity, they shut their ears to all temptations, obstacles were thrown in the way of their going on, and costs and charges so multiplied, that the threatened impoverishment would have become a fact before they reached Manitoba, had they not been resolute and trusted entirely to their own resources. Even when they arrived at Winnipeg the gauntlet had still to be run. In that 'saloon'-crowded village is a knot of touters and indefatigable sympathizers with American institutions, men who had always calculated that our North-west would drop like a ripe pear into the lap of the Republic, who had been at the bottom of the half-breed insurrection, and who are now bitterly disappointed to see their old dream never likely to be more than a dream. These worthies told Grant's party quite confidentially that they had been "so many years" in the country, and had not once seen a good crop. Who could doubt such disinterested testimony? It may be asked, what object can these men have in slandering the country and retarding its development? Is not their own interest bound up in its prosperity? Whatever the motives, such are the facts. But the man who would indignantly deny that there is any connection between great schemes on the other side of the boundary line and Winnipeg pot-house politicians has a very poor idea oi the thorough-going activity of American Railway directors, and Minnesota land agents.

But what of the terrible frost, the deep snow, and the long winters? These must be stern realities. The answer of every man and woman we spoke to, in town or country, was that the winter was pleasanter than in Ontario, Quebec, or the Maritime Provinces. There is no severe weather till the beginning of December. The average depth of snow from that time is two feet, and there is no thaw till March. The severity of the intervening months is lessened by the bright sun, the cloudless skies, the stillness and dryness of the air. On account of the steady cold the snow is dry as meal, and the farmers' wives said that "it was such an advantage that the children could run about all winter, without getting their feet wet." They certainly could not say as much in Nova Scotia. This dryness of the snow is also an important fact as regards Railway construction. Let the rails be raised two or three feet above the level of the prairie, and they are sure to be always clear of snow. In fact there is much less risk of snow blockades in the winter on our western plains than in the older Provinces or in the North-eastern States. In March, and even in April, there are sometimes heavy snow-storms. But this snow soon melts away. It is what was intended for spring rain. Hay is needed in these months more than in the winter, when the horses and even the cattle can paw off the snow and eat the nutritive grasses underneath ; whereas, in March and April a crust is often formed, too hard for their hoofs to remove ; and the more hay that is cut in the autumn the less risk from prairie fires, as well as the better provision for the live stock.

In Grant's house we saw the photograph of an old friend, John Holmes, of Pictou, Nova Scotia, who has been well called "the oldest and youngest Senator of the Dominion ;" and at Prairie Portage, those of the Governor General, the Premier, Sir Francis Hincks, Alexander McKenzie, and others of our public men, adorning the walls, so that we were reminded that, although in a

new land, we were still in our own Country. Everywhere, in conversation with the people, we found the rising of that national
sentiment, that pride in their Country and interest in their
Statesmen, which is both a result and a safe-guard of national
dignity and independence, as distinguished from a petty provin-
cialism. This Western country will, in the future, probably manifest this spirit more than even the Eastern Provinces, and so be
the very backbone of the Dominion ; just as the prairie States of
the neighbouring republic are the most strongly imbued with
patriotic sentiments. The sight, the possession of these boundless
seas of rich land stirs in one that feeling of—shall we call it
"bumptiousness"—that Western men have been accused of dis-
playing. It is easy to ridicule and caricature the self-sufficiency,
but the fact is, one feels like a young giant, who cannot help
indulging in a little "tall talk," and in displays of his big limbs.

At 4 P. M., we prepared to follow our party, but, at this
moment, a body of sixty or eighty Sioux, noble looking fellows,
came sweeping across the prairie in all the glory of paint, feathers,
and Indian warlike magnificence. They had come from Fort
Ellice, had recently travelled the long road from Missouri,
and were now on their way to Governor Archibald to ask
permission to live under the British flag, and that small reserves
or allotments of land should be allowed them, as they were
determined to live no longer under the rule of 'the long knives.'
Some of them rode horses, others were in light baggage-carts or
on foot. All had guns and adornment of one kind or another.
A handsome brave came first with a painted tin horse a foot
long hanging from his neck down on his naked brawny breast,
skunk fur round his ankles, hawk's feathers on his head, and a
great bunch of sweet-smelling lilac bergamot flowers on one arm
to set him off the more. An Indian has the vanity of a child.
We went forward to address him, when he pointed to another as
O-ghe-ma (or chief); and, as the band halted, the O-ghe-ma

then came up with the usual "Ho, Ho; B'jou, B'jou," and shook hands all round with a dignity of manner that whites in the new world must despair of ever attaining. His distinction was a necklace of bears' claws, and mocassins belted with broad stripes of porcupines' quills dyed a bright gold. Next to him came the medicine man, six feet three inches in height, gaunt and wasted in appearance, with only a single blanket to cover his nakedness. They would have liked a long *pow wow*, but we had time only for hasty greetings and a few kindly words with them.

It was late before we reached the tents, for Emilien had gone on to 'the three creeks,' twenty-two miles from Rat Creek—or 'crick' as the word is universally pronounced in the North-west. Every stream, too small to be dignified with the name of river, is a 'crick.'

In to-morrow morning's journey, we are to pass out of the Province of Manitoba. This, then, is probably the best place for a few additional words on it as a home for emigrants; on the subject of emigration generally; and on the settlement of the Indian difficulty in the Province.

How is it that the United States have risen so rapidly from the condition of a fringe of provinces along the Atlantic to that of a mighty nation spreading its arms across a continent? The question is one that the new Dominion ought to ask, for the Dominion also aspires to greatness, and believes that it has within its borders all the resources required to make a nation materially great. A principal cause of the rapid development of the United States is that it has absorbed, especially within the last quarter of a century, so many millions of the population of the old world. It had a great West, boundless expanses of fertile land, and had the wisdom to see that, while the soil is the great source of wealth, untilled soil is valueless; and that therefore every inducement should be held out to the masses, overcrowded in Europe, to seek homes within its borders. Each emigrant who landed at Castle Garden represented the addition of hundreds of dollars to the wealth of the country. He represented the cultivation of some land and an increased value to more, additional imports and exports, taxes and national strength. With the same apparent generosity, but with as cool a calculation of profits as that which sent Stanley to discover Livingstone, free grants of land were therefore offered to the whole world. Homestead laws provided that those farms should not be liable to be seized for debt. As it was necessary that the emigrant should be able to get easily to his farm and to send to market what he raised, companies were chartered to build railways in every direction, the State subsidising them with exemptions, money bonuses, and enormous land grants. The ancient maxim had been, 'settle up the country and the people will build railways if they want them.' The new and better maxim is, 'build railways and the country will soon be settled.' These railway corporations became the emigration agents of the United States, and well have they done the public work while directly serving their own interests. With the one aim of securing settlers, whose labour on parts of their land would make the other parts valuable, they organized, advertized, and worked emigration schemes with a business-like thoroughness that has attracted far less attention than it deserves. What a proud position the United States, as a country, was thus made to occupy in the eyes of the whole world! 'Ho, every one that wants a farm, come and take one,' it cried aloud, and in every language. Poor men toiling for a small daily wage in the old world, afraid of hard times, sickness and old age, heard the cry, and loved the land that loved them so well, and offered so fair. They came in thousands and found, too, that it kept its word ; and then they came in tens and hundreds of thousands, till now less liberal offers have to be made, because most of the public domain that is worth anything has been absorbed. Those hard-working masses prospered, and they made the country great. Some of them who had been rudely expatriated, who had left their mother land with bitterness in their hearts, vowed vengeance and bequeathed the vow to their children. Others, attributing their success to the new institutions, began to hate the forms of government that they identified with their days of penury and misery. Others were wiser, but their interests were bound up with their adopted country, and, when it came to the question, they took sides against the old and with the new. Had the State held aloof, maintaining that any interference or expenditure on its part in connection with emigration was inconsistent with political economy, that the tide of population must be left to flow at its own sweet will, and railways be built only where there was a demand for them, the great west of the United States would not have been filled up for many a year to come. And had the Imperial authorities thought less about imaginary laws of political economy and more about pressing practical necessities, millions, who are now in a strange land, bitter enemies of the British crown, would have been its loyal subjects in loyal colonies.

The past is gone ; but it is not yet too late to do much. We now stand on a more favourable vantage ground than before, not only positively but comparatively, for our vast virgin prairies are thrown open, while there is but little good land left in the United States available for settlement under the homestead laws. The great lines of communication from the seaboard are beginning to touch our North-west territory ; and, if we act with the vigour and wisdom of which our neighbours have set the example, the ever-increasing current of emigration from the old world must flow into Manitoba, and up the Assiniboine, and Saskatchewan rivers.

We must act, to bring about such a result. It will not come of itself. While we stand looking at the river, it flows past. Labour is required to divert it into new channels, or it will flow over the courses that have been made for it, or simply overflow them. We are now able to offer better land, and on easier terms, to immigrants than the United States or any of its railway companies offer, but they will continue to attract them if we fold our arms while they work. They have many influences on their side ; the gravitating force of numbers ; past success on a grand scale ; grooves worn smooth by the millions tramping westward ; a vast army of agents paid in proportion to their success ; every principal railway station in Europe, and even in the Dominion, papered with their glowing advertisements ; floods of pamphlets in every language ; arrangements perfected to the minutest details for forwarding the ignorant and helpless stranger from New York and Chicago to any point he desires ; and perhaps a comfortable log shanty ready for him when he gets there. They offer great inducements to men to organise colonies ; advise neighbours to club their resources and emigrate together, so that one may help the other ; lay off village plats and draw beautiful sketches of future cities ; and cheer the drooping spirit of the foreigner, when he is discouraged with difficulties that had not been advertised, with brilliant prophecies, and an infusion of the indomitable Yankee spirit. They make the doubter believe that it is better to pay their company from $5 to $15 an acre for "the best land in the world," "rich in minerals," with "no long winters," accompanied with free passes over the railway, and long credits, "one-tenth down, the rest when it suits you," than to take up free grants elsewhere.

In all this business, for it is purely a business transaction, though gilded with soft hues of "buncombe," references to downtrodden millions, American generosity, free institutions, and such like, they have hitherto had no competitor ; for, until our Northwest was opened up and proved to contain farms for the million, we could not well compete. What the mass of emigrants wanted was prairie soil ; land that they could plough at once without the tedious and exhausting labour of years required in woodland farming, chopping, rolling, burning, grubbing, stumping and levelling. Such land the Dominion can now offer, and it is therefore, the great and immediate duty of the Government to see that it be opened up, and brought within reach of the ordinary class of settlers.

To what point in the Dominion should the emigrant turn his eyes? Each Province presents special inducements, but no part of America now offers so many as Manitoba. The land farther west and to the north-west is equally good, but, until opened up by railway or steamboats, it is comparatively valueless to the settler; for there is little use in raising stock, wheat, or potatoes, if they cannot be conveyed to market. But Manitoba is now within reach of the emigrant, and there is a good market in Winnipeg. This little village is becoming a town; houses are springing up in all directions with a rapidity known only in the history of western towns; and the demand for provisions, stock, farm implements, and everything on which labour is expended, is so much greater than the supply, that prices are enormously high. The intending settler, therefore, should bring in with him as much of what he may require as he possibly can.

Besides a rich soil, a healthy and—for the hardy populations of northern and central Europe—a pleasant climate, law and order, and all the advantages of British connection, Manitoba offers other inducements to the emigrant.

The Government of the Dominion has opened the country for settlement on the most liberal terms possible. Any person, the subject of Her Majesty by birth or naturalization, who is the head of a family or has attained the age of twenty-one years, is entitled to be entered for one hundred and sixty acres, for the purpose of securing a homestead right in respect thereof. To secure this land he has only to make affidavit to the above effect, and that he purposes to be an actual settler. On filing this affidavit with the land officer, and on payment to him of $10, he is permitted to enter the land specified in his application.　Five years thereafter, on showing that he has resided on or cultivated the land, he receives a patent for it ; or any time before the expiration of the five years he can obtain the patent by paying the pre-emption price of one dollar an acre.　This farm, no matter how valuable it may become, and his house and furniture, barns, stables, fences, tools, and farm implements are declared free from seizure for debt ; and, in addition to the exemption of all those, there are also exempted, "one cow, two oxen, one horse, four sheep, two pigs, and the food for the same for thirty days."

There are, and can be, no Indian wars or difficulties in Manitoba.　This is a matter of the utmost importance to the intending settler.　When we returned from our expedition, the Chief was interviewed at Ottawa by a deputation of the Russian sect of Mennonites, who are looking out for the best place in America for their constituents to settle in, and one of their first questions referred to this.　He answered it by pulling a boy's knife out of his pocket, small blade at one end, corkscrew at the other, and told them that that was the only weapon he had carried while travelling from Ocean to Ocean ; adding that he had used only one end of even so insignificant a weapon, and that end not so often as he would have liked.

As the mode of settlement adopted in Manitoba is based on the system that has been long tested in the older provinces, and that will probably be extended to the whole of the North-west, a few words on the general question may not be out of place. There are three ways of dealing with the less than half-million of red men still to be found on the continent of America, each of which has been tried on a smaller or larger scale.　The first cannot be put more clearly or baldly than it was in a letter dated San Francisco, Sept. 1859, which went the round of the

American press, and received very general approval. The writer, in the same spirit in which Roebuck condemned the British Government's shilly-shally policy towards the Maories, condemned the Federal Government for not having ordered a large military force to California when they got possession of it, "with orders to hunt and shoot down all the Indians from the Colorado to the Klamath." Of course the writer adds that such a method of dealing with the Indians would have been the cheapest, "and perhaps the most humane." With regard to this policy of "no nonsense," thorough-going as selfishness itself, it is enough to say that no Christian nation would now tolerate it for an instant.

The second way is to insist that there is no Indian question. Assume that the Indian must submit to our ways of living and our laws because they are better than his ; and that, as he has made no improvement on the land, and has no legal title-deeds, he can have no right to it that a civilized being is bound to recognize. Let the emigrants, as they pour into the country, shove the old lords of the soil back ; hire them if they choose to work ; punish them if they break the laws, and treat them as poor whites have to be treated. Leave the struggle between the two races entirely to the principle of natural selection, and let the weaker go to the wall. This course has been practically followed in many parts of America. It has led to frightful atrocities on both sides, in which the superior vigour of the civilized man has outmatched the native ferocity of the savage. The Indian in such competition for existence, soon realizing his comparative weakness, had recourse to the cunning that the inferior naturally opposes to the superior strength. This irritated even the well-disposed white, who got along honestly, and believed that honesty was the best policy. It was no wonder that, after a few exchanges of punishment and vengeance, the conviction would become general that the presence of the

Indian was inconsistent with public security; that he was a nuisance to be abated; and that it was not wise to scrutinize too closely, what was done by miners who had to look out for themselves, or by the troops who had been called in to protect settlers. The Indians had no newspapers to tell how miners tried their rifles on an unoffending Indian at a distance, for the pleasure of seeing the poor wretch jump when the bullet struck him; or how, if a band had fine horses, a charge was trumped up against them, that the band might be broken up and the horses stolen; or how the innocent were indiscriminately slaughtered with the guilty; or how they were poisoned by traders with bad rum, and cheated till left without gun, horse, or blanket. This policy of giving to the simple children of the forest and prairie, the blessings of unlimited free-trade, and bidding them look after their own interests, has not been a success. The frightful cruelties connected with it and the expense it has entailed, have forced many to question whether the 'fire and sword' plan would not have been 'cheaper and, perhaps, more humane.'

The third way, called, sometimes, the paternal, is to go down to the Indian level when dealing with them; go at least half-way down; explain that, whether they wish it or not, immigrants will come into the country, and that the Government is bound to seek the good of all the races under its sway, and do justly by the white as well as by the red man; offer to make a treaty with them on the principles of allotting to them reserves of land that no one can invade, and that they themselves cannot alienate, giving them an annual sum per family in the shape of useful articles, establishing schools among them and encouraging missionary effort, and prohibiting the sale of intoxicating liquors to them. When thus approached, they are generally reasonable in their demands; and it is the testimony of all competent authorities that, when a treaty is solemnly made with them, that is, according to Indian ideas of solemnity, they keep it sacredly. They only break it when they believe that the other side has broken faith first.

Such has been the policy of the old Canadas and of the Dominion, and it is now universally adopted in America. True, the agents of the United States Government have often defeated its attempts to do justice and show mercy, by wholesale frauds ; and the Indians, believing themselves deceived, have risen with bursts of fury to take vengeance ; and, like all children, if deceived once, they are very unwilling to believe you the next time. General Howard has therefore advised this year the removal of many of the Indian agents, with the remark that " when agents pay $15,000 for a position, the salary of which is only $1500, there must be something wrong," But this corruption of individual agents is a mere accident, an accident that seems to be inseparable from the management of public affairs in the Republic. The great thing is that the United States Government has taken its stand firmly on the ground that the Indians are to be neither exterminated nor abandoned to themselves, but protected and helped. In a letter to George H. Stewart, dated October 28th, 1872, President Grant writes with his customary directness and plainness of speech : " If the present policy towards the Indians can be improved in any way, I will always be ready to receive suggestions on the subject ; but if any change is made, it must be made on the side of the civilization and christianization of the Indians. I do not believe our Creator ever placed the different races of men on this earth with the view of the stronger exerting all his energies in exterminating the weaker."

It may be said that, do what we like, the Indians as a race, must eventually die out. It is not unlikely. Almost all the Indians in the North-west are scrofulous. But, on the other hand, in the United States and in Canada, they exist, in not a few cases, as christianized self-supporting communities, and have multiplied and prospered. These are beginning to ask for full freedom. It was all right, they argue, to forbid us to sell our lands, when we did not know their value, and to keep us as wards when wecould not take care of ourselves; but it is different now; we are grown men; and it is an injustice to prevent us from making the most we can out of our own.

At all events, there are no Indian difficulties in our North-west. For generations the H. B. Company governed the tribes in a semi-paternal way, the big children often being rude and noisy, sometimes plundering a fort, or even maltreating a factor, but, in the end, returning to their allegiance, as, without the Company, they could not get tea or tobacco, guns or powder, blankets or trinkets.

Since the transfer of the country to the Dominion the Indians have been anxious for treaties, except when operated on by foreign influences. In the year 1871, Governor Archibald made a treaty at the Stone Fort, or Lower Fort Garry, with the Ojibbe-ways and Swampy Crees, the only two tribes in his Province, and a second treaty with the Indians further north, as far as Lake Winnipegosis and Beren's River, and to the west as far as Fort Ellice. This second treaty comprises a tract of country two or three times as large as Manitoba. About four thousand Indians assembled on those occasions, and, after a good deal of preliminary feasting, consulting, and *pow-wow*ing, arrangements were made with them. The objects aimed at by the Governor and the Indian Commissioner were to extinguish the Indian title to the land, and, at the same time, do substantial justice and give satisfaction to the Indians. These objects were accomplished.

The treaty-making process is interesting, as illustrative of several points in the Indian character. Though it took ten days to make the first, yet, in the light lately thrown on the difficul-

G

ties of drawing up a treaty that shall express the same thing
to both parties, the time cannot be considered unreasonably
long.

The Indians first elected chiefs and spokesmen to represent
them. On these being duly presented and invited to state their
views, they said that there was a cloud before them which made
things dark, and they did not wish to commence the proceedings
till the cloud was dispersed. It was found that they referred to
four Swampies who were in prison for breach of contract, and
the tribe felt that it would be a violation of the brotherly
covenant to enter upon a friendly treaty, unless an act of indem-
nity were passed in favour of the four. As they begged their
discharge on the plea of grace and not of right, the Governor
acceded to their petition ; and the Indians thereupon declared
that henceforth they would never raise a voice against the law
being enforced.

The real business then commenced. Being told to state their
views on reserves and annuities, they did so very freely and,
substantially, to the effect that about two-thirds of the province
should be reserved for them. But when it was explained that
their great mother must do justly to all her children, " to those
of the rising sun as well as to those of the setting sun," and that
it would not be fair to give much more than a good farm for
each family, they assented. Fortunately the Governor could
point out to them a settlement of christianized Ojibbeways, numbering some four hundred, between the Stone Fort and the
mouth of Red River, as a proof that Indians could live,
prosper, and provide like the white man. This mission was
established by Archdeacon Cochrane, and has now a full-
blooded Indian for its clergyman. Many of them have well-
built houses and well-tilled fields, with wheat, barley, and
potatoes growing, and giving promise of plenty for the coming
winter.

The Indians of this district form a parish of their own, called St. Peter's, and return a member to the House of Assembly ; they have the honour of being represented by a gentleman who has successively held the offices of Minister of Agriculture, Provincial Secretary, and who is now Provincial Treasurer.

In the end, it was agreed that reserves should be allotted sufficient to give one hundred and sixty acres to each family of five ; that the Queen should maintain a school on each reserve when the Indians required it ; and that no intoxicating liquors be allowed to be introduced or sold within the bounds of the reserves ; also, that each family of five should receive an annuity of $15, in blankets, clothing, twine, or traps ; and, as a mark of Her Majesty's satisfaction with the good behaviour of Her Indians, and as a seal to the treaty, or Indian luckpenny, a present of $3 be given to each man, woman, and child. Every one being satisfied, the treaty was signed, the big ornamented calumet of peace smoked all round, and the Governor then promised each chief a buggy, to his unbounded delight.

One important consequence of these Indians being pleased is that the Indians farther west having heard the news are all anxious for treaties, and have been on their good behaviour ever since.

CHAPTER V.

From Manitoba to Fort Carlton on the North Saskatchewan.

August 5th.—This morning it rained heavily, and delayed us a little ; but, by the time we had our morning cup or pannikin of tea, the carts packed, and everything in its place, the weather cleared up. We got away at 5 A.M., and rode sixteen miles before breakfast ; reaching " Pine Creek," a favorite camping ground ; still following up the course of the Assiniboine, though never coming near enough to get a sight of it, after leaving our first camp from Fort Garry. The next stage was fourteen miles to 'Bog Creek,' and, after dinner, eleven miles more, making forty-one for the day. Instead of the level prairie of the two preceding days, and the black peaty loam, we had an undulating and more wooded country, with soil of sandy loam of varying degrees of richness. Here and there ridges of sand dunes, covered, however, with vegetation, sloped to the south, having originally drifted from the north, probably from the Riding Mountains of which they may be considered the outlying spurs. From the top of any one of these, a magnificent view can be had. At our feet a park-like country stretched far out, studded with young oaks ; vast expanses beyond, extending on the north to the Riding Mountains, and on the south to the Tortoise Mountain on the boundary line ; a beautiful country extending hundreds of square miles without a settler, though

(100)

there is less bad land in the whole of it than there is in the little peninsula of Halifax, or within five or ten miles of any of our eastern cities. This almost entire absence of unproductive land is to us very wonderful. If we except the narrow range of sand-hills, there is actually none ; for the soil, even at their base, is a light sandy loam which would yield a good return to the farmer. The soil about these hills is not what is usually termed prairie, and is not equal to prairie. Its flora is not that of the prairie. Both soil and flora are like those of the Rice Lake plains, and the County of Simcoe in Ontario, where excellent wheat crops are raised. The only question, suggestive of a doubt, that came up was the old one of "Is there plenty of water?" The rivers are few ; the creeks small. Along their banks there is no diffi-culty, but what of the intervening ground? We had heard of wells sunk in different places, and good water found from four to fifty feet down. But, yesterday, Grant informed us that a beautiful stretch of prairie, immediately to the west of his loca-tion, which had been taken up by a friend of his, had been abandoned because no water could be got. They had sunk wells in three places, one of them to the depth of seventy-five feet, but pierced only hard white clay. Grant believed that this stratum of clay extended over a limited area, and that, under it, water would be tapped if they went deep enough. But the matter is of too great importance to be left to conjecture. Test-wells should be sunk by the Government in different places ; and even where there are saline or brackish lakes, or even should the first water tapped prove saline, artesian wells might be tried, so as to get to the fresh water beneath. Till it is certain that good water can be easily had all over the prairie, successful coloniza-tion on a large scale cannot be expected. The general belief is that there is water enough everywhere. There is an abundant rain fall, and the water does not form little brooks and run off, but is absorbed by the rich, deep, porous ground. Still the claims

of our North-west on the attention of emigrants would be
rendered all the stronger, were they assured that the water
supply was unfailing everywhere.   Up to this time the question
has not been started, because much of the land on the river-
banks has not yet been taken up.   But it would be well to be
prepared with an answer.

Nothing could be more exhilarating than our rides across the
prairie, especially the morning ones.   The weather, since our
arrival at Fort Garry, had been delightful, and we knew that we
had escaped the sultry heat of July, and were just at the commencement of the two pleasantest months of the year.   The
nights were so cool that the blanket was welcome, and in the
evenings and mornings we could enjoy the hot tea.   The air
throughout the day was delicious, fresh, flower-scented,
healthful, and generally breezy, so that neither horse nor rider
was warm after a fifteen or twenty miles' ride.   We ceased to
wonder that we had not heard of a case of sickness in one of the
settlers' families.   Each day was like a new pic-nic.   Even the
short, terrific, thunder storm of the day before yesterday had
been enjoyed because of its grandeur.   Grant told us that it was
the heaviest he had ever seen in the country, and that we had
felt its full force.   Three miles away there had been no hail.

August 6th.—Up before four A.M., but were delayed some
time by the difficulty of lassoing the horses that were wanted.
The Doctor had, meanwhile, some shooting round the little
lake by which we had camped ; and getting some more on the
way, Terry, the cook, was enabled to serve up plover, duck and
pigeons, with rice curry for breakfast.   Our morning's ride was
sixteen miles, and brought us to the Little Saskatchewan,—a
swift-flowing pebbly-bottomed stream, running south into the
Assiniboine.   Its valley was about two miles wide and two
hundred and fifty feet deep.   All the rivers of the North-west
have this peculiarity of wide valleys, and it constitutes a serious

difficulty in the way of railroad making; they must be crossed, but regular bridging on so gigantic a scale is out of the question. The hill sides sloping down into the valley or intervale of the river are green and rounded, with clumps of trees, most of them fire-scorched, in the depressions.

We hailed the sight of this flowing stream with peculiar delight; for it was the first thing that looked, to our eyes, like a river in all the hundred and twenty miles since leaving the Assiniboine. The creeks crossed on the way were sluggish and had little water in them, and most of the swamps and lakelets were dried up, and their bottom covered with rank coarse grass, instead of the water that fills them in the spring. This morning, however, we passed by several pretty-well-filled lakes,— plover and snipe about most of them—on the " height of land," from which the ground slopes toward the Little Saskatchewan.

Our second stage for the day was only eleven miles; but the next was fourteen, and we drove or rode along the winding road at a rattling pace, reaching our camping ground, at Salt Lake, an hour before sunset. This lake is bitter or brackish, but, on the opposite side of the road, there is good water; and, although the mosquitoes gave us a little trouble, here we fared well—as at all our camps. This was the first saline lake we had seen, but farther north on the way to Edmonton, there are many such; and grievous has been the disappointment of weary travellers, on drawing near to one of them and preparing to camp. The causes are probably local, for good water is found near, and, all around, the grass is as luxuriant as elsewhere. A white crust forms on the dried up part of the bottom and the shores are covered with marine plants, chiefly reddish-colored, thick, succulent samphire and sea-blite growing together and extending over several acres of ground. The salt in these lakes is sulphate of soda.

A bathe in the little Saskatchewan before breakfast was our

first good wash for two or three days, and we enjoyed it propor-
tionately. Our horses did their forty-one miles to-day, seemingly
with greater ease than they had any previous day's work. Most
of them are of pure native breed; some of them—the largest—
have been crossed with Canadian, and the swiftest with Yankee
breeds. In all our pack there are only two or three bad horses;
none of them looked well at first, but, though small and common looking, they are so patient, hardy and companionable, that
it is impossible for their riders to avoid becoming attached to
them. Hardly two of the saddles provided for our party were
alike. There was choice of English, American, and Mexican
military,—the first kind being the general favorite.

August 7th.—Made a good day's journey of forty-five miles,
from the Salt Lake to the junction of the Qu'Appelle and
Assiniboine rivers. The first stage was ten miles, to the "Shoal
Lake"—a large and beautiful sheet of water with a pebbly or
sandy beach—a capital place for a halt or for camping. The
great requirements of such spots are wood, water, and feed for
the horses; the traveller has to make his stages square with the
absence or presence of those essentials. If he can get a hilly spot
where there are few mosquitoes, and a sheet of water large enough
to bathe in, and a resort of game, so much the better. Arrived
at the ground, the grassiest and most level spots, gently sloping,
if possible, that the head may be higher than the feet, are
selected. The tents are pitched over these, one tent being
allotted to two persons, when comfort is desirable, though sometimes a dozen crowd inside of one. A waterproof is spread on
the ground, and, over that, a blanket. Each man has another
blanket to pull over him, and he may be sound asleep ten
minutes after arriving at the ground, if he has not to cook or wait
for his supper. The horses need very little attention; the
harness is taken off and they are turned loose—the leaders or
most turbulent ones being hobbled, *i. e.*, their fore feet are

fettered with intertwined folds of shaganappi or raw buffalo hide, so that they can only move about by a succession of short jumps. Hobbling is the western substitute for tethering. They find out, or are driven to, the water, and, immediately after, begin grazing around ; next morning they are ready for the road. A morning's swim and wash in Shoal Lake was a great luxury,. and the Doctor had some good shooting at ducks, loons, yellowlegs, and snipe.

Our second stage was twenty-one miles to " Bird's Tail Creek," a pretty little running stream, with valley nearly as wide, and banks as high, as the Little Saskatchewan. It is wonderful to see the immense breadth of valley that insignificant creeks, in land where they have not to cut their way through rocks, have eroded in the course of ages.

At this creek, we were only twelve miles distant from Fort Ellice. The true distance from Fort Garry, as measured by our odometer being two hundred and fifteen miles, and not two hundred and thirty-one, as stated on Palliser's map and by Captain Butler in his book. As our course lay to the north of Fort Ellice, the Chief and two of the party went on ahead to get provisions and half a dozen Government horses that had been left to winter there, and to attend to some business, while the rest followed the direct trail and struck the edge of the plateau overlooking the Assiniboine,—which was running south —just where the Qu'Appelle joined it from the west. The view from this point is magnificent ; between two and three hundred feet below, extending far south and then winding to the east, was the valley of the Assiniboine,—at least two miles wide.

Opposite us, the Qu'Appelle joined it, and both ran so slowly, that the united river meandered through the intervale, as circuitously as the links of the Forth, cutting necks and promontories of land that seemed, and were, almost islands, some of them soft and grassy, and others covered with willows or timber.

The broad open valley of the Qu'Appelle stretched along to the west, making a grand break in what would otherwise have been an unbroken plateau of prairie. Three miles to the south of this valley, and therefore opposite us but farther down, two or three small white buildings on the edge of the plateau were pointed out as Fort Ellice. To the north of the Qu'Appelle, the sun was dipping behind woods far away on the edge of the horizon, and throwing a mellow light on the vast expanse which spread around in every direction.

We descended to the intervale by a much-winding path, and moved on north a little to the "crossing" three miles above the Fort, and immediately above where the Qu'Appelle flows into the main river. Scarcely had the tents been pitched and the fires lighted, when the Chief appeared bringing supplies of flour, pemmican, dried meat, salt, etc., from Fort Ellice. He reported that there were several parties of Indians about the Fort, who had emigrated two or three years ago from the United States, anxious to settle in British territory. One of them, from Ohio, spoke good English, and from him he gained the information about them.

The first portion of the journey from Fort Garry is considered to extend to Fort Ellice, and we had accomplished it in less than six days. The last stage had been over the worst road—a road winding between broad hill-sides strewn with granite boulders, and lacking only brawling streams and foaming fells to make it like Moffatdale, and many another similar dale in the south of Scotland. But here there never had been bold moss troopers, and there were no "Tales of the Borders." Crees, and Sioux and Ojibbeways may have gone in the war path against each other, and have hunted the buffalo over the plains to the west, but there has been no Walter Scott or even Wilson to gather up and record their legends, and hand down the fame of their braves. And there are no sheep grazing on those rich hill-sides, and there was neither wigwam, steading, nor shieling on the last hundred and sixty miles of road. Silence reigned everywhere, broken only by the harsh cry of wild fowl rising from lakelets, 'or the grouse-like whirr of the prairie hen on its short flight. We had seen but a small part, and that by no means the best of the land. The trail follows along the ridges, where there is a probability of its being dry for most of the year, as it was not part of its object to shew the fertility of the country or its suitableness for settlers. But we had seen enough to show that, even east of Fort Ellice, there is room for a large population. Those great breadths of unoccupied land are calling 'come, plough, sow, and reap us.' The rich grass is destroyed by the autumn fires, which a spark kindles, and which destroy also the wood, which formerly was of larger size and much more abundant than now. This destruction of wood seriously affects the water supply. Lakes that once had water all the year round are now dry, except in the spring time. But, when settlers come in, all this shall be changed. The grass will be cut at the proper time, and stacked for the cattle, and then there shall not be the wide spreading dried fuel to feed the fires, and give them ever increasing force. Fields of ploughed land, interspersed here and there, shall set bounds to the flames, and tourists and travellers will be less likely to leave their camp-fires burning, when they know that there are settlers near, whose property would be endangered, and who therefore would not tolerate criminal carelessness on the part of strangers.

8th August.—Being in the neighbourhood of a fort, and having to re-arrange luggage and look after the new horses, we did not get away till nine o'clock. An hour before, greatly to the surprise of Emilien,—for he had calculated on keeping in advance the twenty-two miles he had gained on Sunday,—and greatly to our delight, Mr. McDougal drove up and rejoined us with his man " Souzie." Souzie had never been east before, and the glories of Winnepeg had fairly dazzled him.   He was going home heavy-laden with wonderful stories of all he had seen ;— the crowd hearing Mr. Punshon preach and the collection taken up at the close, the review of the battalion of militia, the splendour of the village stores, the Red River steamboat, the quantities of rum, were all amazing.   When the plate came round at the church Souzie rejoiced, and was going to help himself, but, noticing his neighbors put money in, he was so puzzled that he let it pass.   He chuckled for many a day at the simplicity of the Winnepeggers :—"Who ever before saw a plate handed round except to take something from it ?"   The review excited his highest admiration :—" Wah, wah ! wonderful ! I have seen a hundred men turned into one !"

Our first work this morning was to cross the Assiniboine. The ford was only three feet deep, but the bottom was of shifting sand, so that it did not do to let the horses stand still while crossing The bank on the west side is bold, and the sand so deep, that it is a heavy pull up to the top.   After ascending, we moved west for the first few miles along the north bank of the Qu'Appelle.   The Botanist went down to the intervale and sand-hills near the stream, to inspect the flora, and was rewarded by finding half-a-dozen new species.   We soon turned in a more northerly direction, though, had there been a fortnight to spare, some of us would have liked to have gone a hundred miles up the Qu'Appelle, where, we had been told yesterday by a Scotch half-breed, called Mackay, that the buffalo were in swarms. Mackay was on his way back to Fort Garry with the spoils of his hunt.   He had left home with his wife and seven children and six carts, late in May. joined a party at Fort Ellice and gone up to the high plains, where the source of the Qu'Appelle is, near the elbow of the South Saskatchewan, and obtained his food for the year in the way most pleasing to a half-breed. They had all lived sumptuously while near the buffalo, and when they

FORT ELLICE TO SOUTH SASKATCHEWAN RIVER.

had dried enough meat to fill their carts, at the rate of ten buffalos to a cart, they parted company ; and he and his wife, with the meat and skins, turned homewards, to do little for the rest of the year, but enjoy themselves. This is all very well when the buffalo are plenty ; but as they get scarcer or move farther away, what is to be done ? A man cannot be both a hunter and a farmer ; and, therefore, as the buffalo go west, so will the half-breeds.

But, fascinating as a buffalo-hunt seemed, described in all the glowing language and gesticulations of a successful hunter, the time could not be spared, and so we jogged along our road, hoping that we might fall in with the lord of the prairies as far north as Carlton or Fort Pitt.

The first part of the day's ride, like the last part of the previous day's, was over the poorest ground we had seen—light and sandy—and yet the grass nowhere presented the dried up, crisp, brownish look that is so often seen in the eastern provinces at this time of the year. Still the land about Fort Ellice is not to be recommended, especially when there is so much of the very best waiting to be cultivated.

Nine miles from the Assiniboine, we breakfasted beside a spring in the marsh where the water is good, but where a barrel or some such thing, sunk in the ground, would be desirable. This is every traveller's business, and, therefore, is not done. We are now in "No man's Land ;"—where the Governor of Manitoba has a nominal jurisdiction, but where there are no taxes and no laws ; where every man does what is right in his own eyes, and prays that the great Manitou would prosper him in his horse, stealing or scalping expeditions.

Our next stage was twenty-two miles to "Broken Arm River" —a pretty little stream with the usual deep and broad valley. The soil improved as we travelled west. The grass was richer, and much of the flora that had disappeared for the previous twenty miles began to show again. On the banks of the river there was time before tea to indulge in a great feast of raspberries, as we camped early in the evening, after having travelled only thirty-one miles. The Botanist had found exactly that number of new species,—the largest number by far on any one day since leaving Fort Garry. The explanation is, that he had the valleys of two rivers and several varieties of soil to botanize over.

August 9th.—Last night the thermometer fell to 34 °, and we all suffered from the cold, not being prepared for such a sudden change. There was heavy dew, as there always is on prairies, and at four o'clock, when we came out of the tents, shivering a little, the cold wet grass was comfortless enough ; but a warm cup of tea around the camp fire put all right. We were on horseback before sunrise, and a trot of thirteen miles, over a beautiful and somewhat broken country, fitted us for breakfast. Mr. McDougal told us that in the elevated part of the country in which we were, extending north-west from Fort Ellice, light frosts were not unusual in July or August. They are not so heavy as seriously to injure grain crops ; but still they must be regarded as an unpleasant feature in this section of the country. The general destruction of the trees by fires makes a recurrence of these frosts only too likely, till some action is taken to stop the real fountain of all the evils. If there were forests, there would be a greater rainfall, less heavy dews, and probably no frosts. But it will be little use for the government to issue proclamations in reference to the extinguishing of camp-fires, until there are settlers here and there, who will see to their observance for their own interest. Settlers will plant trees, or give a chance of growing to those that sow themselves, cut the grass, and prevent the spread of fires. But settlers will not come, till there is a railroad to bring them in.

Our second stage for the day was sixteen miles over an excellent road and through a country that evoked spontaneous

bursts of admiration from every one. The prairie was more
than rolling, it was undulating ; broken into natural fields by
the rounded hillocks and ridges crowned with clumps of aspens
—too often, alas ! fire-scathed.   In the hollows grew tall, rich,
grass which would never be mowed ; everywhere else, even on
the sandy ridges, was excellent pasture.

We met a half-breed travelling, with dried meat and buffalo,
skins, to Fort Garry, in his wooden cart covered with a cotton
roof, and he informed us that men were hunting, two days'
journey ahead, about the Touchwood Hills.   This excited our
men to the highest pitch, for the buffalo have not come on this
route for many years, and eager hopes were exchanged that we
might see and get a shot at them.   Wonderful stories were told
of the buffalo-hunts in former days, and men, hitherto taciturn,
perhaps because they knew little English (more, however, than
we knew of French or Indian, which they all spoke fluently)
began explaining volubly—eking out their meaning with expressive gesticulation,—the nature of a buffalo hunt. Fine fellows
all our half-breeds were as far as riding, hunting, camping,
dancing and such like were concerned ; though they would have
made but poor farm-servants.   Two of them had belonged to
Riel's body-guard in the days of his little rebellion.   The
youngest was Willie, a boy of sixteen, who rode and lassoed, and
raged, and stormed, and swore on the slightest provocation, better
than any of them.   He looked part of the horse when on his
back, and never shirked the roughest work. We were horrified
at his ready profanity however, and the Doctor rowed him up
about it ; but, though they all liked the Doctor, for he had
physicked two or three of them successfully, and had even bound
up the sore leg of one of the horses better than they could, the
jawing had no effect.   The Secretary then tried his hand.
Finding that Willie believed in his father, an adventurous
daring Scot, who had married a squaw, he accosted him one day

when none of the others were near, with, "Willie, would you like
to hear me yelling out your father's name, with shameful words
among strangers?" He looked up with a half-puzzled, half-
defiant air, and shook his head. "Well, how can I like to hear
you shouting out bad language about my best friend?" A few
more words "on that line" and Willie was 'converted.' We
heard no more oaths from him except the mild ones, "By
George," by Jing," or "by Golly," and in many an ingenious
way thereafter he showed a sneaking fondness for the Secretary.

We rested to-day for dinner on a hillock beside two deep
pools of water, and the Doctor made us some capital soup from
preserved tomatoes and mutton. Ten or eleven miles from our
dining table brought us to the end of this section of wooded
country, where we had intended to camp for the night, but the
ponds were empty and no halt could be made. We therefore
pushed on across a vast treeless plain, twenty miles wide, with
the knowledge that if there was no water in a marsh beside a
solitary tree four miles ahead, we would have to go off the road
for five miles to get some, and, as the sun was setting, the
prospect for the first time looked a little gloomy. Making
rapidly for the lonely tree, enough water for ourselves and horses
was found, and with hurrahs from the united party, the tents
were pitched. Forty-two and a half miles, the odometer shewed
to be our day's travel.

August 10th.—The night of the 8th having been so cold, we
divided out more blankets the following evening by dispensing
with one tent, and sleeping three, instead of two, in each. The
precaution turned out to be unnecessary, though we kept it up
afterwards for the nights were always cool. This feature of cool
nights after hot days is an agreeable surprise to those who know
how different it is in inland countries, or wherever there is no sea
breeze. It is one of the causes of the healthy appearance of the
new settlers even in the summer months. In the hottest season

of the year the nights are cool on these prairies and the dews abundant, except when the sky is covered with clouds, and then there is usually rain. No wonder that the grass keeps green when elsewhere it is dry and grey.

Our morning's ride was across sixteen miles of the great plain, four miles from the easterly edge of which we had camped. The Secretary walked the distance, and got into the breakfast-place ten minutes after the mounted party. A morning's walk or ride across such an open has a wonderfully exhilarating effect. The air is so pure that it acts as a perpetual gentle stimulant, and so bracing that little fatigue is felt, even after unusual exertion ; seldom is a hair turned on either horse or man.

The plain was not an unbroken expanse but a succession of very shallow basins, enclosed in one large basin, itself shallow, from the run of which you could look across the whole, whereas, at the bottom of one of the smaller basins, the horizon was exceedingly limited. No sound broke the stillness except the chirp of the gopher, or prairie squirrel, running to his hole in the ground. The character of the soil every few yards could be seen from the fresh earth, that the moles had scarcely finished throwing up. It varied from the richest of black peaty loam, crumbled as if it had been worked by a gardener's hand for his pots, to a very light sandy soil. The ridges of the basins were often gravelly. Everywhere the pasturage was excellent, though it was tall enough for hay only in the depressions or marshy spots.

Our two next stages carried us over twenty-five miles of a lovely country, known as the Little Touchwood Hills ; aspens were grouped on gentle slopes, or so thrown in at the right points of valley and plain, as to convey the idea of distance and every other effect that a landscape gardener could desire. Lakelets and pools, fringed with willows, glistened out at almost every turn of the road—though many of them were saline. Only the manor-

H

houses and some gently-flowing streams were wanting, to make
out a resemblance to the most beautiful parts oi England.   For
generations, all this boundless extent of beauty and wealth
had been here, owned by England ; and yet statesmen had been
puzzling their heads over the "Condition of England's Poor,
the Irish Famine, the Land and Labor Questions," without once
turning their eyes to a land that offered a practical solution to
them all. And the beauty in former years had been still greater,
for, though the fires have somehow been kept oft this district for
a few years, it is not very long since both hardwood and ever-
greens as well as willows and aspens, grew all over it ; and then,
at every season of the year, it must have been beautiful.   It is
only of late years that fires have been frequent ; and they are so
disastrous to the whole of our North-west that energetic action
should be taken to prevent them. Formerly, when the Hudson's
Bay Company was the only power in this "Great Lone Land,"
it was alive to the necessity of this, and very successful in
impressing its views on the Indians as well as on its own servants.
Each of its travelling parties carried a spade with which the
piece of ground on which the fire was to be made was dug up,
and as the party moved off, earth thrown on the embers
extinguished them. But since miners, traders, tourists and others
have entered the country, there has been a very different state of
affairs.   Some of the spring traders set fire to the grass round
their camps, that it may grow up the better and be fresh on their
return in autumn.   The destruction of forests, the drying up of
pools, and the extermination oi game by roasting the spring eggs,
are all nothing compared to a little selfish advantage.   And the
Indians and the Hudson's Bay parties seeing this, have become
nearly as reckless.

   This afternoon we had some idea of the lovely aspect that this
country would soon assume, if protected from the fire-demon.
The trees grow up with great rapidity ; in five or six years the

aspens are thick enough for fencing purposes. There was good sport near the lake, and clumps of trees, and Frank shot prairie-hen, partridge and teal, for dinner and next day's breakfast. As he was confined to the roadside, and had no dog, he had but indifferent chances for a good bag. We had to push on to do our forty-one miles, and could not wait for sportsmen. At sunset the camp was selected, by a pond in the middle of a plain, away from the bush so as to avoid mosquitoes; and as Emilien was tired enough by this time, he agreed readily to the proposal to rest on the following day.

August 11th.—Breakfast at 9 a. m., having allowed ourselves the luxury of a long sleep on the "Day of Rest." The water beside our camp was hard and brackish, scarcely drinkable in fact, and not good even to wash with. It gave an unpleasant taste to the tea, and even a dash of spirits did not neutralize its brackishness. Here again the necessity of finding out the real state of the water-supply to this country, was forced on our attention. Even if the pools do not all dry up, the water in them at this time of the year is only what is left of melted snow and the spring and summer rains, tainted with decayed vegetable matter, and filled with animalculæ. The question must be satis-factorily settled; for men must have pure water and plenty of it.

This was a grand day for horses and men. Most of the latter rose early and had their breakfasts and then went to sleep again; others did not rise from under the carts and shake themselves out of their buffalo blankets, till after ten o'clock. At 11.15 all assembled for service—Roman Catholics, Methodists, Episco-palians and Presbyterians. The Secretary sat on a box in front of the tents, with Frank by his side holding an umbrella over both heads, as the sun shone fiercely. The congregation, thirteen in number, sat in the doors, or shade of the tents. Mr. McDougal led the responses, and all joined in devoutly. After the service had been read and hymns sung, a short sermon was preached.

The advantages of resting on the Lord's Day, on such expeditions as this, and also of uniting in some common form of worship, are very manifest. The physical rest is needed by man and beast. All through the week there has been a rush; the camp begins to be astir at three in the morning, and from that hour till nine or ten at night, there is constant high pressure. At the halting places, meals have to be cooked, baggage arranged and re-arranged, horses looked to, harness mended, clothes washed or dried, and everything kept clean and trim; rest is therefore impossible. From four to six hours of sleep are all that can be snatched. The excitement keeps a mere tourist up, so that on Saturday night he feels quite able to go ahead, but if he insists on pushing on, the strain soon becomes too much, and he loses all the benefit to his health that he had gained: and to the men there is none of the excitement of novelty, and they therefore need the periodic rest all the more.

But the great advantages of the day, to such a party, are lost if each man is left the whole time to look after himself,—as if there was no common bond of union,—to sleep, to gamble, to ramble, to shoot, to snare gophers, to read or write, and eat. Let the head of the party ask them to meet for common-prayer or some simple service, let it be ever so short; all will come if they believe that they are welcome. The singing of a hymn will bring them round the tent or hillock where the service is held; and the kneeling together, the alternate reading, a few earnest kindly words, will do more than anything else to awaken old remembrances, to stir the better nature of all, to heal up little bitternesses, and give each that sentiment of common brotherhood that cements into one the whole party.

The large body of Canadians that preceded Milton and Cheadle in their journey across these same plains ten years ago, would hardly have held together, had it not been for their observance of the Sunday rest. In an account of their arduous expedition by this route to the Cariboo gold mines, one of themselves gives the following earnestly-worded testimony :— "The fatigues of the journey were now beginning to have an injurious effect upon our animals, as well as upon the tempers and dispositions of the men, and especially towards the end of the week were these effects more apparent, when frequent disagreements and petty disputes or quarrels of a more serious kind would take place, when each was ready to contradict the other, and, at the slightest occasion or without any occasion, to take offence. But to-morrow would be the Sabbath ; and no wonder that its approach should be regarded with pleasurable anticipations, as furnishing an opportunity for restoring the exhausted energies of both man and beast, for smoothing down the asperities of our natures, and by allowing us time for reflection, for regaining a just opinion of our duties towards one another ; and the vigor with which our journey would be prosecuted, and the cordiality and good feeling that characterized our intercourse after our accustomed rest on the first day of the week, are sufficient evidence to us that the law of the Sabbath is of physical as well as moral obligation, and that its precepts cannot be violated with impunity. We certainly have had much reason gratefully to adore that infinite wisdom and goodness that provided for us such a rest."—All which we endorse as the utterances of sound common sense.

Our Sunday dinner was a good one. Terry had time and did his best. Soup made from canned tomatoes and canned meat gladdened our hearts. The Chief gave a little whiskey to the men, to take the bad taste from the water and kill the animalculæ ; and Emilien took as kindly to resting as if he had never travelled on Sundays in his life.

The afternoon was sultry and thundery. Heavy showers, we could see, were falling ahead and all around, but, although the clouds threatened serious things, we got only a sprinkling, and the evening cleared up with a glorious sunset.

After tea, Mr. McDougal led our "family worship." We did not ask the men to come, but the sound of the hymn brought them round, and they joined in the short service with devoutness, Willie, who had done a good day's work in snaring fat gophers, being particularly attentive. They were all thankful for the rest of the day.

August 12th.—"The 12th" found us up early, as if near a highland moor, and away from camp a few minutes after sunrise. Another delightful day; sunny and breezy. First stage, thirteen miles; the second, sixteen, and the third, fourteen miles, or forty-three for the day; every mile across a country of unequalled beauty and fertility; of swelling uplands enclosing in their hollows lakelets, the homes of snipe, plover and duck, fringed with tall reeds, and surrounded with a belt of soft woods; long reaches of rich lowlands, with hillsides spreading gently away from them, on which we were always imagining the houses of the owners; avenues of whispering trees through which we rode on, without ever coming to lodge or gate.

Our first "spell"* was through the most beautiful country, beautiful simply because longest spared by fire. Many of the aspens were from one to two feet in diameter. Most of the water was fresh, but probably not very healthy, for the lakes or ponds were shallow, and the water tainted by the annual deposition of an enormous quantity of decomposed organic matter. In summer when the water is low, it is difficult to get at it, because of the depth of the mire. When the buffalo ranged through this country and came to ponds to drink, they often sank so deep in the mud that they were unable to extricate themselves, especially if the foremost were driven on by those

---

* The term "spell" is commonly used, all over the plains, to indicate the length of journey between meals or stopping-places; the latter are sometimes called spelling-places, by half-breeds and others.

behind, or the hunters were pressing them. The harder the poor beasts struggled, the deeper they sank; till, resigning themselves to the inevitable, they have been known to disappear from sight and be trampled over by others of the herd. The old deeply indented trails of the herd, in the direction of the saline lakes, are still visible. They used to lick greedily the saline incrustations round the border, as they do still when near such lakes, Like domestic cattle, they instinctively understand the medicinal value of salt. From this point of view, it is doubtful if the saline lakes will prove a serious disadvantage to the stock-raising farmer. In British Columbia and on the Pacific Coast generally, such lakes are found, and the cattle that are accustomed to the water. receive no injury from drinking it.

On our way to dinner, two large white cranes rose swan-like from a wet marsh near the road. Frank with his gun and Willie with a stone made after them. The larger of the two flew high, but Willie's stone brought down the other. As he was seizing it, the big one, evidently the mother, attacked him, but, seeing the gun coming, flew up in time to save herself. The young one was a beautiful bird, the extended wings measuring over six feet from tip to tip. As soon as Willie had killed his game, he rode off in triumph with it slung across his shoulders. In twenty minutes after his arrival at camp, he and his mates had plucked, cooked, and disposed of it, all uniting in pronouncing the meat delicate and ' first-class.'

After dinner a good chance of killing a brown bear was lost. At a turn of the road he was surprised on a hillock, not twenty yards distant from the buckboard that led our cavalcade. Had the horsemen and guns been in front as usual, he could have been shot at once; but, before they came up, he was off, at a shambling but rapid gait among the thickets, and there was not time to give chase. This was a disappointment, for all of us would have relished a bear-steak.

The low line of the Touchwood Hills had been visible in the forenoon ; and, for the rest of the day's journey, we first skirted them in a north-westerly direction, and then, turning directly west, we gained their height by a road so winding and an ascent so easy, that there was no point at which we could look back and get an extended view of the ground travelled in the course of the afternoon. It is almost inaccurate to call this section of country by the name of " Hills," little or big. It is simply a series of prairie uplands, from fifty to eighty miles wide, that swell up in beautiful undulations from the level prairies on each side. They have no decided summits from which the ascent and the plain beyond can be seen ; but everywhere are grassy or wooded, rounded knolls, enclosing natural fields or farms, with small ponds in the windings and larger ones in the lowest hollows. The land everywhere is of the richest loam. Every acre that we saw might be ploughed. Though not as well suited for steam ploughs as the open prairie, in many respects this section is better adapted for farming purposes, being well wooded, well watered, and with excellent and natural drainage, not to speak of its wonderful beauty. All that it lacks is a murmuring brook or brawling burn ; but there is not one, partly because the trail is along the watershed. On a parallel road farther north that passes by Quill Lake, Mr. McDougal says that there are running streams, and that the country is, of course, all the more beautiful.

Our camp for the night was beside two lakelets near forks where the road divides, one going northerly from our course to the old Touchwood trading-post, fifteen miles distant.

So passed 'the 12th' with us. If we had not sweet-scented heather and Scotch grouse, we had duck and plover and prairie hen ; and, beside the cheery camp-fires under a cloudless star-lit-sky, we enjoyed our feast as heartily as any band of gypsies or sportsmen on the moors.

August 13th.—Heavy rain this morning which ceased at sunrise. Got off an hour after, and descended, in our first stage of fourteen and a half miles, the western side of the Touchwood Hills. This side is very much like the other; the descent to us was so imperceptible that nowhere could we see far ahead or feel certain that we were descending, until the most western upland was reached, and then, beneath and far before us, stretched a seemingly endless sea of level prairie, a mist on the horizon giving it still more the look of a sea. Early in the morning we came upon two buffalo-tents by the roadside. In these were the first Indians we had fallen in with since meeting the Sioux at Rat Creek, with the exception of two or three tents at "the crossing" of the Assiniboine. They were two families of Bungys, (a section of the Salteaux or Ojibbeway tribe) who had been hunting buffalo on the prairie to the south-west of us. They had a good many skins on their carts, and the women were engaged at the door of a tent chopping up the fat and meat to make pemmican. Marchaud, our guide, at once struck "a trade" with them, a few handfuls of tea for several pieces of dried buffalo meat. The men seemed willing that he should take as much as he liked, but the oldest squaw haggled pertinaciously over each piece, and chuckled and grinned horribly when she succeeded in snatching away from him the last piece he was carrying off. She was the only ugly being in their camp. The men had straight delicate features, with little appearance of manly strength in their limbs; hair nicely trimmed and plaited. Two or three young girls were decidedly pretty, and so were the little pappooses. The whole party would have been taken for good looking gypsies in England.

The road on this stage was the worst we had travelled over; so full of ruts and boulders that the axle of one of the carts snapped, and as there was not time to make another, the cart had to be abandoned by the road-side till Emilien's return from

Carlton.   It was a marvel how well those Red River carts stood
out all the jolting they got.   When any part broke before, a
thong of Shaganappi had united the pieces.   Shaganappi in this
part of the world does all that leather, cloth, rope, nails, glue,
straps, cord, tape, and a number of other articles are used
for elsewhere.   Without it the Red River cart, which is simply
a clumsy looking, but really light, box cart with wheels six or
seven feet in diameter, and not a bit of iron about the whole
concern, would be an impossibility.   These high wheeled carts
cross the miry creeks, borne up by the grass roots, when ordinary
waggons would sink to the hubs.

After breakfast we entered on a vast plain that stretched out on
every side, but the one we had left, to the horizon.   This had
once been a favourite resort of the buffalo, and we passed in the
course of the day more than a score of skulls that were
bleaching on the prairie.   All the other bones had been of
course chopped and boiled by the Indian women for the oil in
them.   The Chief picked up two or three of the best skulls to
send as specimens to Ottawa.   Great was " Souzie's" amazement
at such an act.   He had been amused at the Botanist gathering
flowers and grasses ; but the idea of a great O-ghe-ma coming
hundreds of miles, to carry home bones without any marrow in
them, was inexplicable.   He went up to Frank and explained
by gestures that they were quite useless, and urged him to throw
them out of the buckboard, and when Frank shook his head he
appealed to Mr. McDougal to argue with us.   All his efforts
failing, he gave it up ; but whenever his eyes caught sight of
the skulls it was too much for even Indian gravity, and off he
would go into fits of laughing at the folly of the white men.

Our second " spell " was nineteen, and the third, nine miles
across this treeless desolate-looking prairie.   Towards evening
the country became slightly broken and wooded, but we had
to camp on a spot where there was not enough wood to make

Pl. 20.

BUFFALO-SKIN LODGE AND RED RIVER CARTS.

the fires for the night. Knowing this, Marchaud passed the word to the men on horseback, two or three miles before arriving at the camp. They dashed into a thicket, pitched some small dead dry wood into the carts, and then each throwing an uprooted tree from fifteen to twenty-five feet long, and four to six inches in diameter across his shoulders or on the pommel of his saddle, cantered off with it, Sancho Panza like, as easily as if it was only a long whip. They had done this several times before, Willie generally picking out the biggest tree to carry, and, no matter how unwieldy the load, they rode their horses firmly and gracefully as ever.

The prairie crossed to-day extends north-easterly to Quill Lake, the largest of the salt lakes. Just on that account, and because all the ponds on it are saline, clearly shown, even where dried up, by the reddish samphire or white incrustations about the edges, one or two test wells should be sunk here; for if good water is found on this plain, it will likely be found every-where.

To-day we had two opportunities of sending to Red River letters or telegrams for home, and—lest one should fail—availed ourselves of both. Tying our packets with red tape, to give them an official look and thus impress Posty with due care, and sealing the commission with a plug of tobacco, we trusted our venture with the comfortable feeling that we had re-established our communications with the outer world. *

All day our men had been on the outlook for buffalo but without result. Marchaud rode in advance, gun slung across his shoulders, but although he scanned every corner of the horizon eagerly, and galloped ahead or on either side to any overhanging lip of the plateau, no herd or solitary bull came within his view.

It is only fair to mention that both messengers, one of them a French, the other a Scotch half-breed and parishioner of Mr. McDougal's, proved trusty. Every letter or telegram we sent from the plains reached home sooner than we had counted on.

They were not far off, for fresh tracks were seen, few in comparison to the tracks of former times, indented in the ground like old furrows and running in parallel lines to the salt lakes, as if in those days the whole prairie had been covered with wood, and the beasts had made their way through in long files of thousands.

August 14th.—The thermometer fell below freezing point last night, but the additional allowance of blankets kept us warm enough. At sunrise there was a slight skiff of ice on some water in a bucket; and, in the course of the morning's ride, we noticed some of the leaves of the more tender plants withered, but whether from the frost, or blight, or natural decay—they having reached maturity,—we could not determine.

The sun rose clear, and the day like its predecessors was warm and bracing, the perfection of weather for travelling. We had hitherto been on "the height of land" that divides the streams running into the Assiniboine from those that run into the Qu'Appelle, and this, in part, accounts for the absence of creeks near our road. To-day we got to a still higher elevation, the watershed of the South Saskatchewan, and found, in consequence, that the grass and flowers were in an advanced stage as compared with those farther east. The grass was grey and ripe, and flowers, that were in bloom not far away, were seeding here. The general upward slope of the plains between Red River and Lake Winnepeg, and the Rocky Mountains, is towards the west. The elevation at Fort Garry is 700 feet, at Fort Edmonton 2088 feet, and at the base of the Mountain Chain 3000 feet above the sea. This rise of 2,300 feet is spread over a thousand miles, but Captain Palliser marked three distinct steppes in this great plain. The first springs from the southern shore of the Lake of the Woods, and, trending to the south-west, crosses the Red River well south of the boundary line; thence it runs irregularly, in a north-westerly direction, by the Riding Mountains towards

Swan River, and thence to the Saskatchewan—where the north and south branches unite. The average altitude of the easterly steppe is from 800 to 900 feet above the sea level. The second or middle steppe, on which we now are, extends west to the elbow of the South Saskatchewan, and thence northwards to the Eagle Hills, west of Fort Carlton. Its mean altitude is 1600 feet. The third prairie steppe extends to the mountains. Each of these steppes, says Palliser, is marked by important changes in the composition of the soil, and consequently in the character of the vegetation.

Our first "spell" to-day was fifteen, and our second, twenty miles, to "the Round Hill," over rolling or slightly broken prairie ; the loam was not so rich as usual and had a sandy subsoil. Ridges and hillocks of gravel intersected or broke the general level, so that, should the railway come in this direction, abundant material for ballasting can be promised.

The prairie to-day had an upward slope till about one o'clock, when it terminated in a range of grassy round hills. For the next hour's travelling the road wound through these ; a succession of knolls enclosing cup-like basins, which in the heart of the range contained water, either fresh or saline. Wood also began to re-appear ; and, when we halted for dinner, at the height of the range, the beauty that wood, water, and bold hill-sides give were blended in one spot. We were certainly three or four hundred feet above the prairie ; the scenery round us was bolder than is to be found in any part of Ontario, and resembled that of the Pentlands, near Edinburgh. It is well to mention this, because of the exaggerated ideas that some people have when a country is spoken of. The hill at the foot of which we camped rose abruptly from the rest, like the site of an ancient fortalice. Horetski described it as a New Zealand pah ; one hill, like a wall, enclosing another in its centre, and a deep precipitous valley, that would have served admirably as a moat, filled with thick

wood and underbrush, between the two.   Climbing to the
summit of the central hill, we found ourselves in the middle of a
circle, thirty to forty miles in diameter, enclosing about a
thousand square miles of beautiful country.   North and east it
was undulating, studded with aspen groves and shining with
lakes.   To the south and west was a level prairie, with a sky line
of hills to the south-west.   To the north-west—our direction—a
prairie fire, kindled probably by embers that had been left
carelessly behind at a camp, partly hid the view.   Masses of
fiery smoke rose from the burning grass and willows, and if there
had been a strong wind, or the grass less green and damp, the
beauty of much of the fair scene we were gazing on would
soon have vanished, and a vast blackened surface alone been
left.

It was nearly 4 P.M. before we left "the Round Hill:" and
then we passed between the remaining hills of the range, and
gradually descended to the more level prairie beyond, through a
beautiful, boldly irregular country, with more open expanses
than the Touchwood Hills showed, and more beautiful pools,
though the wood was not so artistically grouped. Passing near the
fire, which was blazing fiercely along a line of a quarter of a mile,
we saw that it had commenced from a camping ground near the
roadside.   Heavy clouds were gathering that would soon extinguish the flames. As there was the appearance of a terrific thunder
storm, we hurried to a sheltered spot seven or eight miles from
Round Hill, and camped before sunset, just as heavy drops
commenced to fall.   The speed with which our arrangements for
the night were made astonished ourselves.   Every one did what
he could ; and in five minutes the horses were unharnessed, the
tents pitched, the saddles and all perishable articles covered with
waterproofs ; but, while exchanging congratulations, the dense
black clouds drove on to the south, and, though the sky was
a-flame with lightning, the rain scarcely touched us.

August 15th.—Early in the morning rain pattered on our tents, but before day-light it had all passed off, and we started comfortably at our usual hour, a little after sunrise. Our aim was to reach the south branch of the Saskatchewan, forty-six miles away, before night; the distance was divided into three 'spells' of thirteen, seventeen, and sixteen miles.

The scenery in the morning's ride was a continuation of that of last night ; through a lovely country, well wooded, abounding in lakelets, swelling into softly-rounded knolls, and occasionally opening out into a wide and fair landscape. The soil was of the richest loam and the vegetation correspondingly luxuriant ; the flora the same, and almost at the same stage, as that we had first seen on the prairie, a fortnight before, near Red River ;—the roses just going out of bloom; the yellow marigolds and golden-rods, the lilac bergamot, the white tansey, blue-bells and hare-bells, and asters, of many colours and sizes, in all their splendour. We were quite beyond the high and dry region ; and again in a country that could easily be converted into an earthly paradise.

We met or passed a great many teams and "brigades" to-day ; traders going west, and half-breeds returning east with carts well-laden with buffalo skins and dried meat. A number of Red River people club together in the spring, and go west to hunt the buffalo. Their united caravan is popularly called "a brigade," and very picturesque is its appearance on the road or round the camp-fire. The old men, the women and little children are all engaged on the expedition, and all help. The men ride and the women drive the carts. The children make the fires and do 'chores' for the women. The men shoot buffalo ; the women dry the meat and make it into pemmican.

Our breakfast place was a neck of land between two lakes, one of them sweet, the other bitter. The elevation of the two seemed to be the same, but, on a closer look, the fresh lake was seen to be the higher of the two, so that when full it would overflow into the other. This was invariably the case, as far as we saw, when two or more of such lakes were near each other. The salt lakes had no outlet, the natural drainage passing off only by absorption and evaporation.

The country between this first halt and the Saskatchewan consisted of three successive basins ; each bounded by a low ridge, less or more broken. Everywhere the ground was uneven, not so well suited as the level for steam agricultural implements, but the very country for stock-raising or dairy farms. The road was bad, and no wonder, according to the axiom that good soil makes bad roads. The ruts were deep in black loam, and rough with willow roots. Even when the wheels sank to the axles, they never brought up any clay ; moist, dripping, black muck, that would gladden the eyes of a farmer, was all that they found.

Soon after dinner, we came to the last ridge, and before us spread out a magnificent panorama. Fifteen miles farther west rolled the South Saskatchewan. We could not see the river, but the blue plateau that formed our sky line was on the other side of it. And those fifteen miles at our feet, stretching to an inde-finite horizon on the south, and bounded five miles away to the north by Minitchenass or 'the lumping hill of the woods,' showed every variety of rolling plain, gentle upland, wooded knoll, and gleaming lake. Where hundreds of homesteads shall yet be, there is not one. Perhaps it is not to be regretted that there is so much good land in the world still unoccupied. The intense saltness of many of the lakes was to us the only doubtful feature in the landscape. One at our feet several miles long had a shore of brightest red, sure sign of how it would taste. All at the foot of the ridge with one exception are saline ; after going on a few miles and mounting a slope, they are fresh.

The sun set when we were still five miles from the river. Another axle had broken and heavy clouds threatened instant

Pl. 21.

THE SOUTH SASKATCHEWAN RIVER.

rain. Some advised halting; but the desire to see the Saskatchewan was too strong to be resisted, and we pushed on at a rattling rate over the rutty and uneven road. Never were buckboards tested more severely, and no carts but those of Red River could have stood for ten minutes the bumps from hillock to hillock, over boulders, roots, and holes, at a break-neck rate. The last mile was down hill. The Doctor and the Chief dashed on at a gallop, and only drew rein when, right beneath, they saw the shining waters of the river. The rest of us were scarcely a minute behind, and three rousing cheers sent back the news to the carts. In twelve working days, we had travelled five hundred and six miles, doing on this last forty-six; and the horses looked as fresh as at the beginning of the journey; a fact that establishes the nutritious properties of the grasses that were their only food on the way, as well as the strength and the hardihood of the breed.

The first thing the Chief saw to, after pitching the tents, was the preparation of a kettle of whiskey-toddy, of which all who were not teetotallers received an equal share. The allowance was not excessive after nearly a fortnight's work; about three half-pints to thirteen men, six of them old voyageurs; but they had been so abstemious on the road that it was quite enough, and great was the hilarity with which each one drank his mug-full, pledging the Queen, sweethearts and wives, the Dominion, and the Chief. It shakes a company together to share something in common occasionally; and by this time we felt a personal interest in every member of the party, and looked forward with regret to the farewells that would be exchanged to-morrow.

While at supper rain began to fall, and it continued with intermissions all night, but we slept soundly in our tents,—caring nothing, for were we not faring on in good style? A month from Toronto and we were on the Saskatchewan.

I

Augst 16th.—The morning was grey and chilly, and there was some delay in getting the scow, that is now kept on the river by the Hudson's Bay Company, up from a point where it had been left, so that we did not move from camp till 8 o'clock. This delay gave the Botanist an hour or two to hunt for new species, which he did with all diligence, and the rest of us had time for a swim or a ramble up and down the river. Our Botanist had been slightly cast down of late by finding few new varieties. The flora of the five hundred and thirty miles between the eastern verge of the prairie at Oak Point, and the Saskatchewan, is wonderfully uniform. The characteristic flowers and grasses are everywhere the same. We expect, however, to meet with many strange varieties after crossing the two Saskatchewans.

At this point of the river, where the scow is usually kept and where a regular ferry is to be established next year, crossing is an easy matter. When there was no scow, every party that came along had to make a raft for their baggage, and a whole day was lost. Our buckboards, carts, and Mr. McDougal's waggons made two scow-loads ; and the horses swam across. Some were very reluctant to go into the water, but they were forced on by the men, who waded after them—shouting and throwing stones,—to the very brink of the channel. Once in there, they had to swim. Some,—ignorant of "how to do it"— struggled violently against the full force of the current or to get back, when of course they were stoned in again. Others went quietly and cunningly with the current and got across at the very point the scow made. The river for a few minutes looked alive with horses' heads, for that was all that was seen of them from the shore. As the water was lower and the force of the stream less than usual, all got across with comparative ease. The river at this point is from two hundred to two hundred and fifty yards wide. A hand-level showed the west bank to be about a hundred and seventy feet high, and the east somewhat

Pl. 22

SOUTH SASKATCHEWAN TO FORT PITT.

higher. Groves of aspens, balsams, poplars, and small white birch are on both banks. The valley is about a mile wide, narrower therefore than the valley of the Assiniboine or the Qu'Appelle, though the Saskatchewan is larger than the two put together. The water now is of a milky grey colour, but very sweet to the taste, especially to those who had not drunk of 'living water' for some days. A month hence it will be clear as crystal. In the spring it is discoloured by the turbid torrents along its banks, composed of the melting snows and an admixture of soil and sand ; and this colour is continued through the summer, by the melted snow and ice and the debris borne along with them from the Rocky Mountains. In August it begins to get clear, and remains so till frozen, which usually happens about the end of November.

Near the ferry an extensive reserve of land has been secured for a French half-breed settlement. A number of families have already come up from Fort Garry. We did not see them as the buffalo-magnet had drawn them away to the plains. The scantling for a house was on the ground near our camp.

After crossing, most of us drove rapidly to Fort Carlton,— eighteen miles distant, on the North Saskatchewan,—being anxious to see a house, store, and civilized ways and people again. Mr. Clark, the agent, received us with customary Hudson's Bay hospitality. The eighteen miles between the two rivers is a plateau, not more at its highest than three hundred feet above either stream. The soil looked rather light and sandy, but sufficiently rich for profitable farming. There is capital duck-shooting on lakes near the road. From the ancient bank of the river, above the Fort, is a good view of the course of the north stream. It is a noble river, rather broader, with higher banks and a wider valley, than the south branch. The usual square of four or five wooden buildings, surrounded by a high plank fence, constitutes "the Fort," and, having been intended for defence

against Indians only, it is of little consequence that it is
built on the low ground, so immediately under the ancient bank
of the river that you can look down into the inclosure, and
almost throw a stone into it from a point on the bank.   Fifty
miles down stream is the Prince Albert Presbyterian Mission to
the Crees, where there is also the nucleus of a thriving Scotch
settlement.   Fifty miles farther down, in the same north-easterly
direction, the two Saskatchewans unite, and then pursue their
way with a magnificent volume of water—broken only by one
rapid of any consequence—to Lake Winnipeg.

We dined with Mr. Clark on pemmican, a strong but savoury
dish, not at all like 'the dried chips and tallow' some Syba-
rites have called it.   There is pemmican and pemmican
however, and we were warned that what is made for ordinary
fare needs all the sauce that hunger supplies to make it
palatable.

A few hours before our arrival, Mr. Clark had received intelligence from Edmonton, that Yankee free-traders from Belly
River had entered the country, and were selling rum to the
Indians in exchange for their horses.   The worst consequences
were feared, as when the Indians have no horses they cannot
hunt.   When they cannot hunt, they are not ashamed to steal,
and stealing leads to wars.   The Crees and Blackfeet had been
at peace for the last two or three years, but, if the peace was
once broken, the old thirst for scalps would revive and the
country be rendered insecure.   Mr. Clark spoke bitterly of the
helplessness of the authorities, in consequence of having had no
force from the outset to back up the proclamations that had
been issued.   Both traders and Indians were learning the
dangerous lesson that the Queen's orders could be disregarded
with impunity ; and it would cost more before the lesson was
unlearned, than would have taught the opposite at the beginning
of the new regime.   We comforted our good host with the

assurance that the Adjutant-General was coming up with thirty men, to repress all disorders and to see what was necessary to be done for the future peace of the country.

Making all allowances for the fears of those who see no protection for life or property within five hundred or a thousand miles of them, and for the exaggerated size to which rumours swell in a country of such magnificent distances, where there are no newspapers and no means of communication except 'expresses,' it is clear that if the government wishes to avoid worrying, expensive, murderous difficulties with the Indians, 'something must be done.' There must be law and order all over our North-west from the first. Three or four companies of fifty men each, like those now in Manitoba, would be sufficient for the purpose, if judiciously stationed. Ten times the number may be required if there is long delay. The country cannot afford repetitions of the Manitoba rebellion, on account of the neglect of either half-breeds or Indians. The Crees are anxious for a treaty. The Blackfeet should be dealt with firmly and generously; treaties made with both on the basis of those agreed upon in the east; a few simple laws for the protection of life and property explained to them, and their observance enforced; small annuities allowed; the spirit-traffic prohibited, and schools and missionaries encouraged.

On asking Mr. Clark why there was no farm at Carlton, he explained that the neighbourhood of a fort was the worst possible place for farm or garden; that the Indians who come about a fort from all quarters, to trade and to see what they can get, would, without the slightest intention of stealing, use the fences for firewood, dig up the potatoes and turnips, and let their horses get into the grain-fields. He had therefore established a farm at the Prince Albert Mission, fifty miles down the river. With regard to crops, barley and potatoes were always sure, wheat generally a success, though threatened by frosts or early drought, and never a total failure. This year, he expected two thousand bushels of wheat from a sowing of a hundred. The land at Carlton, and everywhere round, is the same as at Prince Albert. Its only fault is that it is rather too rich.

After dinner, three or four hours were allowed for writing letters home, and making arrangements for the journey farther west. We got some fresh horses and provisions from Mr. Clark; said good-bye to Emilien, Marchand, Willie, Frederick, and Jerome; and taking two of our old crew, Terry and Maxime, along with two half-breeds and a hunch-backed Indian from Carlton, crossed the North Saskatchewan before sunset. In addition to Mr. McDougal, two Hudson's Bay officers joined us—one of whom, Mr. Macaulay, had been long stationed at Jasper House and Edmonton, and the other, Mr. King, far north on the McKenzie River. The scow took everything across in two loads, and the horses swam the river; but it was after dark before the tents were pitched on the top of the hill, and nearly midnight when we got to bed.

Pl. 28.

FORT CARLTON.

CHAPTER VI.

Along the North Saskatchewan to Edmonton.

August 17th.—The distance from Fort Garry to Edmonton is nine hundred miles, and is usually regarded as consisting of three portions ; two hundred and fifteen miles to Fort Ellice on the Assiniboine ; three hundred and nine more to Fort Carlton; and about three hundred and eighty up the North Saskatchewan to Edmonton. On this third part of the journey we were now entering.

It rained this morning, but we rose early, as usual, and prepared to start. There was a good deal of confusion and delay, however, as Horetsky, who had employed the new men and made the arrangements, had remained over night at the fort. The new horses could not be found for some time ; and, with one thing and another, it was seven o'clock before we got off on this stage of our journey. The sky soon cleared and the day turned out as suuny and breezy as any of its predecessors.

The road follows the upward course of the Saskatchewan, but as the river soon makes an almost semi-circular sweep, first south and parallel to the South Saskatchewan, then northerly as far as Fort Pitt, the road strikes across the chord of the arc, over a broken and hilly country called the " Thickwood Hills." Lakes are always in sight,—one of them very large and very salt —and extensive views of fine pasture lands are had from every

(135)

elevation. The soil and its productions, greatly to the disappointment of our Botanist, resembled what we had everywhere seen for the last fortnight. The soil in some places was equally rich and deep; but generally not quite as good. Everything indicated a cool and moist climate. There were few of the prairie flowers, but a great variety of grasses, of wild peas and beans all green, succulent herbage; a country better adapted for stock-raising than for wheat. The road was rough with roots, stones, and occasionally deep ruts, and so hilly that the jog-trot had often to be exchanged for a walk. Mr. Clark's horses, with the exception of a span attached to a large waggon of his own that he had kindly lent us, turned out to be miserable beasts; stiff-jointed or sore-backed, and obstinately lifeless; so that we would have fared badly, had it not been for the six government horses brought on from Fort Ellice. The two Carlton half-breeds, employed to drive the carts or horses, were old and stupid, incurable smokers and talkers. The one called Legrace was dried up as a mummy; the other "fat and greasy," popularly known among us as "Haroosh." He owed the name to Terry, who, hearing him drive his red horse with frequent howls of "Ho Rouge! Ho Rouge!" took for granted that this was the "Haroosh" familiar to himself in early days, and the proper north-west cry to lazy horses. Terry, accordingly, never whacked his unfortunate white nag without yelling "Haroosh!" The only acquisition to the party from Carlton, was the young hunchbacked Indian called Keasis or the "little bird."

Our breakfast-place was fifteen miles from camp, beside a marsh or pool on the road, twenty feet wide, and so deep that the water came into the buck-boards and up to the axles of the carts. It is well enough named the "Slough of Despond." Often have carts stuck, and whole brigades come to grief in it. Why the H. B. Company has never bridged it is a puzzle, except on the principle that no company cares to do any work that

will be a public benefit to others as well as to itself, for it
has lost enough by it to build ten bridges.   Where there is any
considerable traffic, nothing is so expensive as a slough, a hole,
or any serious obstruction on the road.

We took dinner fifteen miles further on, beside a pretty little
running stream, and camped before sunset, after making only
eight miles more, beside "The Bears Paddling Lake," a good
place to stay over Sunday, as there is abundance of wood, water,
and pasture.   The lake is very shallow but has a firm sandy
bottom, and the Indians have often seen bears about its shores,
enjoying themselves in the water.   Hence its name, a translation
of which is sufficient for us.

Every one from the Saskatchewan that we previously met,
had spoken so enthusiastically of this river and of the great
country it waters, that we were somewhat disappointed with
what we had seen to-day.   True, we had passed over only a speck
comparatively, and that so elevated that much could not be
looked for from it. The soil appeared good, and the grasses were
so thick that they almost formed a sward ; but the larger wood
had been burnt, and willow bushes, scattered all round, indicated
an indifferent sub-soil.   Besides, we had not got rid of the salt
lakes.   Mr. McDougal, however, ridiculed our doubts : we had
only to go out of our road a little, to find a rich and beautiful
country, extending north to the line of continuous forest, and
to-morrow and every successive day, as we journeyed west, would
show pretty much the same.

Faith in the future of the Saskatchewan and its "fertile belt"
is strong in the mind of almost every man who has lived on it,
and it is impossible to see even the little of the two great
branches of the river that we saw, without being convinced that
they are natural highways along which many steamers will soon
be plying, carrying to market the rich produce of the plains that
extend to the east, west, and north from them.   When the tents

were pitched Souzie went down to the lake and shot four or five
ducks, as a contribution to our Sunday dinner. The night was
cool, as we had expected at the elevation; but there was no
frost.

August 18th.—Took a much-needed long sleep, as usual on
Sunday mornings; breakfasted at nine o'clock and had service
at eleven, Mr. McDougal assisting. We are all much pleased
with Mr. McDougal, and think ourselves fortunate in having
fallen in with him. In his conversation and by his actions he
shows himself thoroughly acquainted with the country, a man of
ready resources and an obliging fellow traveller.

Widely different opinions have been expressed, about the value
of missionary work among the Indians, by the half dozen persons
we have hitherto met who profess to be less or more acquainted
with the subject. One gentleman's information was very decided:
—"The Protestant Missionaries had made no converts; the
Roman Catholic Missionaries had made some, and they were
the greatest scoundrels unhung." Another was qually emphatic
on the other side; and, as positive evidence is worth infinitely
more than negative, we were more disposed to listen to him.
One witness was doubtful, thinking that something could be said
on both sides, and he was, therefore, subjected to a little cross-
examination: — "Many of the Indians are now professing
Christians; but, no doubt, some of them are great hypocrites."
Asked if there was not a share of hypocrisy in all of us, and if
such a charge was not made against Christians everywhere.
Admitted that it was so. Pressed on the point, whether the old
child-like frankness on the part of the Indian along with a vast
fund of reserve on the part of the trader, made the commercial
transactions equally fair to both parties; admitted that it did
not, and that thus the charge of hypocrisy might be retorted in
the wigwam on the trader, or explained in the store on the part
of the Indian. Asked if he could name any positive improve-

ment in morality, that had resulted from the Missionaries' labours. "Yes; Christianized Crees would not steal your horses,—at least not openly—when you were passing through their country." Well, you could not say much more for Christianized Englishmen or Yankees, if so much. Could he mention any other improvement ? "Yes ; they had all been polygamists to as great an extent as they could afford, (a new wife being bought for a horse or a blanket) and they used to exchange wives to suit each others' convenience ; but such practices among several tribes had passed away, or were considered disreputable." Urged, to remember what they were when he first went among them so as to say fairly if there was any other gain. "Yes ; away to the north the Dogribs and other tribes on the McKenzie, had a practice of strangling or smothering all their infant daughters after the first ; even the mother would stuff a handful of grass into the mouth of the poor little thing and choke it ; now the practice was unknown." A decided gain for the daughters. Any more. "Yes ; some of them did keep the Lord's Day after a fashion, treated their women rather better, were more comfortable, a little cleaner, sent their children to school for a while, and—well, there had been improvement, but after all, if, you only knew how superstitious they still are, how dirty, vicious, miserable, you would not consider them much better than pagans."

The style of argument seemed ungenerous. Here were men, self-exiled, toiling all their lives without prospect of earthly promotion or reward, from the Blackfeet on the Bow River to the Loocieux on the Yucan, from Winnipeg to where the McKenzie empties into the Arctic sea; among the Indians of the lakes and the plains, and the still more degraded Indians of the woods; living, many of them, in frozen wildernesses, where the year is made up of a six weeks' summer of West India heat ; six or seven weeks more of warm days and cold nights; and nine months of stern and dreary winter ; and when they see some results of their labour, some small improvements struggling to show themselves in spite of all the dismal surroundings, they find that the necessarily slow process has made men forget the raw material they had to begin upon ; they are sneered at as making hypocrites, or are pointed only to what remains to be done, because their converts are not equal to the descendants of fifty generations of Christian forefathers. It is so easy to forget what once was, or to kick away the ladder by which we ourselves have risen. Changes take place so imperceptibly that even those living among them do not notice there has been change, and they assume that nothing has been done, when a great work is going on around them. Missionaries on the plains say, now that there has been peace for the last two or three years, they can call to mind, only with an effort, the once familiar scenes of bloodshed, and the universal craving for scalps.

The uniform policy of the Hudson's Bay Company was to encourage Missionary effort among the Indians. Their charter bound them to this, and, especially since 1820, they did so to a considerable extent. Sir George Simpson always offered the protection of the Company to Missionaries, on condition that they attended to their own business and did nothing prejudicial to the interests of the Company. When a Missionary was stationed near a Hudson's Bay Fort, he had the position also of Chaplain to the Fort, free passage in and out of the country by the Company's boats, and £50 a year. For some time the Anglican and the Roman Catholic were almost the only churches that entered on the work, perhaps because the Company was most ready to invite and to assist these. During the last quarter of a century the Wesleyans also have worked in this field with their usual energy. They have now nine Missionaries in it, and it is much to the credit of the two Protestant Churches, that they do not interfere with the stations of one another. The Presbyterians have only one mission, that at Prince Albert, and, though in a prosperous state, its work is in a great measure confined to a congregation of half-breed and white settlers.

A practical vindication bo⁺h of the general dealings of the Company with the Indians and of missionary work among them is the fact that, the survey of the Canada Pacific Railway, from the Upper Ottawa to the Pacific coast, has in no case been interfered with. The engineers and others have been welcomed ; and, very often, the Indians have proved extremely serviceable. The contrast with the state of things on the other side of the boundary line,—where surveys have been summarily stopped, engineers killed, and where every Indian scalp is estimated to have cost the country $100,000,—is marked indeed.

Of course the missionary work has another and altogether higher aspect, from which it is only fair to look at it also. We must judge it from its own as well as from the world's standpoint. Christian men and women give their means, their labours, and their lives to the heathen, not for the social, political, or economical results, though they believe that such follow on their success, but for Christ's sake, because the heathen are their brethren, dear to them because dear to their Lord. It is not fair, therefore, to leave the decision as to the value of their labours wholly to men of the world, who judge only from the lower point of view, —whose immediate interests may be injured, or on whose passions a bridle may be put by " the impertinent intermeddling " of Missionaries, or who may even be bitterly opposed to true Christianity—for it is not extravagant to suppose that there have been such men.   To preach the Gospel of the wonderful love of God to a few degraded Indians, may seem a small thing in the eyes of tourist or trader, in comparison with the gospel of plenty of tobacco for peltries.   Far otherwise is it in the eyes of the Missionary and his Master; far otherwise when weighed in the balances of eternity.

August 19th.—Rose at 3 A.M., thanks to the Sunday rest, and got away from camp before sunrise.

Our first 'spell' was thirteen miles, over a rich undulating country, little wooded, but, judging from the strong green grasses and vetches, well suited either for stock-raising or cereals. We breakfasted in a lovely hollow, watered by springs of delicious water, the banks lined with balsam poplars from one to two feet in diameter. The road here is about forty miles from the river on account of the bend, to the south, that the latter makes. The Thickwood Hills are not more than two hundred feet high.

Terry gave us pemmican for breakfast, and, from this date, pemmican was the staple of each meal. Though none of us cared for it raw at first, we all liked it hot. Cooked for a few minutes in a frying pan with a little water and flour, and a dust of pepper and salt, onions added if you have any, it is called "richaud" and a capital dish it is, looking like Rodney, and tasting not very differently from well roasted beef. Pemmican and sun-dried, thin, flitches of buffalo-meat are the great food-staples of the plains, so much so that when you hear people speak of 'provisions' you may be sure that they simply mean buffalo-meat, either dried or as pemmican.

The second 'spell' was twenty miles over round or sloping hills, enclosing lakes and affording good pasturage, though the most of the land was sandy or gravely and not up to the average. The country resembled the Cheviots and the south of Scotland—two or three places reminding us much of Drum-lanrig. The road followed the high lands where the streamlets or 'creeks' that flow into the Saskatchewan, take their rise. We crossed one of these three times, and then halted beside it for dinner. In the afternoon we followed along its course, through a succession of very pretty lakes, that are almost covered with wild fowl, till it issued from the largest of these "Jack Fish Lake." We should have crossed it there, but the water was too high, and we had to follow down its left bank to a ford three miles to the south. When within quarter of a mile of the ford,—the big waggon and buck-boards going before, the carts following at some distance, and the horses driven behind them,—the hump-backed Indian galloped to the front, and pointed back. There was Souzie crossing the river in his light waggon, and the carts and the horses following lead. They floundered across pretty well, except the cart of " Haroosh," which stuck in the mud. Though angry at the " cheek " of the thing, it was thought best to follow, and master Souzie being recalled, and " rowed up " for his impudence, most of the articles that a wetting would damage, were transferred from the buckboards to his waggon and sent safely across. The big waggon, with the Chief and the Doctor mounted on the highest pinnacle, followed ; but, when near the other side, its iron wheels sank in the black muddy bottom, and the horses while struggling to extricate them, broke the whipple-tree and parts of the harness, leaving the waggon and contents in the middle of the stream. Maxime and "the little bird" rushed to the rescue and untackled the horses. The Chief and the Doctor, stripping from feet to waist jumped down into the water, and putting their shoulders to the wheels while the other two pulled, amid cheers from the rest of us on the other side, and countless bites from the mosquitoes, shoved the big thing to the bank. The buckboards fol-lowed, and then "Greasy," who had been left all the time in the middle of the stream, cudgelling his horse, and yelling " Ho Rouge ! Ho Rouge !" supplicated help, as his arm and throat had quite given out. He was told to help himself, and to our great satisfaction, the old fellow had to jump down into the water and shove his cart out. All got safely across, nothing had been hurt, only Souzie looked woebegone for the night, and Greasy continued sulky for two days. We camped at once on the bank, for it was after sunset, though the mosquitoes, that always haunt woods and streams, tormented our horses so much that the poor brutes could not eat, but crowded round the smoke of our fires, making the place look even more like a gipsy encampment than usual.

The Jackfish-lake River runs, through a beautiful park-like country from this point, into the Saskatchewan, fifteen miles to the south. It would be a good location for a missionary or general settlement, for the lakes above are filled with jackfish or pike, and with white fish,—the finest fresh water fish, perhaps, in the world. There is also good water power, as the stream descends about a hundred and fifty feet in the course of the next fifteen miles, and the land is slightly rolling and of excellent quality. It is the favourite ground of a large mixed band of Crees and Salteaux, whom we did not see as they were all away hunting buffalo. On a little hill, near the stream, a great annual "pow-wow," is held in the spring, by the heathen Crees and Salteaux who come from long distances to have a high time. Their "medicine men" who have still much influence among them, take the lead and hold a "revival meeting." All the old incantations and wild dances are practised, and as the excitement gets up, they abandon themselves to the foulest licentiousness.

We had driven forty-eight miles to-day, the longest journey yet made. Except the first and last part, the land was not of the best quality.

August 20th.—Instead of following up the right bank of the stream to the main road near Jack-fish Lake, we struck a new trail direct for Tortoise River, twenty-five miles distant. On the way we saw a fine duck and two or three antelopes, but they were too far off for a shot. In the spring, several varieties of deer come in great numbers to this part of the country, but at this season, most of them are away with their young on the treeless prairies to the south. Halted on the road for breakfast; but, after having unharnessed the horses, found, to our disgust, that the water was salt. A breakfast of dry bread and dry pemmican was hurriedly made; and we found that, on the plains, any meal without tea, is as poor an affair as bacon and beans without the bacon.

At Tortoise River had a most reviving swim and a long halt. Beyond it is Horse Hill, so called from a fight between the Crees and Blackfeet, forty years ago. The Crees were encamped near a thicket at the foot of the hill, and a party of Blackfeet, that had made a successful raid far from their own borders, discovered them and charged. But the Crees were prepared, and, a still larger body of them on the slope of the hill hidden by a ravine, swept round and drove their enemies into it; and though many of the Blackfeet escaped, all their spoil was retaken, and forty horses were killed, an extraordinary number, for the aim is always to capture the horses,—horses, and buffalo being the all-in-all to the Indians of the plains. In their wars the Blackfeet often suffered from similar haste and over-boldness. Not long ago, a party a hundred strong, that was out raiding in the winter time, discovered a Cree camp among the hills, and rushed on it; but as they entered the pass, a second and a third camp appeared on each side of the pass. Their only hope was escape, and they dashed straight on, only to find that they had rushed into a deep hollow, the opposite rim of which was topped high with snow-banks that curled over in folds, so that there was no possibility of mounting it. The Crees closed round with yells of triumph, and for once they had their will on their enemies. It was not a fight but a massacre. Seventy were killed in a few minutes, and then the Crees in a fit of generosity, or because they were glutted with blood, opened out and let the rest go.

Not that the Blackfeet disdain to exercise strategy. Cunning is natural to every Indian, in war and peace, in hunting and

J

trading. We were told of a successful ambuscade of theirs at "the Round Hill," so like a New Zealand pah, on the other side of the Saskatchewan. A large body of Crees had camped by one of the lakes near the open. Towards evening they espied a buffalo grazing on the top of the inner hill. He fed so quietly, that they were a little suspicious at first, but soon others emerged from the coppice in the dip between the two hills. Hungry Crees could be suspicious no longer. They drew near quietly, and were all ready to "run" the buffalo, when every bush opened fire and a score of them dropped. The buffalo became Blackfeet and turning the tables 'ran' the Crees to some purpose.

The characteristic of the Blackfeet braves, however, is daring. Many a stirring tale of headlong valour they tell round their camp fires, as, long ago in moated castles, bards sang the deeds of knights-errant, and fired the blood of the rising generation. Such a story we heard of a Chief called "the Swan," once the bravest of the brave, but now tho' in the prime of life, dying of consumption. Dressing himself one day in all his bravery, he mounted his fleet horse and rode straight for the Cree camp. A hundred warriors were scattered about the tents, and in the centre of the encampment two noted braves sat gambling. Right up to them "the Swan" rode, scarcely challenged, as he was alone, clapped his musket to the head of one and blew his brains out. In an instant the camp was up; dozens of strong arms caught at the reckless foe, dozens of shots were fired, while others rushed for their horses. But he knew his horse, and, dashing through the encampment like a bolt, made good his escape, though chased by every man that could mount.

Many a story of this kind we heard from poor old mummy Legrace, or from others of our party, who boasted for himself in a dignified way that in his time he had killed two Blackfeet, but how much is truth and how much fiction, deponent saith not.

This afternoon we drove sixteen miles, from Tortoise River to English River, another stream running south into the Saskatchewan, and so called from the fact that an Englishman had been drowned while crossing it in the spring time, when very insignificant 'Creeks' are dangerous. The soil all the way was sandy and mossy, except in patches or near either of the rivers where it was excellent; the country was undulating and suited for sheep grazing. At one point, the road ran within two or three miles of the Saskatchewan, and a prominent hill on the other side was recognized by Souzie. 'Ah!' said he to his master, 'I know now where I am'; and, on arriving at the camp, he went up to Frank and formally shook hands with him, to indicate that he welcomed him to his country. He had established confidential relations with Frank from the first, taught him Cree words, and told him long stories, explaining his meaning by expressive gesticulations of fingers, hands, shoulders, mouth, and eyes.

A clump of tall pointed white spruce and branching poplar spruce, on the banks of English River, was the first variety from the universal aspen or occasional balsam poplar, that we had seen since leaving Fort Garry, with the exception of a few white birches on the banks of the Saskatchewan. The aspen, as far as seen by us, is certainly the characteristic tree, just as the buffalo is the characteristic animal of our North-west; the other trees have in great measure been burnt out. Fortunately the aspen is good wood for carpenter work; good also for fuel, being kindled easily and burning without sparks.

In the course of the afternoon "the little bird" having gone in too extensively for pemmican became so sick that he gave out altogether; this generally happens with the new men that are picked up at the forts along the route. They are often half-starved, except when employed, and then it takes them a week to go through the surfeiting and sick stages before shaking down into proper condition. Legrace and Haroosh were far too old hands to get sick, no matter what the quantity they ate. One of us took ' the little bird's ' work, and made him get into a buckboard where he lay prone, head wrapped up in his blanket, till the camping ground was reached. Then he stretched himself beside the fire, the picture of utter wretchedness. The Doctor prescribed castor oil, and Terry put the dose to his mouth. As " the little bird " took the first taste, he looked up and, noticing the comical look about Terry's countenance, thought that a practical joke was being played at his expense, and with a gleam of fire in his eyes spit it out on him. The Doctor had now to come up and with his most impressive Muskeekee ohnyou (chief medicine man) air, intimate that the dose must be taken. 'The little bird' submitted, drank it as if it were hemlock, and rolled himself up in his blanket to die. But in the morning he was all right again though weak ; and gratefully testified that castor oil was the most wonderful medicine in the world.

August 21st.—Our destination to-day was Fort Pitt on the Saskatchewan, but learning that a visit to it involved twelve or fifteen miles additional travelling, as the main road keeps well to the north of the river, it was decided that Horetzky, and Macaulay, óne of the Hudson's Bay officers that joined our party at Carlton, should ride ahead to the Fort for supplies, and meet us if possible in the evening at " the guard." Every station of the Hudson's Bay Company has a " guard," or judiciously selected spot, well supplied with good water, wood, pasturage, and shelter, where the horses are kept. From this depôt we expected to be furnished with fresh horses and men in place of those brought from Carlton.

To-day's travel was through a hilly well-watered country. The first ' spell ' brought us to the base of the Red Deer Hill, close to a spring of cold clear water beside a grove. The soil was of excellent quality all the way, a deep loam. The grasses and flowers resembled those of Ontario and the Lower Provinces rather than the prairie flora. Such common wild fruits as currants, gooseberries, choke-cherries, &c., were in abundance. We seemed to have taken leave of the prairie and its characteristic flowers since crossing the North Saskatchewan, but they were not far off to the north or south. The road from Carlton runs among the sandy hills, that skirt the course of the river, up to Fort Pitt. The nearer the river in this part the more sandy the soil, and the less adapted for cereals, because of droughts, and early frosts which are attributed to the heavy mists that cling about the river banks.

After breakfast, the road ran through a still more broken country and along a more elevated plateau. The windings of the Red Deer and its little tributaries have cut out, in the course of ages, great valleys and enormous 'punch bowls,' resembling the heaviest parts of the south of Scotland, on the rich grassy sides of which thousands of cattle or sheep ought to be grazing to make the resemblance complete. At a point where the plateau is about 400 feet above the level of the Saskatchewan, a round sugar-loaf hill rises abruptly from the road, nearly 200 feet, and is called the Frenchman's Knoll, because long ago a Frenchman had been killed here. We cantered or walked to the top, and had a far extending view of level, undulating, and hilly country. Most of the wood was small because of recent fires, and it was all aspen, except a few clumps of pines far away. The sky line beyond the Saskatchewan was an elevated range with distinct summits, several of which must have been as high as "the mountain" behind Montreal. The smallness and sameness of the wood gave monotony to the view, which was redeemed only by its vastness.

Near this, the trail to Fort Pitt branched off. Keeping the main road for another mile, we halted for dinner, and then moved on, first descending the long winding slopes of a hill to the south, and then going west up a valley that must have

been formerly the bed of a river, or more probably cut out
by an overflow of the Saskatchewan.   In the course of the
afternoon, we crossed three clear streamlets running over soft
black bottoms ; in spite of this abundance of good water the
lakelets in the lowest hollows were saline.   The soil everywhere
was of the rich loam that had become so familiar to our eyes ;
uplands and valleys were equally good.   The grasses were thick
and short, almost forming a sward ; still green and juicy though
they had been exposed to all the summer's heat. In the marshes
the grass was from four to six feet high, and of excellent quality
for hay.

After crossing the last 'creek,' a handsome young Indian
came galloping towards us, to say that Horetzky and Macaulay
were already at "the guard" ahead, with Mr. Sinclair the
Hudson's Bay agent at Fort Pitt.   This was good news, for the
probabilities were that the location of the "guard" had been
changed ; and, at all events, we had calculated on having to wait
several hours for our two outriders. Getting to the "guard" before
sunset, the tents were at once pitched. We had ridden more
than 40 miles, and our avant-couriers about 52, besides attending
to all our commissions at the Fort.

This was the first "guard" we had seen. They are usually at a
distance from the Forts, but it so happened that this one although
ten miles from the Fort was by the roadside. We could not have
seen a better specimen, for, on account of the grasses being so
good, more horses are kept at Fort Pitt than at any other post on
the Saskatchewan.   There are 300 now, and they increase
rapidly though the prairie wolves destroy many of the foals.
All were in prime condition and some of them very handsome.
Not one in ten of those horses had ever got a feed from man,
summer or winter.   They cropped all their own food ; and sleek
and fat as they are now, they are equally so in midwinter:
pawing off the dry snow they find the grasses abundant and suc-

culent beneath. Better witnesses to the suitableness of this country for stock raising on an extensive scale, than those 300 horses, could not be desired.   When weak or sickly, or returned from " a trip," knocked up with hard driving and cudgelling, for the half-breed looks upon cudgelling as an essential and inevitable part of driving, they may be taken into the barn at the Fort for a time and fed on hay, but not otherwise.   At the "guard," only one Indian is in charge of the whole herd.   The horses keep together and do not stray, so fond are they of one another.   The chief difficulty in selecting some for your journey is, to get those you want away from the pack.   There is a thick grove of aspens where they take shelter in the coldest weather, and near it is the tent of the keeper.   His chief work seems to be making little inclosures of green logs or sticks, and build fires of green wood inside to smoke off the mosquitoes. Round these fires the horses often stand in groups, enjoying the smoke that keeps their active tormentors at a little distance.   In considering this fact of horses feeding in the open all winter, it is well to remember that Fort Pitt is between two and three hundred miles farther north than Fort Garry.

After inspecting the horses, we were taken into the keeper's tent to see how he was housed. It was a roomy lodge, called ' a fourteen skin,' because constructed of so many buffalo hides stretched and sewed together ; the smallest lodges are made of five or six, and the largest of from twenty to twenty-five 'skins.' The fire is in the centre, and the family sleep round the side, each member having his or her appointed corner.   The smoke of the fire dries the skins thoroughly, keeps out the mosquitoes, and gives the inmates sore eyes.   We all pronounced it ' very comfortable,' but most of us would probably prefer for our own use a house with more than one room.

Mr. Sinclair showed us the utmost kindness in every way, giving us good advice, good horses, good men, and with no more show than if he had merely run down to the "guard" on his own business. The kindness we appreciated most at the time, it must be confessed, was a huge shoulder of fresh buffalo meat, some tongues, and a bag of new potatoes. Terry was at once set to work on the fresh meat with orders to cook enough for twenty, with a corresponding allowance of potatoes. None of us had ever tasted fresh buffalo before, nor fresh meat of any kind since leaving Red River; and as we had resolved not to go out of our way to hunt, though Mr. Sinclair told us that buffalo were in vast numbers twenty miles to the south of Fort Pitt, it was only fair that our-self denial should be repaid by a good supper at the "guard." And that supper was an event in our journey. Falling to with prairie appetites, each man disposed of his three portions with ease. The prairie wolves were yelping not far off, but nobody paid any attention to them. Tender buffalo steak, and new potatoes in delicious gravy, absorbed every one's attention. The delights of the table when you are in the best of health and keen-set are certainly wonderful; and as a junior member of the party remarked, handing in his plate for a fourth or fifth helping, ' man, what a lot more you can eat when the things are good'! Getting out of the tent after supper with an effort, a spectacle to gladden a philanthropist's heart was presented round Terry's fire. The men were cooking and eating, laughing and joking, old Haroosh presiding as king of the feast. He sat on a hillock, holding tit-bits to the fire on a little wooden spit, for Terry's frying pan could not keep up to him, while his greasy face shone in the ruddy light; so they continued till we went to bed. That they were at it all night cannot be positively affirmed, but in the morning the first sight that met our eyes was Haroosh in the same place and attitude, cooking and eating in a semi-comatose state.

August 22nd.—There was at least an hour's racing and chasing of the "guard" horses this morning, before our quota could be

Pl. 24.

FORT PITT TO FORT EDMONTON.

caught; but, we got such good horses in exchange for our poorest that the delay was not grudged ; and three smart Indians, Louis, Cheeman (the little fellow), and Kisanis (the old man), in stead of the Carlton three. We breakfasted at sunrise and said 'goodbye' to Mr. Sinclair at 7 o'clock. On account of the lateness of the start, we divided the day's journey into two 'spells,' one of nineteen and the other of twenty-one miles.

The country round the "guard" is fertile, and beautiful in outline ; Mr. Sinclair said that it would yield anything. At the Fort and along the sandy banks of the river, their crops often suffered from Indians, droughts, and early frosts ; but it was impossible to have their farm ten miles away from where they lived.

Our first "spelling-place" to-day was Stony Lake ; after dinner we crossed Frog Creek, Middle Creek, and Moose Creek, and camped on the banks of the last named.

This was one of our best days. Everything contributed to make it supremely enjoyable. We had fresh spirited horses under us, a cloudless sky and bright sun above ; and an atmosphere exhilarating as some pure gentle stimulant. The country was of varied beauty ; rich in soil, grasses, flowers, wood, and water ; infinitely diversified in colour and outline. From elevated points, far and wide reaches of the same could be seen ; here was no dreary monotonous prairie such as fancy had sometimes painted, but a land to live in and enjoy life. And last but perhaps to us most important item, Terry had in his cart new potatoes and buffalo steak, good as any porter-house or London rump steak, enough even for our appetites ; man could want nothing more for animal enjoyment. In the forenoon, we rode up two or three hill-sides to get wider views. With all the beauty of former days, there was now what we had often craved for, variety of wood. Clumps and groves of tall white spruce in the gullies and valleys, and along lake sides, branching poplars with occasional white birch and tamarack, mingled with the still prevailing aspen. The sombre spruces were the greatest relief. They gave a deeper hue to the landscape, and their tall pointed heads broke the distant sky line. Recent fires had desolated much of the country, but there was enough of the old beauty left to show what it had been and what it could soon be made. Sometimes our course lay across a wide open, or up or down a long bare slope; and, sometimes through a forest where the trees were far enough apart for easy riding, while a little beyond the wood seemed impenetrably close. In the afternoon we crossed plateaus extending between the different streams that meander to the south; and here the trail ran by what looked like well cultivated old clearings, hemmed in at varying distances by graceful trees, through the branches of which the waters of a lake, or the rough back of a hill gleamed, while high uplands beyond gave a definite horizon. The road was not very good in many places because of the steep little hills near the creeks, or boulders, deep ruts, mole and badger holes; but ten dollars a mile would put it in good repair, and, as it was then, our carts did their usual forty miles easily.

After dinner we came on our first camp of Crees—a small body, of five or six tents, that had not gone after the buffalo, but had remained quietly beside some lakes, living on berries and wild ducks. Two broad-backed healthy young squaws met us first, coming up from a lake with half-a-dozen dogs. One squaw had a bag, filled with ducks, on her neck, and the other had tied her game around the back of a dog. Some of the men came up to shake hands all round and to receive the plug of tobacco they looked for. Others, mostly manly looking fellows, lounged round in dignified indifference, with blanket or buffalo robe, folded gracefully about them,—evidently knowing or hoping that every attitude was noticed. Not a man was doing a single hand's turn, and not a woman was idle. The women wished to trade their ducks for tea or flour; but if we stopped the carts and opened the boxes there would be no getting away from them that night, so the word was passed to push ahead; we were not, however, to be let off so easily. Eight or ten miles further on, two elderly men on horseback—evidently Chiefs,—overtook us, and riding up to our Chief with all the grace of gentlemen of the old regime, again extended their hands. Being welcomed and invited to ride on and camp with us, they bowed with an ease and self-possession that any of us might have envied, and joined our party. There was not the slightest appearance of obsequiousness, although they were really begging for their supper. At the camp, the Chief treated them with great civility, ordering pemmican, as they preferred it to fresh buffalo, and handing them the fragrant tea they love so well; not a muscle of their faces moved, though their souls were rejoicing; a soft smile when they first came upon us, and a more melancholy smile in the morning when departing, were the only indications of feeling that either gave. With the exception of the dull, half-opened, Mongolian, cross-eyes, they were handsome fellows, with well cut, refined Italian features—handsomer than any of us or even than the young English trader, who "never allowed an Indian to enter his rooms; if a Chief came along, he might sit in the kitchen awhile"—so far below the "salt," have the "sons of the soil" to sit now. But "Rolling Mud" and the "Walker with out-turned feet," as our two guests were called, were entitled to move in the highest circles, as far as appearance and a perfect *nil admirari* manner were concerned. They could be guaranteed to look on, without opening their eyes, even at a modern ball.

In the afternoon's drive, the big Carlton waggon, drawn by the span, broke down. The iron bolt, connecting the two fore wheels with the shaft, broke in two. Shaganappi had been sufficient for every mishap hitherto, but this seemed too serious a case for it; but, with the ready help of Mr. McDougal, shaganappi triumphed, and we were delayed only an hour. No one ever seems non-plussed on the plains ; for every man is a " Jack of all trades," and accustomed to make-shifts. When an axle broke, the men would haul out a piece of white birch, shape it into something like the right thing, stick it in, tie it with shaga-nappi, and be jogging on at the old rate before a professional carriage builder would make up his mind what was best to be done.

Both, yesterday and to-day, the sasketoon berries, that are put in the best or " berry pemmican," were pointed out to us, and the creeper which the Indians make into " kinni-kinnick," when they can't get the bark of the red willow to mix with their tobacco. The sasketoon are simply what are known in Nova Scotia as " Indian pears," and the kinni-kinnick creeper is our squaw-berry plant.

Just as the sun was setting behind the Moose Mountain, we had ascended the high ridge that rises from Middle Creek, and were crossing the narrow plateau that separates it from Moose Creek. Getting across the plateau to the edge of the descent to Moose Creek, a glorious view opened out in the glowing twilight. To our immediate left, coming from the west, and winding south and east, the Saskatchewan, not quite so broad as at Carlton, but without any break or sand-bar, flowed like a mass of molten lead, between far extending hills, covered with young aspens ; like the Rhine with its vine-clad slopes near Bingen. Right beneath, was the deep rugged valley of Moose Creek, broken into strange transverse sections by its own action and by swirling overflows of its great neighbour, and running round north and north-west into the heart of the mountain that fed it, and that formed our horizon. Crossing the creek we camped on its bank. Our tents were pitched and fires burning brightly, long before the twilight had forsaken the west. Then a mighty supper of buffalo steak for us, and limitless pemmican for our Cree visitors, rounded off one of the pleasantest days of the expedition.

August 23rd.----Up early and away from camp before sunrise. The sun usually rose and set in so cloudless a sky on the prairies that the Chief had all along roughly determined the longitude of our camps and the local time in a simple way, that may as well be mentioned. His watch kept Montreal time, and he knew that the longitude of Montreal was 73 ° 33 '. Sunset last night was at 9.34 P.M., and sunrise this morning at 7.26 A.M., by his watch. That gave fourteen hours and eight minutes of sunlight : the half of that added to the hour of sunrise made 2.30 P.M, on his watch, to be mid-day. We were thus two hours and a half behind Montreal time, and as four minutes are equal to a degree of longitude, we learned that we were 37 ° 30' west of Montreal, or in longitude 111 °. At the same time we were in latitude 54 °, that is 7 ° or 350 miles north of the boundary line, and 700 miles north of Toronto. Yet the vegetation was of the same general character as that of Ontario ; and Bishop Taché told us that at Lac La Biche, 100 miles further north, they had their favourite wheat ground, where the wheat crop could always be depended on. But we can go still farther north. Mr. King, the second H. B. officer who had joined our party at Carlton, told us that he had never seen better wheat or root crops than are raised at Fort Liard on the Liard river----a tributary of the MacKenzie, in latitude 60 °. This testimony is confirmed by Sir John Richardson who says "wheat is raised with profit at Fort Liard, latitude 60 ° 5' North, longitude 122 ° 31' West, and four or five hundred feet above the sea." And numerous authorities from MacKenzie in 1787, who gave his name to the great river of the Arctic regions, down to H. B. officers and miners of the present day, give similar testimony concerning immense tracts along the Athabaska and the Peace rivers.

There are several reasons why the isothermal lines should extend so far north in this longitude, and why there should be the same flora as farther south, though the summers are shorter.

The low altitude of the Rocky Mountains, as they run north, permits the warm moisture-laden air of the Pacific to get across ; and, meeting then the colder currents from the north, refreshing showers are emptied on the plains. These northern plains of ours have also a comparatively low elevation, while farther south in the United States, on the same longitude, the semi-desert rainless plateaus are from five to eight thousand feet high. Combined with these facts, another may be suggested, that,—the summer days being much longer as you go north,—plants get more of the sun, more light and warmth within the same period of growing weather. The summer days where we are now, for instance, must be two hours longer than at Toronto.

But these and such like general reasons by no means determine the fitness of every section of the country for cereals. Much land south of 54 ° is unsuited for wheat because of drought or early frosts. Probably this is so with much along the banks of the Saskatchewan.   It has been proved at any rate that there is less or more risks, in places ; but those places are as a rule splendidly adapted for stock-raising, and, in such a country as this, cattle and sheep are just as much needed as flour.

To-day we travelled 42 miles. The first ' spell,' ten miles to ' the Little Lake,' was over a cold and moist soil as shown by the more northern character of the vegetation. The ground was profusely covered with the low scrub birch, which is found everywhere in the extreme north.   The second ' spell ' was fourteen miles, over ground that improved as we journeyed west, across Dog-rump Creek and, up the opposite hill, and, four miles farther on, to two beautiful lakes well stocked with wild fowl.   The creek gets its peculiar name from a bluff, projecting beyond a bold ridge that bounds the valley to the west.   A lively fancy sees in the bluff a resemblance to a dog's rump.   Beavers had built a dam a few days before, across the creek below the road, and in consequence the water was too deep for the buckboards. Untackling the horses we ran the buckboards across a slight bridge of willow rods that some good Samaritan had made for foot passengers. The road then wound up to the top of the ridge and gained the plateau beyond, through an extremely picturesque narrow steep pass. From the summit, we had a good view of the creek meandering through valley and lake towards the Saskatchewan.

At the second 'spelling-place' we caught up to a large 'brigade' of Hudson's Bay carts, that had left Carlton for Edmonton a week before us, heavily laden with stores. They were driven by several of Mr. McDougal's people, half-breeds and Crees, from Victoria, an united family of husband, wife, and half-a-dozen young children being at the head of the brigade. The expense of bringing anything into or sending anything out of the country by this old fashioned way is of course enormous. The prime cost of the articles is a bagatelle. Transport swallows up everything. No wonder that the price of a pound of tea, sugar, or salt, is here exactly the same. They weigh the same, and cost the same for carriage. One of the Crees in this brigade, called Jack, was pointed out to us as having in the last Indian war done a very plucky thing. A company of Crees and half-breeds from Victoria were hunting buffalo on the plains. One morning Jack and an old man were left behind to bring up the kitchen and baggage carts, while the main body started ahead for another camp. Just as they got over the first ridge, a war-party of Blackfeet swooped down on them with their usual terrific yells. They turned campwards, from the mere instinct of flight, though there was no relief there. The Blackfeet had just got up to them, shot and scalped the two hindmost, and would soon have massacred every one, but at this moment Jack, who had heard the yells, appeared over the ridge, and firing his gun at the enemy, shouted to an imaginary force behind him,

" hurrah ! here they are boys ; we've caught them at last." The old man at the same moment was seen hurrying up, and the Blackfeet imagining that they had fallen into a trap, turned tail, and fled precipitately.

The third ' spell ' was eighteen miles, over fine meadow land, covered with rich pasturage that extended without break for fifty miles to the north. On the road the Doctor shot some ducks for the pot. Every lakelet had at least one flock among the reeds, or swimming about ; but it was unsatisfactory work shooting them, unless they were close to the shore, not having a dog to bring them out. A little after sunset, we camped near the Riding or Snake Lake.

As we were now only 110 to 120 miles from Edmonton, it was proposed at supper that Horetzky should ride ahead with our letters of introduction to Mr. Hardisty ; order pack-saddles, secure a guide, and make as many arrangements as possible, for our journey over the mountains. At Edmonton, or at any rate at Lake St. Ann's, fifty miles farther west, wheels must be discarded and everything carried on pack horses. A different outfit is required and as some of it has to be made to order, time would be gained for the whole party if one got to the Fort before the others. Macaulay who had been away on a visit to Scotland for the last twelve months, and whose wife and family were at Edmonton, offered to accompany Horetzky. So it was decided that after an early breakfast next morning, the two should ride on rapidly, each taking two horses, a blanket, and some pemmican.

August 24th.—Rose early, but as we breakfasted at the camp, for the sake of Horetzky and Macaulay, it was 6 o'clock before all got away. Our two couriers preceded us by half an hour, but expected to be at Edmonton a day and a half before us. Passed the Riding or—as it is called on Palliser's Map—the Snake Lake. The smell of decaying fish-offal explained the object for which a number of log shanties had been erected, at two points near its shores. The lake swarms with white-fish. Soon after, we crossed the creek that issues from the lake. The cellar of a deserted shanty by the roadside showed the character of the soil; eighteen inches of black loam, and then successive layers of tenacious clay, through the first of which the tissues of plants extended.

The country now became more hilly; the hill-sides covered with heavy wood, and the hollows with marshes or lakelets. Vegetation everywhere was wonderfully luxuriant. Flowers re-appeared, but the general colour was blue in place of the former yellow or lilac; mint, blue bells, a beautiful tall larkspur, but principally light blue and dark blue asters. Our Botanist was disappointed by finding that, amid such wealth of vegetation, there were but few new species. The same plants have kept by us for a thousand miles. Mint and a saxifragaceous plant had accompanied us from Rainy Lake; gentians, asters, castilia, anemones, and golden rods from the eastern verge of the prairie.

We divided the day into two ' spells ;'—sixteen miles of the richest soil and pasturage ; and twenty-four miles to Victoria over a great deal of inferior ground. One large section of this showed little but scrub birch. Another, ten miles broad, near Victoria, was a sandy ridge producing scrub pine, or as the people here called it ' cypress ;' very like the country between Bathurst and Miramichi, N. B., that was burnt over by the great Miramichi fire, and where in the Lower Provinces the scrub pine is chiefly found. The ground was literally covered with cranberries, bearberries, the uva ursi, and other creepers.

In the forenoon the water was in lakes ; in the afternoon in streams, all of which fortunately for us were bridged, roughly indeed, but the worst bridge was a great improvement on deep black quagmire. Pine, White Mud, and Smoking Lake Creeks were the suggestive names of the chief streams, names that we

K

had heard before and probably would again. America has been called the country of inventions,—but it cannot invent names. In the North-west, there are half-a-dozen 'Red Deers,' 'White Muds' 'Vermilions'; and several other names are nearly as popular.

The first part of the day was bright and pleasant as usual, but at two o'clock heavy clouds gathered in the north-west. The wind drifted the thickest masses completely to our right, while all to the left the sky remained a clear bright blue. ' It thundered on the right '; and then we could see the rain falling in half-a-dozen places while intervening districts escaped. At one point, not very far from us, the rain must have been terrific, and right thankful were we that our course had not taken us there, or we would have had Rat Creek over again. The central mass of cloud hung over this point, and all at once seemed to have the bottom knocked out of it, when a deluge either of rain or hail —probably of both—descended, like a continuous pillar, to the ground for a quarter of an hour, uniting the earth to the clouds as if by a solid band. The end of the tail of this cloud swept round over our heads, and gave us first a gust of wind, and then a smart shower of rain and hail for two or three minutes. The sky cleared completely at 3 o'clock ; but, two hours later, as we crossed Smoking Lake Creek, and entered again on good land, thundery clouds rose the second time from the western horizon, and soon covered the sun and sky before us. We were now in the bounds of Mr. McDougal's old mission settlement ; and at his word we "hustled up," that is, pushed our horses to their utmost speed, to reach a good camping ground before the storm would burst. We got to the spot aimed at in time, our course for two miles being up a rich valley that is now behind the northern ridge or bank of the Saskatchewan, but that formerly, when the river was higher, must have been one of its beds, the intervening ridge being then an island. The settlement and

Hudson's Bay fort of Victoria is on the river slope of this ridge, and thus travellers, passing along the main trail up the valley, might be in entire ignorance that there was a settlement near. When we rode up, however, two or three men were making hay in the valley, and, hailing the sight as a sure sign that civilized beings and dwellings must be not far off, we camped at a spring beside them ; and, with a rapidity that astonished them and ourselves, had everything made tight before the rain commenced. After all the threatening the shower did not amount to much, in half an hour the sky was clear again, and the Doctor and Mr. McDougal drove over to the fort, a mile distant, for supplies, and to announce that there would be service in the church next day. They returned after dark with beef, bread, and milk.   Mr. Tait the Hudson's Bay agent, had no fresh meat ; but, hearing of our arrival, with oriental hospitality, had ordered a young ox to be killed and a quarter sent over for our use.

August 25th.—Another day of rest, and a long sleep to begin it with.   At 10 A. M. walked over the ridge to service, at Victoria.   The church, (which is also used as a school-room) the Mission House, and Fort are all at the west end of the settlement.   The log-houses of the half-breeds, (English and Scotch) intermingled with the tents of the Crees, extend in a line from this west end along the bank of the river, each man having a frontage on the river, and his grain planted in a little hollow that runs behind the houses, beneath the main rise of the ridge.   Most of their hay they cut in the valley, on the other side of the ridge where we had camped.

The farming is on a very limited scale, as the men prefer hunting buffalo, fishing, or freighting for the Company to steady agricultural labour, and neither farming nor gardening can succeed well, when the seeds are merely thrown into the ground in spring, and the ground is not looked at again till autumn, when every thing is expected to be ripe and ready for ingathering.   The settlement is seven years old, and consists now of between twenty and thirty families of half-breeds and from ten to a hundred tents of Crees, according to the time of the year, each tent housing on an average, seven or eight souls. It owes its origin to Mr. McDougal who selected the place as a Mission field because the Crees resorted to it ; and as a suitable locality for a half-breed settlement, on account of its advantages of soil, river, lakes abounding in fish and wild fowl, and nearness to the plains where the buffalo are always found.   Last year Mr. McDougal was removed to Edmonton, and the charge of Victoria given to Mr. Campbell who had been conducting a successful Mission among the Stonies at Woodville to the south-west. Mr. Campbell was at present on his way home from Red River, where he had gone to attend the first Wesleyan conference of Manitoba, and consequently there had been no one attending to the Mission for some weeks, except the schoolmaster. This removal of Missionaries from one tribe or even station, where they have gained the confidence of the Indians, to another locality, seems a mistake to outsiders.   The personal influence of the Missionary is the only thing that can be counted upon in work among heathen, or any rude and primitive people, and personal influence can be gained only after long intercourse with them.

When we arrived at the church it was almost filled with about eighty whites, half-breeds, and Crees. The men sat on one side, the women on the other, and the children in a little gallery or loft with the schoolmaster and monitors. The service was in English, but some Cree hymns were sung, and Mr. McDougal announced that there would be service in Cree in the evening, through the medium of an interpreter. The conduct of all present from first to last was most devout, notwithstanding that many present understood but imperfectly what was said. The children led the singing, and though there was lack of bass-voices on account of the absence of the principal members of the choir, it was singularly sweet and correct. Some of us were moved more than we cared to show, when the first Cree hymn was sung.

Service over two of our party dined at the Mission House, and the others at the Fort; and, after a walk through the settlement along the bank of the river, we returned to the church to see the Sunday School. Mr. McKenzie the teacher was about to leave for another mission, and his successor Mr. Snyder was also present. There were sixty names, forty of them half-breeds, and twenty Indians, on the roll; but only thirty-two were present, as whole families were absent, freighting or hunting. We examined the three advanced classes, numbering twenty-one, of the biggest boys and girls. All read the English Bible more or less fluently and with understanding, for they answered every question put to them. Their knowledge of hymns was such as could be found only in a Methodist school; if any of us named a hymn in the collection, the tune was at once raised and all joined in without books. The more ambitious tunes were of course the favourites with the children. The Indians delight in hymn singing, the Missionaries take advantage of this and make it one great means of reaching their hearts. Heathen Crees who come to Victoria only for a few weeks send their children to the school; they pick up some hymns at any rate, and sing them when far away on the plains.

Mr. Snyder had been schoolmaster for the last few years at White-Fish Lake, a settlement of Crees fifty miles to the north, where every one acknowledges that good work has been done. He had eighty Cree children at his school there. When the Indians moved out to the plains to hunt buffalo, the master would pack up his spelling books and slates, and go off with them, setting up his establishment wherever they halted. He spent from two to six months of the year, teaching in this rotary style,—and liked it as every man with a love of the picturesque in him would—hunting half the day, teaching the other half.

The Crees at White-Fish Lake are all Christianized and value the school highly. They are beginning to settle down to steady farming-work too, several families not going to the plains now, but raising wheat, barley and potatoes instead. At Victoria wheat has been sowed for seven successive years, and was a failure only once, the cause then being an extreme local drought. At White-Fish Lake it has never been a total failure. Victoria is on the most northerly bend of the North Saskatchewan; the plateau is very elevated; and many ot the plants in the country round, have more of the sub-arctic character than in any other part of the "fertile belt;" so that we were not surprised when told that there were generally light frosts in July and August. Indeed Mr. McDougal had been warned in planting the settlement, that he was choosing one of the worst spots on the river; the future may show that he was wiser than his friends.

In the evening, we went to church again; more Crees were present than in the forenoon, but not so many of the half-breeds. Mr. Tait acted as interpreter and also led the meeting, with modesty and fervour, in prayer in Cree. It must be a great advantage to a Missionary to have such a man in charge of the Fort.

We had seen enough to-day to convince us, more than all the arguments in the world, that missionary labour among the Indians is a reality, and that the positive language on the other side is the language of ignorance, self-interest or downright opposition to the Gospel. The aims of traders and Missionaries with regard to the Indians are different; the former wish that they should continue hunters, the latter that they should take to steady employment. It is not wonderful then that some traders should feel annoyed at what they regard as a steady working against their interest. But, as the Indian has no chance of existence except by conforming to civilized ways, the sooner that the Government or the Christian people awake to the necessity of establishing schools among every tribe the better. Little can be done with the old, it may be two or three generations before old habits among a people are changed ; but, by always taking hold of the young, the work can be done. A Mission without schools is a mistake, almost a crime. And the Methodists deserve the praise of having seen and vigorously acted on this, and they can, therefore, point to more visible proofs of success in their Indian Missions than perhaps any other church.

It is greatly to the credit of the Indians in British America, that they have never injured or stolen from any Missionary. They have plundered posts, stripped traders naked, and murdered some who perhaps had given them cause ; but even when at war, the Missionary is allowed to enter and speak in their great Councils and is everywhere treated with respect. Reverence is a strong trait in the Indian character. His own language supplies no words for profane swearing ; if he wishes to blaspheme, he must borrow from the French or English. Is not his dignity of speech and manner connected with this veneration for Deity ?

We invited Mr. Tait and the schoolmasters to walk over the ridge and have supper with us. Mrs. Campbell also did us the honour of coming, and, so for the first time, our camp was graced with the presence of a lady. Her presence lighted up everything, and had a very appreciable effect on our style of passing things round the table ; every one was as anxious to help her to something as if she had been Her Majesty in person; Terry, naturally and nationally the soul of politeness, was especially attentive. Rather than let her put preserved peaches on the plate beefsteak had been on, he removed the plate and whipping out his pocket handkerchief, that had not been washed since he left Fort Garry, proceeded to clean it. Luckily the Doctor noticed him in time to snatch the plate away, or—but we must draw a veil over Terry as cook or table-maid ; in no house is it wise to look too closely into how things are done in the kitchen.

Since the commencement of our journey, Sundays had invariably been our most pleasant and profitable days, and this was no exception. The kindness of every one at Victoria was something not soon to be forgotten. They welcomed us for our own sakes, and for the end the expedition had in view, as they had long prayed for the opening up of the country. It was in our favour also here as elsewhere that a Doctor was with us. He visited and prescribed for all the sick in the settlement, and, finding in the Fort a medicine chest that had been sent out as a present by Dr. Ray but had never been used, he explained to Mr. Tait how and when to give the different medicines, and wrote out general directions that could be easily understood and acted upon.

August 26th.—Rose very early, the Doctor acting as campmaster and making every one fly round, so that we got off half an hour before sunrise. The thermometer then stood at thirty degrees, and heavy hoar-frost lay on the rich deep grass. A dense fog rose as the frost exhaled in dew, and, the sun's rays striking on this, formed a beautiful fog-bow that hung before us during fully an hour's travelling. Passing up the valley parallel to the river, to where it turns southerly in a somewhat different direction, we ascended the plateau on the other side and skirted its edge for some distance, going through tall heavy grass and a country which seemed to possess every qualification for successful stockraising. The road showed the influence of recent rains that, the Victoria settlers told us, had been so heavy this August as to have completely stopped haying operations. Every marsh was a bog, every creek swollen, and as good soil makes bad roads, our progress was necessarily slow. Still by getting a good start, and by "pegging away" we made forty-four miles in our three "spells." The first was to the Wassetenow, (or opening in the bank) so called from the cleft it has made, in the ridge, to get to the Saskatchewan. The cleft, instead of showing the usual broad rounded valley, is cut sharp and clean as if with a knife, partly by the force of the stream and partly by land slides. We next passed successively " Sucker " " Vermilion " and " Deep" Creeks, besides several smaller ones, and camped at the last named. The road descended twice to the Saskatchewan, which showed the same clayey look as at Carlton, and ran with almost as great a volume though more than three hundred miles nearer its source. For thirty miles to-day the trail was through thick woods of aspen, poplars, birch, tamarack, spruce and pine. Much of the wood was good timber, from one to two feet in diameter with tall straight shafts, as thick fifty or sixty feet up as when five or six feet from the ground. There are occasionally alternate sections of aspen and spruce for half a mile or so ; in one place the underbrush thick and green ; in another the soil so bare and the trees so branchless, that movement in any direction is easy.

Camped before sunset within twenty-seven miles of Edmonton, and in honour of the event brought out our only bottle of claret. As we had no ice, Terry shouted to "Souzie" to bring some cold water, but no Souzie appearing he varied the call to "Pimmican!" This brought Souzie to the front, and great was his indignation when a bucket was put into his hands, instead of the rich pemmican he was never tired of feasting on. Terry had a decidedly Irish contempt for Indians, half-breeds, or "coloured gentlemen " of any kind ; and Souzie was especially obnoxious, because of his magnificent appetite, and because with Indian carelessness he often mislaid the belongings of the party, as if, remarked Terry confidentially to the Secretary :— " I carried tillygraph wires in my head."

August 27th.—Off this morning again before sunrise, and breakfasted fourteen miles from camp at a little Creek near " Horse Hill, " where the " guard " of Edmonton was formerly located. On the way crossed a strong rapid-running stream

called Sturgeon Creek, from which twenty-five pound fish are
often taken.   We had left the thick woods last evening, and the
country to-day was open and elevated.   Thirty miles to our left
the Beaver Hills, on the other side of the Saskatchewan, formed
a bold background of deep blue.   Mr. McDougal pointed out a
spot near our breakfast "spelling place," where his predecessor had
a remarkable escape when travelling. He had intended to camp
on Horse Hill but when within a mile of it, so furious a storm
came on that he dismounted and crouched for protection under
a bank with overhanging low willow bushes.   When the storm
passed over, he rode on to the hill and found on the very spot
he would have camped on, a horse that had just been killed
by the lightning.

At eleven o'clock, arrived at Edmonton and found that
Horetsky had made arrangements to enable us to start next day·
Mr. Hardisty in the quiet business-like way, and with the same
kindness that many a traveller has experienced before, had done
everything to forward our views. We pitched tents on the bank
three quarters of a mile down the river from the Fort, near Mr.
McDougal's house and the new Church he is building, and had
the whole party photographed ; tents, carts, buck-boards, with
Terry, seated on his pots and pans, mending his pants and
smoking the inevitable inseparable cutty, in the foreground.

The first great half of our journey, the prairie as distinguished
from the mountain part, was over. It had not been all prairie
or anything like it, and the second part would not be all mountain.   We were not obliged to discard our carts for another
fifty miles, and the mountains were still two hundred miles
distant. But, Edmonton may be considered the end of the
journey across the plains and the beginning of the woods ; and
is the point at which to prepare for crossing the Rocky Mountains.
It is the headquaters of the Company's posts on the Saskatchewan, and here we were to take our leave of the great river

Pl. 25.

FORT EDMONTON.

Up to this point it had been all plain sailing, but now we were told to expect toil and trouble.

At Edmonton we looked with great interest for the section of coal that crops out on the river bank. 'Is it coal or not', was the question. Some had called it bitumenous shale, with very little bitumen, and others lignite. A bushel or two was brought up from the river side at our request; it looked like shale, or dull dried stuff from which most of the bitumen had leaked out. Trying it in the smiddy, it burnt well and gave a good heat when the bellows was applied, but it would be very difficult to kindle without the bellows. It keeps burning a long time and leaves a great deal of dirt, dust and ash, worse in this respect than the Pictou coal, that Captain Davidson used to declare yielded " at the rate of two ton of ashes to one of coal." The section at Edmonton is only three feet thick, and it crops out in several places, with a conglomerate beneath it that resembles ironstone in nodules ; but, at the Pembina river, seventy miles to the west there is a seam ten feet thick that we would see ; and Mr. Hardisty informed us that at the Rocky Mountain House, one hundred and forty miles distant to the south-west, the seam is ten feet, the coal of a much superior quality, and used regularly in the forge. Many other seams are found over a wide extent of country, and it is but reasonable to infer that several of these will yield good fuel, for even in the richest coal countries there is no such abundant outcrops as here. What we tried was picked up from the river or from the outcrop ; and was hard and shaly and therefore inferior as fuel; but had it not been very hard it would probably have crumbled away by exposure to the air and rain and snow and frost, and its face been covered up completely with earthy and vegetable matter, so that no surface traces of its presence would have been left. A little boring would soon settle the question, for the beds are horizontal and not very deep. It is desirable that the whole

truth should soon be known on the subject, for if there is
abundance of good coal, the point most important, next to the
water supply on the plains, in the future of our North-west will
be decided in our favour. The Edmonton specimens being
evidently inferior, we resolved not to make up our own minds
until we saw the Pembina seams.

The Company works a large farm at Edmonton, and with a
success that is very encouraging, especially when it is remembered
that the methods are comparatively rude, and that there is much
better land to the north, south and east. They have raised
wheat for thirty years, and it has failed only two or three times;
barley and potatoes and turnips are sure crops. The usual
difficulties from the Indians camping near a Fort have been
experienced. A band of strange Indians come along, and,
without the slightest idea that they are doing anything objec-
tionable, use the fences for tent poles or fuel ; and their horses
then getting into the fields destroy much of the crop. But in
spite of these and other hindrances, a thousand bushels of wheat
are usually stored from a sowing of a hundred ; and last year,
two hundred and fifty kegs of potatoes (eight gallon kegs used
instead of bushels) were planted, and about five thousand were
dug. The same land has been used for the farm for thirty
years, without any manure worth speaking of being put on it.
Part is intervale and part upland.

The uplands do not yield such good crops because there is a
slight infusion of alkali in the surface soil, which subsoil plough-
ing would probably do away with.

In the evening the Secretary held Divine service in ' the ball
room " of the Fort. About fifty men, most of them employed
about the post, were present. There were also some miners
who had recently arrived from Peace River, and whose reports
of the Ominica gold-mines were not very encouraging. The
men who wash the Saskatchewan sand bars for gold make on an

average four dollars per day, but that does not satisfy them ; five dollars a day is called " wages." This year there are only fifteen miners on the Saskatchewan.

Three. or four intend starting to-morrow for the Red Deer, a tributary of the Bow River, in some canyons of which heavier grains of gold than usual have been found.

On the North Saskatchewan the gold miners or washers range up and down for about one hundred and thirty miles, Edmonton being the central point of this distance. It was for a long time supposed that all the gold in the Saskatchewan and the other rivers—in the same longitude—came from the Rocky Mountains, and these were diligently ' prospected ' near their sources. But not a trace of gold has been found there, and it is now thought more probable that a stratum of gold-bearing quartz extends across the country, some distance on the west side of the mountains. " Float" silver is also found in some of the rivers, but not in sufficient quantities to encourage prospecting.

This seems the proper place, before going on with our diary, for some general observations on the country, between the North-west Angle of the lake of the Woods and Edmonton ; particularly with a view to its capabilities as a great field for colonization. We can speak positively only of what we saw, and that includes a very narrow strip. All admit that the line of our route does not show the best land, however much they differ as to the quantity that is available for settlement. Some observers, long resident in the country, declare that the fertile belt practically means the whole distance between the North and South Saskatchewan, and other vast regions to the east, north, and west, especially a broad belt along the bases of the Rocky Mountains to the south of Edmonton, two hundred miles long by fifty broad, the home of the Blackfeet, and pronounced by many to be the garden of the North-west. Others maintain that, as far as the Saskatchewan country is concerned, only a narrow belt along such rivers as the Battle, Vermillion, and Red Deer can be cultivated with success.   It is not necessary to decide between those views now. We know on the authority of Captain Palliser, who crossed and re-crossed the plains several times, that the central American desert does extend a short way into British Territory forming a triangle, having for its base the forty-ninth parallel from longitude 100 ° to 114 ° W., with its apex reaching to the fifty-second parallel of latitude.   But the first emigrants will select land along the courses of streams, especially the navigable rivers, and they will soon find out all about the intervening districts.

Speaking generally of Manitoba and our North-west, along the line we travelled, it is impossible to doubt that it is one of the finest pasture countries in the world, and that a great part of it is well adapted for cereals.   The climatological conditions are favourable for both stock raising and grain producing.   The spring is nearly as early as in Ontario; the summer is more humid and therefore the grains, grasses, and root crops grow better ; the autumn bright and cloudless, the very weather for harvesting; and the winter has less snow and fewer snow-storms and though, in many parts colder, it is healthy and pleasant because of the still dry air, the cloudless sky, and bright sun. The soil is almost everywhere a peaty or sandy loam resting on clay.   Its only fault is that it is too rich.   Crop after crop is raised without fallow or manure.

As regards the practical experience of farmers on the subject there is little to appeal to, and that little is chiefly favourable. The only large settlement is about Red River.   The farms there are most inconveniently shaped, being very narrow, very long strips ; none of the people were skilled farmers to begin with, and, till the last two or three years, they had no market except what the H. B. Company took from them.   But the Scotch

farmers there are all making money now, and their testimony is
uniformly in favour of the country being the best in the world
for farming purposes.

The other settlements are few and far between, on the edges
of rivers or lakes, where wood and water are easily obtainable.
The population of these consists entirely of half-breeds, and
their method of farming is unique. They are farmers, hunters,
fishermen, voyageurs, all in one; the soil is scratched, three
inches deep, early in May, some seed is thrown in, and then
the whole household go off to hunt the buffalo. They get back
about the first of August, spend the month haying and harvesting, and are off to the fall hunt early in September. Some are
now so devoted to farming that they only go to one hunt in the
year. It is astonishing that, though knowing so well ' how not
to do it,' they raise some wheat and a good deal of barley, oats
and potatoes. There is a great difference, however, between the
Scotch and French half-breeds. The French who intermarried
with the Indians in some respects became as the Indians ; just as
the Spaniards in Mexico and South America who intermarried
with the natives, sank to their level. The squaw was treated as
his wife. Her people became his people, but his God her God. The
children have all the Indian characteristics, the habits, weak-
nesses, and ill-regulated passions of nomads. They excel the
Indian in strength of body and endurance. They beat him on
his own field of hunting, running, riding, power of eating or when
necessary of abstinence ; with these are united much of French
vivacity, love of amusement, hospitality, patience, courtesy of
manner, and warmth of affection. When a Scotchman married
a squaw, her position, on the contrary, was frequently not much
higher than a servant's. He was 'the superior person' of the
house. He continued Christian after his fashion, she continued
pagan. The granite of his nature resisted fusion in spite of
family and tribal influences, the attrition of all surrounding cir-

cumstances, and the total absence of civilization ; and the wife
was too completely separated from him to be able to raise her
self to his level.   The children of such a couple take more afte
the father than the mother.   As a rule they are shrewd, steady
and industrions.   A Scotch half-breed has generally a field of
wheat before or behind his house, stacks, barn, and provision for
a year ahead, in his granary.   The Métis has a patch of potatoes
or a little barley, and in a year of scarcity draws his belt tighter
or starves.   It is interesting as one travels in the great North-
west to note, how the two old allies of the middle ages have left
their marks on the whole of this great country.   The name of
almost every river, creek, mountain or district is either French
or Scotch.

The climate and the soil are favourable !   What about water,
fuel, and the summer frosts, the three points next in importance?

A large population cannot be expected unless there is
good water in the form of rivers, lakes, springs, or wells.   In
many parts of the prairies of the U. S., dependence is placed
mainly on rain water collected in cisterns ; but such a supply is
unwholesome, and to it may be attributed much of their prairie
sickness.   In connection with this question of water, the existence of the numerous saline lakes, that has been again and again
noted, forces itself on our attention ; the wonder, is that former
observers have said so little about them.   Palliser marks them
on his map in two places, but they are really the characteristic
feature of the country for hundreds of miles.   In many parts
they so completely outnumber the fresh water lakes, that it is

> "Water, water, everywhere
> And not a drop to drink."

Some of them are from five to twenty miles long, others only
little pools.   Some are so impregnated with salt that crystals of
sulphate of soda are formed on the surface, and a thick white
incrustation is deposited round the shores.   Others are brackish

or with a salt taste that is scarcely discernible. We noted several facts about these lakes that may be stated. (1) That they have no outlet. (2) That they are often side by side with fresh water lakes, and that, in these cases, the latter occupy the higher situation and their outflow consequently falls into the former. (3) That a few feet away from their immediate shores, on which marine plants grow, the usual flora and grasses of the country flourish. (4) That the tracks of the buffalo show that the water is drank by them, and horses drink it when they cannot get fresh water, though it acts medicinally on them.

Whence have they originated? Several theories may be suggested. Here is one that explains all the facts so far as known to us. Suppose that formerly a superabundant quantity of alkaline matter was diffused through the soil generally, over our Northwest, as we know it is over a wide extent of the American desert and in sections on the Pacific coast. We found it so in some places where there are no lakes, and where it could be carried off by rivers. On the bank of the Assiniboine near Fort Ellice, similarly on the Saskatchewan near Edmonton, and at other points it was observed. If it had once been generally diffused through the soil what must have happened in the course of centuries wherever there was an ordinary rainfall? The water, percolating through the soil, would carry off the alkali matter into lakes and rivers, and it would be retained only in those lakes that had no outlet. This theory explains all the features of the case, and starts no new difficulties. It suggests too, that the one great reason why the American Desert must remain both desert and bitter is, that there is no rainfall on it, while farther north in the same longitude there is abundance of rain.

Apart from those saline lakes, is there a sufficient supply of water? In brief we must answer that, in many parts there is, in others we do not know yet. Test wells must be sunk and

L

then we can speak positively; in the meantime all the indications are in our favour.

The question of fuel is next in importance in a country
where the winters are severe, for corn cannot be grown for fuel
in our North-west as it has been on the prairies of Illinois.   At
present, on account of the destructive prairie fires for successive
years, there is little wood except along the rivers and creeks, and
on some of the hills, until we go back to the continuous forest
on the north, or to within two hundred miles of the Rocky
Mountains.   This scarcity of wood is of little consequence, if
the vast coal-measures, that extend from the Red Deer and Bow
Rivers to the McKenzie, prove to contain good coal in large
enough seams to be worked with profit. By river or rail, coal can
be carried in all directions for every purpose; and it is highly
probable, as will be pointed out hereafter, that we have the
most extensive, perhaps the finest, coal fields in the world. The
importance of definitely ascertaining the quality of each prominent seam is very great.   But even though wood may not be
absolutely required for fuel, every encouragemnnt for its growth
should be given.   Wood is needed for many purposes, and the
plains would be warmer in winter if they were not treeless.

The remaining difficulty is the recurrence of summer
frosts. In many localities these are dreaded more than anything else. At one place in June or July, at another in August,
sharp frosts have nipped the grain, and sometimes even the
potatoes. At Edmonton, 2088 feet above the sea, there is
invariably a night or two of frost between the 10th and 20th of
August. At Victoria and Fort Pitt to the east, and still more
so at the R. C. Mission of Lake St. Albert and Lake St. Ann
to the west of Edmonton, the grain has suffered more or less
frequently from the same cause.   This enemy is a serious one,
for against it man seems powerless. But admitting to the full
that there are such frosts, admitting that they cannot be avoided,

that no improvement will ensue on the general cultivation of the land, the draining of bogs, and the peopling of the country, there remain large and fertile tracts free from them, and, where the frosts are frequent, other crops than wheat can be raised, and the pasturage remains unhurt and unrivalled.

It is only fair to the country to add, that the power of those frosts to injure must be judged not by the thermometer, but by actual experience. It is a remarkable fact, that frost which would nip grain in many other countries is innocuous on the Red River and the Saskatchewan. Whatever the reason, and Mr. Spence in a recent pamphlet on 'Manitoba and the North-west of the Dominion,' has assigned several,—such as the dryness of the atmosphere, the heat-retaining character of the soil, and the sudden change of temperature that enables vigorous plants to bear an atmosphere at 20 ° better than at 35 ° when the latent heat of the earth and the plants has been given off,—the fact is undoubted. Due regard to times and seasons will also enable the farmer to escape very often the dangers peculiar to a locality. Thus, at Edmonton, if they sow late and the wheat is in the milk when the frost comes, it is injured. Of course the remedy is to sow early.

Looking fairly at all the facts, admitting all the difficulties— and what country has not its own drawbacks, it is impossible to avoid the conclusion that we have a great and fertile North-west, a thousand miles long and from one to four hundred miles broad, capable of containing a population of millions. It is a fair land; rich in furs and fish, in treasures of the forest, the field, and the mine; seamed by navigable rivers, interlaced by numerous creeks, and beautified with a thousand lakes; broken by swelling uplands, wooded hill-sides, and bold ridges; and protected on its exposed sides by a great desert or by giant mountains. The air is pure, dry and bracing all the year round; giving promise of health and strength of body and length of days. Here we have a home for our own surplus population and for the stream of emigration that runs from northern and central Europe to America. Let it be opened up to the world by rail and steamboat, and in an incredibly short time the present gap between Manitoba and British Columbia will be filled up, and a continuous line of loyal Provinces extend from the Atlantic to the Pacific.

———

Pl. 27.

EDMONTON TO JASPER HOUSE, AND YELLOW HEAD PASS.

CHAPTER VII.

From Fort Edmonton to the River Athabasca.

August 28th.—It is proverbially difficult to get away in a hurry from an Hudson's Bay Fort, especially if outfit is required; but, we were furthered, not only by the genuine kindness of Mr. Hardisty but by a false alarm that quickened every one's movements, and so we got off early in the afternoon.

A foolish report reached Edmonton in the forenoon, that the Crees and Blackfeet were fighting on the other side of the river, a report based, as we afterwards learned, on no other ground than that 'some one' had heard shots fired, at wild duck pro-bably enough. Where there are no newspapers to ferret out and communicate the truth to every one, it is extraordinary what wild stories are circulated ; and how readily they are believed, though similar 'on dits' have been found to be lies time and again. As we would be detained with long pow-wows, if either party crossed the river, every one helped us to hurry off. We had to say "good bye" not only to the Indians who had come from Fort Pitt, and to Mr. McDougal and the gentle-men of the Fort ; but also to Horetsky and to our Botanist, as the Chief had decided to send these two on a separate expedition to Peace River, by Fort Dunvegan, to report on the flora of that

(181)

country, and on the nature of the northern passes through the
Rocky Mountains. We parted with regret, for men get better
acquainted with each other on shipboard, or in a month's travel
in a lone-land, than they would under ordinary circumstances in
a year. Souzie was more sorry to part with Frank than with any
of the rest of us. He had been teaching him Cree, and Frank had
got the length of twenty-four words which he aired on every
possible occasion, to his tutor's unbounded delight. Souzie
mounted his horse and waited patiently at the gate of the Fort
for two hours, without our knowledge. When Frank came out
he rode on with him for a mile to the height of a long slope ;
then he drew up and putting one hand on his heart, with a
sorrowful look, held out the other ; and, without a word, turned
his horse and rode slowly away.

Our number was now reduced to four. We were to drive
out fifty miles to Lake St. Ann's, and "pack" our travelling
stores and baggage on horses there ; taking with us the faithful
Terry as cook, and three new men ; a guide and two packers.
Mr. Hardisty kindly accompanied us ten miles out, to the guard
at Lake St. Albert, to see that we got good horses. The road
is an excellent one, and passes through a rolling prairie, dotted
with a great number of dried marshes on each side, from which
immense quantities of natural hay could be cut.

Crossing the same Sturgeon River that we had crossed yesterday morning on our way to Edmonton, a hill rose before us
crowned with the Cathedral Church of the Mission, the house of
the Bishop, and the house of the Sisters of Charity ; while, up
and down the river extended the little houses and farms of the
settlers. We called on Bishop Grandin and found him at home,
with six or seven of his clergy who fortunately happened to be
in from various missions. The Bishop is from old France. The
majority of the priests, and all the sisters, are French Canadians.
The Bishop and his staff received us with a hearty welcome,

showed us round the church, the school, the garden, and introduced us to the sisters. The church represents an extraordinary amount of labour and ingenuity, when it is considered that there is not a saw mill in the country and that every plank had to be made with a whip or hand saw. The altar is a beautiful piece of wood-work in the early Norman style, executed as a labour of love by two of the fathers. The sacristy behind, was the original log church and is still used for service in the winter.

This St. Albert mission was formed about nine years ago, by a number of settlers removing from Lake St. Ann's in hope of escaping the frosts which had several times cut down their grain there. It grew rapidly, chiefly from St. Ann's and Red River, till two years ago, when it numbered nearly one thousand, all French half-breeds. Then came the small-pox that raged in every Indian camp, and, wherever men were assembled, all up and down the Saskatchewan. Three hundred died at St. Albert. Men and women fled from their nearest and dearest. The priests and the sisters toiled with that devotedness that is a matter of course with them; nursed the sick, shrived the dying, and gathered many of the orphans into their house. The scourge passed away, but the infant settlement had received a severe blow from which it is only beginning to recover. Many are the discouragements, material and moral, of the fathers in their labours, as they frankly confessed. Their congregation is migratory, spends half the year at home and the other half on the plains. The children are only sent to school when there are no buffalo to hunt, no pemmican to make, or no work of greater importance than education to set them at. The half-breed is religious, but he must indulge his passions. It is a singular fact that not one of them has ever become a priest, though several, Louis Riel among the number, have been educated at different missions, with a view to the sacred office. The yoke of celibacy is too heavy; and fiddling, dancing, hunting, and a wild roving life have too many charms.

The settlement now numbers seven hundred souls. The land is good, but, on account of its elevation, and other local causes, subject to summer frosts; in spite of these, cereals, as well as root crops, succeed when any care is taken. Last year they reaped on the mission farm twenty returns of wheat, eighteen of barley, sixteen of potatoes. Turnips, beets, carrots and such like vegetables, grow to an enormous size. A serious drawback to the people is that they have no grist mill; the Fathers could not get them to give up the buffalo for a summer and build one on the Sturgeon. They would begin it in the fall and finish it in the spring; but the floods swept it away half-finished, and the Fathers have no funds to try anything on a solid and extensive scale.

The sisters took us to see their orphanage. They have twenty-four children in it, chiefly girls; two-thirds of the number half-breeds, the rest Blackfeet or Crees who have been picked up in tents beside their dead parents, abandoned by the tribe when stricken with small-pox. The hair of the Indian boys and girls was brown as often as black, and their complexions were as light as those of the half-breeds. This would be the case with the men and women also, if they adopted civilized habits. Sleeping in the open air, with face often turned upward to a blazing sun, would soon blacken the skin of the fairest European.

Last Sunday we noticed, in the congregation at Victoria, that while some of the old Indians had skins almost as black as negroes, the young men and women were comparatively fair. The simple explanation is that the young Crees are taking now to civilized ways. People at Fort Garry told us that when the troops arrived under Colonel Wolsely, some of them, who had slept or rowed the boats bare-headed under the blazing sun, were quite as dark-complexioned as average Indians. The gentle

Christian courtesy and lady-like manners of the sisters at the mission charmed us, while the knowledge of the devoted lives they lead must impress, with profound respect, Protestant and Roman Catholic alike. Each one would have adorned a home of her own, but she had given up all for the sake of her Lord and His little ones. After being entertained by the bishop to an excellent supper, and hearing the orphans sing, we were obliged to hurry away in order to camp before dark. The Doctor, however, remained behind for an hour to visit three or four who were sick in their rooms, and arrange their dispensary. Taking leave of Mr. Hardisty also, we drove on three miles farther and camped. Five of us occupied one tent; our own party of four and Mr. Adams, the H. B. agent at Lake St. Ann's who was returning from Edmonton to his post.

August 29th.—Some of the horses were missing this morning, but an hour after sunrise all were found except Mr. Adams' and another, whose tracks were seen going in the St. Ann's or homeward direction. Knowing that we would overtake them the start was made. After a third and fourth crossing of the Sturgeon river, we halted for breakfast. We then crossed it for the fifth and last time, caught up to the two horses quietly feeding near the wayside, dined at mid-day, and rode on in advance with Mr. Adams to St. Ann's, leaving the two carts to follow more leisurely. We reached the post an hour before sunset, having ridden nearly forty miles, though, as we had presented the odometer to Mr. McDougal, our calculations of distances were now necessarily only guess work. The carts got in an hour after, and the tent was pitched and the carts emptied for the last time. From St. Ann's the road is only a horse-trail through the woods, so often lost in marshes or hidden by windfalls that a guide is required. Tents, for the sake of carrying as little weight as possible, were discarded for the simple "lean to"; and wheels had to be discarded for pack horses. Our guide was Valad, a three-quarters-Indian, and our packers—Brown a Scotchman, and Beaupré a French Canadian; both old packers and miners and first rate men. They said that the whole of next day would be required to arrange the pack-saddles, but they were told that we *must* get away from the post immediately after dinner, so that one "spell" might be made on the 30th, and a long day on the 31st.

The road travelled over to-day was through a beautiful country, hilly and wooded, creeks winding round narrow valleys and others that beaver dams had converted into marshes, on which were growing great masses of natural hay, that there was no one to cut. The vegetation on the hill-sides was most luxuriant. The grass reached to the horses' necks, and the vetches, which the horses snatched at greedily as they trotted past, were from four to six feet high. The last twelve miles of the day's journey resembled a pleasure drive; the first half amid tall woods through which the sunlight glimmered, with rich green underbrush of wild currant, mooseberry, and Indian pear, the ripe fruit of which we plucked from our saddles. Through these our road led down to the very brink of Lake St. Ann's, a beautiful sheet of water, stretching away before us for miles, enlivened with flocks of wild duck and pelican on the islets and promontories that fringed it; and then round the south west-side of the lake, for the last six miles, to Mr. Adams' house. Mrs. Adams had a grand supper ready for us in half an hour, and we did full justice to the cream and butter, and the delicious white-fish of Lake St. Ann's. This fish (*albus coregonus*) is in size and shape and even taste very like the shad of the Bay of Fundy; but very unlike it in the number and intricacy of its bones. It is an infinite toil to eat shad; and with all possible care little prickly bones escape notice and insinuate themselves into the throat; but with white-fish a man may abandon himself to the simple pleasure of eating. Lake St. Ann's is the great storehouse of white-fish for supplying this part of the country. It provides for all demands up to Edmonton. Last year thirty thousand, averaging over three pounds each, were taken out and frozen for winter use.

This was the worst place for summer frosts that we had yet seen. A field of potatoes belonging to the priest was cut down to the ground, and Mr. Adams pointed out barley that had been nipped two or three times, but from which he still expected half a crop.

August 30th.—"Packing" the horses was the order of the day till two o'clock, and Brown and Beaupré showed themselves experts at the work. A pack-saddle looks something like a miniature wooden "horse" such as we have all seen used in our backyards for sawing sticks of cordwood. Wooden pads suited to the shape of the horse's back, with two or three plies of buffalo robe or blanket underneath, prevent the cross legs and packs from hurting the horse. All the baggage, blankets, provisions, and utensils are made up into portable bundles as nearly equal in size and weight as possible. Each of the packers seizing a bundle places it on the side of the saddle, another bundle is put on the top between the two, where the log of wood to be sawed would be placed, and then the triangular shaped load is bound in one by folds of shaganappi twisted firmly but without a knot, after a regular fashion called the "diamond hitch."

The articles which experience had shown to be not indispensable or not required for the mountains, were now discarded, and other things of exactly the right sort obtained in their stead ; the object being to give as light loads as possible to the horses, that they might travel the faster. A horse with a hundred weight on his back can trot without racking himself : when he has from one hundred and sixty to two hundred pounds he can only walk, not only because of the weight but because the load catches in the bushes and between trees and rocks, and jars him constantly. If the horse is at all restive and breaks from the path, he crashes

through dead wood and twists through dry till he destroys the
load, or is brought up all standing by trees that there is no getting through.

In the Mexican and United States Rocky Mountains, where a
great deal of business has long been done with pack-horses, the
saddles are of a much superior kind, called appara-hoes. With
those the horses carry over three hundred pounds, and a day's
journey is from twelve to fifteen miles. As our object was speed we
dispensed with tent, extra clothing, tinned meat, books etc., and
thus reduced the loads at the outset to a hundred or a hundred
and thirty pounds per horse. That weight included food for
thirty days for eight men, and everything else that was absolutely
necessary.

There was now before us a journey of about six hundred miles,
through woods and marshes, torrents, and mountain passes ;
for we could not depend on getting supplies of any kind or fresh
horses on this side of Kamloops ; though there were probabilities
of our meeting with parties of engineers between Jasper House
and Yellow Head Pass.

Mr. Adams was of infinite service in all these arrangements.
The luxuries of white-fish, fresh eggs, cream, butter and young
pig bountifully served up for us at his table, were duly appreciated at breakfast and dinner, but we valued still more highly
the personal exertions, made as earnestly and with as much simplicity and thoughtfulness as if he had been preparing for his
own journey. He was the last of the Hudson's Bay officers that
we would be indebted to till we got to the Pacific slope, and
parting from his post was like parting from the Company that
has long been the mainstay of travellers, the only possible
medium of communication, and the great representative of
civilization in the vast regions of the North and North-west.
From our meeting with the chief Commissioner at Silver Heights
until our departure from St. Ann's we had experienced the hos-

pitality of its agents, and had seen the same extended to all who claimed it, to the hungry Indian, and the unfortunate miner, as well as to those who bore letters of recommendation. It was on such a scale as befitted a great English corporation, the old monarchs and still the greatest power in the country.

At two P. M. all was ready; eight horses packed, eight others saddled for riding, and a spare horse to follow. Mr. Adams accompanied us a short distance ; but, as the line of march had to be Indian file, we soon exchanged the undemonstrative " good-bye " with him, and plunged into the forest. For the first five miles the trail was so good that the horses kept at their accustomed jog-trot, though some of them were evidently unused to, and uneasy under their pack-saddles. Valad rode first, two pack-horses followed, Brown next, and so on till the Chief or some other of the party brought up the rear of the long line on the seventeenth horse. If any of the pack-horses deviated from the road into the bush, the man immediately' behind had to bring him back. The loud calls to the obstinately lazy or straying " Rouge, " " Brun," " Sangri," " Billy," " Bischo," varied with whacks almost as loud on their backs, were the only sounds that broke the stillness of the forest ; for conversation is impossible with a man on horse-back in front of or behind you, and there is little game in these woods except an occasional partridge. After the first day, the horses gave little trouble as they all got accustomed to the style of travelling, and recognized the wisdom of keeping to the road. Two or three old hands at the work always aimed at getting one of their companions between them and a driver, so that their companions might receive all the occasional whacks, and they share the benefit only of the loud calls and objurgations ; but the new ones soon got up to the trick, and their contentions for precedence and place were as keen as between a number of old dowagers before going in to dinner. These old hands carried their burdens with a swinging, waddling motion that eased their backs, and saved them many a rude jar.

In the course of the afternoon we passed one or two deserted tents, and "sweating booths," but no Indians. Three miserable starved looking "Stonies" or Wood Indians had entered Mr. Adams' house while we were there, and, in accordance with invariable Indian etiquette, shook hands all round, before squatting on the kitchen floor and waiting for something to eat ; but, with the exception of the few scattered round each of the Company's posts, who as a rule are invalids or idlers, we had not seen an Indian since leaving the Assiniboine, except the small camp near Moose-Creek and the Crees at Victoria. That they were buffalo hunting or that their principal settlements are off the line of the main road, does not give the whole truth. The Indians are evidently decreasing ; " dying out " before the white man. Now that the Hudson's Bay monopoly is gone, "free traders," chiefly from the south, are coming in, plentifully supplied with a poisonous stuff, rum in name, but in reality a compound of tobacco, vitriol, bluestone and water. This is completing the work that scrofula and epidemics and the causes that bring about scrofula and epidemics were already doing too surely : for an Indian will part with horse and gun, blanket and wife for rum. There is law in abundance forbidding the sale of intoxicating liquor to Indians, but law, without force to execute law, is laughed at by rowdies from Belly River and elsewhere.

The "sweating booths" referred to should have been explained before. They are the great Indian natural luxury, and are to be found all along the road, or wherever Indians live even for a week. There was scarcely a day this month that we did not pass the rude slight frames. At first we mistook them for small tents. They are made in a few minutes of willow wands or branches, bent so as to form a circular enclosure, with room for one or two inside ; the buffalo robe is spread over the frame

work so as to exclude the air as much as possible, and who-
ever wants a Russian bath crawls into the round dark hole.   A
friend outside then heats some large stones to the highest point
attainable, and passes them and a bucket of water in.   The
"insides" pour the water on the stones, steam is generated, and,
on they go pouring water and enjoying the delight of a vapor
bath, till they are almost insensible.   Doctor Hector thought the
practice an excellent one, as regards cleanliness, health and pleasure ; but the Indians carry it to an extreme that utterly enervates
them.   Their medicine-men enlist it in aid of their superstitions.
It is when under the influence of the bath, that they become
inspired ; and they take one or two laymen in with them, that
they may hear their oracular sayings, and be able to announce
to the tribe where there is a chance of stealing horses or of
doing some other notable deed with good prospect of success.
It is easy to see, too, what a capital opportunity the medicine-
man has, when thus inspired to gratify his private malice or vengeance, or any desire.   Many a raid and many a deed of darkness has been started in the sweating booth.

The first five miles of the road, this afternoon, was a broad
easy trail, through open woods which showed fine timber of
spruce, aspen, and poplar, some of the spruce being over two
feet in diameter ; but had we formed from it any conclusion as
to our probable rate of speed, the next four miles would have
undeceived us.   Crashing through windfalls or steering amid
thick woods round them, leading our horses across yielding
morasses or stumbling over roots, and into holes, with all our
freshness we scarcely made two miles an hour, and that with an
expenditure of wind and limb that would soon have exhausted
horse and man.   But the road again improved a little, and by
6.30 P.M., we had accomplished about twelve miles, and reached
a lake called " Chain of lakes " or " Lac des Iles," out of which
the Sturgeon river flows before it runs into Lake St. Ann's.   In

an open ground near the lake, covered thick with vetches, a
simple 'lean to' or screen for the whole company was constructed.
In the morning all decided that the 'lean to' was a preferable
home to the round or closed tents we had hitherto used. You
require for the former only a large cotton sheet in addition to
what the forest supplies at any time. Two pairs of cross-poles
are stuck in the ground, as far apart as you wish your lodging
place for the night to be long; a ridge pole connects these, and
then half-a-dozen or more poles are placed slanting against the
ridge pole. Cover the sloping frame with your cotton sheet, or
in its absence, birch bark, and your house is made. The ends
are open and so is the front, but the back is covered, and that,
of course, is where the wind comes from. The ventilation is
perfect, and as your fire is made immediately in front, there is
no lack of warmth.

From this date the whole party had one tent of this description to sleep under, and one table to eat from. The days were
getting shorter, the horses could not go fast, and time therefore
had to be economised in every possible way.

August 31st.—As packing eight horses takes twice as long as
harnessing twice the number, it was 6.30 P.M., before we started.
Hereafter, and for the same reason—the time needed to unpack
and pack,—only one halt and two "spells" per day were to be
made.

Six hours' continual travel at an average rate of three miles an
hour, brought us to the Pembina river, where we halted for two-
and-a-half hours. The road was through thick woods and along
the "Chain of lakes," with an upward incline until we came to
the watershed between the Saskatchewan and the rivers running
north-east which fall into the McKenzie, and through it into the
Arctic sea. The country then opened, and we could see before
us four or five miles to a ridge, on the other side of which the
guide said was the Pembina. The timber in the morning was

not as large as that nearer St. Ann's ; and it became smaller as
we advanced, till in the open it was poor and scrubby, and the
land here and all over the drive to the Pembina looked cold
and hungry, with occasional good spots. In the neighbourhood
of coal the land is usually poor, and we had been told that the
banks of the rivers showed abundant indication of coal for sixty
miles up and down from where the trail struck it. After passing
the " Chain of lakes " the road led along a small round lake that
empties on the other side ; and, soon after, over a ridge from
which a fine amphitheatre of hills, formed by a bend of the river
beneath, opened out before us, in the valley of which we saw the
broad shallow Pembina flowing away to the north. The underbrush on the hill-sides had decided autumn tints, the red and
yellow showing early frosts, although there would be nearly three
months yet before winter. The top of the opposite bank was a
bold face of sandstone, with what looked like enormous clusters
of swallow's nests running along the upper part ; underneath the
sandstone, clay that had been burnt by the spontaneous combustion of the coal beneath, ash and burnt pieces of shale like
red and white pottery on the surface, half hidden by vegetation ;
and down at the water's edge a horizontal bed of coal. We
forded the river which is about a hundred yards wide, and looking back saw on the east side a seam of coal about ten feet thick,
whereas on the west side to which we had crossed only about
four feet showed above the water. Pick in hand the Chief made
for the coal, and finding a large square lump that had been
carried down by the river, he broke some pieces from it to make
a fire. In appearance it was much superior to the Edmonton
seam ; instead of the dull half-burnt look, it had a clean glassy
fracture like cannel coal. Carrying a number of pieces in our
hands we proceeded to make a fire and had the satisfaction of
seeing them burn, and of cooking our pemmican with the
mineral fuel. It was evidently coal, equal for fuel, we considered,

M

to the inferior Cape Breton kinds, burning sluggishly, and leaving a considerable quantity of grey and reddish ash, but giving out a good heat. Beaupré, who all this while had been washing sand from the river in his shovel for gold, and finding at the rate of half a cent's worth per shovel full, was amazed at our eagerness, or that there should have been any doubt about its being coal. He and his mates when mining on different rivers, had been in the habit of making fires with it whenever they wished the fire to remain in all night ; and he and Brown both said, that the exposure of coal on Pembina was a mere nothing compared to that on the Brazeau or North Fork of the North Saskatchewan ; that there were seams eighteen feet thick there ; that in one canyon was a wall of seam on seam as perpendicular as if it had been plumbed, and so hard that the weather had no effect on it ; and that on all the rivers, for some distance east of Edmonton, and west to the Rocky Mountains, are abundant showings of coal.   This is perhaps the proper place to mention that on our return to the east, Ex-Governor Archibald presented the Secretary with a little box full that had been sent him as a sample from Edmonton ; the sample was exactly like what we picked up in the Pembina and tried with the results just stated.

The Secretary submitted it to Professor Lawson of Dalhousie College, Halifax, for analysis, and received a letter of which the following is an extract, and may be regarded as settling the question more favourably than we could even have hoped for :

" My analysis of your coal is by no means discouraging :—
Combustible matter - - - - - - - - - - - 97.835 p. c.
Inorganic Ash - - - - - - - - - - - - - 2.165 p. c.

Total   100.000

" The proportion of sulphur, chlorine, and other obnoxious impurities,
" is quite small. The coal burns with a flame, and also forms a red cinder,

" but is a slow burner; and, although the absolute amount of ash is so
" small, yet a much larger amount of apparent ash will be left in the grate
" from imperfect combustion.   Yet, if we view this as a surface sample—
" and such are invariably of inferior quality,—I think it offers great en-
" couragement, for the percentage of ash is less than the average of the
" best marketable coals in Britain.   Of course this analysis of a very small
" sample can only be regarded as a probable indication, not a demonstra-
" tion, of the nature of the extensive beds of coal or bituminous shale
" described in your letter."

The simple fact is that the coal deposits of the North-west are
so enormous in quantity that people were unwilling to believe
that the quality could be good.

Here then is fuel for the future inhabitants of the plains,
near water communication for forwarding it in different directions.

Captain Palliser also reports the existence of iron ore near
several coal seams.

After dinner we rode on for three and a half hours to a good
camping ground on the Lobstick river, about eleven miles from
the Pembina; and had the horses watered and everything made
snug for Sunday before sunset.

On the way several creeks had to be crossed, or valleys where
creeks had run till beavers dammed them up, and, as all had
high steep banks, the work was heavy on the horses.   But the
road so far had agreeably disappointed us.   It was not at all so
bad as travellers' tales had represented.   True, it is better at this
season of the year and for the next six weeks, than at any time
except in the winter; but we felt confident that in another week
Jasper House would not be far off, unless the roads became
very much worse, instead of fifteen days being required as every
one at Edmonton and St. Ann's had said.   So, after a talk with
Brown and Beaupré about their mining and Blackfeet experiences, we threw ourselves down on a fragrant grassy bed, a

little tired, but in good spirits and glad enough that we were not to be called early in the morning.

September 1st.—When we looked out at our wide open door, between six and seven o'clock, a good fire was blazing, and by it sat Valad smoking. He might have been sitting there for centuries, so perfect was the repose of form and feature.

Brown enquired if he had seen the horses and the answer was a wave of the hand, first in one direction and then in another, not only enough to say that he had, but also where they were, without disturbing any of us who might be asleep.

He looked more like a dignified Italian gentleman than an obscure Indian guide. With the lazy movements peculiar to Sunday morning in a camp, one after another of his bed-fellows shook himself out of his blanket. We had now time to look around, and see what kind of a place we were camping on. A bluff had stopped the course of the stream on its way east, and made it swing round to the south. On the bluff, just at the elbow, our tent was pitched. A rich grassy intervale along the river, and vetches in a little valley on the other side of our camp, gave good feed for the horses. On the opposite bank of the stream, and a little ahead, stood three "lobstick" spruce trees in a clump. From these probably the stream gets its name. A lobstick is the Indian or half-breed monument to a friend or to a man he delights to honour. Selecting a tall spruce or some other conspicuous tree, he cuts off all the middle branches leaving the head and feet of the tree clothed and the body naked, and then writes your name or initials at the root. That is your lobstick and you are expected to feel highly flattered, and to make a handsome present in return to the noble fellow or fellows who have erected such a pillar in your honour.

There is an old superstition that your health and length of days will correspond to your lobstick's. As this belief proved inconvenient in some cases it has been quietly dropped, but the custom still flourishes and is greatly favoured by the half-breeds.

Whether such a simple way of getting up a monument is not preferable to piling brick upon brick to the height of a tree, to show how highly you honour a hero, is a question that might bear discussion.

At morning service the whole party attended.   We did not ask any of the men "what denomination he was of," but took it for granted that he could join in common prayer, and hear with profit the simplest truths of Christianity.   With none of our former crews had we been on such friendly terms as with this one.   All the men were up to their work, prompt and respectful, but the relation seemed more like that of a family than simply master and servant.

The weather was beautiful as usual.   Last night it clouded up and in the early morning there was a light drizzle of rain, but not enough to wet the grass as much if there had been the ordinary heavy dew of a clear night.   The forenoon was cool enough to keep the black flies away, but they came out with the sun and the mosquitoes in the afternoon.   At sunset the black flies vanish, but the mosquitoes keep buzzing round till the night is sufficiently cold to drive them off to the woods ; this usually happens about nine o'clock.   Warm as the days now were the nights were so cold, though there was no actual frost, that we usually kept our clothes on, in addition to the double blanket.   Our bag or boots served for pillow, and none of us were ever troubled with wakefulness, or complained in the morning that there had been a crumpled rose leaf under blanket or pillow.

There was little to mark this Sunday except the pleasant peaceful enjoyment of it.   The murmuring of the river over its pebbly bed was the only sound that broke the Sabbath stillness.   The rest was peculiarly grateful after the week's hurry and changes ; and the horses looked as well pleased with it as

we. They ate till they could eat no more : and then they affec-
tionately switched or licked the flies off one another, or strolled
up to the camp to get into the smoke of the fire. Had they
been able to speak, they would certainly have given thanks for
the institution of a day of rest for beast as well as man.

We had one source of annoyance however. Two stray dogs
had joined our party uninvited, a brown one at Edmonton, and
a black at St. Ann's. They had been hooted, pelted and driven
back, but after going on a mile or two further we would see them
slinking after us again. Pemmican could not be spared, as we
bought sufficient for our own wants only, and to-day they looked
particularly hungry. What was to be done with them? Go back
they would not. To take them to Kamloops was out of the
question. To let them die of starvation would be inhuman. There
seemed nothing for it but to shoot or drown them, and though
each and all of us promptly declined the part of executioner,
their prospects looked so gloomy that Frank, who had pleaded
for them all along, resolved to try and provide for them outside
of our regular supplies. Getting permission to do what he could,
on the plea that it was both necessity and mercy, he rigged a
fishing line, and persuaded Brown and Valad to take a gun and
try for beaver or duck. While all three were away, the brown
was caught in the act of stealing pemmican. This aggravated
their case, but, though all condemned, none would shoot. The
hunters too came back empty handed, except with a pan-full of
cranberries that Brown had picked, and that he stewed in a few
minutes into a delicious jam. The dogs puzzled us, so we
postponed further consideration of the problem till next day.

Instead of the usual three meals of pemmican, bread and tea,
we had only two to-day, and a simple lunch at one o'clock. At
six, dinner was served with all the delicacies we could muster,
Berry-pemmican, pork and cranberry jam made a feast so
delicious that no one thought of the dogs.

September 2nd.—Up at four and away at half-past five, or twenty minutes after sunrise. Another bright and sunny day, though the woods were so thick in some places that, at one o'clock the dew was still on the grass.

Our first spell was six hours long. We crossed the Lobstick a little above our camp, and followed up its course without once seeing it again, to Chip Lake, from which it flows. The road ran through a fertile undulating country at first, then through inferior land which forest fires had desolated. There were few flowers or berries and no large trees. The dogs roused a great many partridges, but no one felt disposed to follow them into the bush. Brown shot a fine fat one from the saddle with his revolver and divided it between the dogs, so that they had a meal and therefore a respite for another day.

Our progress was so slow, averaging only two miles an hour, that we were all dreadfully tired. The trail was not bad in itself, with the exception of a few small morasses, some of black muck, and others of a tenacious clay, but at every four or five yards a tree, or two or three branches were lying across, as firmly set by having been trodden on as if placed in position, and they prevented the horses from getting into a trot. These obstacles were not recent windfalls. They had evidently been there for years, and an expenditure of five or ten dollars a mile would clear most of them away. But the H. B. Company could hardly be expected to make a road for free-traders to Jasper House, and it is everybody's business, not a hand is put to the work. Our dining place was at a small creek that runs into Chip Lake, a lake half as big as St. Ann's, that the thick woods prevented our seeing. The ground was plentifully covered with creepers that yielded blueberries smaller and more pungent than those in the Eastern Provinces.

A little after two P.M., we crossed the creek, and wound up the opposite hill-side into a broken well-wooded country, the hollows in which were furrowed with beaver dams. After an hour of this we reached a hill-top, from which a great extent of thickly-wooded country opened out, first level and then with an undulating upward slope to the watershed of the McLeod. The horizon far beyond this slope in a due westernly direction was bounded by dim mountains, that we hailed with a shout as the long sought Rocky Monntains, but Beaupré checked the cheer by calling back that they were only the "foot hills" between the McLeod and the Athabasca. At any rate they were the outliers of the Rocky Mountains, and in exactly a month from our saying goodbye to Governor Archibald at Silver Heights we had our first glimpse of them.

The road now descended to lower ground, and passed over the beds of old creeks destroyed by beavers. Had it not been for half-decayed logs lying across the path, the horses could have trotted the whole way. As it was, they made fully four miles an hour, in the afternoon spell of three-and-a-quarter hours. Before five o'clock we came to a beautiful, clear, cold stream and Valad advised camping, but the Chief, learning that there was a suitable place with good water and feed four miles farther on, gave the word to continue the march. This ground like much that we had gone over in the morning, consisted either of old willows and alders, dry marsh, or sandy and gravelly ridges covered with scrub pine. It was part of the level region we had seen from the hill-top, and had a decidedly poverty-stricken look. In an hour we had reached the camping place and prepared our lodging for the night, well pleased with the progress that had been made during the day. The spare horse, however, which as usual had been left to himself to follow in his own way, was missing. Terry, who had brought up the rear, had seen him lounging and looking back when within a mile of the camp. Beaupré at once started in pursuit bridle in hand, but returned at dusk without him. He had seen him near the creek we had crossed at five o'clock, evidently on his way home or in a state of bewilderment, not knowing where he was going. Beaupré had tried to drive him into camp, but he plunged into the woods and refused to be driven back; so Beaupré, afraid of losing the trail in the darkness, returned. As the horse could not well be spared, Valad was asked to go after him early next morning, try his luck and catch up to us before dark, while we went on under the guidance of Beaupré for the day.

The evenings were getting long now and, after our slow and tedious journeying, it was pleasant to sit in the open tent before a great pine fire and talk about the work of the day, the prospects of to-morrow, and hear some story of wild western life from the men. Brown gave us the particulars of the horrible massacre of the Peigan Indians by Colonel Baker, the kindly views of it taken by the Montana citizens, and their memorial to Washington in his favour when he was threatened with court-martial. Brown and Beaupré themselves judged the massacre from a miner's stand point.

But none of their stories of lawless and cruel deeds roused in us such indignation as what they told concerning villanies done recently in our own North-west. Perhaps the worst had happened only three weeks before our arrival at Edmonton, within one hundred yards of the Fort. A young Métis of eighteen summers, son of a well known hunter called Kiskowassis (or "day child," born in the day) had murdered his wife, to whom he had been married only a few months and who was enceinte. Last year he had slashed a woman with his knife in the wrist and made her a cripple for life. That was a small affair. But, having gone to the plains and formed an intimacy with another girl, he wanted to get rid of his wife. Luring her down to the river side, so that suspicion might fall on a party of Blackfeet camped on the other side, he stabbed but only wounded her, and she fled up the hill, he chasing and striking at her. Some of the Blackfeet on the opposite bank cried *manoyo, manoyo,* (murder), but there was no one near to help the poor creature, and soon a surer blow stretched her dead. This was too serious to be altogether passed over, so her brothers promptly called on Kiskowassis about it. Charley—the murderer—was not at home, but Kiskowassis acknowledged that he had gone too far, and proffered two horses that he extolled highly, the one as " a hunter " and the other as " a carter," in atonement. The elder brother went out and came back in a few minutes, saying : " They're pretty good horses, I guess we'd better take them." And thus the affair was amicably settled ; and, at the same price, as far as law on the Saskatchewan is concerned, Charley may go on and have his six wives more easily than Henry the eighth. An uncle of Charley, on the plains two months ago, shot a man who had offended him ; and Beaupré extolled the whole family as " very brave." Charley had tried to enlist Beaupré last year in a promising enterprise of killing some Sursees who owned good horses : but Beaupré was not " brave " enough. There is a young brother, aged fourteen, who Beaupré says is sure to beat even Charley : " he is bound to steal a horse this very summer from the Black-feet."

We asked Brown why at any rate the miners did not lynch Charley, since no one else acted. He said that there was such a proposal, but it was decided that as they were strangers enjoying the "protection" of the country, it would not be seemly for them to interfere.

September 3rd. — Awoke at four A.M., and found the fire burning brightly and Valad away in pursuit of the missing horse. Partly owing to his absence the start was an hour later than yesterday's. Leaving his saddle and some bread and pemmican on a tree we moved on. The trail was a continuation of the willow and alder marsh of last evening, but instead of being dry it was swampy, and the travelling heavy. The brown dog caught a musk-rat that made a meal for the two, and gave them another day's respite.

For the first eight or ten miles the road was almost wholly swamp, till a creek was crossed that runs into Chip or Buffalo Lake, and from it by the Lobstick into the Pembina. The watershed of the McLeod then rose in a long broken richly-clothed slope. In five hours from camp, at an average rate of three miles an hour, Root River that runs into the McLeod was reached. The trail, which at no time was better than a bridle path, was so heavily encumbered in places with fallen timber that no trace of it could be seen. A rough path had to be broken round the obstacle, and sometimes Beaupré had difficulty in finding the trail again. Indian pears and moose-berries—the largest we had seen—grew along the hill-side, in such quantities that you could often fill your hand by leaning from the saddle, as the horse brushed past the bushes. We halted two hours and a half at Root River, and, as there was a birth-day at home, slap-jacks, mixed with berry pemmican were made as a substitute for plumpudding, and, at dinner, the Chief produced a pint bottle of Noyeau, which had been stored for some great occasion, and Minnie's health was drunk in three table-spoonfulls a piece. Just as dinner was over, Valad made his appearance. He had had a hard day of it following the track of the horse, but came up to him at our yesterday's dining place, moving quietly home-wards. Three times he turned him, but the horse always got away by dashing into the brush. Valad then went ahead and set a wooden trap on the road, but the horse avoided it, and Valad gave up the chase. On his way back—he found that the squirrels had eaten his breakfast. Shouldering his saddle, he followed our trail, and rejoined us at two P.M., having walked forty-one miles and eaten nothing. His moccasins had been cut with the stumps and thorns ; but, though footsore in consequence, he made light of it and went to work with his usual promptness.

Beaupré had been looking for half an hour, but quite in vain, among the long grass and shrubs, for a bit that had dropped off one of the bridles. "We're all right now" was his judicious remark, when Valad appeared, "the old man will smell it if he can't see it."

Our afternoon spell was heavy work; crossing a branch of the Root River, we came on a barren swamp, burned over so thoroughly that there was not a trace of water nor of the trail for two miles; the once heavily-timbered slopes all round had been devastated. On our right a forest of bare poles, looking in the distance like a white cloud, clung to the hill-side. Dead logs, poles, branches, strewed the ground so abundantly that the horses could pick their steps but slowly. After the barren, came the last ascent, and so gradual was it that we did not know when we were at the top, and then instead of a rapid descent to the McLeod, stiff marsh succeeded that got stiffer every mile. The sun set before we got through half of the marsh, but at one spot, a dry ridge intervening with good water near, Valad advised camping. In answer to our question, 'how far off is the McLeod still?' he pointed to the sky saying 'the sun will be over more than half of that again before we see it.' This settled the question, though in a disappointing way, as it put an end to the hope of getting to Jasper's this week. Three of the horses, too, were a little lame, and things did not look quite as bright as when we started in the morning.

September 4th.—The three lame horses were looked at immediately after breakfast. The cause of lameness in all three cases was, that sharp strong stobs or splinters had run into or just above their unshod hoofs; we half wondered that some of them had not pulled their hoofs off, in struggling to extricate them from tough and sharp fibrous roots. The splinters were easily extracted from two, and, the third horse, allowing no one near his hind leg, was managed dexterously by Valad. Passing

one end of his shaganappi lasso twice round his neck, he made
two turns of the other end round his body, and gradually slipped
those turns down over his hind legs, and tightened them.
Tightening the rope at his neck now, the horse resisted, but his
legs being tied, his own struggles with a little shove threw him,
and when thrown he lay quiet as a lamb.

It had rained during the night, and the morning was cloudy
and threatening.   At 9 A.M., the rain came on again, after we
had been two hours on the road, if the expression is allowable
when there was no road.   The rain made travelling across the
muskeg still more difficult and uncomfortable.   In six hours and
a quarter we fought through ten miles, six or seven of them
being simply over a continuous muskeg covered with windfalls.   The horses stumbled over roots and timber to sink into
thick layers of quaking moss, and sometimes through these to
the springs underneath.   The greater part of the ground bore
tall beautifully shaped spruce and poplar, chiefly spruce, from
one to three feet in diameter.

After crossing a little creek, the trail improved somewhat till
it led to the ancient bank of the McLeod, at the foot of which
yawned a deep pool with a bottom of tenacious clay, that had to
be struggled through somehow.   The horses sinking almost to
their bellies, floundered in the mud at a fearful rate, with such
effects on our clothes as may be conceived ; fortunately by this
time we were quite indifferent on the subject of appearances.
The river was only a hundred yards from this, but the trail led
for half a mile up through a wooded intervale to "the crossing."
A little creek seamed the intervale, and the first open spot was
strewed with as many chips as would furnish a carpenter's shop,
beside several logs, two of them stripped of their bark and
others cut into junks for transportation.   We had disturbed a
colony of beavers, in their work of building a dam across the
creek and of laying in their winter supplies.

The sight of the McLeod was a relief, for we had found the
way to it "a hard road to travel," as the Canadians who pre-
ceeded Milton and Cheadle evidently had also. The Chief came
upon their testimony chalked with red keil on a large spruce tree
in the swamp, five or six miles to the east of the river. Only the
following words and half-words could be made out :—

> AUGUST 10TH, 1862,　* * * * * * * * * * * * * * *
> *
> * * * * East Tilbury　* * * . * * * * * * * * *
> * * * * * * * * * * and　* * * * * * * * * *
> * * * * * * * * * * * Robert Campb　* * * * *
> *
> * * * * * * * * * for Cariboo　* * * * * * * *
> * * * * * * * * * * * * a hard road to travel.

Poor fellows! some of them found the North Thompson a harder
road.

The McLeod heads inside of the first range of the Rocky
Mountains. Where we crossed, it is a beautiful stream about 110
yards wide, running north-easterly with a rapid current over a
pebbly bed. Its breadth is not much greater than the Pembina,
but it has three times the volume of water. At this season of the
year, it can be forded at almost any point where there is a little
rapid, the water in such places, not coming up to the horses'
necks. Crossing, we came upon a few acres of prairie, to the rich
vetches on which the horses abandoned themselves as eagerly as
our party did to the *richaud* and tea that Terry hurried up. Fortunately too, the rain ceased, though the sky did not clear, and
Valad made a big fire at which we dried ourselves partially.
Brown advised that, as this was a good place, some provisions
should be cachèd for those of the party who were to return from
Jasper's; and Valad, selecting a site in the green wood, he and
Beaupré went off to it from the opposite direction, with about
twenty-five pounds of pemmican and flour tied up, first in canvass and then in oil-skin, as the wolverine—most dreaded plun-
derer of cachés—dislikes the smell of oil. Selecting two suitable

pine trees in the thick wood, they "skinned" (barked) them to prevent animals from climbing; then placing a pole between the two, some eighteen feet from the ground, they hung a "St. Andrew's Cross" of two small sticks from the pole, and suspended their bag from the end of one, that the least movement or even puff of wind would set it swinging. Such a caché Valad guaranteed against bird and beast of whatever kind. "And now," Beaupré summed up, "if no one finds that, we will be in good luck; but if somebody finds it, we will be in bad luck; that's all."

Our course from this point was to be up the McLeod for nearly seventy miles of very bad road. As we had had enough of that for one day, we listened eagerly to Beaupré saying that it was possible to dodge the first eight miles by creeping along the shore of the river, and crossing and recrossing wherever the banks came down too close to permit travelling. Though Valad didn't know this way and Beaupré himself had not tried the crossings, having on a former occasion made the trip up the river in a canoe, and not by the shore, it was decided to try. A very pleasant change on the forenoon's journey it proved to be, and quite a success; for we arrived at the proposed camping ground, after four crossings, before sunset. The river was low and the shore wide, consisting of rough pebbly stretches or sand bars, covered, near the bank, with wild onions, sand grasses, and creepers. Beaupré said that the sand would yield gold at the rate of a cent a shovelful, but that would give only $2 or $3 per day. Where the banks came near the river in bold bluffs, they showed sections chiefly of different kinds of clay and sandstone separated by black slate. No coal beds appeared except a four-inch seam that looked like coal, but may have been only a roof of shale to the coal beneath.

At the camp a roaring fire of pine logs was soon kindled, and a line hung along one side for our wet clothes; but the steady drizzling rain recommenced and continued all night. We warmed ourselves at any rate, and 'turned in' as comfortably as the circumstances permitted.

September 5th.—It rained steadily through the night and was drizzling in the morning. Though it hurts the horses' backs to saddle them when wet, there was no alternative, and so after getting ready with great deliberation, in hopes that it would clear up, we moved away at 7.30 A.M.

Our first "spell" was the hardest work of the journey, so far, with the least to show for it. We made about five miles, and it took as many hours to make the distance. The road followed the upward course of the McLeod, crossing the necks of land formed by the doublings of the river. These so-called, 'portages' were the worst part of the road, though it was all so bad that it is invidious to make comparisons. The country was either bog or barren—both bad,—for the whole had recently been burned over, and every wind had blown down its share of the burnt trees. There was no regular trail. Each successive party that travelled this way, seemed to have tried to make a new one in vain efforts to escape the difficulties. Valad went ahead, axe in hand, and between natural selection and a judicious use of the axe, made a passage; but it looked so tangled and beset, that the horses often thought they could do better; off they would go, with a swing, among the bare poles, for about two yards before their packs got interlaced with the tough spruce. Then came the tug; if the trees would not give, the packs had to, and there was a delay of half an hour to tie them on again. We often wondered that the packs came off so seldom; but Brown understood his business; besides the trees had been burnt, and some of them were uprooted or broken with comparative ease. Of course the recent rains had not improved the going. Beaupré said that it had not been worse last summer, after the spring frosts had come out and the spring rains gone in. Take it all in all, the road was hopelessly bad,—deserving all the hard things that had been said of it,—and called for a large stock of the Mark Tapley spirit, especially when, by wandering from the trail, the horses got mired in muskegs or stuck between trees, or when the blackened, hard, tough spruce branches, bent forward by a pack horse, swung back viciously in the face of the unfortunate driver.

The road could only have been worse by the trees being larger; but then it would have been simply impassable, for the windfalls would have barricaded it completely. The prospect, too, was dismal and desolate looking enough for Avernus or the richest coal fields : nothing but a forest, apparently endless, of blackened poles on all sides. Only when an angle or bend of the river came into view, was there any relief for the eye.

Towards midday, when every one's thoughts were on pemmican, 'ho,' 'ho,' was heard ahead, and two Indians appeared holding out hands to Valad. They had left Jasper's four days ago, and were bound for Edmonton, trusting to their guns or the berries to supply them with food on the way. The offer of a pemmican dinner turned them back with us for quarter of a mile, to a little creek where the halt had to be called, though there was but poor feed for the horses among the blackened trees. The Indians had no dog, and were glad to take the black—as he would be useful in treeing partridges—back to Mr. Adam's, to whom the Doctor thought he belonged. They promised also to drive home the spare horse if they could track him. We wrote a note by them to Mr. Adams, telling him what commissions we had entrusted them with. These Indians had straighter features and a manlier cast of countenance than the ordinary wood-Indians. On inquiry, we learned that they were Iroquois from Smoking River, to the north of Jasper's, where a small colony has been settled for fifty years back. Their ancestors had been in the employment of the North-west Fur Company, and on its amalgamation with the Hudson's Bay, had settled on Smoking River, on account of the abundance of fur-bearing animals and of large

N

game such as buffalo, elk, brown and grizzly bears, then in that
quarter.

After dinner, the march was resumed at the mile per hour rate.
More discouraging was the fact that scarcely two-thirds of that
modest speed was progress ; for the trail twisted like a ship
tacking, so that at times we were actually progressing backwards.
In struggling across creeks the difference between the Lowland
Scot and the Frenchman came out amusingly. Brown continued
imperturbable no matter how the horses went. Beaupré, the
mildest mannered man living when things went smoothly, could
not stand the sight of a horse floundering in the mud. Down
into the gully he would rush to lift him out by the tail. Of
course he got spattered and perhaps kicked for his pains. This
made him worse, and he had to let out his excitement on the
horse. Gripping the tail with his left hand, as the brute struggled
up the opposite hill swaying him from side to side as if he had
been tied to it, he whipped with his right ; *sacré*-ing furiously,
till he reached the top. Then feeling tha. he had done his part,
he would let go and subside again into his mildest manners.

Towards evening the road improved so that the luxury of a
smart walk was indulged in—with occasional breaks—for an
hour or two. When we camped, the tally for the day was twelve
miles, representing perhaps an air line of six or eight, for ten
hours, hard work. A bath in the McLeod, and a change of socks
followed by supper, put us all right, although the hope of seeing
Jasper's before next Wednesday had completely vanished.

September 6th.—It rained last night, but the morning gave
signs of a fair day. Renewed the march at 6.45 A.M. Yesterday's
experiences were also renewed, except that the road, as well as the
day, was better—enabling us to make two miles an hour,—and
kept closer to the river, revealing many a beautiful bend or long
reach. The timber was larger and less of it burnt. Poplar,
cottonwood, and spruce, chiefly the latter, predominated. The

opposite bank had escaped fires. Before noon, we got a glimpse of the mountains away to the south, and soon after reached a lovely bit of open prairie covered with vetches, honey-suckle, and rose-bushes out of flower. Here, the McLeod sweeps away to the south and then back to the north, and the trail instead of following its long circuit cuts across the loop. This 'portage' is twenty miles long, and a muskeg in the middle—on one or the other side of which we would have to camp to-night—is the worst on the road to Jasper's. Halted for dinner at the bend of the river, having travelled nine or ten miles, Frank promising us some fish, from a trouty looking stream hard by, as a change from the everlasting pemmican. Not that any one was tired of pemmican. All joined in its praises as the right food for a journey, and wondered why the Government had never used it in war time. It must be equal or superior to the famous Prussian sausage, judging of the latter, as we needs must, without having lived on it for a month. As an army 'marches on its stomach' condensed food is an important object for the commissariat to consider, especially when as in the case of the British Army, long expeditions are frequently necessary. Pemmican is good and palatable uncooked and cooked, though most prefer it in the *richaud* form. It has numerous other recommendations for campaign diet. It keeps sound for twenty or thirty years, is wholesome and strengthening, portable, and needs no medicine to correct a tri-daily use of it. Two pounds weight with bread and tea, we found enough for the dinner of eight hungry men. A bag weighing a hundred pounds is only the size of an ordinary pillow, two feet long, one and a half wide, and six inches thick. Such a bag then would supply three good meals to a hundred and thirty men. Could the same be said of equal bulk of pork? But as Terry—an old soldier too—indignantly remarked "the British Gauvirmint wont drame of pimmican till the Prooshians find it out."

Frank came back to dinner with one small trout, though Beaupré said that he and his mate last summer had caught an hundred in two hours, some of them ten pounds in weight. Perforce we dined on pemmican and liked it better than ever.

The sun now shone out, making the day warm and pleasant, as all September usually is in America. At 2 P. M. got into line again to cross the long portage. The course was westerly, by the banks of the stream called the Medicine, at the mouth of which we had dined. A great part of the road was comparatively free from fallen timber, so that we enjoyed the novelty of a trot, and, except near two creeks that ran into the Medicine,—free from the still worse obstruction of muskegs. An hour before sunset, the Medicine itself had to be crossed, and on the other side of it was the bad muskeg. Beaupré drew a long face when he saw the river, for the recent rains had made it turbid and swollen to an unusual height, and this augured ill for the state of the ground on the other side. For the first mile, however, we got on well enough, as the road took advantage of a ridge for two-thirds of that distance; but, then came the dreaded spot. It looked no worse than the rest, but the danger was unseen. Deep holes formed by springs abounded underneath the soft thick moss, in which horses would sink to their necks. The task was to find a line of sure ground, and by avoiding Scylla not to fall into Charybdis. As Valad with Indian, and Brown with Scotch caution were trying the ground all round, Beaupré leading his horse by the bridle dashed in close to the swollen river, at a most unlikely spot, exclaiming " I'll chance it any way." The words were only out of his lips when he fell into a pool up to his middle; but, undismayed he scrambled out and keeping close to beds of willows and alder, actually found a way so good that all the rest followed him. Only one pack-horse sank so hopelessly deep, into a hole, that he had to be unpacked and lifted out, Beaupré hoisting by the tail with a mighty hoist—ior the man

had the strength of a giant. An hour after sunset, we arrived at
an ascent where it was possible to camp, though the bare
blackened half-burnt poles all round gave a cheerless aspect to
the scene.   All were too tired to be critical ; thankful besides
that the worst was over, and that to-morrow, according to Valad
there would be 'un beau chemin.'

To-day we had travelled twenty miles, representing probably
fourteen on the map. As more could not have been done, no
one grumbled, though all devoutly longed for a more modern
rate of speed. Crossing muskegs, it is impossible to hurry horses,
and when fallen timber cannot be jumped or scrambled over, a
single tree on the path may necessitate a detour of fifty yards to
make five.   How the heavily laden pack-horses of the Hudson's
Bay Company get along such a road, is rather a puzzle ?

September 7th.—We got away from camp at 6.45 A.M. ; and
in less than two hours came again in view of the McLeod ;—narrower and much more like the child of the mountains than at
the first crossing.   Instead of sand bars as there, ridges and
masses of rounded stones and boulders are strewn along its
shores, or piled up with drifted trees and rubbish in the shallower
parts of its bed. The trail led up stream near the bank, descending headlong to the river two or three times, and then ascending
precipitous bluffs that tested the horses' wind severely.   From
these summits, views of a section of the Rocky Mountains, sixty
or seventy miles away to the south-west, rewarded our exertions,
and were the only thing that justified Valad's phrase of ' beau
chemin.' The deep sides of the mountains and two or three of
the summits were white with snow, and under the rays of the
sun one part looked green and glacier-like. We should have
crossed and then recrossed the McLeod hereabouts to escape the
worst part of the road, but Valad, to his own intense mortifica-
tion, missed the point where the trail led off to the ford. There
was nothing left, therefore, but to keep pegging away at the rate

of a mile an hour, up and down hill, through thick underbrush of willows and aspens that had sprung up round the burnt spruce and cotton-wood, which still reared aloft their tall blackened shafts.

At 1 o'clock, we dined beside the river on the usual breakfast and supper fare, having travelled twelve or thirteen miles in six hours and a quarter. Muskegs and windfalls delayed us most, the former being always near creeks, and worse than the latter. The only hard ground was on the sandy or gravelly ridges separating the intervening valleys, and on these, windfalls had accumulated from year to year, so that the trail in many places was buried out of sight. While at dinner, clouds gathered in the west and quickly overspread the whole sky. This hurried our movements, but the rain was on—with thunder and lightning—in ten minutes. After the first smart shower, a lull followed which the men took advantage of to pack the horses, drying their backs as well as possible before putting on the saddles.

A little after 3 P.M., we were on the march and on rather a better road, though of the same general character as in the morning. Heavy thunder showers broken by gleams of sunlight dispelling the leaden clouds from time to time, gave a sky of wonderful grandeur and colour. The river and the finely wooded hilly country beyond, for hereabouts too the opposite banks had escaped the ravages of fire—probably because there was no trail and no travelling on that side, displayed themselves in magnificent panoramic views from every bluff we climbed, while far to the west and south-west beyond the hills, masses of clouds concealing the mountains but assuming the forms and almost the solidity of the mountains, made an horizon worthy of the whole sky and of the foreground. At sunset we descended for the last time to the river, and skirting it for two miles or crossing to long islets where the current divided itself, reached a beautiful prairie and camped under the shade of a group of spruce and

poplars. This was the point Valad had aimed for, as a good place
for the Sunday rest, chiefly because of the feed ; and here we
were to take leave of the McLeod, and cross to the Athabasca—

'No more by thee our steps shall be
For ever and for ever,'

or at least until there is a better road, was gladly chorussed,
for we were all heartily sick of the McLeod.   From its watershed to this point was less than eighty miles, and to get over
that distance had occupied four and a half days of the hardest
travelling.   The tally of the week was 120 miles, and every one
was satisfied with it because more could not have been done.
And when, on the only occasion in the week on which spirits
were used, the whole party gathered round the camp-fire after
supper to have the Saturday night toasts of 'wives and sweethearts' and 'the Dominion and the Railroad,' immediately after
the Queen,' the universal feeling was of thankful content that
we had got on without casualties, and that to-morrow was
Sunday.   The men being without waterproofs had not an inch
of dry clothing on them, but they dried themselves at the big
fire as if it was the jolliest thing in the world to be wet.   Valad,
under the influence of a glass of the mildest toddy, relaxed from
his Indian gravity and taciturnity, and smiled and talked
benignantly.   'When with gentlemen' he was pleased to inform
us, 'he was treated like a gentleman ; but when with others he
had a hard time of it.'   Poor Valad ! what a lonely joyless life
he lived, yet he did his duty like a man, and bore himself with
the dignity of a man who lived close to and learned the lessons
of nature.   Some will blame us for giving toddy to an Indian, or
for taking it ourselves, and perhaps more severely for not sup-
pressing all mention of the fact. Our only answer is that a little
did us good and we were thankful for the good, and that the one
merit this diary aspires to is to be a frank and truthful narrative.

It would have been mean to have left Valad out; and to show an Indian that it was possible to be temperate in all things, possible to use a stimulant without abusing it, seemed to us on the whole a better lesson to enforce practically, than to have preached an abstinence that he would have misunderstood.

September 8th.—Another Day of rest, with nothing to chronicle save our ordinary Sunday routine. But no,—this is doing great injustice to the Doctor who eclipsed all his former efforts, in the way of providing medical comforts, by concocting a plum-pudding for dinner. The Doctor's prescriptions smelled of the pharmacopœia as little as possible. Was an old woman that he met on the way complaining of 'a wakeness?' Send her a pannikin of hot soup. Were Valad's legs inflamed by rubbing all day against his coarse trowsers in the saddle? Make him a present of a pair of soft flannel drawers. Was a good 'Father' at the mission in failing health? Fatten him up with rich diet, even on fast days. And finally were we all desirous of celebrating a birth-day, and did the thought make us a little homesick, the only sickness that our own party ever suffered from? Get up a plum-pudding for dinner.

But how? We had neither bag, suet, nor plums. But we had berry pemmican, and pemmican in its own line is equal to sha-ganappi. It contained buffalo fat that would do for suet, and berries that would do for plums. Only genius could have united plum-pudding and berry pemmican in one mental act. Terry contributed a bag, and, when the contribution was inspected rather daintily, he explained that it was the sugar bag, which might be used as there was very little sugar left for it to hold. Pemmican, flour and water, baking soda, sugar and salt were surely sufficient ingredients; as a last touch the Doctor searched the medicine-chest, but in vain, for tincture of ginger to give a flavour, and in default of that, suggested chlorodyne; but the Chief promptly negatived the suggestion, on the ground that if we ate the pudding the chlorodyne might be required a few hours after.

At 3 P.M. the bag was put in the pot, and dinner was ordered to be at 5. At the appointed hour everything else was ready; the usual *pièce de résistance* of pemmican, flanked for Sunday garnishing, by two reindeer tongues. But as we gathered round, it was announced that the pudding was a failure; that it would not unite; that buffalo fat was not equal in cohesive power to suet, and thar instead of a pudding it would be only boiled pemmican. The Doctor might have been knocked down with a feather; Frank was loud and savage in his lamentations; but the Chief advised 'more boiling,' as an infallible specific in such cases, and that dinner be proceeded with. The additional half hour acted like a charm. With fear and trembling the Doctor went to the pot; anxious heads bent down with his; tenderly was the bag lifted out and slit; and a joyous shout conveyed the intelligence that it was a success, that at any rate it had the shape of a pudding. Brown, who had been scoffing, was silenced; and the Doctor conquered him completely by helping him to a double portion. How good that pudding was! A teaspoonful of brandy on a sprinkling of sugar made sauce; and there was not one of the party who did not hold out his plate for "more," though, as the Doctor belonged to the orthodox school of medicine, the first helping had been no homœopathic dose. To have been perfect the pudding should have had more boiling; but no one dared hint a fault, for was not the dish empty? We at once named the place Plum-Pudding Camp, and Brown was engaged on the spot to make a better if he could at the Yellow Head Pass Camp.

In all respects save weather the day was as pleasant as our former Sundays; but gusts of wind blew the smoke of the fire into the tent, and the grass was too thoroughly soaked with rain for pleasant walking. The sun struggled to come out but scarcely succeeded, and towards evening a cold rain, that would be snow on the mountains, set in. Valad had pitched a separate camp for himself under a grove of pines, that sheltered him beautifully from the wind and rain. So cozy was it that during the day one after another resorted thither, for a pipe or a quiet read, when eyes could no longer endure the big tent's smoke.

The usual morning and evening services were attended by all. Without them the day would have been a rest, but otherwise not of much profit. Each time that we united as one body in worship, our thoughts were raised from earth and the bond that united us became stronger and more sacred.

September 9th.—Up very early this morning, but it was 7 before we said 'goodbye' to Plum Pudding Camp and the McLeod river. In packing horses, the more haste the less speed. Any twist of the shaganappi omitted is sure to avenge itself at the most inconvenient place. And as none but Brown and Beaupré could do this work, it took a long time.

The night had been cold and the grass in the morning was crisp with frost, but the sun rose bright and soon dissolved the hoar into dew. We started in high spirits, under the warm rays of the sun, with good hopes of soon seeing the Athabasca. The trail to it leads up an intervale of the McLeod for a mile, and then crosses a hilly portage thirteen miles long. The portage consists of ridges of gravel intermixed with clay, supporting a growth of pines and spruce large enough for railway or building purposes. At the bottom of each ridge is a creek of clear cold water, running over black muck or whitish clay. Half way across, a lake, that empties into the Athabasca, lies under the shadow of the Foot Hills; and from this point successive steep descents, lead to streams running in deep valleys over pebbly beds, and through the woods glimpses are had of blue wooded heights on the other side of the Athabasca. Instead of going directly west to the river, the trail trends more to the south, ascending the river at a distance from it, and we thus missed the large alluvial flat a little north called Le Grand Bas-fond, where is the only good grass for miles. At 1 o'clock we got our first sight of the Athabasca, from a high bluff, and beyond it to the south-west, fifty miles off but seemingly close at hand, the Rocky Mountains covered with snow. It was time to halt, but the pasture under the pines and spruces was so scant that it would have been a mockery to turn the horses loose. We resolved therefore to keep moving and make only one spell for the day. For two hours longer the patient creatures toiled on, as willingly as when fresh; the trail winding for five or six miles up and down the steep banks of the river, and crossing several mountain streams, and for the next five going along a smooth terrace of shingle, now a hundred feet above the river but once its bed. Here the trail was so good that, with few interruptions the jog trot was maintained. At length on a burnt tract, rich heavy bunch-grass—enough for the night—showed, and the trail descending to another bench only ten feet above the present bed of the river, we camped on the lower, and drove the horses back to the upper terrace after watering them. In a continuous march of ten hours about twenty-five miles had been travelled.

Valad shook his head when he saw the white peaks and the river. He had never known the former so covered with snow, nor the latter so swollen at this season of the year. There must have been severe weather in the mountains, with the probable consequence for us, that instead of fording we would have to construct a raft opposite Jasper House.

The Athabasca at this early point of its course is nearly as large as the Saskatchewan at Edmonton, of the same clay colour, and running with a more rapid current. It varies in breadth according as it is hemmed in by cliffs of sandstones, shales, and clay; or as its shores expand into intervales or broad terraces rising one above the other. These successive terraces are marked very distinctly in several places on both sides of the

stream.   Dr. Hector measured their heights with the aneroid at
' Le Grand Bas-fond,' and found that the three lowest and most
distinctly marked were fifteen, a hundred, and two hundred and
ten feet above the alluvial bottom of the valley, while one above,
not so uniformly distinct, was three hundred and seventy feet.
These terraces are covered with spruce and pine, most of which
has escaped fires.

From the terrace above our camp, the mountains seemed
immediately beyond the wood on the opposite side of the river
They towered up in a grand silver-tipped line closing the western
horizon so high up, that the sun always sets here more than half
an hour sooner than on the plains.

At length we had come to the bases of the Rocky Mountains,
and the sight of them was sufficient reward for all the toil of the
preceding fortnight.

While hacking with his axe at brush on the camping ground,
just where our heads would lie, Brown struck something metallic
that blunted the edge of the axe. Feeling with his hand he drew
out from near the root of a young spruce tree, an ancient sword
bayonet, the brazen hilt and steel blade in excellent preserva-
tion, but the leather scabbard half eaten as if by the teeth of
some animal.   It seemed strange in this vast and silent forest
wilderness thus to come upon a relic that told, probably, of the
old days when the two rival fur companies armed their agents
to the teeth, and when bloody contests often took place between
them. Brown presented the "treasure trove" to the Chief, for
his museum, as a memento of the Athabasca, and from it, this
our forty-fourth camp, since leaving Thunder Bay, received the
name of Bayonet Camp.

To-night we rest under the protection of the Rocky Mountains.

CHAPTER VIII.

The Rocky Mountains.

September 10th.—The Athabasca fell six inches during the night. Got away from camp at 7.30 A.M., and for two hours had a delightful ride to Prairie River. The trail ran along a terrace of shingle or alluvial flats, and was free from fallen timber and muskegs. Most of the flowers were out of blossom, but in the spring and summer these open meadow-like places must be gay with anemones, roses, vetches, and a great variety of compositæ—none of which were now in bloom, except a light-blue aster that had accompanied us from the North Saskatchewan, and all the way through the wooded country. The burnt ground shewed a brilliant crimson flower from which red ink is made, and which we had seen on the Matawan.

Few, however, thought of plants to-day or of anything but the mountains that stood in massive grandeur, thirty miles ahead, but on account of the morning light, in which every point came out clear, seemingly just on the other side of each new patch of wood or bit of prairie before us.

They rose bold and abrupt five or six thousand feet from the wooded country at their feet,—the western verge of the plains, the elevation of which was over three thousand feet additional above the sea,—and formed in long unbroken line across our path, save where cleft in the centre down to their very feet, by the

(221)

chasm that the Athabasca, long ago forced, or found for itself. "There are no Rocky Mountains" has been the remark of many a disappointed traveller by the Union and Central Pacific Railways. The remark will never be made by those who travel on the Canadian Pacific; there was no ambiguity about these being mountains, nor about where they commenced. The line was defined, and the scarp as clear, as if they had been hewn and chiselled for a fortification. The summits on one side of the Athabasca were serrated, looking sharp as the teeth of a saw; on the other, the Roche à Myette, immediately behind the first line, reared a great solid unbroken cube, two thousand feet high, a "forehead bare," twenty times higher than Ben An's; and, before and beyond it, away to the south and west, extended ranges with bold summits and sides scooped deep, and corries far down, where formerly, the wood buffalo, and the elk, and now the moose, bighorn, and bear find shelter. There was nothing fantastic about their forms. Everything was imposing. And these too were ours, an inheritance as precious, if not as plentiful in corn and milk, as the vast rich plains they guarded. For mountains elevate the mind, and give an inspiration of courage and dignity to the hardy races who own them, and who breathe their atmosphere.

> For the strength of the hills we bless thee
> Our God, our fathers' God.
> Thou hast made our spirits mighty
> With the touch of the mountain sod.

The scene had its effect on the whole party. As we wound in long Indian file along the sinuous trail, that led across grassy bas-fonds under the shadow of the mountains that were still a day's journey distant, not a word was heard nor a cry to the horses for the first half-hour. Valad led the way, clad friar-like in blue hooded capote which he wore all regardless of the fact that the sun was shining; Brown next, in rugged miner costume half-leathern half-woollen, and Beaupré in the same with a touch of colour added ; the Chief and the Doctor in their yellow moose-hide jackets; even Terry, who of late invariably brought up the rear, ceased to howl " git up out o' that " to the unfortunate animal he sat upon, dropped his stick, and put his pipe in his waistcoat pocket. He had seen Vesuvius, the Himalayas and the Hill of Howth, but they were "nauthin to this." Before us, at times, a grove of dark green spruce, and, beyond the sombre wood, the infinitely more sombre grey of the mountains ; where the wood had been burnt, the bare blackened poles seemed to be only a screen hung before, half revealing, half concealing, what was beyond. The mountains dwarfed and relieved everything else. There was less snow than had appeared yesterday, the explanation being that the first and least elevated mountain range only was before us now that we were near, whereas, when at a greater distance, many of the higher summits beyond were visible.

Soon after crossing Prairie River, the trail led away to the east from the Athabasca among windfalls of the worst kind, or muskegs, and up and down steep banks. Little progress was made for the next two hours, but the mountain air told so on our appetites that at midday a halt of an hour and a half was imperatively demanded, although it had to be on the borders of a swamp among blackened poles.

After dinner we resumed the march and soon crossed another Prairie River, formed apparently by the union of three streamlets, winding by different valleys down a wooded range that lies at the foot of the mountains, and extends east by north for some distance. By one of these valleys there is a direct road to the McLeod, and probably a route may be found by the same for the railway. The view of the mountains all this afternoon more than made up for the difficulties of the road. Instead of being clearly outlined, cold, and grey as in the morning, they appeared indistinct through a warm deep blue haze ; we had come nearer but they seemed to have removed farther back.

When on the other side of Prairie River, the wooded range from which it flowed was on our left, and the high wooded hills beyond the Athabasca on our right. Woods and hills in front closed up the lower part of the gorge from which the Athabasca issued, and completely divided the Rocky Mountains into two ranges, right and left ; thus an amphitheatre of mountains closed round while we were making for the open that yawned right in front.

It was now only 4.30 P.M. and the travel of the day not more them 17 miles ; but Valad stated that there was no other good place for the horses to rest on this side of the south end of Lac Brulé, and that it would take four hours to reach it. Reluctantly the order was given to camp ; and to improve the time, Frank and Valad went off to hunt, and the Chief and the Secretary to climb a hill and note the surrounding country. Bear and fresh moose tracks were seen by the latter two, and fresh otter trails leading down into the river. On their return they fell in with Frank carrying a beaver ; he and Valad had fired at two and shot one. The Doctor in their absence had fished in most primitive style, with a tent pole and twine, and a hook baited with pemmican, and had caught two fine trout. Having this varied provision, supper without *richaud* was unanimously decreed, and Valad set to work at once on the beaver and Terry on the fish. In fifteen minutes Valad had the animal skinned, boned, the whole of the meat stretched out in one piece on a brander of sticks and exposed to the fire to grill ; the tail on another stick, and the liver on a third. We waited impatiently for supper, the Secretary making toast of Terry's under-done bread to keep himself from murmuring. In due time everything was ready, and the five who had never tasted beaver, prepared themselves to sit in judgment. The verdict was favourable throughout ; the meat tender, though dry, the liver a delicious morsel, and the tail superior to the famous moose-muffle. Within an hour after that beaver had been industriously at work on his dam, he formed part of the interior economy of eight different stomachs, and scarcely a scrap was left to show what he once had been. More sudden and complete metamorphosis, surely, is not in Ovid. The trout were excellent, so that it may be understood that a "straight meal" was made. In honour of the great event of the evening, this, our forty-fifth, was named Beaver Camp.

Having lost an hour and a half of sunlight by not knowing whether there was grass ahead, and by not wishing the horses to run the risk of going supperless to bed, we made arrangements to start early to-morrow for a long spell.

This was to be our last night on the plains. To-morrow night we would be in the embrace of the mountains.

September 11th.—Away this morning at 6.15 A.M., and halted at 1 P.M., after crossing the Rivière de Violon or Fiddle river, when fairly inside the first range. It was a grand morning for mountain scenery. For the first three hours the trail continued at some distance east from the valley of the Athabasca, among wooded hills, now ascending, now descending, but on the whole with an upward slope, across creeks where the ground was invariably boggy, over fallen timber, where infinite patience was required on the part of horse and man. Suddenly it opened out on a lakelet, and right in front, a semi-circle of five glorious mountains appeared ; a high wooded hill and Roche à Perdrix on our left, Roche à Myette beyond, Roche Ronde in front, and a mountain above Lac Brulé on our right. For half a mile down from their summits, no tree, shrub, or plant covered the nakedness of the three that the old trappers had thought worthy of names; and a clothing of vegetation would have marred their massive grandeur. The first three were so near and towered up so bold that their full forms, even to the long shadows on them, were reflected clearly in the lakelet, next to the rushes and spruce of

O

its own shores. Here is scene for a grand picture equal to Hill's much admired painting of the "Yo Semite Valley." A little farther on, another lakelet reflected the mountains to the right, showing not only the massive grey and blue of the limestone, but red and green colourings among the shales that separated the strata of limestone. The road now descended rapidly from the summit of the wooded hill that we had so slowly gained, to the valley of the Athabasca. As it wound from point to point among the tall dark green spruces, and over rose bushes and vetches, the soft blue of the mountains gleamed through everywhere, and when the woods parted, the mighty column of Roche à Perdrix towered a mile above our heads, scuds of clouds kissing its snowy summit, and each plication and angle of the different strata up its giant sides boldly and clearly revealed. We were entering the magnificent Jasper portals of the Rocky Mountains by a quiet path winding between groves of trees and rich lawns like an English gentleman's park.

Crossing a brook divided into half a dozen brooklets by willows, the country opened a little and the base and inner side of Roche à Perdrix were revealed ; but, it was still an amphitheatre of mountains that opened out before us, and Roche à Myette seemed as far off as ever. Soon the Rivière de Violon was heard brawling round the base of Roche à Perdrix and rushing on like a true mountain torrent to the Athabasca. We stopped to drink to the Queen out of its clear ice cold waters, and halted for dinner in a grove on the other side of it, thoroughly excited and awed by the grand forms that had begirt our path for the last three hours. We could now sympathise with the daft enthusiast, who returned home after years of absence, and when asked what he had as an equivalent for so much lost time,— answered only " I have seen the Rocky Mountains."

After dinner, a short walk enabled us to take bearings. The valley of the Athabasca from two to five miles wide, according as a sandy bas-fond or intervale along its shore varied in width, extended up to the west and south, guarded on each side by giant forms. We had come inside the range, and it was no longer an amphitheatre of hills but a valley ever opening, and at each turn revealing new forms, that was now before us. Roche Ronde was to our right, its stratification as distinct as the leaves of a half opened book. The mass of the rock was limestone, and what at a distance had been only peculiarly bold and rugged outlines, were now seen to be the different angles and contortions of the strata. And such contortions ! One high mass twisting up the sides in serpentine folds, as if it had been so much pie-crust ; another bent in great waving lines like petrified billows. The colouring too was all that artist could desire. Not only the dark green of the spruce in the corries which turned into black when far up ; but autumn tints of red and gold as high as vegetation had climbed on the hill sides ; and above that, streaks and patches of yellow, green, rusty red, and black relieving the grey mass of limestone ; while up the valley, every shade of blue, came out according as the hills were near or far away, and summits hoary with snow bounded the horizon.

There was a delay of three hours at dinner because the horses as if allured by the genii of the mountains, had wandered more than a mile up the valley, but at four o'clock all was in order again and the march resumed in the same direction. A wooded hill that threw itself out between Roches à Perdrix and à Myette had first to be rounded. This hill narrowed the valley, and forced the trail near the river. When fairly round it, Roche à Myette came full into view, and the trail now led along its base.

Myette is the characteristic mountain of the Jasper valley. There are others as high, but its grand bare forehead is recognized everywhere. It is five thousand eight hundred feet above the valley, or over nine thousand feet above the sea. Doctor Hector with the agent in charge of Jasper House climbed to a sharp peak far above any vegetation, three thousand five hundred feet above the valley, but the great cubical block which formed the top towered more than two thousand feet higher. A hunter who has given his name to the mountain, is the only one that ever ascended this cube. He made the ascent from the south side, every other being absolutely inaccessible. Dr. Hector gives the following description of the composition of Myette. "It is composed of a mass of strata, which have at one time formed the trough of a huge plication ; viz :

		ft.
(*a*)	Hard compact blue limestone and shale, with nodules of iron pyrites...	2,000
(*b*)	Fossil shales almost black..	300
(*c*)	Hard grey sandstone..	100
(*d*)	Shales towards the upper part with green and red blotches..	500
(*e*)	Cherty limestone and coarse sandstone obscured by timber..	3,000

The ridge we had ascended is formed of cherty limestone and capped by yellow shales with beds of black sandstone forming the highest point."

The views this afternoon from every new point were wonderfully striking. Looking back on Roche à Perdrix it assumed more massive proportions than when we were immediately beneath. A huge shoulder stretched up the valley, one side covered with bare poles, grey as itself, and the other with sombre firs. From it the great summit upreared itself so conspicuously, that it filled the back ground and closed the mouth of the valley. Valad in grave tones told the story of his old partner—an unfortunate half-breed,—who when hunting bighorn on its precipitous slopes, twenty-two years ago, was carried over one of them on a snow slide and dashed in pieces.

A good photographer would certainly make a name and perhaps a fortune, if he came up here and took views. At every step we longed for a camera. On the opposite side of the river a valley opened to the north, along the sides of which rose mountain after mountain with the clearly defined outlines that the secondary formation of the rocks here gives to them. On the same side the range from Roche Ronde was continued further up the Athabasca by a hump-shaped rock, and then by a vast mass, like a quadrilateral rampart, with only two sides of the square visible, the sides furrowed deep, but the line of the summit unbroken. At the base of this—Roche Suette—is Jasper's House and opposite it, Roche Jacques showed as great a mass, with two snow-clad peaks, while the horizon beyond seemed a continuous bank of snow on mountain ranges. But the most wonderful object was Roche à Myette, right above us on our left. That imposing sphinx-like head with the swelling Elizebethan ruff of sandstone and shales all around the neck, save on one side where a corrugated mass of party coloured strata twisted like a coil of serpents from far down nearly half way up the head, haunted us for days. Mighty must have been the forces that upreared and shaped such a monument. Vertical strata were piled on horizontal, and horizontal again on the vertical, as if nature had determined to build a tower that would reach to the skies. As we passed this old warder of the valley, the sun was setting behind Roche Suette. A warm south-west wind as it came in contact with the snowy summit formed heavy clouds, that threw long black shadows, and threatened rain; but the wind carried them past to empty their buckets on the woods and prairies.

It was time to camp, but where? The Chief, Beaupré, and Brown rode ahead to see if the river was fordable. The rest followed, going down to the bank and crossing to an island formed by a slew of the river, to avoid a steep rock, the trail along which was fit only for chamois or bighorn. Here we were soon joined by the three who had ridden ahead, and who brought back word that the Athabasca looked ugly, but was still subsiding, and might be fordable in the morning. It was decided to camp on the spot, and send the horses back a mile for feed. The resources of the island would not admit of our light cotton sheet being stretched as an overhead shelter, so we selected the lee side of a dwarf aspen thicket, and spread our blankets on the gravel ; a good fire being made in front to cook our supper and keep our feet warm through the night. Some of us sat up late, watching the play of the moonlight on the black clouds that drifted about her troubled face, as she hung over Roche Jacques ; and, then we stretched ourselves out to sleep, on our rough but truly enviable couch, rejoicing in the open sky for a canopy, and in the circle of great mountains that formed the walls of our indescribably magnificent bed chamber. It had been a day long to be remembered. Only one mishap had occurred ; the Chief's bag got a crush against a rock, and his flask, that held a drop of brandy carefully preserved for the next plum-pudding, was broken. It was hard, but on an expedition like this the most serious losses are taken calmly and soon forgotten.

September 2nd.—We slept soundly our first night in the mountains, and after a dip in the Athabasca and breakfast, Valad went off on horse-back to try the fords. Though the river had fallen six inches since last night, he found it still too deep for pack horses, and there was nothing for it but to construct a raft, —a work of some difficulty when a big one is needed, and there is no auger and only one axe to cut down the wood. We had time now to take a good view from our Island Camp. Looking forward, Roche Jacques closed the horizon on the left ; to his right and farther up the river, the Pyramid Rock barred the way, a graceful conical shaped mountain like Schiehallion, but grander, his front-face a mass of snow. Between these two our road lay after crossing the river. Opposite the camp to the north, the hump of Roche à Bosche, stood out prominently ; separated from it by the Indian Snake River, and two or three miles

Pl. 28.

JASPER HOUSE *(looking towards Roche à Miette.)*

farther up stream, the great wall of Roche Suette, at the foot of which Jasper house is situated, blocked the western way.

The forenoon looked as if it meant rain. Sunrise gilded with fire the tops of the mountains ; but the light soon died away. Clouds and mists gathered round Roches Jacques and Suette, but hung there instead of coming down, and the white face of the Pyramid Rock, that divided the two, stood out clear and untouched by the rolling vapour.

The Chief made some pencil sketches, while the men went up stream a mile to a suitable part of the river and worked hard preparing a raft till 10.30 A.M., by which time they had enough logs for the purpose cut and carried down to the bank. Returning to camp for an early dinner of tea and cold pemmican, they then "packed" the horses, carried everything up to the raft and unpacked there. Fifteen or sixteen logs bound together by three strong crosspoles, and tied each to each with folds of rope, composed the raft. Between the crosspoles a number of smaller ones were laid, to serve for a floor and keep the luggage from getting wet. The Chief and the two packers were then left to manage the raft, and the rest stripped to the middle and rode across— Centaur like—driving before them the unsaddled pack-horses. At the crossing the river is divided by sand bars into three parts, and at two of these the water reached to the pommel of the saddle. All got over safely, though there was some danger on account of the strength of the current ; and the raft followed, after a delay caused by the weight of the cargo necessitating the addition of two big logs to make the ship float lightly enough. A ride of two miles took us to Jasper's, where we arrived exactly fifteen days after leaving Edmonton, two of them days of rest and a third lost by the obstruction of the Athabasca. It is hardly fair to speak of it as lost however, for there was no point at which the delay of a day was so little unacceptable to us. The mountains of the Jasper valley would have repaid us for a week's detention.

This station is now all but abandoned by the Hudson's Bay Cy. It was formerly of considerable importance, not only from the number of fur-bearing animals around, but because it was the centre of a regular line of communication between Norway House and Edmonton on the one side, and the Columbia District and Fort Vancouver on the other. An agent and three or four men were then stationed at it all the year round. Even in Dr. Hector's time the house must have been of a somewhat pretentious order, for he speaks of it as "constructed after the Swiss style, with overhanging roofs and trellised porticos." Now there are only two log houses, the largest propped up before and behind with rough shores, as if to prevent it being blown away into the River or back into the Mountain gorges. The houses are untenanted, locked, and shuttered. Twice a year an agent comes up from Edmonton to trade with the Indians of the surrounding country and carry back the furs.

The Chief expected to meet at this point, or to hear some tidings of one of his parties that had been instructed to explore from the Pacific side of the mountains in the direction of the Jasper valley. As no trace of any recent visit could be found, we moved on up the Athabasca ; the trail leading along the sandy beach of Lake Jasper for two miles to a little opening on the hill side above, where as there was a species of small bunch-grass growing, and no one knew of feed farther on, camp was pitched for the night about five P.M.

Our four miles travel to day on the west bank of the river was a succession of magnificent mountain views. After crossing the Athabasca the valley of Rocky River, which runs into it, opposite Jasper House, opened out, extending away to the south east, bordered on both banks by ranges of serrated bare peaks while seemingly in the very centre rose a wooded conical hill. Round all these, masses of mist were enfolding themselves, and the sun shining at the same time brought out the nearest in clear relief.

Pl. 29.

JASPER HOUSE (looking West.)

Jasper House itself is one of the best possible places for seeing to advantage the mountains up and down the valley. It is situated on a pretty glade that slopes gently to the Athabasca, sufficiently large and open to command a view in every direction. Roche à Myette, distant five or six miles, is half concealed by intervening heights and is here less conspicuous than elsewhere even when seen from greater distances, but a gleam of sunlight brightens his great face and makes even it look lighsome. A score of miles to the south, the Pyramid Rock gracefully uplifts its snowy face and shuts in the valley, the space between being filled by the mountains of Rocky River and the great shoulders of Roche Jacques. Looking westerly, and behind the House, is Suette, his rampart rising cold, stern, and grey above his furrowed sides. Other peaks overhang the valley to the north, and between them deep wooded valleys are dark as night. Separated from these by the Snake Indian River, the true proportions of Roche à Bosche are seen for the first time. Away to the south the masses of snow on the Pyramid speak of coming-winter.

There is a wonderful combination of beauty about these mountains. Great masses of boldly defined bare rock are united to all the beauty that variety of form, colour, and vegetation give. A noble river with many tributaries each defining a distinct range, and a beautiful lake ten miles long, embosomed three thousand three hundred feet above the sea, among mountains twice as high, offer innumerable scenes, seldom to be found within the same compass, for the artist to depict and for every traveller to delight in.

Valad informed us that the winter in this quarter is wonderfully mild, considering the height and latitude ; that the Athabasca seldom if ever freezes here, and that wild ducks remain all the year instead of migrating south, as birds farther east invariably do. The lake freezes, but there is so little snow that travellers prefer fording the river to trusting to the glare ice.

Our tent was pitched among firs on a slope above Lake Jasper. Gusts of wind came from every point in the compass, and blew about the sparks in a way dangerous to the blankets, but before we were well asleep rain began to fall and dispelled all apprehensions on the score of fire.

September 13th.—The rain that had been brewing all yesterday came down last night in torrents. One awakened to find the boots at his head full of water; the feet of another, the head of a third, the shoulders of a fourth, were in pools according to the form of the ground, or the precautions that each had taken before turning in. The clouds were lifting, however, and promised a fine day, and nobody cared for a little wetting, but everybody cared very much, when the Chief announced that the flour bag was getting so light that it might be neceesary to allowance the bread rations. That struck home, though there was abundance of pemmican and tea. By 6.45 A.M. we were on the march again, to go deeper into the mountains.

The trail led along Lake Jasper and was so good that we made the west end of the lake, which is ten miles long, in two hours. Practically we were now without a guide; for Valad had not been beyond Jasper House for twenty years, and twice before dinner he missed the trail. Every mile we advanced revealed new features. Roche Jacques rises on the opposite side of the lake, and one deep valley in his sides would be bright as an autumn garden, up to the line of snow; the next, sombre with firs. Each of those valleys is seamed transversely by a number of streamlets, that divide it into a succession of plateaus rising higher and higher till the wall of steep bare rock is reached. But there is no sharp line dividing vegetation from the naked rock. A belt of harder rock intervening breaks the forest; one or two hundred feet above, the trees may reappear in a long thin streak along the side of the mountain, like a regiment in line, or in a dense grove, like a column; and a different stratification above

JASPER LAKE *(looking South.)*

stops them again. The same change of strata, probably accounts for the absence of snow from belts which have snow above and beneath them; far away these bare belts look like highways winding round the mountain. Behind, Myette reared his head over us, seemingly as near as ever; the Pyramid Mountain supported by a great rampart of rock, from which his lofty head rose gracefully, still closed the view; and a cluster of snow clad peaks surrounded him at a respectful distance. From time to time we passed through woods that usually grow along the sides of burns rushing down into the lake; and these prepared us for a fresh prospect beyond, so that the eye had a perpetual feast.

At one point the trail led up some steep rocks, and from these the most charming views of the lake and the mountains were had. Towards the west end, a lakelet, separated from Lake Jasper by two low narrow pine clad ridges, presented in its dark green waters, that reflected the forest, a striking contrast to the light sunny grey of the larger lake reflecting the sky.

Rounding the lake, the trail was encumbered with fallen timber, and from this point to the halting place for dinner at two o'clock we travelled slowly, doing altogether not more than eighteen or nineteen miles in the seven and a quarter hours. A great part of the last half of this distance, was through wood, some of it injured by fire, but most of it good. At the end of Lake Jasper, a strath, from two to five miles wide, which may still be called the Jasper valley, bends to the south. Our first look up this valley showed new lines of mountains on both sides, closed at the head by a great mountain so white with snow that it looked like a sheet suspended from the heavens. That, Valad said, was "La montagne de la grande traverse," adding that the road to the Columbia country up the formidable Athabasca Pass, lay along its south eastern base, while our road would turn west up the valley of the River Myette. He mentioned the old local titles of the mountains on this side, but every passer by thinks that he has a right to give his own and his friends' names to them over again.

In going through the woods we saw several broken traps. This was a famous place in the olden time for trappers, and on that account a foaming torrent that comes down between Pyramid Rock and three great crags to the north, like Salisbury Crags, Edinburgh, on a large scale, is called "Snaring River."

Some of the timber here is three feet in diameter, chiefly fir, but near Snaring River a growth of small pines has sprung up on burnt ground.

This torrent will be remembered by us because of the danger in crossing it, and because beside it we found the first traces of one of the parties we expected to meet in the Jasper valley. It is a foaming mountain torrent, with a bed full of large round boulders which it piles along its banks, or hurls down its bed to the Athabasca. These make the footing so precarious that if a horse falls, there is little hope for him or his rider. Valad crossed first. As the water came up to his horse's shoulder, and the horse stumbled several times, it was evidently risky. Just at this moment, Brown who had gone down stream to look for another ford, called out that he saw footprints of men and horses. Off went the Chief, and at the same moment Valad screamed across the torrent that white men had just been there. All followed the Chief, and Valad came back at a lower crossing. The traces of three men and three shod horses, (showing that they did not belong to Indians) were clearly made out going down in the direction of the Athabasca; but though guns were fired as a signal, no response was heard; and the word was passed to cross at the lower ford. Beaupré took some pemmican in his pocket, as a precaution, in case all hands but himself were lost; notwithstanding the omen, we reached the other side safely, and pushed across a pine flat, and then a quaking bog like Chatmoss to a little lake, with treacherous quicksands on its shore and in its bed. On the other side is an extensive sandy bas-fond where we halted for dinner, sorely regretting that the men who were on their way to Jasper's for the very purpose of meeting us, had missed us by being on a different trail or on no trail, for as the old one had been burnt over, neither party had found it. But the packs were scarcely off the horses' backs when a Shuswap Indian rode up the bank so quietly, that he was in our midst before we saw him, and after the usual hand-shaking, delivered a slip of paper to the Chief. Hurrah! it was from Moberly, and stated that he had just struck fresh tracks and had sent back this Indian to learn who we were. Valad spoke to the Indian in Cree, and Beaupré in French, but he was from the Pacific side and only shook his head in answer. Brown then tried him in Chinook, a barbarous lingo of one or two hundred words, first introduced by the Hudson's Bay agents, for common use among themselves and the Pacific Indians ; and, generally spoken now all through Oregon, B. Columbia, and the north, by whites, Chinese, Indians, and all nationalities. The Shuswap's face brightened, and he answered in Chinook to the effect that Moberly was five or six miles back : that they had come three day's journey from their big camp, where there were lots of men and horses. Brown asked if they had enough to eat at the camp; 'Oh! hy-iu, muck à muck! hy-iu iktahs!' 'Lots of grub, lots of good things'—was the ready answer. He was offered some pemmican and took it, but said that he had never seen such food before. A note was at once sent back to Moberly that we would move on, and that he would probably overtake us on the morrow.

After dinner the march was resumed for seven miles up the valley. On the east side a succession of peaks ressembling each other with the exception of one—'Roche à Bonhomme'—hemmed us in : while on the west, with lines of stratification parallel to lines on the east side, the solid rampart at the base of the Pyramid rose so steep and high, that the snowy summit behind could not be seen. The valley still averaged from two to five miles wide, though horizontal distances are so dwarfed by the towering altitude of the naked massive rocks on both sides, that it seemed to be scarcely one fourth of that width. What a singularly easy opening into the mountains, formed by some great convulsion that had cleft them asunder, crushed and piled them up on each side like cakes of ice, much in the same way as may be seen in winter on the St. Lawrence or any of our rivers, on a comparatively microscopic scale, in ice-shoves! The Athabasca finding so plain a course had taken it, gradually shaped and finished the valley, and strewn the bas-fonds, which cross-torrents from the hills have seamed and broken up. It looks as if nature had united all her forces to make this the natural highway into the heart of the Rocky Mountains.

Myette and all his companions of the first range, that had become so familiar to us in the last few days, were completely hidden by the turn of the Athabasca ; and the mountains ahead, that had shown at the bend, were also hidden from view ; but at sunset we came to another bend that the river makes again to the west, and " La grande montagne de la traverse " came fully out in his snowy raiment, and the Pyramid peeped over the great wall, that girds his body and flows down over his feet, to see our backs. We turned with the river and, after going another mile encumbered with fallen timber, camped on a terrace overlooking the river and surrounded on all sides with snow-capped mountains. As this was to be our last night by the Athabasca and perhaps the last on the eastern slope of the mountains, we named this camp, the forty-eighth from Lake Superior, " Athabasca."

September 14th.—The trail this morning led along the Athabasca for seven miles, to where the Myette runs into it, opposite the old " Henry House." With the exception of a difficulty soon after starting, caused by the disappearance of the trail near the

Pl. 31.

CALEDONIAN VALLEY (*looking towards Jasper Valley.*)

river and the forcing a path through thick brush till we found it
again, the road was excellent ; passing for four or five miles over
beautiful little "prairies,"—which had not been touched as yet by
the frost, and on which grew the bunch-grass that horses prefer
to any other feed,—and for the next two or three miles through
small and middling sized pines, so well apart from one another
that it was easy to ride in any direction. The day was warm and
sunny, and the black flies that had left us for a week reappeared
here. This valley, which seemed as beautiful on the other side
of the river, is so completely sheltered, that the winter in it must
be very mild.

The highest mountains that we had yet seen, showed this morning away to the south in the direction of the Athabasca Pass,
and "the Committee's Punch Bowl." This Pass is seven thousand
feet high, and snow lies on its summit all the year round, but
our road led westward up the Myette ; and, as the Athabasca here
sweeps away to the south, under the name of Whirlpool river,
the turn shut out from view for the rest of our journey, both the
valley and the mountains of the Whirlpool.

With the Myette bad roads began again. Just as they commenced, Moberly caught up to us, having ridden on in advance
of his men. He had left Victoria, Vancouver's Island, for
the Columbia, having organized large provision-trains in the
spring on pack-horses, and brought them on over incredible
difficulties to " Boat encampment " at the most northerly bend
of the Columbia. From Boat encampment they were to cross
to the Athabasca Pass and move on to the Jasper valley, to afford
autumn and winter supplies to the parties operating from that
centre. He himself had crossed in advance direct to the lake
on the other side of the Yellow Head Pass, where he met one of
the parties under his command, making a trail in the direction of
the Pass from the west. Hearing nothing about us from them,
he had loaded three horses with flour and bacon, and come on

to meet us. But by taking the river trail from Snaring River, two
hours before our arrival there, he had missed us yesterday.
Except the two Iroquois on the MacLeod, his was the first face
we had seen since leaving St. Ann's, and to meet him was like
opening communication with the world again, although we, and
not he had the latest news to give.—How welcome he was, we
need not say !

The first five miles up the Caledonian valley, as the valley of
the Myette is called in the old maps and in Dr. Hector's journals,
we made in about three hours, and a little after midday halted
for dinner.   Fallen timber was the principal cause of the slow
rate, though the steep sharp rocks hurt the horses so much, that
they had to tread softly and slowly.   The rocks are hard rough
sandstone, with a slaty or a peculiar pebbly fracture.   The trail
so far was scarcely worthy of the bad name travellers had given
to it, and we began to imagine that the remaining fifteen miles
to the Yellow Head Pass, could be made before nightfall.
Moberly quietly said that it was a fond imagination, and that
if the next five miles were got over by dark he would be satisfied,
as it had taken him a whole day to make seven miles on his way
down.   Myette has such unpretending portals, especially when
compared with the magnificent ranges about the Athabasca, it's
current is so quiet, almost sluggish, near the mouth, and the valley
is so short that no one would fore-cast any formidable difficulties,
in ascending it to the Pass.   But the afternoon proved that the
valley is worthy of its old name ' Caledonian,' if the name was
meant to suggest the thistle or the " wha' daur meddle wi' me !"

The Myette has a wonderful volume of water for its short
course.   It rushes down a narrow valley fed at every corner by
foaming fells from the hill-sides, and by several large tributaries.
A short way up from its mouth it becomes simply a series
of rapids or mad currents, hurling along boulders, trees, and
debris of all kinds.   The valley at first is uninteresting, but five

Pl. 32.

CALEDONIAN VALLEY (*looking towards Yellow Head Pass.*)

miles up and for much of the rest of the way, is quite picturesque, two prominent mountains, that rise right above the Pass and the lake at the summit, closing it in at its head.

Moberly's three men and horses, came up just as we were rising from dinner ; and they passed on ahead, axes in hand, to improve the trail a little. It certainly needed all the improvement it got, and a good deal more than they could give in an afternoon. Long swamps that reminded us of the muskegs on the MacLeod, covered with an under-brush of scrub birch, and tough willows eight to ten feet high, that slapped our faces, and defiled our clothing with foul-smelling marsh mud, had to be floundered through. Alternating with these, intervened the face of a precipice, the rocky bed and sides of the river, or fallen timber, stumps, and blackened poles, to climb, to scramble over, or to dodge. No wonder that Milton and Cheadle bade adieu to the unkindly Myette with immense satisfaction. We had to cross and recross the river or parts of it seven or eight times in the course of the afternoon, for the trail sought low levels and avoided as often as possible ascending the bluffs and walls of rugged rock that rise sheer from the water. The middle ten miles of the Caledonian valley present formidable difficulties for a road of any kind. Four hours hard work took us over five miles, and by that time every one was heartily sick of it, and full of longing to reach Moberly's camp ; although as yet no suitable camping ground had offered. As we stumbled about on a patch recently burnt over on the south side of the river, one of his Indians that he had thoughfully sent back, met and guided us to a desolate looking spot, the best camping ground he had been able to find. Some little grass had sprung up on the blackened soil, and no one was disposed to be particular. Supper was left in the hands of Tim—Moberly's Indian cook—and he prepared a variety of delicacies that made up for all other deficiencies ; bread light as Parisian rolls, Columbia flour being as different

P

from Red River as Tim's baking from Terry's; delicious Java coffee, sweetened with sugar from the Sandwich Islands, that now supply great part of the Pacific coast with sugar; and crisp bacon, almost as great a luxury to us as pemmican to Moberly's men. All the hardships of the afternoon were forgotten as the aroma of the coffee steamed up our nostrils, and when Tim announced that he had oatmeal enough to make porridge for breakfast, our "luck" in meeting him was declared to be 'wonderful,' and 'Caledonian Camp' was voted the jolliest of our forty-nine. An hour after, the united party gathered round the kettle to drink the three Saturday night toasts, with three times three and one cheer more.

Consulting Moberly about the programme for next day, he advised that we should move on in the morning four miles to the last recrossing of the river and rest there for the day; for the two reasons, that by so doing we would get good feed for the horses, and probably fall in with the camp of his trail makers, who worked in advance of the surveying party. Both reasons were so good that the advice was taken *nem. con.*

September 15.—Had the promised porridge for breakfast, after some more of the good bread and bacon, and found it quite up to our anticipations. Left the " Caledonian Camp " at eight A.M. for our Sabbath day's journey, and found it not much better than yesterday afternoon's as far as quality was concerned. As every one needed rest and was tired of the Myette and its swamps, willows, and rocks, the sight of the crossing was hailed with general joy, and all the more when those in front called out that there was a fresh trail on the other side. Sure enough, as Moberly had expected, the trail party had reached the river, and their camp was only a quarter of a mile off. Our difficulties had come to an end, we supposed, for there would be a reasonably good trail now all the way to Kamloops; and the North Thompson canyons especially need no longer be dreaded. The conclusion

Pl. 33.

THE YELLOW HEAD PASS (looking West.)

proved to be somewhat hasty, but it cheered us at the time and was substantially correct. We rode up to the camp, and gave and received hearty greetings. An old-countryman named McCord was at the head of the trail party. He had pitched tents for the Sunday rest on a gentle incline beside the river, which flowed without rapids all the way from our last camp. We had been at the entrance of the " Yellow Head Pass " then, for though the actual summit was six miles farther west than where we met McCord, there was little or nothing of a rise up from our last night's camp. The two mountains that we had seen from near the bottom of the valley, closing its head, now appeared as the southern peaks of a noble ridge that bounded the pass to the north. The nearer to us of the two was almost conical and the other resembled the frustum of a cone, serrated into a number of peaks, like a cross-cut saw, the big teeth in the centre and the small ones at the ends. These two mountains on which the snow rests the whole year are still nameless, strange to say. As the most prominent points on the Canadian Pacific Railway, we would suggest that the statesmen who have been most identified with the great project should have the honor of giving names to them.

After a hearty lunch on pork and beans—the favourite dish of miners and axemen, divine service was held. The congregation consisted of twenty-one men, including English, Scotch, Irish, Indians from both sides of the Rocky Mountains, and representatives of all the six provinces of the Dominion. We joined in singing Old Hundred and in common prayer, and a sermon was then preached—not very short on the plea that the majority of the Congregation had not heard a sermon for three months. As usual the worship had the effect of awakening old hallowed associations, and making us feel united in a common sacred life. In the evening all hands of their own accord gathered round our tent to share in the family worship.

McCord had selected his camping ground judiciously. Good wood, water, and pasture in his immediate neighbourhood ; a beautiful slope covered with tall spruce, amid which the tents were scattered ; an open meadow and low wooded hills to the Northwest round which the low line of the Pass winding in the same direction, could easily be made out ; and the horizon, bounded by a bold ridge which threw out its two great peaks to overhang the Pass. This was one of the most picturesque spots in the Caledonian Valley, combining a soft lowland and woodland beauty, with stern rocky masses, capped with eternal snow. We were 3,700 feet above the sea, but the air was soft and warm. Even at night it was only pleasantly cool. We were all delighted with this our first view of the Yellow Head Pass.

Dinner was ordered for six o'clock and Brown set to work on his pemmican plum pudding in good time. It had to be made so large, however, that at six o'clock it required at least another hour's boiling. Fortunately McCord's cook, in ignorance of what Brown was about, had prepared at his fire a genuine old fashioned plum-pudding ; and full justice was done to this, till the pemmican one was ready. It was then proposed to keep it for break-fast, but the Dr. was impatient to put Brown's skill to the proof, and an hour after dinner, all gathered around our tent, to try the second pudding and decide on Brown's reputation. Terry in preparing the sauce had used salt instead of sugar, and the Dr. was accused of having put him up to the mistake to spoil the dish ; but the pudding was a decided success, though eaten under the great disadvantage of no one being very hungry, and plates were handed in for the second helping. Altogether this was a great day. The pleasure of meeting friends, of believing that our difficulties were practically at an end, the establishment of communication with the Pacific parties, the beauty of the prospect, the many novelties—to us luxuries of the table, the general good feeling, the quiet Sunday rest, the common worship.

all contributed to heighten our enjoyment ; and to make us rise from our second plum-pudding with the plough boy's sentiment in our hearts if not on our lips, " I'm fu', and as thankfu'."

CHAPTER IX.

Yellow Head Pass to the North Thompson River.

September 16.—Our aim to-day was to reach Moose Lake where Mohun's party was surveying. The distances given us were ; six miles to the summit of the Pass, six thence to Yellow Head Lake, four along the Lake, and fourteen to Moose Lake. These we found to be correct except the last which is more like sixteen than fourteen, and unfortunately Mohun's party was near the west end of Moose Lake, and this added eight more, so that instead of thirty, we had to do forty. Besides, not having been informed that the second half of the trail was by far the worst, no extra time was allowed for it, and hence we had five hours of night travelling that knocked up horses and men, as much as or more than a double day's ordinary work would have done. In fact, the day began well and ought to have ended well, but instead of that, it will always be associated in our minds with the drive to Oak Point from the North-west Angle on July 30th. Worse cannot be said of it.

The first half of the day was more like a pleasure trip than work. The six miles to the summit were almost a continuous level, the trail following the now smooth-flowing Myette till the main branch turned north, and then a small branch till it too was left among the hills, and a few minutes after the sound of a rivulet running in the opposite direction over a red pebbly bottom was heard.

(246)

Pl. 34.

Mitchell's Lake

Tete Jaune Cache

Sep.18

Yellow Head Pass

Albreda L.

Sep 21&22

M'Broad

Sep 23rd

Boat Encampment

Lat 52°

Sep 24

200?

Mt Arthur

Inm tum L.

Sep

Lost C.

Dal

Tranquille

L. des Roches

27th

Seymour

C. Newman C.

Adams L.

Lat 51°

Shuswap Lake

Indian band

Little Shuswap L.

Sep 28&29th

Kamloops L.

Kamloops

YELLOW HEAD PASS TO KAMLOOPS

We had left the Myette flowing to the Arctic Ocean, and now came upon this, the source of the Fraser hurrying to the Pacific. At the summit, Moberly welcomed us into British Columbia, for we were at length out of " No man's land," and had entered the western province of our Dominion.   Round the rivulet running west, the party gathered, and drank from its waters to the Queen and the Dominion. No incline could be more gentle than the trail from the Atlantic and Arctic to the Pacific slope.   The road wound round wooded banks, a meadow with heavy marsh grass extending to the opposite hill. There had been little or no frost near the summit, and flowers were in bloom that we had seen a month ago farther east.   The flora was of the same character on both sides of the summit ; eight or nine kinds of wild berries, vetches, asters, wild honey-suckle, &c., &c. Good timber, the bark of which looked like hemlock, but that the men called pine, covered the ground for the next few miles to Yellow Head Lake.   This beautiful sheet of water, clear and sparkling up to its firm pebbly beach, expanding and contracting as its shores recede or send out promontories, was absurdly called " Cowdung Lake " formerly, but ought always to bear the same name as the Pass.   Towards the western end where we halted for dinner, its woods have been somewhat marred by fires that have swept the hill sides, but wherever these have kept off, its beauty is equal to, though of a different kind from Lake Jasper.   Low wooded hills intersected with soft green and flowery glades rise in broken undulations from its shores.   It is on those and up to the line of vegetation that a botanist should go ; for there are few varieties along the low ground, but evidently many higher up.   Above and behind the hills on the south side, towers a huge pinnacle of rock, the snow on whose summit is generally concealed by clouds or mist.   On the north, the two mountains that we had seen yesterday, bounding the Pass on that side, and which had been hidden all the forenoon by the woods at their

base, through which the trail runs, now looked out from right
over our heads ; riven masses of stratified rock, in a slightly
curved line, forming a gigantic cross-cut saw. Through the Pass,
slate cropped out in several places, and boulders of granite strewed
the ground, but the granite was not observed *in situ*. Probably,
slate is what gold miners term "the bed rock," and Brown and
Beaupré pointed out quartz veins that they had no doubt were
gold bearing.

After dinner the trail, from the nature of the soil, was so rough
that the horses could go only at a walk of three miles an hour
It ran either among masses of boulders, or through new woods,
where the trees and willows had been cut away, but their sharp
stumps remained. It was dark before we reached the east end of
Moose Lake, and if all our party had been together, we would
certainly have camped beside one of the many tributaries of the
Fraser, that run down from every mountain on both sides, after it
emerges from Yellow Head Lake, and make it a deep strong river
before it is fifteen miles long. One of those mountain feeders that
we crossed was an hundred feet wide, and so deep and rapid in
two places, that the horses waded across with difficulty, and had
almost to swim. Our company, however, was unfortunately
separated into three parts, and no concerted action could be taken.
Moberly and the Doctor had ridden ahead to find Mohun's Camp
and have supper ready ; the pack-horses followed three or four
miles behind them; and the Chief, Frank, and the Secretary were
far in the rear, botanising and sketching. Every hour we expected
to get to the Camp, but the road seemed endless. In the dense
dark woods, the moon's light was very feeble, and as the horses
were done out, we walked before or behind the poor brutes, stumbling over loose boulders, tripped up by the short sharp stumps
and rootlets, mired in deep moss springs, wearied with climbing
the steep ascents oi the lake's sides, knee-sore with jolts in
descending, dizzy and stupid from sheer fatigue and want of

YELLOW HEAD LAKE AND PASS.

sleep. A drizzling rain had fallen in showers most of the afternoon, and it continued at intervals through the night ; but our
exertions heated us so much that our clothes became as wet, on
account of the waterproofs not allowing perspiration to evapo-
rate, as if we had been thrown into the lake ; and thinking it
less injurious to get wet from without than from within, we took
off the waterproofs, and let the whole discomfort of the rain be
added to the other discomforts of the night. The only consolation was that the full moon shone out occasionally from rifts in
the clouds, and enabled us to pick a few steps and avoid some
difficulties. At those times the lake appeared at our feet, glim-
mering through the dark firs, and shut in two or three miles
beyond by precipitous mountains, down whose sides white
torrents were foaming, the noise of one or another of which
sounded incessantly in our ears till the sound became hateful.

This kind of thing lasted in the case of the three in the rear
fully five hours. The men with the pack-horses had got in to
camp half an hour, and Moberly and the Doctor two hours
before them. None of us were in good humour, because we felt
there had been stupid bungling or carelessness on the part of
those who should have guided us, as no one would have dreamed
of attempting such a journey if proper information had been
given. And to crown this disastrous day, there was no feed
about Mohun's camp, and his horses that we had expected to
change with ours, had left a few days previously for Tête Jaune
Cache. His men had a raft made on which to transport their
luggage and instruments up to the east end oı the lake, as their
first work for to-morrow. They had completed the survey along
the west end and centre. Our poor horses, most oı which had
now travelled eleven hundred miles, and required rest or a
different kind oı work, had had a killing day of it and there was
no grass for them. Reflecting on the situation was not pleasant,
but a good supper of corned-beef and beans made us soon forget

our own fatigue. After supper, at 2 P.M., wrapping dry blankets round our wet clothes, and spreading waterproofs over the place where there were fewest pools of water, we went in willingly for sweet sleep.

The Doctor had completely forgotten his fatigue before our arrival under the influence of a present of the spoon and fishing line of Milton and Cheadle's "Headless Indian." One of the packers had found the skeleton, and had also found the head lying under a fallen tree, a hundred and fifty yards from the body. As the body could not have walked away and sat down minus the head, the explanation of the packers was that the Assiniboine on his unsuccessful hunt for game had killed and eaten the Shuswap, and turned the affair into a mystery by hiding his head. Poor Mr. O'B., of whom we heard enough at Edmonton to prove that his portraiture is faithfully given in "the North-west Passage by land," will accept this solution of the mystery if no one else will. The Doctor put the old horn spoon, and the fishing line—a strong native hemp line, among his choicest treasures, and took minute notes of the position of the grave that he might dig up the head.

The two descriptions in Milton and Cheadle that have been generally considered apocryphal, and that have discredited the whole book to many readers, are those concerning Mr. O'B., and 'the headless Indian.' Not only did we find both verified, but the accounts of the country and the tale of their own difficulties are as truthfully and simply given as it was possible for men who travelled in a strange country, chiefly in quest of adventures that they intended to publish, and who naturally wished to get items with colour for their book. The pluck that made them conceive, and the vastly greater pluck that enabled them to pull through such an expedition was of the truest British kind. They were more indebted than they perhaps knew as far as "Slaughter Camp," to the trail of the Canadians who

NEAR THE GRAND FORKS OF THE FRASER RIVER.

had preceded them, on their way to Cariboo; but from that point, down the frighful and unexplored valley of the North Thompson, the journey had to be faced on their own totally inadequate resources. Had they but known it, they were beaten as completely as by the rules of war the British troops were at Waterloo. They should have submitted to "the inevitable" and starved. But luckily for themselves and for their readers, they did not know it; and thanks to Mrs. Assiniboine, and their own intelligent hardihood that kept them from giving in even for an instant, they succeeded where by all the laws of probabilities they ought to have disastrously failed.

We had now crossed the first range of the Rocky Mountains, and were on the Pacific slope, on the banks of a river that runs into the Pacific Ocean. One or two of our party seemed to think that difficulties were therefore at an end; that all that had to be done now was to follow the Fraser to its mouth, as so great a river would be sure to find the easiest course to the sea. A party of gentlemen ignorant of the geography of the country and deserted by their guides, in endeavouring to cross the Rocky Mountains a few years ago farther south, argued similarly when they struck the Columbia river. 'So great a river cannot go wrong: its course must be the best; let us follow it to the sea.' And they did follow its northerly sweep round the Kootanie or Selkirk range, for one or two hundred miles, till inextricably entangled among fallen timber, and cedar swamps, they resolved to kill their horses, make rafts or canoes, and trust to the river. Had they carried this plan out, they would have perished, for no raft or canoe can get through the terrible canyons of the Columbia. But fortunately two Shuswap Indians came upon them at this juncture, and though not speaking a word that they knew, made them understand by signs, that their only safety was in retracing their steps, and by getting round the head waters of the Columbia, reach Fort Colville by the Kootanie Pass.

Just as the Columbia has to sweep in a great loop round the Selkirk range, so in exactly a similar way farther north or north-west, has the Fraser to loop round the Gold range. Those two ranges may be considered one, with a gap or long break in it between the northern bend of the Columbia and the point called " Tête Jaune Cache " where the Fraser has to turn to the north. It is evident then that the true course for a traveller, from Yellow Head Pass to the west, since he cannot cross the Gold Mountains, which stretch in line across his direct path, is to turn south east a little, try for a road by this gap, and overcome the Gold Mountains by flanking them.

The reader must understand, that although there are many cross-sections and subdivisions of the Rocky Mountains called by different names, there are three main ranges that have to be traversed in going to the Pacific. In the United States and Mexico these ranges bear different, but all well known names. As compared with the mountains farther north, two points may be noted concerning them. First, that they are not cloven by river passes. A Railway therefore has to climb to the high plateau that is nearly as high as the summits. Secondly, that they stretch, especially in the United States, over a far greater extent of country from east to west than is the case in British America.

Our three ranges are the Rocky Mountains proper ; the Selkirk and Gold, which may be considered one ; and the coast range or Cascades. The passage from the east through the first range, is up the valley of the Athabasca and the Myette, and we have seen how easy it is, especially for a Railway. The average height of the mountains above the sea, is nine thousand feet ; but the Yellow Head Pass is only three thousand seven hundred feet. On each side of the valley are mountains that act as natural snow-sheds.

The next question is, are there similar valleys and passes through the other two ranges ? Yes, but not so direct and broad, and there are many obstacles to be overcome. How to get through the second range has always been considered the great difficulty.

First, we have to get to it from Yellow Head Pass. This is done by following the Fraser, as we did to day to Moose Lake, and as we shall to-morrow, to Tête Jaune Cache. There we expect to see the Gold range stretching in unbroken line before us, forcing the Fraser far to the north, and us somewhat to the south east and then the south. Oh! for a direct cut through to the Cariboo gold fields like that which the Athabasca cleaves the Rocky Mountains with! Search for such a Pass has not been given up, and even though no Pass be found, there is hope that a short tunnel may yet "cut the knot," and solve all difficulties. But in the mean time our only course from Tête Jaune Cache, will be to slip in between the Gold and Selkirk ranges till we strike the North Thompson, and continue the flanking process, by going down its banks southerly till we get to Kamloops at the junction of the North and South Thompson, where we can recommence our westerly course, along the comparatively low lying plateau, extending between the second range, and the third called the Cascades.

September 17.—We are now in the heart of the Rocky Mountains, between the first and second great ranges, nearly a day's journey on from Yellow Head Pass, with jaded horses, and a trail so heavy that fresh horses cannot be expected to average more than twenty miles of travel per day.

This morning the consequences of last night's toil and trouble showed plainly by a multitude of signs. Breakfasted at 9 A.M., started from Moose Lake Camp at midday, and crawled ahead about four miles, the horses lifting their feet so spiritlessly that at every step we feared they would give out wholly. At an open glade here, the feed was pretty good, though cropped closely by the dozen horned cattle, kept for the purpose of furnishing fresh beef for Mohun's party, and it was decided that it would be wise to camp.

The delay was not lost time, however vexatious the mismanagement that necessitated it. The Chief had to receive reports about all that had been done by the engineers in this quarter, inspect the line of survey and the drawings that had been made; and give instructions not only for Moberly's parties, but through him for others. Besides, all of us needed a long night's rest, and a big fire to dry our clothes and blankets at before going farther. For assurances were volunteered all round that we had a full fortnight of no holiday travel before reaching Kamloops.

Mohun accompanied us until we should fall in with the pack-train on its way up from the Cache, in order to arrange about an exchange of our jaded and unshod horses for others fresh and shod.

Moose Lake that we struck last night but only got a tolerable view of to day, is a beautiful sheet of water, ten or eleven miles long, by three wide. It receives the Fraser, already a deep strong river fully a hundred and fifty feet wide, and also drains high mountains that enclose it on the north and south. The survey for the Railway is proceeding along the north side, where the bluffs though high appeared not so sheer as on the south. The hillsides and the country beyond support a growth of splendid spruce, black-pine, and Douglas fir, some of the spruce the finest any of us had ever seen. So far in our descent from the Pass, the difficulties in the way of railroad construction are not formidable nor the grades likely to be heavy. Still the work that the surveyors are engaged on requires a patience, hardihood, and forethought that few who ride in Pullman cars on the road in after years will ever appreciate.

September 18th.—Got away from camp at 8 o'clock. Soon after, struck the Fraser, rushing green and foaming through a narrow valley, closed in by high steep rocks wooded beneath, and bare from half-way up. As we advanced, a change in the vegetation, marking the Pacific slope, began to show distinctly. The lighter green of cypress mingled with the darker woods till it predominated,—white birch and small maples also coming in. Our jaded horses walked quietly along, at the two-and-a-half miles per hour step, on a trail heavy in the best places, across mountain streams rushing down to join the Fraser the worst of them roughly bridged with logs and spruce boughs ; around precipitous bluffs and hills, and through mud-holes sprinkled heavily with boulders. Frequently we came on the stakes of the surveying party who had used the trail where there was but one possible course for any road. After travelling nine miles Mohun invited us to tie our horses to the trees, and go down two hundred yards to see the first canyon of the Fraser. A canyon is simply a mountain gorge in which the river is obliged to contract itself, by high rocks closing it in on both sides. A river, however, is not needed to form a canyon ; for walled rocks, enclosing a narrow waterless valley constitute a canyon. At this first canyon, the rocks closed in the river for some hundred yards to a width of eight feet, so that a man could jump across. Down this narrow passage, the whole of the water of the river rushed, —a resistless current, slipping in great green masses from ledge to ledge, smashing against out-jutting rocks, eddying round stony barriers till it got through the long gate-way. In some places these canyons are merely rocks near the stream ; in others they are bluffs extending far back, or perhaps one great bluff that had formerly stretched across the river's bed, and had been riven asunder. In either case, they present formidable obstacles to railroad construction.

A mile beyond, we came to the " Grand Fork of the Fraser," where the main stream receives from the north-east, a tributary important enough to be considered one its sources. It flows in three great divisions, through a meadow two miles wide, from round the bases of Robson's Peak,—the monarch of the mountains hereabouts, and his only less mighty satellites whose pyramidal forms cluster in his rear. A mile from the first division, we came to the second, and found the first section of Mohun's pack-train in the act of crossing it towards us. This first section consisted of horses ; and the second of mules led by a bell horse, under the supervision of Leitch, the chief packer, followed a mile behind. A general halt was called, and Leitch sent for. No difficulty was found in making new arrangements. He gave us four fresh pack horses which would now be sufficient for our wants, five saddle horses, and two packers, and took all our horses, and Brown, Beaupré, and Valad to help him—Valad being specially entrusted with the duty of taking back six horses of the Hudson Bay that were among ours. This was an entire reorganization, and again Terry was the only one of the old set that remained with us. He wished to go on to Cariboo and make his fortune at the mines there. A vision of gold nuggets, picked up as easily as diamonds and rubies in Arizona, more than any sentimental attachment to us was at the root of his stedfastness. But it grieved all to part from the other three, and they seemed equally reluctant to turn their backs on us. Beaupré's only consolation was that he would get pemmican again, for he declared that life without pemmican was nothing but vanity ; and we had made the huge mistake of exchanging our pemmican with McCord for pork. The next day and every day after we rued the bargain, but it was too late. Beaupré and Valad had suffered grievously in body from the change, and for an entire day had been almost useless. The Doctor was reduced practically to two meals a day, for he could not stand fat pork three times. Indeed all, with the single exception of Brown, lamented at every meal, as they picked delicately at the coarse pork, the folly of forsaking that which had been so true a stand by for three weeks. The Chief gave Brown and Beaupré letters to

Pl. 37.

NEAR THE GRAND FORKS OF THE FRASER RIVER.

Moberly, the latter having returned to the Jasper valley two days ago. In now taking leave of these fine fellows, it is with the hope that they may be entrusted with positions in which they will be able to exercise their good qualities in the service of the country. Valad made his adieus, and received the gratuity that the Chief gave him, with a dignity that only an Indian or a gentleman of the old school could manifest. And so exeunt, Brown, Beaupré and Valad.

It was only two P.M. when Leitch came up; but his horses had been travelling all day, and as we were in a good place for feed and for our own dinner, he advised that camp should be pitched, and no movement onward made till the morrow, as time would really be gained by the delay. This was agreed to, the more readily because the Chief had further instructions to write and send back by Mohun, and because the clouds that had been floating over the tops of the hills all day, and obscuring the lofty glacier cone of Robson's Peak, began to close in and empty themselves. Looking west down the valley of the Fraser, the narrow pass suddenly filled with rolling billows of mist. On they came, curling over the rocky summits, rolling down to the forests, enveloping everything in their fleecy mantles. Out of them came great gusts of wind that nearly blew away our fires and tents; and after the gusts, the rain in smart showers. Once or twice the sun broke through, revealing the hill sides, all their autumn tints fresh and glistening after the rain, and the line of their summits near, and bold against the sky; all, except Robson's Peak which showed its huge shoulders covered with masses of snow, but on whose high head masses of clouds ever rested.

Brown made us a plum cake for tea, and in honor of the occasion, a tin of currant jam that had been put up to be eaten with mutton, if bighorn were shot, was produced. On being opened, it turned out to be only tomatoes, to our great disap-

Q

pointment, but still it was a variety from the routine fare, and relished accordingly.

Sept. 19th.—It rained during the night and the morning looked grey and heavy with clouds ; but the sun shone before eleven o'clock, and the day turned out the finest since crossing the Yellow Head Pass. At 7.30 A.M. got off from the camp, giving a last cheer to Brown, Beaupré, and Valad ; and casting many a longing look behind to see if Robson's Peak would show its bright head to us. But only the snow-ribbed giant sides were visible, for the clouds still rested far down from the summit. Three miles from camp, beside the river, at a place called " Mountain view," his great companions stood out from around him ; but he remained hidden, and reluctantly we had to go on, without being as fortunate as Milton and Cheadle.

Our new horses were in prime condition ; but the road for the first eleven miles was extremely difficult ; and last night's rain had made it worse. The trail follows down the Fraser to " Tête Jaune Cache," when it leaves the river and turns south-east to go to the North, Thompson, at right angles to the main course we had followed since entering the Caledonian Valley. The Fraser at the same point changes its westerly for a northerly course, rushing like a race horse, for hundreds of miles north, when it sweeps round and comes south to receive the united waters of the North and South Thompson, before cutting through the Cascade Range and emptying into the ocean. Tête Jaune Câche is thus a great centre point. From it the valley of the Fraser extends to the north, and the same valley extends south by the banks of the Cranberry and of the Canoe Rivers to the head of theColumbia,—a continuous valley being thus formed parallel to the East range of the Rocky Mountains, and separating them from the Gold and Selkirk ranges.

Our first " spell " to-day was eleven miles over a road so heavy that it cost our fresh horses three and a half hours tough work.

It hugged the banks of the river closely, passing through timber of the finest kind—spruce, hemlock, cedar, (a different variety from the white or red cedar in the eastern provinces) white birch and Douglas fir. Small maples, Mountain ash, and other varieties also showed. An old Iroquois hunter, known in his time as Tête Jaune or Yellow Head, probably from the noticeable fact in an Indian of his hair being light coloured, had wisely selected this central point for caching all the furs he got in the course of a season on the Pacific slope, before setting out with them to trade at Jasper House. He has given his soubriquet forever, not only to the Cåche, but to the Pass and the Lake at the summit. Two or three miles to the east is a roaring linn of the Fraser with a fall of from fourteen to twenty feet ; but we did not go off the road to see it. At the Câche, lofty, glacier clothed mountains rose in all directions up and down the valley of the Fraser, the Cranberry, and the Canoe—enough peaks to hand down to posterity the names of all aspiring travellers and their friends for the next century. The Gold Mountains formed in unbroken line right across our path, forbidding any further progress west, and forcing us to go south-east to flank them, as they forced the Fraser to the north. To our great comfort there is stationed at the Câche a large boat of the C. P. R. S. and into it were pitched saddles and packs, and we rowed ourselves across while the horses swam. The Fraser, at this early stage of its course, is as broad and strong as the Athabasca below the Jasper valley. As the packs were off the horses, we halted for dinner, and at one o'clock were on our way again, "hustling" at a great rate to make up for the slow progress of the last two days. Jack and Joe, our new packers proved to be no idlers. The one was a New Bruswicker who had spent years among the Rocky Mountains, chiefly in the United States ; the other an Ontarian, settled in British Columbia,—both sharp, active fellows, knowing a good deal of human and still more of horse nature.

Our second "spell" was twenty miles, south-east and south to the crossing of the Canoe River. The trail here was in excellent condition, and for great part of the way a buggy might have been driven on it. A sandy ridge like a hog's-back runs up the east side of the valley of the Cranberry, and the trail is along it's top. This valley is the connecting link between the Fraser and Canoe rivers. The valley of the Canoe is the larger link again, extending to "Boat encampment" at the northern end of the valley of the Columbia. The black pines on the ridge are so well apart that there is no difficulty in diverging from the trail, and going in different directions. Before us, as we journeyed south with a little easting, snowy peaks rose on each side of the wide valley, dwarfing it, in appearance, to an extremely narrow width ; while right ahead a great mountain mass that marked the beginning of the main valley of the Canoe, seemed to close our way. The trees struggled far up the sides, fighting a battle with the bare rocks and the snows,—the highest trees heavily dusted with last night's snowfall. Crossing a little stream called the McLennan that issues from a pass in the side hills, we rounded Cranberry Lake and saw the valley of the Canoe stretching far up in the direction we had been going, while our road was across the river and up the dividing line S.S. W. to Albreda Lake and River, flowing into the Thompson.

Although only five o'clock, the sun was now setting behind the mountains to the west from which the Canoe issues, and the road here was heavy with recent rainfall, boulders, and mudholes, so that there was no use of pushing on much farther. At the "Crossing" of the Canoe, there was a raft on the other side, but as the river had fallen two feet in the course of the day, we tried the ford and found it quite practicable,—the water not coming much higher than the horses' shoulders ; so that the "Crossing" which had so nearly cost Lord Milton and Mrs. Assiniboine their lives did not delay us ten minutes.

The rapidity with which these mountain torrents increase or decrease in depth is an astonishing feature to those who have been accustomed only to Lowland rivers. A warm day melts the snows high up, and there is an increase in depth by the afternoon, of from six inches to two or three feet. A cold night succeeds, and down the stream falls by morning. That the Canoe had fallen during the day, was proof th..t though warm in the valley, the air was cold in the mountains. This is pretty much the state of matters as regards weather all through the winters here. The high mountains not only protect the valleys from much of the cold, but also from much of the snow. They act as natural snow fences. As the sun had now disappeared, though his light still shone on the double range of high peaks stretching away down the Canoe, camp was pitched on the other side of the river, Jack and Joe proving themselves as expeditious and obliging as even Brown and Beaupré. It was amusing to listen to the slang terms of the Pacific that garnished their talk. "Spell" we found had crossed the mountains, and "spelling place" and a "good spell" were as common on the one side as the other. But Jack's câll to his horses was new to us. "Git" probably the abbreviated form of our "get up," and Terry's "git up out o' that," was the only cry ever addressed to them, and the sound of it would quicken their walk into a trot when no other words in the language would have the slightest effect. This transatlantic sententiousness and love of abbreviations, from which come their "Sabre cuts of Saxon speech" characterized all their conversation. Without intending the faintest disrespect, they addressed the Doctor always as "Doc." "Good morning Doc," meant no more than "good morning my Lord" would mean. Even the grandeur of the mountains did not secure to them their name in full. "They call them 'the Rockies,'" said Jack, jerking his head in their direction, with an air that indicated that no further information was required about such things. Every adjective and article that could, in any way, be dispensed with was rejected from their English; and if syllables could be lopped off long words so as to bring them down to one syllable, the axe was unsparingly applied. Thus, San Fransiseo was always " Frisco," and Captain —a name applied indiscriminately to every stranger—never longer than " Cap."

September 20th.—Up early this morning and, after breakfast on bread and pork—very unlike Irish pork—for not a solitary streak of lean relieved the fat, got away at 6.30 A.M., before the sun had looked out over the mountains. From our camp a singular radiation of valleys could be observed. That of the Canoe ran almost north and south, inclining more to the west up stream. Between the west and south, the valley of one of its tributaries joined it. Along this tributary called the Camp River—from the fact of one of the surveying parties wintering on it last year—our course was to be to-day. Between the east and north the valley of the Cranberry, along which we had travelled yesterday afternoon, extended away to the Fraser.

Our aim to-day was to reach the North Thompson. Between our camp and it, thirty-three miles of bad road had to be travelled.

Broad gravel benches, supporting a growth of small black pines, rose one above another like terraces, the highest attaining a height of four or five hundred feet. Up these the trail led, heading across to Camp River. Similar benches of sand or gravel, or of sand mixed with boulders are a characteristic of all the rivers in British Columbia. They are distinctly defined as the successive banks of the smallest as well as of the largest rivers. Those along the Canoe, are so extensive as to show that a much greater volume of water once flowed over or rested in the valley. It may be that the Columbia, before the present canyons through which it now runs to the south were riven, flowed thus far or farther north.

MOUNT MILTON FROM ALBREDA LAKE.

It seemed to us a great mistake that the old Indian trail had not been abandoned here, and a new trail made. The terraces are so steep and high, and the descent on the other side to the valley of Camp River so sudden, that the only explanation we could suggest of the trail facing up and down instead of rounding them, was that Tête Jaune had first made it when chasing a chamois or bighorn, and that he and all others thereafter, McCord's party included, were too conservative to look for another and better way.

At the summit of the divide, Camp River flows opposite ways from the two ends of a sluggish lake, the part that runs down to the Thompson assuming the name of the Albreda. The valley is narrow and closed in at its south-west end by the great mass of Mount Milton which fronted us the whole day. This mountain that Dr. Cheadle selected to bear the name of his fellow traveller is a mass of snow-clad peaks that feed the little Albreda with scores of torrents, ice-cold and green coloured, and make it into a river of considerable magnitude before it flows into the Thompson. It is on the south of the Albreda and not on the north as stated by them, and the trail winds round its right or north side leaving it on the left. Soon after entering the valley of Camp River we saw it before us, towering high above the hills that enclosed the narrow valley, and seeming to bar our further progress to the south and south-west. A semi-circle of five peaks, enclosing a snowy bosom, forms the left side ; and, next to these, four much higher rise, the highest and largest in the centre showing a broad front of snow like a field, inclined down till hidden by a forest of dark firs on a range of lower hills. Our road which at first was up the narrow fire-desolated, stony valley, led next round the base of these lower hills, and from the difference of soil and of elevation, changed from a succession of bare, stony ridges, into a succession of mud-holes and torrents— bridged, fortunately for us, by the trail party—till we came to the first crossing of the Albreda. The timber here was of the largest size, but many of the noblest looking cedars were evidently not of much worth from internal decay. It was after sunset when we passed over the wooded slopes and along the banks of the river, and as the dark forest opened here and there, one white peak after another came out through a broad rift in the wooded hills. The underbrush consisted chiefly of a great variety of ferns of all sizes, from the tiniest to clusters six feet high, or of the broad aralea which so monopolized all light and moisture where it grew that there was no chance for grass. In some marshes a water-lily, with leaves three feet long, in seed at this season, hid the water as completely as the aralea the ground. Everything on this side of the mountains is on a large scale,—the mountains themselves, the timber, the leaves, ferns, etc.

It was still eight miles to the crossing of of the Thompson. Since starting in the morning we had halted only once, and yet had made barely twenty-five miles. But as the fast gathering darkness, twice as deep too because of the forest, compelled it, our fifty-fifth camp from Lake Superior was pitched beside the Albreda.

September 21st.—Up this morning at 4.30, in the dark, and on the road two hours later. The days were now so short, because of the season of the year and the mountain-limited horizon, that as it was impossible to travel on the trail after night-fall, the most had to be made of the sunlight.

The trail for the first eight miles was as bad as well could be, although a great amount of honest work had been expended on it. Before McCord had come through, it must have been simply impassable except for an Indian on foot,—worse than when Milton and Cheadle forced through with their one pack-horse at the rate of three miles a day ; for the large Canadian party had immediately preceded them, whereas no one attempted to follow

Pl. 39.

ABOVE THE FORKS OF THE NORTH THOMPSON.

in their steps till McLellan in 1871, and in the intervening nine years much of the trail had been buried out of sight, or hopelesly blocked up by masses of timber, torrents, landslides, or *debris.* Our horses, however, proved equal to the work. Even when their feet entangled in a network of fibrous roots or sunk eighteen inches in a mixture of bog and clay, they would make gallant attemps at trotting ; and by slipping over rocks, jumping fallen trees, breasting precipitous ascents with a rush, and recklessly dashing down the hills, the eight miles to the crossing of the Thompson were made in three hours.

The early morning was dark and lowering, and at eight o'clock a drizzle commenced which continued all the forenoon. Struggling through sombre woods and heavy underbush, every spray of which discharges its little accumulation of rain on the weary traveller as he passes on, is disheartening and exhausting work. The influence of the rain on men and horses is most depressing. The riders get as fatigued as the horses ; for jumping on and off at the bogs, precipices, and boulder slides thirty or forty times a day is as tiresome as a circus performance must be to the actors.

We crossed the Thompson at a point where it divides into three, the smallest of the three sections being bridged with long logs, the two others, broad and only " belly deep," as Jack phrased it. Riding down the west side, too wet and tired to notice anything, the men in advance passed a blazed tree with a piece of paper pinned to the blaze ; but the Secretary, being on foot, turned aside to look ; and read,—

" In V's Cache
There is a box for S. Fleming
or M. Smith."

He at once called out the good news, and V's Cache in the shape of a small log shanty was found hard by. Jack unroofed it in a trice and jumped in ; and among other things, stored for

different engineering parties, was the " box." A stone broke it
open, and as Jack handed out the contents, one by one, a general
shout announced their nature.—Candles and canned meats;
good. "Hooray," from the rear! Two bottles of Worcester sauce
and a bottle of brandy! better; sauce both for the fat pork and
for the plum-pudding next Sunday. Half a dozen of Bass' Pale
Ale, with the familiar face of the red pyramid brand! Three times
three and one cheer more! After this crowning mercy, more canned
meats, jams, and a few bottles of claret evoked but faint applause.
The wine and jams were put back again for Mr. Smith. Four
bottles of the ale, a can of the preserved beef, and another of
peaches were opened on the spot, and Terry producing bread
from the kitchen sack, an impromptu lunch was eaten round the
Cache, and V's health drank as enthusiastically as if he had
been the greatest benefactor of his species. As the *finale*, we
deposited the empty bottles and cans at the foot of the blazed
tree, and wrote our acknowledgments,—

> " Gratefully received
> The above ;
> *Vide infra.*"

On one side, "God bless V!" and on the other, "*Si vis monumen-
tum, despice*," and decorating the paper with red and blue pencil
marks as elaborately as time and our limited resources permitted,
we rode off with merry hearts, the rain ceasing and the sun shining out at the same time as if to be in unison with our feelings.
Is it necessary here to implore the ascetic and the dignified
reader to be a little kind to this ebullition on our part? It was
childish, perhaps, but then what were we but "babes in the wood?"
Circumstances alter cases ; and our circumstances were peculiar.
We would have gushed over a mere "bowing" acquaintance,
had he come upon us in that inhospitable valley, those melancholy
woods, under those rainy skies. Probably we might have fallen on

the neck and wept over an old friend. Is it wonderful that the "red pyramid" looked so kindly, and touched a chord in our hearts?

Two miles farther on, the sound of a bell was heard. Jack said that it must be the bell-horse of another pack-train; but in a few minutes a solitary traveller, walking beside his two laden horses, emerged from the woods ahead. He turned out to be one John Glen—a miner on his way to prospect for gold on hitherto untried mountains and sand-bars. Here was a specimen of Anglo-Saxon self reliant individualism more striking than that pictured by Quinet of the American settler, without priest or captain at his head, going out into the deep woods or virgin lands of the new continent to find and found a home. John Glen calculated that there was as good gold in the mountains as had yet come out of them, and that he might strike a new bar or gulch, that would "pan out" as richly as "Williams Creek" Cariboo; so putting blankets and bacon, flour and frying-pan, shining pickaxe and shovel on his horses, and sticking revolver and knife in his waist, off he started from Kamloops to seek "fresh fields and pastures new." Nothing to him was lack of company or of newspapers; short days and approach of winter; seas of mountains and grassless valleys, equally inhospitable; risk of sickness and certainty of storms; slow and exhausting travel through marsh and muskeg, across roaring mountain torrents and miles of fallen timber; lonely days and lonely nights;—if he found gold he would be repaid. Prospecting was his business, and he went about it in simple matter-of-course style, as if he were doing business 'on change.' John Glen was to us a typical man, the modern missionary, the martyr for gold, the advance guard of the army of material progress. And who will deny or make light of his virtue, his faith, such as it was? His self reliance, surely, was sublime. Compared to his, how small the daring and pluck of even Milton and Cheadle? God save thee, John Glen! and give thee thy reward!

Glen was more than a moral to us. He brought the Chief a letter from the Hudson Bay agent at Kamloops, of date August 24th, informing him that our personal luggage from Toronto *via* San Francisco had arrived, and would be kept for us. This was another bit of good fortune to mark the day.

In hopes of getting to Cranberry marsh, twenty-two miles down from the crossing, we pushed on without giving the horses any rest except the lunch half-hour at V's Cache; but the roads were so heavy that when within four miles of the marsh the packers advised camping. The horses continued to go with spirit ; but the long strain was telling on them, and they had to be our first consideration. The road had seemed to us—if not to the horses—to improve from V's Cache ; but it was still a "hard road to travel," the valley of the Thompson being almost as bad as the valley of the Albreda. In our eighteen miles along it to-day, there was not a mile of level. It was constant up and down, as if we were riding over billows. Even where the ground was low, the cradle hills were high enough to make the road undulating. The valley of the Thompson is very narrow for a stream of its magnitude ; in fact it may more fitly be called a mountain gorge than a valley. Only at rare intervals is there a bit of flat or meadow or even marsh along its banks. High wooded hills rise on each side ; and, beyond these, a higher range of snowy peaks, one or another of the highest of which peeps over the woods at turns of the river, or when the forest through which you are toiling opens a little to enable you to see. The forest is of the grandest kind—not only the living but the dead ; for everywhere around, lie the prostrate forms of old giants, in every stage of decay, some of them six to eight feet through, and an hundred and fifty to two hundred feet in length. Scarcely half-hiding these, are broad leaved plants and ferns in infinite variety, while the branchless columnal shafts of more modern cedars tower far up among the

Pl. 40.

MOUNT CHEADLE.

dark branches of spruce and hemlock, dwarfing the horse and his rider, that creep along across their interlaced roots and the mouldering bones of their great predecessors.

It was not quite five o'clock when we camped; but the sun had set in the narrow valley, and it was quite dark before the horses had been driven to the nearest feed, and the tent put in order for the night. Terry set to work as usual to hurry up the tea; but, to his and our dismay there was no tea kettle. It had fallen by the way from the pack to which it was tied. Jack was sure he had seen it on, four miles back; but as "*Nulla vestigia retrorsum*" was our motto, whatever the loss sustained, no one proposed to turn back and look for it; and our only other pot, — the one used for pork and porridge boiling and all other purposes was laid under requisition for the tea. The two frying pans had also had their handles twisted off; but Joe tied the two handles together and made a pair of pincers out of them that would lift one; and Terry notched a crooked stick and made a handle for the other. Supper was prepared with these extemporised utensils. The Doctor and Frank fried slap-jacks and then boiled canned goose in the one pan. Terry fried pork in the other; and boiled dried apples in the pot before making the tea in it. The Chief and the Secretary assisted with bland smiles and words of encouragement, and by throwing a few chips on the fire occasionally; and a jolly supper, between the open tent and the roaring fire, was the grand finale.

September 22nd.—The first meal this morning, there being only one pot, was a plate of porridge, eaten at 8.30 A.M., after a dip in the ice cold Thompson. Two hours after Terry announced *dejeuner à la fourchette*. The Doctor and Frank roused themselves from their second sleep to enjoy it; but Jack was absent. Not taking kindly to the porridge, he had gone off without saying a word, in search of the missing kettle, and service was postponed till his return.

Looking round at the site of our camp, we could see nothing on our own side of the river but a willow thicket, and the dense forest rising beyond.   On the other side, and up stream, a snow-clad, round topped mountain looked over the lower hills.   Four or five miles down stream a lofty pyramid showed us its snowy face, with a twin peak a little to the south, and a great shoulder also snow-covered, extending farther beyond in the same direction.   This 'biceps Parnassus' we inferred was Mount Cheadle, and in honor of the man the camp was dubbed 'Camp Cheadle.'

Before mid-day Jack returned in triumph with the tea kettle—which he had found less than four miles back—slung across his shoulders.   A cup of tea was at once made in it for him as reward. The Dr. now prepared the pudding, and when it was deposited in the pot for its three hours boil, the bell was rung for divine service.

Just as the Secretary commenced, the pot to the dismay of every one tumbled over.   Half-a-dozen hands were instinctively stretched out, but Terry put it right, with the coolness of a veteran, and the service proceeded with no more trouble, except that gusts of wind blew the smoke into our eyes, making Jack in particular weep enough to gratify any preacher.

Dinner was ordered for four o'clock, and it need hardly be said, the pudding was a success.   It rolled from the bag on to the plate, in the most approved fashion of oblong or rotund puddings.   The Dr. garnished it with six ferns for the six Provinces of the Dominion.   The Chief produced V's brandy, poured some over the pudding and applying a match, it was set on the table in a blaze of blue light, that gladdened every one with old memories.

Before sunset, the wind had blown away the clouds and the snowy mist that had been falling up on the mountains.   When it was dark the stars came out in a clear sky, promising fine weather on the morrow.   After some general talk and calculations as to whether we could get to Kamloops for next Sunday, in which hope weighed down the heaviest improbabilities, all gathered round the hearthstone fire for family worship. It was the time that we always felt most solemnized ; thankful to God for his goodness to us, praying His mercy for our far away homes, and drawn to one another by the thought that we were in the wilderness, with common needs, and entirely dependent on God and each other.

CHAPTER X.

Along the North Thompson River to Kamloops.

September 23rd.—Jack rose this morning at 3 A.M., and made up the fire by kicking the embers together and piling on more wood. In a quarter of an hour after, all hands were up—folding blankets, and packing. We breakfasted by moonlight, and would have been off by five, but two of the horses had wandered and it was some time before they were found. Jack tracked them to an island in the river and had to wade across for them. Notwithstanding the delay we left camp at 5.45 A.M.

This was the first occasion on which any of the horses had strayed even a short distance away from the bell. They had always kept within sound of it on the journey and during the night. The bell is hung round the neck of the most willing horse of the pack, and from that moment he takes the lead. Till he moves on, it is almost impossible to force any of the others forward. If you keep back your horse for a mile or two when on the march, and then give him the rein, he dashes on in frantic eagerness to catch up to the rest. Get hold of the bell-horse when you want to start in the morning, and ring the bell and soon all the others in the pack gather round.

We had never seen the gregariousness of horses so strongly exhibited as in the case of those Pacific pack-trains. And the mule

(272)

AT THE CONFLUENCE OF MUDDY AND N. THOMPSON RIVERS.

shows the sentiment or instinct still more strongly. A bell-horse is put at the head of the mule train, and the mules follow him and pay him the most devoted loyalty. If a strange dog comes up barking, or any other hostile looking brute, the mules often rush furiously at the enemy, and trample him under foot, to shield their sovereign from danger or even from insult. Altogether the bell-horse was a novelty to us, though his uses are so thoroughly understood here, that Jack and Joe were astonished at our asking any questions about so well established an institution.

The night had been frosty, and the ground in the morning was quite hard, but after we had been on the road for an hour, the sun rose from behind Mount Cheadle, and warmed the air somewhat, though it continued cold enough all day to make walking preferable to riding. For the first four miles the road was similar to Saturday's. We then came to a mountain stream, towards the mouth of which the view opened and showed us Mount Cheadle rising stately and beautiful from the opposite bank of the Thompson. What had seemed yesterday a great shoulder stretching to the south was now seen to be a distinct hill, but in addition to the cone or pyramid with the twin heads of Mount Cheadle, a third and lower peak to the north east now appeared. Beyond the stream is Cranberry marsh. The trail here goes along the beach for a short distance, and then turns into the woods and hills again, giving us a repetition of Saturday's experiences. Eight miles from camp we crossed another and larger stream on the other side of which the valley widened and the country beyond opened. The landscape was softer and the wild myrtle and the garden waxberry mixed with the ruder plants that had held entire possession of the ground farther up. Eight miles more brought us to open meadows along the banks of the river, overgrown in part by willows and alders, and in part covered with marsh grass. Here a halt of two

R

hours for dinner was called. We had travelled about sixteen miles in five hours, and had only ten more to travel, to reach Goose Creek, where camp was to be pitched for the night. It was expedient to get there as early as possible, that the horses might have a good feed, for there would be no grass along to-morrow's road, which was also said to be the worst between Yellow Head Pass and Kamloops.

During the last two or three days the river had fallen very much, and at our halting place it was eight or nine feet below its high water mark. The valley was wide enough to enable us for the first time to see on both sides the summits of the mountains that enclosed it. At this point they are remarkably varied. A broad deep cleft in the heavily timbered hills on the west side of the river, showed an undulating line of snowy peaks, rising either from or behind the wooded range ; and the opposite side was closed in nearer the river, by a number of separate mountains, probably from four to six thousand feet high, that folded in upon or rose behind one another.

The afternoon drive was along a level, for the next six or seven miles to Blue River, where our progress was slow from the stubs or short sharp stumps of the alders, that dotted and sometimes completely filled up the trail. Blue River gets its name from the deep soft blue of the distant hills, which are seen from its mouth well up into the gap through which it runs. A raft is kept on this river for the use of the survey. We made use of the Cache or shanty on the bank, opening it for a small supply of beans and of soap. A diligent search was made for coffee but without result.

The timber here is small and much of it has been destroyed by fires. After crossing the river, the trail winds round a bluff that extends boldly to the Thompson. Timber that had fallen down the steep face across the trail delayed us several times. Frank shot a large porcupine as it was climbing a tree, and

SKULL OF THE HEADLESS INDIAN.

pitched it on the kitchen pack to be tried as food. Three miles more brought us to Goose Creek where we camped an hour before sunset. This was the spot the Doctor had been told to examine for the bones of "the headless Indian," and therefore as soon as he had unsaddled his horse, he selected a shingle shaped stick and, without saying a word, set off on his exploration with all the mystery and deliberation of a resurrectionist. In a few minutes he came on a bit of board with the following inscription pencilled on it :—

" Here lie the remains of the "Headless Indian," discovered by Lord " Milton and Dr. Cheadle, A. D. 1863. At this spot we found an old " tin kettle, a knife, a spoon, and fishing line; and 150 yards up the bank " of the river we also found the skull, which was sought for in vain by " the above gentlemen.

" T. Party, C. P. R. S.

" June 5th, 1872."

Scratching the ground with his wooden spade the Dr. was soon in possession of the skull and of the rusty scalping knife, that had been thrown in beside it, and finding the old kettle near, he appropriated it too, and deposited all three with his baggage, as triumphantly as if he had rifled an Egyptian tomb. Terry did not like the proceedings at all, and could only be reconciled to them on the plea that they might lead to the discovery of the murderers; for nothing would persuade him that the man's head had dropped off, and been carried to a distance by the wind or some beast. He had seen heads broken, or cut off, but he had never heard before—and neither had we as far as that goes—ot a head rolling off; and therefore concluded that "there had been some bad work here."

Frank and Jack skinned the porcupine, and prepared it for cooking; and Jack boiled some beans to be eaten with it. A leg being spitted and broiled before the fire as a test morsel, was pronounced superior to beaver; and the carcase was consigned to Terry, who decided to cut it up, parboil, and then fry it for breakfast.

September 24th.—There was no need to look at the thermometer when we got up, to know that there had been frost. Every one felt it through the capote and pair of blankets in which he was wrapped. The Chief rose at midnight and renewed the fire. Frank then got up and curled himself into a ball within a few inches of the red embers. At 3 A.M., all rose growling, stamping their cold feet, lingering about the fire, lighting pipes, and considering whether washing the face wasn't a superstitious rule to be occasionally honoured in the breach rather than the observance. Everything was done slowly. It was nearly sunrise before any one even thought of looking at the thermometer, which then indicated 17 ° : not so very low, but we had been sleeping practically in the open air, and in a cold wind with rather light covering. Three-quarters of an hour were spent in cooking the porcupine ; and as it did not come up to our expectations, from inherent defects or Terry's cooking, very little of the meat was eaten ; and no one proposing to carry a piece in his pocket for lunch, it was left behind,—the only thing in the shape of food that had ever been wasted by us on the journey.

At 6.15 A.M. we were on the march, expecting a heavy day's work, as the road lay over the Great Canyôn that had all but defeated Milton and Cheadle's utmost efforts, and past the 'porte d' enfer' of the Assineboine. The first three miles after crossing the Creek were partly round and partly over a heavy bluff ; and the next five along the river, which ran like a mill-race between high hills. These hills on our side afforded space for the road either along their bases, or on the first bench above. The next ten or twelve miles were to be through the dreaded canyôn ; a pass as much more formidable than Killiecrankie as the Thompson is greater than the Garry. While climbing the first bluff near the entrance to the canyôn, the bell-horse of a pack-train was heard ahead. Fortunately there was space for us to draw aside and let the train pass. It was on its way up to Tête Jaune Cache with supplies, and consisted of fifty-two mules led by a bell-horse, and driven by four or five men, representing as many different nationalities. Most of the mules were, with the exception of the long ears, wonderfully graceful creatures; and though laden with an average weight of three hundred pounds, stepped out over rocks and roots firmly and lightly as if their loads were nothing. This was the first train that had ever passed through the canyôn without losing at least one animal. The horse or mule puts its foot on a piece of innocent-looking moss; underneath the moss there happens to be a wet stone over which he slips; at the same moment, his broad unwieldly pack strikes against a rock, outjutting from the bluff, and as there is no room for him to recover himself, over he goes into the roaring Thompson, and that's the last seen of him unless brought up by a tree halfway down the precipice. Two months before a mule fell over in this way. The packers went down to the river side to look for him, but as there was no trace to be seen, resumed their march. Five days after, another train passing near the spot heard the braying of a mule, and guided by the noise looked, and found that he had fallen on a broad rock half way down, where he had lain for some time stunned. Struggling to his feet, fortunately for him the apparaho got entangled round the rock, and held him fast till he was relieved by the men of the train from his razor bridge over the flood. This was a more wonderful deliverance than that of Bucephalus when abandoned by Mr. O'B.

For several miles, the river here is one long rapid, dashing over hidden and half-hidden rocks scattered over every part of its bed. The great point of danger is reached at 'Hell Gate.' A huge arch had once stretched across the present channel, and had been rifted asunder, leaving a passage for the river not more than thirty feet wide. The rock looked as if it had recently parted, a depression on the one side exactly fitting into an over-hanging rock opposite, as if it were possible for a counter con-vulsion to groove and tongue the two together again. Through this passage the river raged, and the whole force of the current ran under the overhanging black rock, so near its roof that at high water the river is forced back. From this point the Canyon continues for six or seven miles down, at one point the opposing rocks being only fifteen feet apart. The river there boils and spurts up as if ejected from beneath out of an hydraulic pipe.

Half a mile below ' Hell Gate,' a bell was again heard ahead. This, to our great delight belonged to a mule train accom-panying Mr. Marcus Smith—the deputy of the Engineer in chief on the Pacific side. Our pack-horses were sent on while we halted to exchange greetings and news. Mr. Smith was on his way to Tête Jaune Cache to try and find a Pass across the Gold range. He had spent the greater part of the summer on the Pacific coast, in the Cascades, and the Chilcoten District in order to find a practicable line for the railway from Bute Inlet through to Tête Jaune Cache. After a long consultation and a lunch of bread and cheese—cheese produced by Smith and eaten so freely by us who had not tasted any for two months, that Smith ruefully declared our lunch to be " cheese—and bread," the Chief advised him to return with us to Kamloops, as it was too late in the season to adventure into the heart of the Gold range from the east side. It being also of importance that the two should compare notes for a few days, the two parties became one.

Following up our pack-horses, we came in the course of the next few miles to the bottom of the Canyon, and all at once, to a totally different aspect of the river and road. The river ceases to descend rapidly for the next twelve miles, and the valley opens out to a breadth of two or three miles. The road runs through this level; but, though a great improvement on the breakneck hills we had been going up and down all day, the clumps of willow and alder stubs and roots kept the horses from venturing on much beyond a walk,—except the Secretary's, a mad brute called "the fool" which dashed on after the "bell" at such a rate that the rest of the party in following more slowly looked round to pick up the remains. The river here, as if exhausted with its furious racing, subsides into a smooth broad lake-like appearance, and calmly reflects everything on its banks· Hence the name of this district—"Stillwater." Four miles along this brought us to our men unpacking the horses at the point agreed on in the morning. Half a mile ahead, they said, were the tents of the U. and V. parties who had been surveying all summer between Kamloops and Tête Jaune Cache. They had met at this central point, the work on both sections being just finished. Going on to their camp, we found Mr. John Trutch, the engineer in change of both parties, and our friend V. Their encampment seemed to us a great affair, unaccustomed as we had been for weeks to new faces. Each party consisted in all of sixteen or eighteen men, with two Indians,—one the cook's slavey, and the other—slavey to the officer in charge, cabin boy, and general messenger. Besides the two parties there was a third in charge of a pack train, so that the valley was alive with men and mules;—all busy packing up to start for Kamloops in the morning. Most cordial were the greetings on both sides. They at once set to work to prepare supper for us, though they had had their own already, and men were sent back to bring our tent down beside their encampment. The latest news was eagerly asked and given. We heard for the first time scraps of general election news, the item of most recent interest being the election of Sir Francis Hincks as M.P. for the Vancouver District; but the one that delighted us most being the victory of the Canadian team at Wimbledon in the competition for the Rajah of Kolapore's cup against the eight picked shots of the United Kingdom. The names of the eight were read out, and a special cheer given for Shand of Halifax who scored highest.

A mighty supper was soon announced, and as we looked at the tent floor, laden with what to us were the rarest delicacies, and knew that we had appetites to do full justice to them all, one after the other, our hearts warmed within us. Never were men in better condition for the table. Beefsteak, bacon, stuffed heart, loaf bread and a bottle of claret ; a second course of fried slices of the remains of a plum-pudding with which they had entertained Mr. Smith the day before, seasoned with blueberry jam made by themselves,—a feast for a king,—a feast the memory of which shall long gladden us. There was so much to talk and hear about, such a murmur of voices, the pleasant light of so many fires, the prospect of a warm sound sleep, and of more rapid journeying hereafter, that there was nothing wanting to make our happiness complete, except letters from home, and those were at Kamloops, not far away.

September 25th.—Rose at 5.30 refreshed, and as ready for a Highland breakfast as if we had not eaten an English dinner last night. It was arranged that Mr. Trutch should accompany us to Kamloops, V. remaining behind to bring on everything, and that at the Clearwater River, sixty-two miles distant, we should take the survey boat, and go down the Thompson for the remaining seventy-three miles to Kamloops.

As the Chief had letters to write to different parties, it was nine o'clock before we got away from the pleasant Stillwater Camp, bidding good-bye to V., not without the hope of soon meeting him in Ottawa, for we heard that there was a probability that in his absence, and without canvassing, he would be elected on this very day as a member of the House of Commons. Our pack-horses had gone on two hours before with instructions to camp at Round Prairie, twenty-five miles from Stillwater.

Soon after starting, we caught np to the beef-cattle and the pack-train of mules that had gone in advance with U's camp. As the trail is narrow and mules resent being passed on the road —occasionally flinging their heels back into the face of the too eager horse, it took some time and engineering to get ahead ; but when this was accomplished we moved at a rapid walk, breaking now and then into a trot.   From the canyôn to Kamloops the trail steadily improved.   Our morning journey was for ten miles along the grassy or willow covered meadow on the west side of the Thompson's Stillwater. The river looked like a long lake.   The sand over the trail and the *debris* strewn around showed that, in some years at any rate, the river overflowed the low meadow; but an embankment of very moderate height would protect a railway line from all danger.

We halted for lunch at the south end of the Stillwater, fortunately coming on U's advance party who supplied us with some bread, while the Doctor produced two boxes of sardines he had prudently " packed." One of the men, an old Ontarian, was diligently perusing the *Toronto Globe* of August 9th; and as it contained the latest news, he kindly presented it to the Chief. The paper, as was natural at the season, was filled with electioneering items ; but though we would have preferred a larger infusion of European news, very little was left unread. Another of the men gave Mr. Trutch a pair of willow grouse he had shot the day before. British Columbia boasts of having seven or eight varieties of the grouse kind, the most abundant being the sage hen, the blue grouse, the ptarmigan, and the spruce partridge or fool-hen, that is oftener knocked over with a stick than shot.

After its long repose the Thompson now begins to brawl and prepare for another rush down hill. Its height above sea level at the bottom of the canyôn is 2,000 feet and at Kamloops 1,250. It falls more than two-thirds of this 750 feet of difference in thefortyfive miles immediately above Clearwater. In the seventy-three miles below Clearwater the fall is only 240 feet. The meadow now ceased, and the valley contracted again. We could easily understand the dismay with which Milton and Cheadle beheld such a prospect. The valley had opened before, below Mount Cheadle, as if the long imprisonment of the river, and with it their own, was coming to an end; but the Great Canyôn had hedged it in again more firmly than ever. Next at Stillwater and down for twelve or fourteen miles, everything looked as if the river wearied with its long course between high overhanging hills, was at last about to emerge into an open country of farms and settlements; but again the hills closed in, and the apparently interminable narrow valley recommenced.

There was no gloom, however, in our party. No matter what the road, the country, or the weather, everything was on our side ; fair trail, friendly faces, commissariat all right, and the prospect of a post office before the end of the week. The day too was warm and sunny ; the climate altogether different from the rainy skies and cold nights higher up the slope; and we were assured that an hundred miles farther down stream, no rain ever fell except an occasional storm or a few drops from high passing clouds,—an assurance more welcome to us than to intending settlers.

The aspect of the hills too was changing. They were lower and more broken, with undulating spaces between, giving promise of escape to the imprisoned traveller, sooner or later. Distinctly defined benches extended at different points along the banks, and on these the trail was comparatively level. About 4 P.M. we came to a bit of open called "Round Prairie," and found the men unpacking for the night, as there was no other good place for the horses nearer than sixteen miles off.

This had been the easiest day's journey since entering the mountains, for though we had travelled twenty-four miles, there was no fatigue, so that it was really like one of the pic-nic days of the plains. The early camping gave another chance to read the papers, of which every one took advantage, though it seemed odd to be devouring with avidity papers nearly two months old.

September 26th.—It rained heavily this morning, and the start from camp was made with the delays and discomforts that rain produces. The cotton tent weighes thrice as much as when dry. The ends of the blankets, clothes, some of the food, the shaganappi, etc. get wet. The packs are heavier and the horses' backs are wet; and it is always a question whether or not water-proofs do the riders any good. This morning one of the pack-horses could not be found. Everything had to be packed on the three others; Jack remained behind to look for the fourth, and soon found the poor brute sheltered from the rain, in a thicket near where "the bell" had been.

The country to-day resembled that of yesterday; but even where it opened out, the steady drizzle and the heavy mists on the hills hid everything. Cedars had entirely disappeared, and the spruce and pines were comparatively small. The aralea gave place to a smaller leaved trailer with a red berry like the raspberry; and a dark green prickly-leaved bush like English holly, called the Oregon grape, and several grasses and plants new to us covered the ground.

Six miles from camp we came to Mad River, a violent mountain affluent of the Thompson, crossed by a good bridge; and ten miles farther on to "Pea Vine Prairie," where as the rain ceased and enough blue sky "to make a pair of breeches" showed, the halt for dinner was called. Here we saw for the first time the celebrated "bunch-grass," which has no superior as feed for horses or cattle; especially for the latter, as the beet that has been fed on it is peculiarly juicy and tender. The name explains its character as a grass. It consists of small narrow blades—ten to fifty of them growing in a bunch from six to eighteen inches high, and the bunches so close together in places that at a distance they appear to form a sward. The blades are green in spring and summer, but at this season they are russet grey, apparently withered and tasteless, but the avidity with which the horses cropped them, turning aside from green and succulent marsh grass and even vetches, showed that the virtue of the bunch grass had not been lost.

The clouds now rolled up like curtains from the hills, and the sun breaking out revealed the river, three or four hundred feet below, with an interval on each side that made the valley at least two miles across to the high banks that enclosed it. There was a bend in the river to the west, so that we saw not only a little up and down, which is usually all that can be seen on the North Thompson, but round the corner; a wide extent of landscape of varied beauty and soft outlines. The hills were wooded, and the summits of the highest dusted with the recent snow, that had been rain-fall in the valley. Autumn hues of birch, cottonwood, and poplar blended with the dark fir and pine, giving the variety and warmth of colour that we had for many days been strangers to, and which was therefore appreciated by us all the more. The face of the bank on which we stood presented a singular appearance. It was of whitish clay mixed with sand, the front hard as cement by the action of the weather ; there had been successive slides of the bank behind in different years, but the old front had remained firm, and was now standing out along the face, away from the bank, in pyramidal or grotesque forms, like the trap or basalt rocks, spires, and columns along the east coast of Skye, springing from debris at the base. Similar strange forms of cemented whitish clay are to be found in several places on the Fraser.

As Smith and Trutch now messed with us, the different cooks contributed to the common stock and to the cooking, with the two advantages of greater variety to the table, and greater speed in the preparation. After a short halt at "Pea Vine" we got into the saddle again, and made ten miles before sunset; the trail leading across sandy benches intersected by numerous little creeks, the descent to which was generally so direct that every one had to dismount, both for the down and the up hill stretch. Camp for the night was pitched at one of these creeks, twelve miles to the north of the Clearwater, and Frank who had become quite an adept at constructing camp fires, built up a mighty one, at which we dried wet clothes and blankets. Our camp presented a lively scene at night. Great fires before each tent lit up the dark forest, and threw gleams of light about, that made the surrounding darkness all the more intense. Through the branches of the pines, the kindly stars—the only spectators— looked down on groups flitting from tent to tent, or cumbered about the many things that have to be cared for even in the wilderness, cooking, mending, drying, overhauling baggage, piling wood on the fire, planning for the morrow, or "taking notes." How like a lot of gypsies we were in outward appearance, and how naturally every one took to the wild life! A longing for home and for rest would steal over us if we were quiet for a time, but a genuine love for camp life, for its freedom and simplicity and rude happiness, for the earth as a couch and the sky for a canopy, and the wide world for a bed-room, possessed us all; and we knew that, in after days, memory would return, to dwell fondly over many an old camping ground by lake or river side, on the plains, in the woods, and among the mountains.

September 27th.—Six miles travel like yesterday's brought us this morning to Raft River, a broad stream, whose ice cold pellucid waters, indicated that it ran from glaciers, or through hard basalt or trap rock that yielded it no tribute or clay to bring down ; and six miles more along gravelly benches to the Clearwater, whose name is intended to express a similar character, and the difference between itself and the clay coloured Thompson

it empties into.   The Clearwater is so large a stream that after
its junction, the Thompson becomes clearer from the admixture.
At the junction there is a depot of the Canada Pacific Railway
Survey, with a man in charge, and a three ton boat used to bring
up supplies from Kamloops, which we had arranged with V. to
take down, leaving Jack and Joe to bring along the horses, at a
leisurely pace.   From Clearwater to Kamloops by the trail is
between seventy and eighty miles, and by the river probably
ninety.   Aided by the current we hoped to row this in a day
and a half, and so get to Kamloops on Saturday night.   V. had
given us four men to row the boat, and as she lay at the river
bank, the loads were taken from the horses' backs, and thrown
in without difficulty.

After dining in front of the shanty, we said "good-bye" to
Jack and Joe, and gave ourselves up to the sixth lot of men, we
had journeyed with since leaving Fort Garry, and the fourth
variety of locomotion ; the faithful Terry still cleaving to the
party, and really seeming to get fond of us, from force of habit,
and the contrast of his own long tenure of service with the short
periods of all the others.

At two P.M., twelve got into the boat ; our five, the crew,
Smith, Trutch, and his man Johnston who was to steer and help
Terry.   Up to two o'clock the day had been cloudy and cold,
but the sun now came out, and we could enjoy the luxury of
sitting in comfort, talking or reading, knowing too that no delay
was occasioned by the comfort.   The oars were clumsy, but the
men worked with a will, and the current was so strong that the
boat moved down at the rate of five or six miles an hour, so that
after four and a half hours, Trutch advised camping, though there
was still half an hour's twilight, for at the same rate we would
easily reach Kamloops on the morrow.

In this part of its course the river did not seem materially
larger, or different from what it was much farther up.   It still

THE ASSINIBOINE BLUFF.

ran between high rugged hills, that closed in as canyons at intervals. Its course was still through a gorge rather than a valley. Any expanse was as often up on a high terrace, that had once been its bed, as down along its present banks. Seventeen miles from the Clearwater we passed the "Assineboine's bluff," a huge protuberance of slate that only needs a similar rock on the other side, to make it a formidable canyon. At some points the forms of the hills varied so much that the scene was picturesque and striking, but these hills are merely outliers, and not high enough to impress, or to do away with the feeling of monotony. Besides, we had been so sated with mountains that it needed much more to attract our admiration now than would have sufficed a month ago.

Our crew were expert in managing a boat and in putting up a tent. Before dark everything was secured, and we were enjoying our pork and beans, with a plate of porridge before and after the heavier dish; and soon after supper lay down, as we expected, for the last time in this expedition—in our "lean to"—*sub Jove frigido*. This—our 'Thompson River Camp'—was the 60th from Lake Superior, and as we wrapped the blankets round us, a regretful feeling that it would probably be the last, stole into every one's mind.

September 28th.—Raining this morning again, but as there were no horses to pack, it was of less consequence. By 7.30 the boat was unmoored and we were rowing down the river, having fifty-two miles by the survey line and probably sixty-five by the river to make, if at all possible, before night. Behind and above us the clouds were heavy, but we soon passed through the rainy region, to the clearer skies that are generally in the neighbourhood of Kamloops. For the first half of our way the river scenery was very similar to that of yesterday, except that the flats along the banks were broader and more fertile, and the hills covered more abundantly with bunch grass. A few families

of " Siwashes," as Indians on the Pacific slope are universally
called, in the barbarous Chinook,—probably from " Sauvages,"
are scattered here and there along the flats.   Their miserable
little tents looked like salmon smoking establishments ; for as
the salmon don't get this far up the river till August and September, the Siwashes have to catch and dry them for winter
use very late in the year.

Small pox has reduced the number of Siwashes in this part of
the country to the merest handful. A sight of one of their winter
residences, is a sufficient explanation of the destructiveness of
any epidemic that gets in among them. A deep and wide hole is
dug in the ground, a strong pole with cross sticks like an upright
ladder stuck in the centre, and then the house is built up with
logs, in conical form, from the ground to near the top of the
pole, space enough being left for the smoke and the inmates to
get out.   Robinson Crusoe like, instead of a door, they use the
ladder, and go in and out of the house during the winter, by the
chimney.   As this is an inconvenient mode of egress they go
out as seldom as possible ; and as the dogs live with the family,
the filth that soon accumulates can easily be estimated, and so
can the consequence, should one of them be attacked with fever
or small pox. They boast that these houses are " terrible warm,"
and when the smoke and heat reach suffocation point, their
simple remedy is to rush up the ladder into the air, and roll
themselves in the snow for a few minutes. In spring they emerge
from their hybernation into open or tent life ; and in the autumn,
they generally find it easier to build a new house or bottle to shut
themselves up in, than to clean out the old one.   This practice
accounts for the great number of cellar-like depressions along
the banks of the river; the sites of former dwellings resembling
the sad mementoes of old clans to be seen in many a glen in the
Highlands of Scotlands, and suggesting at the first view that the
population in former years had been very large.   But as one

Siwash family may have dug out a dozen residences in as many years, the number of houses is no criterion of what the tribe numbered at any time.

For the first ten or fifteen miles of to-day's course, the river ran rather sluggishly. The current then became stronger, and as it cut for several miles through a range of high hills that had once stretched across its bed, there was a series of rapids powerful enough to help us on noticeably, and of course to hinder much more a boat going upstream. The valley here became a gorge again. Emerging from the range at mid-day, Trutch pointed out blue hills in the horizon, apparently forty or fifty miles ahead, as beyond Kamloops. We halted for twenty minutes to take a cold lunch, and then moved on.

An hour before sunset we came to the first sign of settlers,— a fence run across the intervale from the river to the mountain, to hinder the cattle from straying farther up. Between this point and Kamloops there are now ten or eleven farms or "ranches" as they are called on the Pacific slope, all of them taken up since Milton and Cheadle's time. The first building was a saw-mill about fifteen miles from Kamloops, the proprietor of which was busy sawing boards to roof in his own mill, to begin with. Small log cabins of the new settlers, each with an enclosure for cattle called "the corral" close to it, next gladdened our eyes, so long unused to seeing any abodes of men. For all time, the names and technical expressions on the Pacific coast are likely to show that settlement proceeded from the south and not across the mountains. But such Californian terms as 'ranch,' 'corral' and others from the lips of Scotchmen sounded strangely in our ears at first.

Stock raising is the chief occupation of farmers here ; for though the ground produces the very best cereals and vegetables, irrigation is required as in the fertile plains and valleys of California ; and the simplest methods of irrigating—even where a

S

stream runs through the farm—are expensive in a country where farm labourers and herdmen get from $30 to $75 a month and their 'board'; and where stock raising pays so well on account of the excellence of the natural grass. Common labourers on the roads in British Columbia get $50 a month, about $20 of which they pay for 'board'; and teamsters and packers from $100 to $150.

The farmers who have settled on the North or South Thompson are making money; and beef commands higher prices every year. As there are very few white women, most of the settlers live with squaws, or Klootchmen as they are called on the Pacific; and little agricultural progress or advance of any kind can be expected until immigration brings in women, accustomed to dairy and regular farm-work, to be wives for white men.

The ranches taken up are near little creeks that supply water to irrigate them. In the valley of the South Thompson are large extents of excellent land beside, fit at once for the plough, that will not be settled on, till it is proved that water can be profitably raised from the river, or be had from wells in sufficient quantity. Neither way has yet been tried, simply because all the land along the creeks has not yet been taken up, and there has been no necessity for experimenting.

As we drew nearer Kamloops, characteristics of a different climate could be noted with increasing distinctness. A milder atmosphere, softer skies, easy rolling hills; but the total absence of underbrush and the dry grey grass everywhere covering the ground were the most striking differences to us, accustomed so long to the broad-leaved underbrush and dark green foliage of the humid upper country. We had clearly left the high rainy, and entered the lower arid, region. The clouds from the Pacific are intercepted by the Cascades, and only those that soar like soap-bubbles over their summits pass on to the east. These float over the intervening country till they come to the second

Pl. 44.

KAMLOOPS.

range, a region high enough to intercept them.   Thus it is that while clouds hang over Kamloops and its neighbourhood, little rain or snow falls.   The only timber in the district is a knotty red pine, and as the trees grow widely apart, and the bunch-grass underneath is clean, unmixed with weeds and shrubs, and uniform in colour, the country has a well-kept park-like appearance, though there is too little of fresh green and too many signs of aridity for beauty.

The North Thompson runs smoothly for ten miles above Kamloops, after rippling over a sudden descent, and making a sharp bend round to the north-west and back again to the south.   In the afternoon a slight breeze had sprung up, and a tent was hoisted for a sail: but the wind shifted so frequently that more was lost than gained by it, and at sunset we took it down and trusted to the heavy clumsy oars.   We had only four or five miles to make when it became so dark that the shoals ahead could not be seen; and as none of the crew knew this part of the river, the steering became mere guess-work, and the doctor as the lucky man was put at the helm.   We grounded three or four times, but as the boat was flat-bottomed, and the bed of the river hard and gravelly, she was easily shoved off. The delays were provoking, all the more because there might be many of them; but about 8 o'clock, the waters of the South Thompson, running east and west, gleamed in the darkness at right angles to our course.   The North branch, though the largest, runs into the South branch.   A quarter of a mile down stream from the junction is Fort Kamloops.

The boat was hauled in to the bank; and Trutch went up to the Fort.   Mr. Tait, the agent, at once came down, and with a genuine H. B., which is equivalent to a Highland, welcome, invited us to take up our quarters with him.   Gladly accepting the hospitable offer, we were soon seated in a comfortable room beside a glowing fire.   We were at Kamloops! beside a Post

Office, and a waggon road ; and in the adjoining room, the
half-dozen heads of families resident in or near Kamloops were
holding a meeting with the Provincial Superintendant of Education, to discuss the best means of establishing a school.   Surely
we had returned to civilization and the ways of men !

Were we to judge from what we have seen of the country
along the Fraser and Thompson rivers, the conclusion would be
forced on us that British Columbia can never be an agricultural
country.   We have not visited, however, the Okanagan and
Nicola Districts, or the Chilcoten Plains ; and we have heard
good accounts of the fertility of the former, and the rich park-
like scenery of extensive tracts in the latter.   But the greater
part of the mainland is, "a sea of mountains" ; and the Province will have to depend mainly on its rich grazing resources,
its valuable timber, its fisheries, and minerals, for any large
increase of population.   Even that part of the country lying
between the second range of "the Rockies" and "the Cascades"
where we now are, is an elevated plateau, broken by hills.   The
indications are that it once was submerged under water, with
the hill tops then showing as islands, and with the long line o₁
the Cascades separating the great elevated lake from the sea.
In process of time clefts riven in the Cascades made ways for the
waters to escape.   By these clefts the Fraser, the Homathco,
the Skeena, and the Bella Coula now run in deep gorges through
granite and gneissic or trap and basalt rocks to the sea.   Originally the waters emptied by a series of falls the magnificence of
which it is scarcely possible to conceive.   The successive sub-
sidences of the water are now shown by the high benches of
gravel and silt along the river valleys, and on account of the
great depth cut down by the rivers, there are no bottom

lands or meadows worth speaking of.   As a general rule, with only a few exceptions, all the water channels are found in deep gorges, and for this reason the great rivers of the Province cannot overflow their banks. They must be content with rising higher up the steep hill-sides, between which, for the greater part of their course. they are pent.

CHAPTER XI.

From Kamloops to the Sea.

Sept. 29th.—A long sleep in real beds under a raftered roof, and a dip in the Thompson prepared us for such a breakfast as some at least of us never expect to eat again. "Turtle soup out of a gold spoon" is meagre fare compared to Kamloop's beef. After a few samples at breakfast, we were willing to subscribe to all that had ever been said in favour of bunch-grass as feed for the cattle of kings. Mealy potatoes, eggs, and other luxuries that need not be mentioned, lest those who never knew want should scorn our "simple annals," explained satisfactorily the process by which Dr. Cheadle added forty-one pounds to his weight in a three week's stay at Kamloops. The dip was a pleasure too and not merely the duty it had sometimes been felt; for though the branches of the river are united, the currents of the two keep distinct for several miles down; and the Fort being on the south side, we bathed in the South branch, which is so much warmer than the North that in summer, people who are anxious for cold water often cross in a canoe to the other side for a bucketful.

(294)

Pl. 45.

FROM KAMLOOPS LOOKING NORTHERLY.

Soon after breakfast, people began to assemble for the public worship that had been intimated immediately on our arrival The service was held in the dining room of the fort. About thirty attended ;—our own party, several gentlemen from other parts of the Province, the seven or eight inhabitants of Kamloops, and four or five farmers from the neighbourhood. Mr. Tait's two little girls represented the female population of the place ; for the three or four white women of the settlement were either absent from home or otherwise unable to attend ; and the men who lived with " Klootchmen," as might be expected, did not bring them to church. It may seem wonderful that these prosperous farmers should not have white wives ; but the remoteness of the place must be remembered, and they say too that the Victoria girls are unwilling to give up the pic-nics and gaieties of the capital for farm-life and hard work in the interior. Of course there are no servant girls at Kamloops. A young Chinaman, answering to the common name of " John," was cook and maid of all work at the fort ; and he did the work in a quiet pleasant thorough way that made us wish to steal him for our own use.

Lunch at one, and dinner at five o'clock came in not too rapid succession, though a walk to the nearest hill-top was all that even the most energetic of the party took in the interval. From the hill-top is a magnificent view of the country round Kamloops : the North Thompson valley for twenty miles up ; the South Thompson extending to the east, and the united stream running west for seven miles,—when it expands into a beautiful sheet of water—eighteen miles long—called Kamloops Lake The hills in the neighbourhood have the clean cultivated park-like appearance that we noticed yesterday ; and several farms on the flats, at the junction of the two branches, gave a look of life and field work, to which, as well as to the universal soft mellow colouring imparted by the bunch grass, our eyes had long been unaccustomed. Ten miles away among the hills on the opposite or north side of the Thompson is the " guard " with the four or five hundred horses of the fort, which, had time allowed, we would have visited, to compare the horses with those of the plains. One keeper suffices for the guard, for the horses cluster in bands round their own stallions, and give no trouble except when some, being required for use or sale, have to be separated from the rest. On such occasions, the whole guard has to be " coralled " or penned, and the selection made. It would be impossible for a thief to steal one except by " coralling " the band. Last year the Company was offered $12,000 for their Kamloops collection of horses. The offer was not accepted, but it gives us an idea of the value of animals that cost their owners only the pay of one keeper.

Our Sunday dinner was again crowned with a pemmican plum-pudding. The Doctor had fraternized with ' John,' and prepared it as a surprise. Nothing can be said concerning its excellence more forcible than that it stood the test of being eaten after Kamloops roast beef, and a dinner worthy in all respects of Hudson Bay hospitality. Few guessed the ingredients of the pudding, but all praised it as having a " peculiar " flavour.

Dinner was scarcely over, when people began to assemble for the evening service that had been announced in the forenoon. It was ' rough, mighty rough ' on some of the party round the table, this sudden transition from material to spiritual food. The Doctor looked beseechingly at the Secretary, and formed on his lips without syllabling it a word that could easily be interpreted ' short '! But he, with callous indifference, preached for nearly an hour, because the congregation was larger than in the morning, and would not get a sermon again for six months.

September 30.—On Saturday night our disappointment had been intense on learning that there were no letters or papers for

Pl. 46.

KAMLOOPS TO NEW WESTMINSTER.

us. All grumbled, and one threatened to leave out the last half of the weekly toast of "sweethearts and wives"; but hearing that the paymaster of the Canada Pacific Railway Survey had left Victoria for up country, we comforted ourselves with the hope of meeting him, with the budget in his pocket at Cache Creek, where the Kamloops road joins the Cariboo waggon road, or at Ashcroft six miles farther down the Thompson.

Ashcroft is fifty-five miles from Kamloops, and if we were to get there to-night, an early start was necessary. But the proverbial difficulty of getting away in a hurry from an Hudson Bay fort held good. New arrangements require to be made ; men taken on or paid off; horses or boat, and baggage to be seen to ; instructions to be left; and all the time loafers and interviewers are in the way. We took advantage of odd minutes to be weighed, and a table giving our respective weights at Toronto and Kamloops is enough to prove that the expedition had not told severely on our physique.

	Weight at Toronto, July 16.	At Kamloops, Sept. 30.
The Chief - - - -	174 lbs.	177 lbs.
The Doctor - - - -	184 "	187 "
Frank - - - - - -	142 "	160 "
The Secretary - - -	142 "	160 "

Or a sum total, for the four, of 42 lbs. gain.

The order for the day was to row down twenty-five miles to Savana's ferry at the foot of Kamloops Lake, and there take horses to Ashcroft. This plan would both ease the horses, and enable the Chief to examine a bluff on the south side of the Lake, that had been represented as a formidable obstacle to the Railway line projected along the Thompson.

It was 8 o'clock before a start from the fort was effected, and a head wind springing up soon after, our rate of progress was very slow. The river gradually expands into the Lake, and the scenery would be exceedingly beautiful were it not for the grey and arid or California look that vegetation here presents. The hills are diversified in form and colouring, as they are in age ; some heavy bluffs of trap and basalt jutting out into the lake, intermingled with carboniferous rocks; and beyond them elevated plateaus, composed of a silt of mingled sand and clay, retreat in more or less distinctly defined terraces on which the subsiding waters had successively rested. These plateaus again have been broken and twisted by small streams and side waters. On those broken, narrow, winding plateaus, and the hill sides that bound them, is abundant grazing for ten times the number of cattle or sheep now seen on them.

While rounding the great bluff, the wind—which generally blows directly either up or down stream—blew so freshly up that the boat made little or no headway. We landed at midday to eat a cold lunch, resolving to take to the horses if they could be seen on the other side of the bluff, and leave Terry in the boat to look after the luggage. Fortunately Mr. Tait had accompanied Jack, (who had made a forced march from Clearwater, arriving at Kamloops on Sunday afternoon), and noticing that the wind kept the boat back, they waited for us in a little cove beyond the bluff, nine miles from the ferry. We gladly mounted into the saddle again at 3 P.M., and in an hour and a half reached the end of the lake, where the Thompson issues from it as a broad deep noble-looking river. Ferrying across, a council was held at Savona's to decide what was to be done. It would be sunset before refreshment could be taken ; and it looked a little Dick Turpin-ish to start at such an hour for a thirty mile ride over a new road in a cloudy moonless night. Learning, however, that the Governor had been on his way to Kamloops to meet us, but had turned back to Ashcroft on hearing that we would probably be there to-night, our usual word "Vorwärts" was given. A jolly-looking Boniface and Mrs. Boniface hurried

SAVONAS FERRY, NEAR OUTLET OF LAKE KAMLOOPS.

up a capital supper of Kamloops beef and vegetables, coffee and cake; and promised one 'that would make the hair curl' to any who could remain over night.   Such a temptation, aided doubtless by a variety of circumstances, induced Smith to remain; but at 6 o'clock the rest of us were in the saddle.

Four hours after, we reached Cache Creek, having rested only ten minutes on the way at the house of a French Canadian settler.   The road followed the course of the Thompson, except for the last six or eight miles, when it turned a little northerly up the valley of the creek that runs into the Buonaparte, a tributary of the Thompson.   There are good farms along the road, but night and the fact that it was after harvest made it necessary to accept the testimony of others on the point.   The ground is a sandy loam, and will produce anything if irrigated, and nothing without irrigation.   At Cache Creek the hotel was full, as it generally is, because at a junction of several roads.   We learned here that the paymaster had gone in the Cariboo direction some days previously, perhaps carrying our letters on his person, as amulets.   There was a letter for us from the Governor, and his trap waiting to take us on to Ashcroft.   After waiting a little at Cache Creek to give the Dr. time to examine a patient, we got into the trap, and reached Ashcroft Hotel at 11 o'clock, and in half an hour after were in bed.   The Governor had taken up his quarters at Senator Cornwall's, hard by, and would see us in the morning.

October 1st.—After breakfast, a decision had to be come to with regard to our future movements in British Columbia.   The Governor, not expecting our arrival so soon, had concluded that we would not be able to take the steamer for San Francisco till the 27th inst.   He had arranged to accompany us to Bute Inlet on the 11th, and advised us to visit in the interval the Upper Fraser river and Cariboo.   It was important, however, that we should leave Victoria a fortnight earlier, if at all possible, and that necessitated our going on directly to New Westminster. No special object would be served by the Chief visiting Cariboo. The Governor, therefore, very kindly waived his own wishes, and telegraphed to Victoria for a steamer to meet us on Saturday at Burrard's Inlet.

We had now to wait a day at Ashcroft for an express to Yale, where the steamer to New Westminster connects with the stage coach from Cariboo. Nothing would be gained by going on at once, for there would have to be delay at Yale, if not here. We therefore spent the day in seeing the country, and in the evening dined at Senator Cornwall's.

The country about Ashcroft is sparsely peopled, and men accustomed to the rich grassy plains on the other side of the mountains, might wonder at first sight that it is peopled at all. In appearance, it is little better than a vast sand and gravel pit, bounded by broken hills, bald and arid except on a few summits that support a scanty growth of scrub pines. The cattle had eaten off all the bunch-grass within three or four miles of the road, and a poor substitute for it chiefly in the shape of a bluish weed or shrub, called "sage grass" or "sage bush" has taken its place. The cattle eat this readily, and fare well on it in winter; but it grows thinly, dotting rather than covering the sandy soil, and giving a "pepper and salt" look to the near hill-sides. This poor looking land however is no more a desert than are the rich valleys of California. Like them, it will grow anything, if irrigated. Unfortunately the clouds pass and repass, driving forward only to sail high up, and beyond to the mountains, or to eddy back; but even with this great drawback, and the high price of labour, and the lack of capital or enterprise, farming here pays well. There is abundance of water in the Thompson to irrigate all those arid slopes, and the time is coming when this shall be done with success.

At lunch to-day, a lumberer from the other side of the river, came in and inquired for the Doctor. A log had fallen on a Chinaman employé, and broken his leg. As there was no Dr. within a hundred miles, the employer had come over to telegraph for a druggist 30 miles off, as the nearest approach to a regular practitioner. "John," he said, "was a wonderful Chinaman; he would as lief live with him as with a white man." The Doctor went at once on the errand of mercy, and having to extemporise everything required for setting the leg, it was eight o'clock at night before he got back. He reported the patient to have exhibited the greatest fortitude, and to be doing well.

All the domestic servants we had seen as yet were Chinamen. They are paid from $20 to $45 a month, but as servant girls ask nearly as much, "John" is usually preferred. Though all gamble and most smoke opium, such vices do not materially interfere with their duties as servants. They are bowling out not only the cooks and servant-girls, but the washer-women on the Pacific coast. And we must look to them as the future navvies and miners of our West. There are now 18,000 of them in San Francisco out of a population o. 160,000; 60,000 in California, and about 100,000 altogether on the Pacific side of North America. It would have been difficult to build, and it would now be difficult to work the Union Pacific Railway without them. Is it wonderful then that there should be a prejudice against them in the breasts of the white working-classes they are supplanting. The true-blue Briton of last century hated the French, because "they were all slaves and wore wooden shoes." Why should not the Yankee labourer hate the Chinese, when they not only wear wooden shoes, but are the best of workmen, cleanly, orderly, patient, industrious, and above all cheap?

This evening we met Judge O'Reilly whose praises had been often sung by Brown and Beaupré, in contrast with judges on the other side of the boundary line. "There isn't the gold in

British Columbia that would bribe Judge O'Reilly," was their
emphatic endorsement of his dealings with the miners. They
described him, arriving as the representative of British law and
order, at Kootanie, immediately after thousands had flocked to
the newly discovered gold mines there. Assembling them, he
said that order must and would be kept ; and advised them not
to display their revolvers unnecessarily, " for, boys, if there's
shooting in Kootanie, there will be hanging." Such a speech
was after the miners' own hearts, and after it, there were no
disturbances in Kootanie.

The judge in his turn praised the miners, as manly law-abiding
fellows. He never had the least difficulty in preserving order
among the thousands gathered from all quarters of the earth,
though the available force at his back usually consisted of two
constables.

Left this morning for Lytton, forty-eight miles down stream,
in an express, as the mail waggon from Cariboo was sure to be
full of passengers at this season of the year. The waggon road
on which we travelled is the principal public work of British
Columbia ; constructed as a government work with great energy
soon after the discovery of the Cariboo gold mines. It was a
creditable undertaking for the infant colony, for most formidable
engineering difficulties had to be overcome at the Canyons of
the Fraser and the Thompson, and the expense was necessarily
heavy.

Before it's construction there was only a trail to Cariboo, along
which the gold hunters toiled night and day, driving pack-horses
that carried their blankets and provisions, or if too poor to afford
horse or mule, packing everything on their own backs. Men
have been known to start from Yale on foot, for the gold fields,
with 150 lbs weight on their backs, and when they got to their
destination, their difficulties only commenced. Gold was and is
found in every sandbar oₓ the river and in every creek ; but it

had to be found in large quantities to enable a man to live. A pound of flour cost a dollar and a half, and everything else sold at proportional prices. The gold was in largest quantities near the bed rock, and this was generally covered with a deposit of silt from five to forty feet thick, containing but little of the precious metal near the surface. The country presented every obstacle to "prospecting." Range upon range of stern hills wooded from base to summit, through which a way could be forced only with incredible toil, and at the daily risk of starvation; it is little wonder that the way to Cariboo, and the country itself proved to be the grave of many an adventurous gold seeker. A few made fortunes, in a week or a month, which as a rule they dissipated in less than a year; hundreds gathered moderately large sums, which they took away to spend elsewhere; thousands made "wages;" and tens of thousands, nothing. It had been the same in California, when gold was discovered there: but then the masses who were unsuccessful could not get out of the country, and they had,—fortunately for themselves,—to hire out as farm servants and herdmen. In British Columbia they could get back to Oregon and California, and back they went, poorer than they had come, but leaving the Province little the better for their visit.

At various points on the river, all down the road, miners are still to be found. These are chiefly "Siwashes" and Chinese, who take up abandoned claims, and wash the sand over again, being satisfied with smaller wages than what contents a white man. Their tastes are simple and their expenses moderate. None of them dream of going to the wayside "hotels," and paying a dollar for every meal, a dollar for a bed, a dollar for a bottle of ale, or twenty cents for "a drink." The Chinaman cultivates vegetables beside his claim; these and his bag of rice suffice for him, greatly to the indignation of the orthodox miner. The Siwash catches salmon in his scoop net from every eddy of the river, and his wife carries them up to the house and makes his winter's food. These two classes of the population, the one representing an ancient civilization, the other scattered nomads with almost no tribal relationships, resemble each other in appearance so much, that it would be difficult to distinguish them, were it not for the long tail or queue, into which the China-man braids his hair, and which he often folds at the back of his head, instead of letting it hang down his back. The Pacific Indian is Mongolian in size and complexion, in the shape of the face, and the eyes. He has neither the strength of limb, the manly bearing, nor the dignity so characteristic of the Indians on the east side of the Rocky Mountains.

Salmon are the staple of the Siwash's food, and these are so abundant that they generally sell them for ten to twenty-five cents apiece; and ten cents in British Columbia is equivalent to a penny elsewhere, for there is no smaller coin than the ten cent piece in the Province. Servants here and on the Fraser river would probably bargain as they used to bargain when "hiring" in Scotland, that they were not to be expected to eat salmon oftener than four times a week, if there was the slightest neces-sity of their making any stipulation. But master and mistress know their places too well to dream of imposing that or any other hardship on them. We passed several Chinamen travelling along the road, each man carrying all his worldly goods suspended from the ends of a pole slung across one of his shoulders. So habituated are they to this style of carrying weight, that when they possess only one bundle, inconvenient to divide, they are said to tie a stone to the other end of the pole to balance the load.

Next to the bold and varied scenery, and the dangers of the road, the chief objects of interest to a stranger travelling down the Thompson and the Fraser, especially after entering the Cascade range, are the Indian graves. Whatever these poor people can accomplish in the way of architecture or art, is reserved for their dead. A house better than they live in is built, or a good tent erected, and in it are placed all the valuables of the deceased,—his gun, blanket, food, etc.; in front hang scalps, or bright shawls, and white flags; his canoe is placed outside, and beside it the hide of his horse or mule over a wooden skeleton; rude painted images representing the man, woman, or family, as the case may be, are ranged in front. It is an article of faith with them that no Indian ever desecrated or robbed a grave; and this is probable enough, for seldom has an Indian been known to steal or disturb even the "cache" of another, though the cache of dried salmon on the Pacific slope is usually hung on a tree by the wayside. The provincial law, very properly im- poses severe penalties on those who violate Indian graves; but that the temptation may not be too strong, the canoe is generally riddled, and the lock of the gun taken off, before being deposited beside the dead. All those possessions so valuable in the eyes of a Siwash are left exposed to the winds of heaven and the beasts of the forest, and the age of the grave can be read in the condition in which you find them.

Driving for three hours over a country resembling that round Ashcroft, we came to Cook's Bridge, where the Thompson is crossed, and soon after to the foot hills of the Cascade range. Everywhere the soil looked poor and arid; yet every- where that cultivation was attempted, it produced cereals, roots, and fruits of the best kind. Tomatoes, water and musk melons ripened in the open air; and no farmer has fewer than fifty head of cattle, while some have ten times as many. Now, how- ever, we were about to enter another rainy region, and the heavy mists resting on the hill-tops ahead, were the first indications of the change. The river's narrowness about Ashcroft had astonished us; but here it contracted still more, looking smaller than either its North or South branch away up at Kamloops.

T

What it is forced to lack in breadth it makes up in depth. As the rocky outliers of the mountains cannot be levelled into meadows, the river has to dam itself up their sides or dig a deeper ditch. The road followed its course, winding along the bases of the hills, or climbing over the canyôns, while far down, so immediately under us, that a stone could be dropped into the deep water, the river lay, like a green serpent, now at peace, and now rearing a crested head to pierce deeper into the overlapping barriers before it.

Towards sunsetting, cold rain with strong gusts of wind came on ; and as the road was often only a narrow ledge, cut out of the side of a precipice, we were thankful when the driver pointed out a hill in front, as the one on the other side of which was our resting place, the village of Lytton, at the junction of the Thompson with the Fraser.

We soon saw the lights of the village, and drove up to a house, the mean outside of which gave little promise of the good things for the inner man, in the dining room. M. Hautier, a Frenchman, and his pretty little Flamand wife, kept the house, and had comfortable rooms prepared for us, and a *petit goût de mouton*, with fixings, for supper. The only unpleasant creature in the house, was a half drunken loafer, who carried the credentials of his nationality in his nose, and who was so disgusted at our having a separate sitting room, that he swore at large for an hour or two, consigning all " big bugs " to unmentionable places. Nobody answering or taking any notice of him, he at length subsided into mere growling and snoring, one or the other of which he kept up through the night, as a democratic protest against " big bugs."

October, 3rd.—The village of Lytton can scarcely be considered worthy of its aristocratic name. A single row of frail unpainted sheds or log shanties, the littleness and rickettiness of which are all the more striking from the two noble rivers that

Pl. 48.

THOMPSON RIVER ABOVE LYTTON.

meet here and the lofty hills that enclose the two valleys, is the
sum total of Lytton. Its population of perhaps an hundred
souls is made up of Canadians, British, Yankees, French, Chinamen, Siwashes, half-breeds; all religions and no religion. An
Episcopalian Missionary who has his headquarters at Lytton,
was reported in a recent Exeter Hall speech to have four
thousand baptized Siwash catechumens on his roll. A cipher
or two must have slipped in through a clerical mistake, for the
best authorities say that there are not as many Siwashes on the
Thompson and Fraser, all told, and that the great majority are
Roman Catholics or heathen. If the converts were baptized by
any Church into cleanliness and industry, travellers would be
more likely to believe in their conversion.

To judge by the outside appearance of the village of Lytton,
there must be something rotten in its state.—No sign of progress
or improvement of any kind; the use of paint or whitewash
considered a sin; though, perhaps even whitewash would be too
good for such tumble down little huts. But go into the hotel,
and all is changed. The inside is as different from what the
outside would lead you to expect, as if it was the house of a rich
Jew, in the middle ages. "All the comforts of the Saut-market"
are to be had, and everyone, inside and outside the house,
appears able to pay for them. A dirty looking miner calls for
drinks all round, at twenty-five or fifty cents a drink, and con-
siders himself half insulted if any one in the room declines the
friendly invitation. "Go through the form so as not to give
offence," whispered a gentleman to the Doctor, as he saw him
backing away from the freely proffered claret, champagne, and
brandy. The meat, fish, vegetables, and sweets on the table are
all excellent, and well cooked. There are no poor men in the
Province, and no such thing as bad living known. The explanation of this contrast, huts in which the tenants live like fighting
cocks—is that none of the people came here to stay. They

came to make money and then return home. Therefore it is
not worth their while to build good houses or furnish them
expensively ; but they can afford to live well ; and the gold
miner's maxim is " Eat, drink, and be merry, for to-morrow we
die."

This state of things has been the millstone round the neck of
British Columbia. The discovery of gold in 1858, on the Fraser,
brought the first rush of people to the mainland, and resulted in
the formation of the colony. All California was delirious.
Thirty thousand men left the States for the Fraser, or, as it was
popularly called, "the Crazy River." The rush to Pike's Peak
was nothing to the rush for Victoria. But in the course of the
next two or three years, the thousands died or drifted back
again, and only the tens remained. Then, in 1862 the Cariboo
mines were discovered, and the second rush was greater than
the first ; but again, not an emigration of sober, steady house-
holders, whose aim was to establish homes, and live by their
own industry, but of fever-heated advevturers from all parts
of the world,—men without a country and without a home. San
Francisco was deserted for a time. Thousands sold their lots
there, and bought others in Victoria or claims in Cariboo.
Cariboo was four hundred miles from the sea, and there was no
road but an old Indian trail, winding up and down mountains
and precipices, across deep gorges and rivers, through thick
woods without game; but the obstacles that would have stopped
an army were laughed at by miners. Of course the wave soon
spent itself. Had the colony been wisely governed, some thousands of the gold crusaders might have been retained as farmers,
whose labour would have enriched the country ten times as much
as all the gold of Cariboo. But the Province was not wisely
governed in those days. It "knew not the times of its visitation."
At least this was the reason assigned by most persons we
conversed with on the subject; and their testimony is confirmed

Pl. 49.

THE GREAT BLUFF ON THE THOMPSON RIVER.

in a work published in 1862 by D. G. F. M'Donald C. E., on British Columbia and Vancouvers Island, Here is his pretty strong language, page 59:—

" What has been done to forward the peopling of the country? The
" answer is short and simple,—nothing. The policy pursued has been
" disastrous in the extreme, unexampled in the history of any other
" dependency of the British Crown, and pertinaciously persisted in for
" reasons unexplained to the public, and to them incomprehensible.
" Greviously, indeed, have those persons complained who have given
" consideration to the subject of colonization, and who have felt deeply
" interested in the prosperity of the colony ; but without avail. Every
" obstacle had been cast in the way of the agriculturist, who desired to
" settle and battle with natural impediments. This, no conscientious man
" can be found to gainsay. The inflexible reply to one and all had been
" that land could not be had even at Government prices, or upon any
" terms until first surveyed and put up at auction; and that *squatting or*
" *pre-emption would not only not be tolerated, but such aggression would be*
" *visited with the summary process of ejectment by the stern arm of the law.*
" Such has been the discouraging announcement which greeted hundreds
" of hardy industrious emigrants, who finding themselves in the colony,
" and having been at the expense of landing there, had determined upon
" giving it a trial ; and these men had a full knowledge of all the natural
" obstacles incident to such settlement and many had ample means to im-
" prove their allotments, and provide for their immediate support. Lands
" denied by the marvellous blindness of officials—a blindness as culpable
" as it is inexplicable ! Has not the colony been strangled in its infancy?"

Mr. McDonald then proceeds to give a number of facts to prove his assertions, p. 60 to 67 ; but, it's no use "crying over spilt milk."

From that day, until recently, the colony has been going back, or as some gloomily say : "getting into its normal condition." Within the last ten years, millions of dollars in solid gold have been taken out of the colony. No one thought of remaining in it except to make a fortune ; no one was interested in its political life ; no one of the thousands of foreign immigrants became a subject of the Crown. It was a mere finger-joint separated from its own body. But all this is now changing. With Confederation came the dawn of a brighter future ; and, although British Columbia may never have the population of California or Oregon, an orderly development is commencing that will soon make it rank as a valuable Province of the Dominion. It has now the prospect of being no longer a dissevered limb, but of being connected by iron, as well as sympathetic, bands with its trunk ; and it is already receiving the pulses of the larger life, Had the Columbia River, instead of the 49th parallell been made its Southern boundary line, i. e., had it received its natural and rightful boundary instead of a purely artificial one, it could compete with California in cereals as well as in gold mining, But in this, as in every case of disputed lines in Amerifia, U. S. diplomatists knew the value of what they claimed, and British diplomatists did not. Every one in the Province believes that they lost the Columbia, because the "salmon in it would not take a fly." At the time of the dispute, when, too, the Secretary for War was using brave words in the House of Commons, the brother of the Prime Minister happened to be stationed on the Pacific coast, and fished in the Columbia without success, because the salmon were too uneducated to rise to a fly. He wrote home to his brother that "there was no use making a fuss about the country for it wasn't worth a ――――." And so the worthless region, now considered the most valuable on the Pacific, was gracefully given up. And why not, when it was the privately if not publicly announced aim of a school of British politicians to get rid of the whole of British America, and thus gradually work out Benjamin Franklin's problem of how "a great nation may be made into a very little one." But enough of this. We still have more good land than we know what to do with.

FRASER RIVER (17 miles above Yale.)

Our first spell to-day was thirty-two miles down the Fraser from Lytton to Boston Bar,—once a sand-bar celebrated for its rich gold deposits, and still rich enough to be washed by China-men and even a few not over ambitious whites. The road for the first ten or eleven miles ran chiefly across broken gravelly benches; and then over, or when possible, around canyons that overhung the river. The highest of these was " Jackass Mount-ain," a huge bluff of pudding stone, probably so called because before the waggon-road was made, the trail must have been strewn with the carcases of the gold seekers' mules. The road now is at an elevation of seven or eight hundred feet above the river; and a thousand feet higher up may be seen a bridge at one time only two feet wide, stretched, like a spider's web, across a deep gulch on the old trail. Many a miner, in 1862, had crawled across this on his hands and knees, with heavy packs on his shoulders, well knowing that if he slipped, there was nothing to save him from rolling and pitching over sheer perpendicular rocks, from point to point, for eighteen hundred feet into the Fraser.

The waggon road, in many places, had to be hewed sideways out of the rock, or cloven through it, or built up with log or mason work in the hollows; and the cribbing is now so much out of repair, that one couldn't help feeling uneasy occasionally. The heavy rain last night had both brought down boulders on it from the rocks above and loosened the soil at its outward edge, leaving but little firm ground for the waggon between the mountain and the edge of the bank. The slightest carelessness or recklessness in driving would have hurled the whole of us into the deep muddy torrent that rolled along swiftly at the bottom of the gorge. But the ribands were in the hands of a steady New Brunswicker, who had been on the road since it was built, in summer and winter, day-light and dark, storm and shine, and who had never once missed time or come to grief in any way.

Steve and a brother New Brunswicker, who drove the mail-coach, were now, as they deserved to be, partners in the concern. Better whips there are not; and we, therefore, cordially recommend tourists who wish to travel over a road far more grand and picturesque than the celebrated Corniceé between Genoa and Nice, to trust themselves to either of them.

We dined at Boston Bar; and by one o'clock, were on the road again, hoping to get over the remaining twenty-four miles to Yale before dark. The scenery all the way was of the same frightfully grand character as it had been for most of the forenoon, with the exception of a small patch of open ground here and there, cultivated by an enterprising settler, and on which fruits and roots of the finest kinds grow readily. Eleven miles from Yale we crossed to the west side of the Fraser over a pretty suspension bridge, and, a mile beyond had to halt, as it seemed at first, for the night. A gang of men were busy rebuilding the bridge over a strong mountain torrent, called Spuzzum's Creek, from a patriarchal Siwash chief of that ilk, who had gathered a colony around him near the bridge, in decent looking huts superior to those of the town of Lytton; and as only the stringers had been laid, there seemed nothing for it but to camp, or cross on foot and walk to Yale through a thick drizzle which had commenced. Several of the huge freight waggons used in British Columbia, each drawn by twelve or sixteen oxen, and fully a hundred pack mules had come on before us, to cross; but having been told that there was no chance, their drivers had unharnessed or unpacked them, and were idling about. Steve, however, was equal to the occasion. He offered ten dollars if the men would stop their work and place loose planks across the stringers. The bargain was struck, and in an hour the job was done. Steve unharnessed his horses and walked them across, and the men dragged after him not only his waggon, but also the mail coach which by this time had caught up to us. A

Pl. 51.

VALE OF ... (looking ... East.)

number of Siwashes were engaged on the bridge, and seemed to work on a footing of equality with the whites, with the grand exception that their wages were only $20 a month, while the whites got from $40 to $60 and their board. The general report was that the Siwash was a good fellow, obedient and industrious as long as he had " a mind to work," if liquor could be kept from him ; but that liquor made him mad. He could neither resist it nor stand it. Again we were struck with the Asiatic cast of countenance ; and some of them were handsomer, from having decidedly straighter noses, than any Chinaman we saw. But the Fraser and Lilloet Indians are said to be the best in the Province the best featured and the most industrious.

It was not quite dark when we saw the lights of Yale. Our first resort was to the Post Office armed with authority from the Governor to open the Kamloops bag. No difficulty was made, and in it were found letters and papers for everyone of the party but the Secretary. Unfortunate man ! Never did Briton look more like pariah than he as he sat looking gloomily at the others. They dealt generously by him, even handing him their own to read. He smiled and made light of it, but they instinctively felt it would be better to say nothing. The newspapers were the first things that gave relief. In their company he found solace till the "wee short hour."

October 4th.—At Yale, we said good bye to horses. Henceforth, steam, the nineteenth century horse would carry us down the river, along the coast, and across the continent homewards. Canoe and barge, buck-board and cart, saddle and pack-horse, buggy and express waggon belonged to the past of the expedition.

To-day the steamer " Onward," that runs twice a week down the Fraser from Yale, was to take us to New Westminster, the Capital of British Columbia, previous to its union in 1866 with Vancouver's Island. There, another steamer connects for Victoria, but our intention was to examine some of the harbours on the mainland before crossing to Vancouver's Island. The "Onward's" usual hour of starting is 7 A.M., but she delayed to-day till noon to oblige several gentlemen who had come up the river as far as Hope, to examine a new silver lead discovered in the mountains seven miles back from that settlement, and who wished to get back to Victoria this week. The delay gave us time to walk round Yale and up the river. The village itself has a neat, clean, and thriving appearance, as if its inhabitants had settled down to live in the country. The scenery in the neighbourhood is of the grandest kind, varying with every bend of the river. Hills rise in gradual wooded slopes for five, six, or eight hundred feet ; and above, bald rocks shoot up plumb for ten or twelve hundred feet higher. The valley is narrow, affording but little room for the farmer.

The steamer started at noon, and nine hours after reached New Westminster, distant 95 miles. The current is so strong that she could run down in six hours—subtracting stoppages, while it takes two days to work up. None of the stopping places, are of much importance, though one or two are reported to be "growing," especially the agricultural settlement of Sumass, which is beginning to supply New Westminster and Victoria with beef cattle. A little more work 'on that line' is what the Province needs most; for at present, instead of keeping her gold within her own borders, she has to export it all to buy the necessaries of life.

Soon after passing Hope, where every one got specimens o the new silver mine, the Fraser turns from its southerly to a south-westerly and then a westerly course ; and the valley begins to broaden and give some room and verge for farms. But the good land near the river does not amount to much. The Fraser has gold in its sandbars and salmon by the hundred thousand in its pools and channels ; but spite of its great length and force, the mountains between which it forces its way are too powerful for it to accomplish the usual work of rivers. It cannot overflow, no matter how immense the volume of water it rolls down to the sea ; it can only rise higher up the sides of its rocky barriers. We could see the high water mark twenty-five feet above the present level.

On board the "Onward" we met Chief Justice Begbie, another name held in profound respect by the miners, Siwashes, and all others among whom he has dealt out justice. Judge Lynch has never been required in British Columbia, because Chief Justice Begbie did his duty, and maintained the dignity of his Court as effectually as if it had been held in Old Westminster. It is a grand sight to a rightly constituted mind when two or three policemen scatter a street mob. It must have been a grander to see a British judge backed by one or two constables maintaining order at the gold mines among the tag-rag and bob-tail, the rough and tumble, fever-heated classes of miners, gamblers, claim 'jumpers,' and cuthroats who congregate at such places. For "the yellow fever" seizes upon the most daring and the most abandoned of humanity, the strongest and the weakest. And where there is no previously settled population to enforce order, what can be expected round every rich creek or gulch but a miniature "Norfolk Island" without the keepers? In such communities, especially at the outset, justice or even a little more than justice is true mercy. That Scotch Lord Braxfield who gleefully told an unfortunate wretch that 'he would be nane the waur o'a little hanging' would have been a very guardian angel in California in 1849. It is a proud thought to us that British America has proved herself a worthy daughter of the Old Mother in her judiciary ; that in no Province has a judge ever been accused as corrupted or corruptible. In British Columbia the difficulties in the way of preserving order were greatest, yet the laws have always been respected and enforced, and two or three constables proved sufficient for every emergency. The results have been simply marvellous. *The Times* Cariboo correspondent could write in 1862 :—" As to security of life I consider it just as safe here as in England." Every week for the last nine years the mail coach has carrid a box or boxes of gold dust from Cariboo with no defender but " Steve" or his partner ; and though running through a country roamed over by the lawless of every nation, where ambuscades could be planned at every turn, where for long stretches there is neither house nor shanty, it has never been plundered nor even attacked. Though comparisons are odious, they ought to be made sometimes. It is almost impossible to take up a newspaper, published on the other side of the line, without reading accounts of violent deeds in the gold fields, or of mail-coaches plundered. One fact that came under our own notice is sufficiently illustrative. On our return, the train stopped for an hour at Ogden in the Utah Territory. The first thing that attracted our attention was a series of placards on the railway station describing four different cases of highway robbery in the territory that month, and offering rewards varying from hundreds to thousands of dollars for the discovery of the highwaymen.

They tell many good stories in British Columbia of the Chief Justice's dignity on the Bench, and the terror he inspires not only the guilty but sometimes the innocent with. The last we heard ought to be true if it is not. He sternly told a witness who hesitated considerably, that he believed he was prevaricating. —" And h-how can a fellow h-help prevaricating who has l-lost his front teeth ?" was the half-frightened, half-piteous response of the poor man expecting nothing less than an order for his instant execution.

On our arrival at New Westminster, several gentlemen of the place waited on the Chief to offer him a public dinner. He felt obliged to decline, with thanks for the courtesy ; and after making arrangements to start for Burrard's Inlet in the morning, we turned into our berths in preference to going to an hotel. The Secretary got his letters at New Westminster, and as a recompense for last night's disappointment received twice as many as any other of the party.

October 5th.—The programme for the day was to drive nine miles across the spit of land, on one side of which is New Westminster, to Burrard's Inlet on the other side; see as much of the Inlet as possible; and when the steamer that the Governor had telegraphed for arrived, proceed in her to Bute Inlet, visiting on the way the surveying parties who had been at work all summer on the coast. Several New Westminster gentlemen accompanied us to Burrard's Inlet; and as the member for the district, the senior member for Victoria, and a senator from Cariboo were in town, the Chief invited them to join us in our coasting trip to the north.

As this enlargement of the party occasioned an hour's delay, there was time to look round New Westminster, before starting, The population of the little town is less than a thousand, but the importance of a town in America is not estimated so much by its population, as by its position and the extent of country it supplies. New Westminster is the only town on the delta of the Fraser, and as the delta may be said to extend east and west from Sumass to the sea, and from Boundary Bay on the south to Burrard's Inlet on the north, or over sixty miles in length by twenty in breadth, a district including much land fit for agriculture, the population and importance of the country and town are sure to increase. Its being near the mouth of the Fraser, a river seven hundred miles long, does not help it much, not only because the Fraser drains comparatively little fertile land that is well adapted for cultivation, but because the entrance is intricate on account of the tortuous channel and shifting shoals that extend out for some distance into the Gulf of Georgia. The excellent harbour of Burrard's Inlet, nine miles to the north, will therefore be generally preferred for shipping purposes. This has been already proved to a certain extent. The New Westminster proprietors of a large steam saw-mill finding Burrard's Inlet the fitter port for their shipments of lumber, transferred the machinery and set up their mill on the north side of the Inlet; so that now, little or nothing is exported from New Westminster, except fish and cattle from the neighbouring settlements. A practically unlimited quantity of fish ought to be exported ; for salmon go up the Fraser from the sea in countless numbers. They are said to be inferior in quality to those of the Atlantic coast, though we did not unanimously think so, and they would probably be quite as good for "canning." The first "trade" we saw this morning was a Klootchman selling four salmon for twenty-five cents ; and that in a country where twenty-five are less valuable than ten cents in the Eastern Provinces. A sturgeon in the fish market weighed over 300 lbs. They are sometimes caught from six to nine hundred weight, and the flavour of this fish is considered by many superior to salmon. But the Province is very young, and requires capital and enterprise before it can compete on a large scale with the fish-curing establishments on the Columbia River.

We paid a visit to the Assaying office, and the agent in charge explained the process by practical illustrations. Where there is no assay office, the miner in selling his gold is at the mercy of itinerant dealers. Now he takes his precious dust or nuggets to the office, where it is fused into ingots and the exact market value of each ingot stamped on it for a quarter per cent, or $1 for $400. The New Westminster office assayed last year of the products of the Fraser mines $100,000. The Cariboo office of course does a much more extensive business.

At 10 A.M. the united party started for Burrard's Inlet, and arrived in two hours. A lover of ferns would be charmed with this bit of road, so surprising a variety can be gathered, especially near the Inlet. Many, such as the shield, the winter, the rock, the lady fern, and the bracken, are similar to those found in the Atlantic provinces, but other varieties were altogether new to us.*

A steamer, so diminutive and toy-like that each man stepped on board tenderly for fear of upsetting or breaking her, was in waiting to take us across the Inlet to the large saw-mill owned by a firm, of which the enterprising M. P. for New Westminster is a partner. Thirteen million feet of lumber were exported last year from this, and about as much from another mill on the south side of the inlet owned by a company. All the lumber is the famous Douglas pine. Logs four to five feet in diameter were being hauled up and sawed by two circular saws, the one placed above the other, as it is easier to work on such huge subjects with two ordinary sized than with one very large saw. The workmen represented the various nationalities scattered everywhere along the Pacific coast, Whites, Chinese, Siwashes, Kanakas or Sandwich Islanders, etc.

The aborigines work well till they save enough money to live on for some time, and then they go up to the boss and frankly say that they are lazy and don't want to work longer. They are too unsophisticated to sham sickness, or to 'strike.' Another habit of the richer ones, which to the Anglo-Saxon mind borders on insanity, is that of giving universal backshish or gifts to the whole tribe, without expecting any return save an increased popularity that may lead to their election as Tyhees or chiefs when vacancies occur. An old fellow, "big George," was pointed out to us as having worked industriously at the mill for years

---

* A small collection chiefly made about Burrard's Inlet, includes the following varieties, besides two new ones that we could not make out:—Polypodium vulgare ; P. Dryopteris ; Asplenium Trichomanes ; Allosorus crispus ; Cystopteris montana ; C. fragilis ; Pteris Aquilina ; Blechnum boreale ; Polystichum acrostichoides ; P. Lonchitis ; Lastrea dilatata ; Botrychium Virginicum ; B. Lunaria ; B. lunarioides.

till he had saved $2,000. Instead of putting this in a Saving's Bank, he had spent it all on "stores" for a grand "Potlatch," summoning Siwashes from far and near to come, eat, drink, dance, be merry, and receive gifts. Nearly a thousand assembled; the festivities lasted a week; and everyone got something, either a blanket, musket, bag of flour, box of apples, or tea and sugar. When the fun was over, "big George," now pennyless, returned to the mill to carry slabs at $20 a month. His reputation mounted to an extraordinary height because of so magnificent a "potlatch," and he stood a good chance of the Tyhee-ship; but two rivals, "Supple Jack" and "Old Jim," were preparing to outdo him; and if Siwashes are at all like civilized beings, the "popularis aura" shall fill their sails before long.

Very naturally Siwashes measure all excellence by the grub or gifts they get. It is said that when a Church of England Bishop lately visited a tribe that one of his missionaries had laboured among for some time, they all gathered to meet him, being told that he was "hyass Tyhee" or great chief of the praying men. The Bishop addressed them at great length, and apparently with effect, but when done, a grave and reverend fellow rose and snuffed out his lordship with half a dozen words, which in vernacular Chinook, are even more emphatic than in any slang English they can be rendered into, "lots of gab; no grub, no gifts; all gammon." A delightful gentleman to convert certainly!

The workmen at the mill live in comfortable little houses, perched on rocks at the foot of a lofty wooded hill overhanging the shore. There is no soil except what has been made on the beach from chips and sawdust. Round the nearest point is a small tract diligently cultivated by a few Chinamen. The men have a large reading-room with an harmonium, and a well selected library. No intoxicating liquors can be sold on the premises. Their pay is good and they save money. The manager of the mill on the other side of the Inlet told us that he would give $200 a month to any competent overseer we would send him.

The woods all round these shores are well stocked with deer. The usual way of hunting is to send the dogs into the woods, and drive the deer down into the harbour, where they are at the mercy of the sportsman. The overseer informed us that in this way he could shoot a deer any day within two hours.

After lunch, we embarked on a large steamer belonging to the mill for a sail round the Inlet. At this moment, the *Sir James Douglas* the steamer the Governor had telegraphed for, arrived from Victoria. The captain came on board to put himself at the orders of the Chief, and it was arranged to start with him as soon after midnight as possible. In the meantime he proceeded with us down the Inlet.

Burrard's Inlet is naturally divided into three divisions, that are really three distinct harbours. The saw-mills are on the opposite shores of the middle one. This middle harbour narrows at both extremities, and an outer and a further inner harbour are thus made. We had time to visit only the outer and the middle, both safe and capacious harbours, with easy entrance and good anchorage. At seven P.M. we got back to the mill, and after dinner said good-bye to the New Westminster gentlemen who had kindly accompanied us. The little cabin of the *Sir James Douglas* was to be our dining and sleeping room for the next week, our last week, for after it "the home stretch" would begin.

———

The little that we saw of the mainland of British Columbia does not warrant us to say much about it as a field for emigrants. There can be no reasonable doubt that it can support in comfort a much larger population than it now has. The resources of the

U

colony are considerable, but all its industries are in their infancy, cramped from want of capital, and obliged to compete with the immense and consolidated establishments of similar industries on the other side of the boundary line. Its distance from the countries that supply emigrants, and the expense of travelling from place to place, on account of the magnificent distances within the Province itself, are great drawbacks. But on the other hand, the high price paid for all kinds of labour, the ready market for all products of the soil, and the healthiness of the climate are immense attractions to the ordinary class of emigrants. While lumbering, mining, and the fisheries offer the richest prizes to men of capital and experience, mechanics and the labouring classes can command such wages that the economy of a few years puts them in the position of small capitalists. Farm labourers especially ought to be able to buy and stock good farms of their own out of the savings of four or five years ; and then they are comfortable and independent for life. We heard the Province styled "the poor man's paradise ;" and as 10 per cent is given everywhere, with undoubted security, for the use of money, the rich man has no reason to be dissatisfied.

STRAITS OF GEORGIA AND PART OF VANCOUVER ISLAND.

Pl. 52.

CHAPTER XII.

The Coast, and Vancouver's Island.

October, 6th.—Before any of us came on deck this morning,
the good *Sir James Douglas* had steamed out of Burrard's
Inlet, and past the lofty mountains that enclose the deep fiords
of Howe Sound and Jervis Inlet, into the middle of the Straits
of Georgia. Our first sight was of the Island of Texada on our
right, and the bold outline of Vancouver's Island farther away
on our left.

After breakfast, divine service was held in the cabin. On
those inland waters of the Pacific that, folding themselves round
rocky mountain and wooded island, looked to us so lovely, we,
who had come four thousand miles from the Atlantic, united our
voices in common prayer with fellow subjects who call these
shores of the vaster Ocean of the West, their home. Again, all
found that prostration before Him, who is our Father, and also
King of Nations, not only evokes the deepest feelings of the
human heart, but also purifies them. The tie of a common
nationality, especially if the nation has a great history, is holy.
The aim of our work was to bind our country more firmly
together, and this thought elevated the work ; while worshipping
together made us feel more powerfully than any amount of
feasting and toasting the flag—that inhabitants of the same

(323)

Dominion, subjects of the same Sovereign, and heirs of the same destinies, must ever be brothers.

Towards mid-day, our course took us out of the Straits of Georgia, north-easterly up into Bute Inlet, another of those wonderful fiords of unknown depth that seam this part of the Pacific coast. The chart makes it 40 fathoms deep, with a mark over the figures signifying that the naval surveyors had sounded to that depth without finding bottom.

The object of going up this Inlet, another of the proposed ter-mini for the Railway, was to enable the Chief to get such a birds-eye view of it as he had already obtained of the prairie and the mountain country, and at the same time to meet two parties of the C. P. R. Survey, who had been at work in this quarter all summer.

On the question of which is the best western terminus, there are two great parties in British Columbia, one advocating the mainland, the other Vancouver's Island. On the mainland, New Westminster, Burrard's Inlet, and other points are proposed. If a harbor on Vancouver's Island be chosen, then the railway must cross to the shores of Bute Inlet, and follow the easiest possible route from its head through the Cascade Mountains. The advocates of the island termini, Victoria, Esquimalt, and Alberni, always asserted that it was a simple matter to cross the Straits of Georgia to the mouth of Bute Inlet by Valdes Island, which on the map does seem to block them up almost completely; then, that the line could be made along the shore of the Inlet to the mouth of the Homathco River, and up its course, through the Cascades, to the Chilcoten plains. Two main routes had there-fore to be surveyed : one, from the mouth of the Fraser River, and up the Thompson ; the other, from Vancouver's Island across to Bute Inlet, and, up the Homathco to the Upper Fraser, from whence the line could be carried by the North Thompson valley, if no direct passage across the Gold-range to the Canoe River, or Tête Jaune Cache could be found.

PITTY INLET. (looking towards Negille Peak Mountain.)

A short time after the latter survey was commenced, the engineers reported that Valdes Island, although represented on the Charts as one, really consisted of a group of three islands. The naval surveyors had seen channels piercing into Valdes Island, but had not followed them up, their business being to lay down the soundings only along the through channels, and Valdes Island, not having been explored, had always been considered an unit. The discovery of the true state of the case complicated the question, and rendered a Hydrographic survey, of four or five, instead of two "Narrows," necessary. This was work for one party, the line up Bute Inlet being assigned to another, and up the Homathco through the Cascades to a third.

On board the *Sir James Douglas* we had the member for New Westminster a zealous advocate of Burrard's Inlet, and the member for Victoria—a true believer in an Island terminus. To a student of "human natur" it was amusing to notice with what different eyes each looked at or refused to look at the difficulties of the rival routes. The former gazed exultingly on the high bluffs and unbroken line of mouutains, that rose sheer from the waters of Bute Inlet. But his sarcasms were invariably met by a counter reference to the canyôns of the Fraser and the Thompson. The Senator from Cariboo acted the part of a free lance, now backing the one and next moment the other.

There was not one of us who had ever seen anything like the Inlet we steamed up this afternoon. The inlets which cut deep iuto this coast, from the straits of Fuca northward for twelve degrees of latitude, probably resemble the fiords of Norway, but none of our party could speak of those from personal observation.

It is a singular fact that, while there is not a single opening in the coast for seven hundred miles north of San Francisco, except the bad harbour of Astoria at the mouth of the Columbia river, the next seven or eight hundred miles should be broken by

innumerable inlets. The case is paralleled on the Atlantic side
of North America. From Florida to Maine there are very few
good ports, while north of Maine, embracing the coast of New
Brunswick and Nova Scotia, there are scores. The openings in
the ironbound coast of Nova Scotia are not unlike those on the
Pacific side, except that on the Atlantic the indentations do not
cut so deep into the land, and the shores are low.

Up into the very heart of the Cascade range through a
natural passage, which could not have been formed by the
Ocean, for the coast is protected here from its erosions by Vancouver's Island, we sailed to-day for forty miles, over water
almost as deep under our keel as the snow-capped mountains
that hemmed the passage were high above our heads. The
Inlet varies in breadth from one to two-and-a-half miles, and so
deep is it in every part that a ship may sail up and down close
enough to the shore, in most places, for a man to jump to the
rocks.

A mist, followed by a drizzliug rain, came on early in the
afternoon, and hid the snmmits of the mountains, but the gleam
of scores of white cataracts could be seen ; and, like furrows
amid the dark spruce, the clean sides of the rocks in long
straight lines showed where avalanches had swept every thing
before them into the deep waters below. Half way up the Inlet,
we saw a tent on the shore. A whistle brought it's tenant out to
us in a canoe ; and he proved to be a commissary who had preceded X party a few miles, in order to make necessary arrangements for their advance. An hour after, we passed camp X., but,
as the mist had thickened and our captain had never been in
these waters before, he steamed on without stopping, for
Waddington harbour at the head of the Inlet. This point he
reached after dark, and at once sent a boat's crew ahead to
sound for an anchoring place. After some delay, between seven
and eight P.M., the boatswain held up a lantern in the boat to

Pl. 54.

THE HAMATHCO. *(looking up from head of Bute Inlet.)*

indicate where soundings had been found.   Steaming up to the light the anchor was let go in twenty-five fathoms, quarter of a mile from the shore and from the head of the Inlet.

October 7th.—A magnificent view awaited those early on deck this morning.   Nearly two hours were spent in weighing anchor, and then the steamer went round the harbour to enable us to see it on all sides.   Rain had fallen steadily through the night, and, now that it had ceased, mist clouds hung about the great masses of rock that on all sides rose perpendicularly into the region of eternal snow.   Here and there, rifts in the mist, as it was broken by projecting peaks, revealed mountain sides curtained with glaciers.   The only sound which broke the awful stillness was the muffled thunder of cataracts, multiplied by last night's rain, gleaming far up among the scanty pines, washing down the slippery rocks in broad white bands, or leaping from bluff to bluff an hundred feet at a time, for more than a thousand feet down to the sea.   We were at the head of Bute Inlet.   The salt sea water could cut no deeper into the range that guards the western side of our continent.   The mountains stood firm except where the Homathco cuts its way through, in a deep gorge, sentinelled on each side by snow-clad warders.

By this water-highway of Bute Inlet, the late Mr. Waddington had urged the Government of British Columbia to make their road to Cariboo.   On their adopting the Fraser River route, he organized a private company and began its construction, so convinced was he, that, its superiority would attract to it the travel between Cariboo and the outside world, and that a toll on goods carried over it would soon repay the cost of construction.   His project was a steamer from Victoria to the head of Bute Inlet, and a waggon road thence up the Homathco to Cariboo ; the distance being 175 miles less this way than by the Fraser.   After spending $60,000 on surveys and on trail making, his men were murdered in 1864 by a tribe of Indians to whom provocation

had been given. The Government secured the arrest of the
murderers, and had them hung up at Quesnel mouth; but, from
that day, the Coast and Chilcotin Indians have been regarded as
dangerous and blood-thirsty. The C. P. R. parties, who travelled
the country this year, had no trouble however; and Mr. Smith
reports that the Chilcotins are the manliest and most intelligent
Siwashes in the Province.

From the description that Mr. Smith gave us of the scenery
on the Homathco, we would fain have landed and gone at least a
few miles up the river : but time did not permit. He had worked
up from the head of the Inlet through the Cascades in July last,
overcoming by sheer determination not to be beaten—all difficulties of forest, canyons, torrents, and lazy treacherous Indians ;
getting surveys at great risk of neck and limb, by felling trees
across deep chasms from one to two hundred feet wide, and letting men down by ropes to the foot of high cliffs. The following
extracts from one of his private letters to the Chief give more
vivid pictures than any plate can, of scenes up the river. Here
is what he says of the canyon, 31 miles from the head of the
Inlet, and immediately above the rope ferry used by Mr. Waddington which is shown, as it then existed, in one of the plates.—
" I commenced the survey of the canyon, following the river
on the new trail commenced by Waddington, as far as it went,—
about half a mile,—when it terminated at an inaccessible bluff
on which blasting had been commenced. The scene here is
awfully sublime. The towering rocks, thousands of feet high ;
—far above these again the snow-clad peaks, connected by huge
glaciers ; and in a deep gorge beneath, a mountain torrent—
whirling, boiling, roaring, and huge boulders always in motion—
muttering, groaning like troubled spirits, and ever and anon
striking on the rocks, making a report like the booming of
distant artillery. But with all this wildness, there is the fresh
beauty of vegetation. Wherever there is a crevice in the rocks

Pl. 55.

THE HAMATHCO BELOW THE DEFILE.

large enough to hold a few inches of soil, trees are growing and wild flowers blooming."

After getting through "the core of the Cascade range," he came upon "the murderers' camp, where thirteen of Waddington's men were murdered eight years ago. The spot looks as if it had never before been visited by man since the massacre. The number of tents could be counted by the cedar bark forming the beds. Strewed around were various tools,—a blacksmith's anvil, sledge-hammers, crowbars, grindstone, vice, picks, and half a dozen shovels carefully placed against a tree ready for the morrow's work ; also pieces of clothing, amongst which were at least one pair of woman's boots—too surely indicating the source of the trouble." This last clause suggests the origin of more than one "Indian atrocity." It's a fair question to ask always, "Who struck the first blow?" So much for the Homathco.

The forenoon was spent by us in coasting down the northerly side of the Inlet until we came to camp X. After inspecting their work we proceeded on our way down, Mr. Gamsby, the engineer in charge of party X. accompanying us. He reported that the Indians, far from giving any trouble, had been of material assistance in many ways, acting as servants or messengers, and selling deer, wildfowld, fish etc., at moderate prices. He pointed out a stream, running into the Inlet on the east side, at the mouth of which, on a recent visit, he had seen hundreds of thousands of dead salmon strewn along the shore ; while thousands of crows, kites, vultures, and eagles filled the air. In similar places, such sights must have been common when white men first came to the country. These Pacific waters swarm with fish, that struggl. up brawling streamlets to spawn, in spite of rapids, cascades, rocks, and shallows. No wonder that people, who have only eaten salmon caught inland, say that the Pacific varieties are inferior. They were good when they entered the river's mouth ; but, when caught a few hundred miles up the

Fraser, often the head is bruised by rocks and falls, and the scales, fins, and even the tail rubbed or worked off. No wonder that half of them perish by the way, and that none return to the sea. It is asserted as a fact, every where in British Columbia, that none of the salmon entering the Fraser river, and even the smaller streams, ever return to the sea.

We were struck with the beauty of Gamsby's canoe, and indeed of all the Indians canoes on this coast. Each is a model of architectural grace, although the lines reminded us of Chinese or Japaness rather than of British models. The canoes are generally made out of a single large log. After scooping out the log, they steam it in the following primitive manner.—Filling it with water, they throw in heated stones to make the water boil, and at the same time build a bark-fire round the outside. The wood "gives" several inches, until the central part of the canoe is made broader at the top, and the requisite curvature given to its sides. The proper shape is secured by putting in stretchers like a boat's thwarts : outside and inside are then painted ; an ornamental figure-head set on, and the canoe is complete.

By midday the mouth of Bute Inlet was gained, but instead of returning in the direction of Burrard's Inlet, we ran through Arran Rapids in order to pass round the north side of Valdes' Island. At every turn, the beautiful views which an archipelago affords, met our eyes. The islands of every possible variety of form, were wooded from lofty summits to the brink of deep channels. At one time we were in cross-roads where four different channels opened out, north, south, east, and west ; soon after in a narrow winding strait, or shooting swiftly through tidal rapids, or in a broad bay where snowy peaks could be seen behind the green foothills. After passing through Seymour Narrows, where, if there is to be a continuous line from an Island terminus, the bridge between Valdes' and Vancouver must be built, we rounded into a beautiful land-locked harbor, called Menzies

Bay, and cast anchor for the night. Between the Narrows and the Bay, the tents of Y. party were picturesquely pitched, on an open easy slope, under the shadow of the forest. A whistle from the steamer brought Mr. Michaud, who is in charge of the party, on board, and, after dinner, all rowed off to his encampment, the Chief to inspect plans, the rest to see the camp. As compared with all the others, Y. party has been in clover from the beginning of their work. They were near Victoria, had a monthly mail, and could renew their supplies as they ran out. Their store-house filled with bags of flour, flitches of bacon, pork, molasses, split peas, beans, pickles, and a keg of beer, suggested good cheer; while any day, they could buy from the Indians a deer, weighing from 120 to 160 lbs., for one, or according to circumstances, two dollars; and salmon, trout, wild-geese, duck, or mallard, for trifling sums. They had no deer-meat in camp to-day, but they generously presented us with two wild-geese, each weighing ten or eleven lbs.

October 8th.—Our programme for the day was to reach Nanaimo Coal Mines as soon as possible, for the steamer's bunkers needed replenishing, and we all wished to see something of the mines, which promise to be of more benefit to British Columbia than all the gold-fields. Accordingly at 4 A.M. the anchor was weighed.

We were now getting into waters familiar to our captain; for strange as it may appear, not one on board with the exception of Mr. Smith, had ever been up Bute Inlet or round Valdes Island before this trip. Nothing shows more clearly the youthful and imperfectly developed condition of the Province than such a fact. Her representative men, those most likely to be best acquainted with her resources, know little beyond their own neighbourhood or the line of their one waggon-road. Distances here are so great, the means of communication so limited, and the mountainous character of the country renders travelling so difficult, that the dwellers in the few towns and settlements have hitherto seen but little of the Province as a whole.

When we appeared on deck about 7 o'clock, the steamer was running down the Straits of Georgia, over a rippling, sun-lit sea. The lofty Beaufort range, on our right, rose grandly in the clear air, every snowy peak distinct from its neighbour, and the blue sky high above the highest. Victoria, and the twin peaks Albert Edward and Alexandra, ranging from 6,000 to over 7,000 feet in height, were the most prominent; but it was the noble serrated range as a whole, more than separate peaks, that caught the eye. The smaller Islands to the left were hidden by a fog-bank that gradually lifted. Then stood out, not only islet after islet in all their varied outline, but also the long line of the Cascade range behind. Yesterday had been charming from 10 o'clock, when the sun pierced through the mists; but to-day was "all white." A soft warm breeze fanned us, and every mile disclosed new features of scenery, to which snow-clad mountain ranges, wooded plains, and a summer sea enfolding countless promontories and islands, contributed their different forms of beauty. The islands are composed of strata of sandstone and conglomerate; the sandstone at the bottom worn at the water line into caves and hollows; the conglomerate above forming lofty cliffs, wooded to the summits, and overhanging winding inlets and straits most tempting to a yachtsman. From the southern point of Valdes Island down to Nanaimo, a considerable area of low lying and undulating land extends between the central mountain range of Vancouver's Island and the Straits of Georgia, well adapted for farming purposes. At two points, Comox and Nanoose, settlements have been formed within the last few years, and are prospering; but where there is one settlement there ought to be twenty, if the island is to raise its own grain and hay, and to cease sending out of the country all its wealth. There is little or no immigration to Vancouver's Island, and but little has been done to induce it, or to smooth the way for those who arrive. When an immigrant reaches the country, he finds it difficult to obtain information as to where there is good land to take up; and how is it possible for him to go out among a sea of mountains to search for a farm? The island should be thoroughly surveyed according to the simple system long practised in the United States and lately adopted in Manitoba; the amount of good land known, divided into sections and subsections, and numbered; so that, on arriving at Victoria, the immigrant could go into the Crown Land office, learn what land was pre-empted, and where it would be expedient for him to settle. There are many obstacles in the way of immigrants reaching this distant colony, and therefore special efforts are required to bring them, and to keep them when they come; for, until there is a large agricultural population, the wealth of the country must continue to be drained out of it, in order to buy the necessaries of life and every article of consumption, from Oregon, California, Great Britain, and elsewhere.

We were sorry at not being able to visit Comox. Our information about it is therefore second-hand; but testimony was unanimous concerning the good quality of the land, the accessibility to markets, and the prosperity of the settlers, notwithstanding the short time they have been in the country.

By noon we had left the Beaufort range behind, and Mount Arrowsmith came into view; while far ahead on the mainland, and south of the 49th parallel, what looked a dim white pyramid rising to the skies, or a white cloud resting upon the horizon, was pointed out to us by the Captain as Mount Baker. Soon after, we rounded into the northern horn of Nanaimo harbour, called Departure Bay, and drew alongside the pier where a lately organized Company is shipping coal from a new seam that has been opened, three miles back from the point of shipment.

Landing here, and leaving the steamer to coal, most of us walked by a trail to Nanaimo through the woods, along a channel that connects Departure Bay with the old mines. The channel, which is an excellent roadstead is between the mainland of Vancouver and a little Island called Newcastle, on the inner side of which another excellent coal mine, within ten feet of navigable water, has just been opened. There are two seams at Newcastle, averaging three feet each and separated by three feet of fire clay, which as the miners proceed becomes thinner, the coal seams becoming thicker. From this convergence it is supposed that the clay will soon give out, and the two seams of coal unite into one. Near this Newcastle mine, is a quarry of light colored freestone of excellent quality, from which the mint at San Fransisco has just been built, and which is sure to be of immense service and value in the near future. There is no such freestone quarried on the Pacific coast ; and its convenience for shipping makes it doubly valuable.

At Nanaimo proper, is a population of seven or eight hundred souls,—all depending on the old or Douglas mine. The manager informed us that they would probably ship fifty thousand tons this season, while last year they shipped less than thirty thousand ; and that, next year, they would be in a position to ship an hundred thousand or more. They could give employment to fifty or sixty additional men at once, at wages averaging from two to three dollars a day. A new seam, nine feet thick, had lately been discovered, below the old one ; and we went down the shaft three hundred feet to see it. The coal was of the same excellent quality as that of the old mine, which is the best for gas or steam purposes on the Pacific coast. But the miners had come upon "a fault" in the seam, caused by the dislocation of the strata, immediately above and below, intruding a tough conglomerate rock that they were now cutting away in the hope of its soon giving out. The coal measures which these few seams now worked represent, extend over the whole eastern coast of Vancouver Island, and like those on the east of the Rocky Mountains are cretaceous or of tertiary age. They are considered as valuable as if they were carboniferous and are certain to be fully developed before long.

It is provoking to know, however, that the agricultural settlements in the neighborhood, which, though small, are the most extensive on the island, are not able to supply the present population of Nanaimo with food; and that no steps are taken to bring in new settlers, though there is abundance of good land all round. If this state of things continues, even though the mining population of Vancouver's Island increase ten fold in as many years, most of the wealth will be sent out of the country, as was the gold of Cariboo, and the country in the end be as poor as ever.

Nanaimo does not look like a coal mining place. The houses are much above the average of miners' residences in Britain or in Nova Scotia. Scattered about, often in picturesque situations, with gardens, and not in long, mean, soot-covered rows, as if laid out with the idea that men who see nothing of beauty underground cannot be expected to appreciate it above. The view from the town, of the Cascades range, on the other side of the Straits is almost equal to the view of the long semi-circular line of the Alps from Milan. At sunset, when warmed with the roseate light, or, a little later, when a deep soft blue has displaced the *couleur de rose*, the beauty is almost inconsistent with the ash heaps and tenements of a mining village. Though not a believer in the " God made the country ; man made the town " sentiment, the contrast irresistibly suggests the words.

In the evening a concert was held on behalf of the Episcopal Church of the place, and all our party went to see ' the beauty and fashion, the bone and sinew' of Nanaimo. The hall, which holds about two hundred was well filled, and the entertainment

consisted of music, vocal and instrumental, and magic lantern
views.   The prologue by the Rector, the songs, the dresses of
the ladies, reminded us of a world left behind three months ago.
We had got back to civilization.   The Ontario papers that
reviled the constituency that returned Sir F. Hincks, should send
reporters to Nanaimo ; for only men who have been accustomed
to describe such assemblages could do justice to the beauty of
the women, the intelligence of the men, the musical taste of the
Rector and the choir.   If an impartial report concerning the
Nanaimo concert were given, no further doubt would be entertained in the East, of the Vancouver districts' right to have a
Cabinet Minister for their representative.

October, 9th.—Another day of glorious weather ; such weather
as Vancouver's Island has, almost without interruption, from
March till October or November ; warm enough for enjoyment
and cool enough for exercise.   Our course was down the Gulf
of Georgia to Victoria ; past the agricultural districts of Cowichan
and Saanich on the Vancouver side, and the various islands
that line the mainland on our left.   Mount Baker was the great
feature in the landscape all day.   We could hardly help feeling
envious that the United States instead of ourselves possessed
so glorious a landmark ; especially as it still bears the name of
the British Naval Officer in Capt. Vancouver's ship who first saw
it, and is in the country that was formally taken possession of,
for the British Crown in 1792, and that had been, up to 1846,
held by a British Company.   Indeed, it is difficult even to conceive of any plausible excuse that the United States could have
brought forward, in claiming the country round Puget's Sound.
They knew its value, and the British Premier, not only did not,
but his brother had assured him that the whole country wasn't
worth talking about, much less the risk of war ; for " the
salmon wouldn't take a fly."

On the fourth of April 1792, the birthday of King George III, after whom he had named the Straits of Georgia, Captain Vancouver took formal possession of all the waters of Puget Sound, and of the coast north and south along which he had sailed, for His Majesty, whose commission he carried. All the prominent capes, points, harbours, straits, mountains, bear to this day, the names of his lieutenants or friends, just as he named them on his great voyage. He changed nothing. As the old Portuguese navigator, Juan de Fuca, had discovered the Straits of Fuca, his name was honorably preserved, and as Vancouver met a Spanish Squadron that had been sent out to give up Nootka and other Spanish claims on the coast to Great Britain, he adopted the names that the Dons had given to any channels or islands, such as Valdez, Texada, Straits of Melaspina, etc. Puget Sound, he named from his second lieutenant ; Mount Baker, from his third ; Cape Mudge, from the first ; Mount Rainier, from Rear Admiral Rainier ; Capes Grey and Atkinson, Burrard, Jervis, and Bute Inlets, Fort Discovery, Johnstone's Channel, and a hundred others were all alike named by him ; and if Britain had no right to those south of the 49th parallel, she had no right to those farther north.

Still more astonishing : in 1846 when Britain yielded the Columbia River and the whole Pacific side of the continent up to the 49th parallel, not a single citizen of the United States had settled to the north of the Columbia. Swarms from the Western States had flocked into Oregon in the ten preceding years of joint occupation, and so the Government at Washington might plead the will of the settlers against the Imperial rights of Britain ; but that plea could have carried them, at the farthest, only to Astoria. If Oregon had to be ceded, the Columbia River should have been the boundary.

It may be said that all this is a reviving of dead issues, out of place and useless now. But the history of the past throws light on the present, and is a beacon for the future. Had the

V

San Juan difficulty been viewed, not merely in the light of the literal wording of the Treaty of 1846, but in the light of all the facts, the decision of the Emperor of Germany must have been different.

Before noon we entered the Haro Strait that separates San Juan (pronounced here "San Wân") from Vancouver's Island. Between the northern part of the Haro Channel and Vancouver's Island, are several islets and two narrow channels, that ships going to Victoria may take. South of these, there is nothing between San Juan and the southern extremity of Vancouver, but the Haro Strait, six or seven miles wide. It is therefore evident that while San Juan would be useless to Britain for military purposes, its possession by the United States is a menace to us; for it commands the entrance to British waters, British shores, a British river, and a British Province. There is a hill on San Juan about a thousand feet high, a battery on which would command the whole Strait.

There are many conjectures here as to the effect of the Emperor's judgment, should it be adverse, some think his decision would throw a heavy sword into the scale against New Westminster or Burrard's Inlet as a terminus for the Canadian Pacific Railway.

The sail down the Straits of Haro was all that a pleasure party on board a steam yacht could have desired. On the mainland, the long line of the Cascades or Coast range broken by the Delta of the Fraser extended to the south,—though dwarfed into comparative insignificance by the mighty mass of Mount Baker, rising up in the midst. Farther south, the line swept round the deep gulf of Puget Sound, then north-westerly and away as far west as the entrance of the Straits of Fuca, under the name of the Olympian range. When under the lee of San Juan the snowy pyramid of Mount Baker looked out on us over the Island, while far to the south, in the back ground of the Olympian range, the dim form of Mount Rainier was seen lifting

Pl. 56.

JUAN DE FUCA STRAIT TO THE PACIFIC OCEAN.

itself up in the sky. Rounding the southern point of Vancouver's Island, we came to the spit of land that is cut into by the harbour of Victoria and four miles further west by the much superior harbour of Esquimalt. We steamed first into Victoria to get letters and telegrams, and proceeded immediately thereafter to Esquimalt, returning at 4 P.M., some of us by land, over a good macadamized road, and some in the *Sir James Douglas*.

The harbour of Victoria has a narrow entrance, is small, inconveniently shaped, and accommodates only vessels of eighteen feet draught of water ; but as Esquimalt is near enough to serve as an additional harbour, Vicioria does not suffer. Esquimalt harbour is a gem ; not very large, but the anchorage is excellent, and it has all the other requisites of a first-class harbour ; and in " the Royal Roads " outside, along the coast as far as Race Rocks, any number of slips can ride safely. In Esquimalt, one U. S. and four British men-of-war lay, two of the latter having been just paid off. We were astonished to find that the British Government had not constructed a dock at Esquimalt, and that now it is not even the headquarters of the Pacific squadron, the foreign port of Valparaiso having been selected instead. Esquimalt is our own, our interests are along the coast, coal is near, China and Japan only fifteen days distant, and the Admiral could be in daily communication when necessary with the Home authorities. The only reasons assigned on the other side are that British Commercial interests in South America are paramount, and that sailors desert at Esquimalt and get off easily to the States. The same reasons ought to be conclusive against Halifax as the head-quarters of the North American squadron, and in favour of adopting Rio or some other South American port in its stead.

The terms of confederation with the Dominion included a guarantee of the interest on £100,000 stg. for ten years from the completion of the work, for a first-class Graving Dock at Esquimalt, and the Provincial Government has accordingly taken steps to commence its construction.

On our return to Victoria in the afternoon, one of the first persons we met in the street was Terry. Having no further need of his services, we had parted with him last week at New Westminster. He had gone on to Victoria direct and had monopolized the lionizing intended for the whole party; had been interviewed about our marvellous north-west passage by land, with results as given in the newspapers, that spoke quite as much for Terry's imagination as for his memory. He had conjured up a Canyon on the Canoe River twenty miles long, where no Canyon is or ever had been; had described us as galloping down the Yellow Head Pass till arrested by the sight of quartz boulders gleaming with gold, and rocks so rich that Brown and Beaupré had deserted to go back and mine; and, with many another fact or fancy equally readable, made the hearts of reporters glad. "Drinks" had probably been the reward, and the consequences to Terry proved serious. For on the first day after being paid in full at the office in Victoria for his long trip, he had been plundered of every dollar. He was now looking round for work; and before we left Victoria, hired as general servant on board a ship going north. Thus disappeared Terry into space. Should any one in future wish to engage him, we hereby certify him as a good servant, a good tailor, a good cobbler, and indeed anything but a good cook, the post which, unfortunately for us, he filled. In his own words, "he never liked being boss; but could be understrapper to any any one," and, such a man is a treasure in America.

A walk through the streets of Victoria showed the little capital to be a small polyglot copy of the world. Its population is less than 5,000; but almost every nationality is represented. Greek fishermen, Kanaka sailors, Jewish and Scotch merchants, Chinese washerwomen or rather washermen, French, German and

Yankee restaurant-keepers, English and Canadian officeholders and butchers, negro waiters and sweeps, Australian farmers and other varieties of the race, rub against each other, and apparently in the most friendly way. The sign-boards tell their own tale: "Own Shing, washing and ironing"; "Sam Hang," ditto; "Kwong Tai & Co., cigar store"; "Magasin Français"; "Teutonic Hall, lager beer"; "Scotch House"; "Adelphic" and "San Francisco" saloons; "Oriental" and "New England" restaurants; "What Cheer Market," and "Play me off at ten-pins," are all found within gunshot, interspersed with more common-place signs.

The senior member for the city had invited several gentlemen to dine with us at the Colonial Hotel at 5 o'clock. A better dinner could not be served in Montreal. We were only sorry that we had to leave at 7, to go on board the *Sir James Douglas*, and proceed to Alberni Channel, one of the proposed termini on the west coast of Vancouver's Island. But time was precious, as the San Francisco steamer was expected to be in every hour. Parting with Mr. Smith, and adding the second member for Victoria to our number, we went down to our little steamer and started on this, our last expedition, at 7.30 P.M.

October 10th.—The distance between Victoria and the Pacific by the Straits of Fuca is sixty miles. The *Sir James Douglas* made that by midnight, and then turned north for the spacious Archipelago of Barclay's Sound, from the head of which Alberni Canal, or to use the modern word Channel, a deep narrow fiord like those on the main land, cuts its way up into the interior of Vancouver's Island. Barclay Sound has three entrances, separated from each other by groups of islets and rocks, and as the nearest is the best for ships from the south, the Captain intended to run up by it into Alberni. The weather during the night was so favourable that he over-ran his distance, and never having been in the sound before, he waited for daylight to compare the coast with the charts. Those who came early on deck had thus an opportunity of seeing the Pacific breaking on the iron shores of Vancouver. Away behind us the great ocean stretched unbroken to Japan and China, sleeping peacefully—under the morning light that was shining over the mountains to the east—with no motion save a slow voluptuous roll of long billows that seemed gentle enough to be stayed by a child's hand. But to know their strength, even in a calm, turn and look where these same billows meet the headlands. Over the first they break with a heavy roar ; and then, as if amazed to be resisted, they gather up their forces and rush with a long wild leap, like white-maned war-horses charging, among the inner breakers, to meet the fate that a gallant ship would meet if it mistook the entrance to the sound. When a gale is blowing from the west, the surf must be tremendous, for there is nothing to break the roll of the Pacific for 2,000 miles ; but the entrances into the sound are wide, and one or two lighthouses would obviate all risk. The most prominent mark about the southern entrance at present is Ship Island, probably so called from a number of bare trees on it like the masts of a ship. Beyond the coast line a bold range of serrated mountains runs along the centre of the island, like a backbone, north and south, into the heart of which Alberni Channel pierces.

Passing up the sound, several canoes with from two to half-a-dozen Indians in each hailed us with friendly shouts. They are squat in shape, dirtier, more savage, with a more decided cross-eye than the Indians on the main land. In all probability this side of America was peopled from Asia, and not necessarily round by Behring's Straits and the Aleutian Islands. Even in this century Japanese junks, dismasted in a typhoon or otherwise disabled, after drifting for months about the North Pacific have stranded on the American continent or been encountered by whaling ships, and the survivors of the crews rescued, in those cases where all had not perished of hunger.

Pl. 57.

There are two or three trading posts and several Indian villages on Barclay Sound. The traders come to the posts in schooners at certain seasons of the year, and trade for peltries, seal-oil, and fish. The scenery along the sound and up the channel resembles Bute Inlet, except that the hills do not rise so sheer and high from the water and the wood is better. There are also larger extents of open alluvial ground at the mouths of streams that run into the sea, and along the valleys between the hills that they drain. At the head of Alberni, is the Sumass, a river of considerable size that drains large lakes in the interior and is said to be bordered by extensive tracts of fertile soil. At its mouth is enough good land for several farms, but there are no settlers. An English Company formerly worked saw-mills at this point, from which in 1862 over eight million feet of lumber were exported. The working of the mills has been abandoned, as the speculation did not pay, and the premises are now going to ruin. A walk round showed us one reason at least of the failure. Too much money had been sunk in house, orchard, outhouses, and other "fixtures" and improvements that yielded no return. No sane man would have started on such a scale with his own money. It was a sorry spectacle to see so many good buildings doorless and windowless, falling into decay or broken up by the Siwashes for wood to burn. In a country whose lumbering interests require development it is too bad that capitalists should be deterred by such an example.

Alberni harbour offers such decided advantages as a terminus that it may prove a formidable rival even to Esquimalt.

After a bathe in the harbour, the water being wonderfully warm for the time of year, we steamed out into the Ocean again, and got back in time to see a glorious sunset on the Pacific. The twilight continued for an hour after ; a band of carmine that shaded into orange and, higher up, into mauve, lingering so long over the horizon that we ceased to look at it,

and only when turning into our berths, noticed that it had given
way to the universal deep blue of the night sky.   The sea was
smooth and the night calm and beautiful as the preceding ; and
in consequence we were at the wharf in Victoria harbour
between four and five A. M., to the astonishment of the citizens
who had not expected us back till the afternoon or next day.

October, 11th to 14th.—It had been assumed that the *Prince*
Alfred steamer would leave Victoria for San Francisco on the
twelfth ; but her day was changed to the fourteenth as she had
to go to Nanaimo to coal.   We had thus three days to spend in
Victoria instead of one, and so great was the hospitality of the
people that three months might have been spent enjoyably.
Various as are the nationalities and religions represented in
Victoria ; the people are wonderfully fused in one, and there is
a general spirit of mutual toleration, kindness, and active good
will that makes it a pleasant town to live in.   Like the whole
colony it is a poor man's paradise.   Everyone seems to have
plenty of money ; and every kind of labour receives enormous
prices.   There is no copper currency and the smallest silver piece
is what is called 'a bit' ; the ten cent and the English sixpence
though of different values being alike called 'bits,' and given to
children or put in church-door plates (there are no beggars) as
cents or coppers are in all other countries.   This absence of
small coins has much to do with the general cost of living and
the indifference to small profits characteristic of all classes here.
The merest trifle costs 'a bit' ; and though there are 25 and 50
cent pieces in currency, yet, if anything is worth more than a
bit, with a lofty indifference to the intermediate coins, the price
is generally made a dollar.   Emigrants on landing and men
with fixed incomes are the chief sufferers from this state of
things ; for as mechanics, labourers, and servants are paid accordingly, they like it, and speak with intensest scorn of the unfor-
tunates who would devide 'a bit' because they perhaps think

it too much to give for a paper of pins or an apple. "John" who comes across the Pacific to make money and then return to the flowery land doesn't heed their scorn; and so, most of it was reserved before Confederation for canny Canadians who received the flattering appellation of North American Chinamen. The Californians being as well supplied with gold and as lavish with it as the Victorians themselves.

All this was very well in the halcyon days of the young Province, when gold-dust was accounted as nothing; when miners who had been six months in Cariboo would come down to the capital and call for all the champagne in an hotel to wash their feet; eat £10 notes as pills, or as a sandwich with a slice of pork, or light their pipes with them; and when town lots commanded higher prices for the moment than in Frisco. But the tide turned; the gold flowed out of the country to buy the champagne, and more necessary articles, instead of being spread abroad among resident farmers, or manufacturers; Cariboo yielded less abundant harvests; and the inflated prosperity of Victoria collapsed. Lots that had been bought at from $10,000 to $25,000 have been sold since, it is said, for $500; the 15,000 people who lived around the city in tents have taken flight, like wild geese to more Southern climates; and the then reputed millionaires are now content with a modest business. The *virus* however is still in the blood of the Victorians. They half expect that the good old times, when every man got rich without effort on his part, will come again; that something will turn up; new mines, or the railway being now the chief objects of reliance, to make business brisk. This delusion which belongs to the gambling rather than the true trading spirit retards the growth of the city: for it makes men hold on to house and business lots, or demand sums for them far beyond their real value. A mere rumour last winter that Esquimalt was to be the terminus of the railway, at once sent

up real estate in its neighbourhood four or five fold.   The balloon
has been accustomed to gas, and is easily inflated again.   Great
part of the four miles between Esquimalt and Victoria is owned
by a company called " the Puget Sound."   This land is held at
prices too high for settlers or gardeners to buy and improve,
and thus it is that the suburbs do not present the cultivated
appearance that might have been expected from the soil and
fine climate.   High prices for land and for everything else in
and around the town, and extreme difficulty of obtaining information about good land elsewhere; what condition of affairs
could be more discouraging for emigrants or intending settlers?

An infusion of new blood is required.   At present the classes
that ought to come are servant girls, labourers, mechanics,
miners, farm-servants and such like, for these would get remu-
nerative employment at once ; and, gradually, land would be
taken up, and money diffused in so many hands that there would
be a healthy flow instead of the present comparative stagnation
and universal waiting for " better times."

In looking at Victoria and the surrounding coast the situation
is so commanding that it is difficult to avoid speculating a little
as to its probable future.   The Island is at the end of *the west*
and the beginning of *the east*.   Behind it, over the mountains,
stretch the virgin plains of our North-west extending to the
Great Lakes.   Fronting it, are the most ancient civilizations and
the densest masses of humanity on the surface of the globe.
With such a position, the harbours, minerals, fish, and timber of
this colony all become important.   If the " golden gate " be one
passage-way between the old world and the new, the straits of
Fuca and its harbours, the channels of Vancouver's Island and
the inlets of the mainland are many.   To our railway terminus
will converge the products of Australia and Polynesia as well as
of China and Japan ; and all that the busy millions of Great
Britain need can be sent to them across their own territory, in-

dependently of the changing phases of the eastern question. Neither the Suez Canal nor the Euphrates Valley can ever belong to England. But let there be a line of communication from the Pacific to the St. Lawrence through a succession of loyal Provinces bound up with the Empire by ever-multiplying and tightening links, and the future of the Fatherland and of the Great Empire of which she will then be only the Chief part is secured. With such a consummation in view, should not he be considered an enemy to the Common-weal who would dissever the western or American portion of so great an Empire from its foundation, from its capital and centre, simply because a belt of Ocean intervenes ; a belt too that is becoming less of an obstacle every year. For in a few years we shall have a Railway with but one break from the Pacific coast to the extreme easterly side of Newfoundland, and from thence daily steamers will cross the Atlantic in a hundred hours. Canada will be as near London then as Scotland and Ireland were forty years ago. It will then be easier to make the journey from Victoria to London than it was to make it from the North of Scotland at the beginning of the century. These results, however marvelous, will be due to steam alone. How much nearer to the core of the Empire may not Canada be considered with the means of instantaneous telegraphic communications extended to every part of the Dominion ?

But it would be unworthy of our past to think in this connection only of material progress and national consolidation and security. Loftier have ever been the aims of our forefathers. It is not enough for us to allow Chinamen to come to our shores merely that, while living, they may do our rough work cheaply, repelled the while from us by systematic injustice and insult, and that when dead a Company may clear money by carrying their bodies back to their own land. A nation to be great must have great thoughts ; must be inspired with lofty ideals ; must have men and women

willing to work and wait and war 'for an idea.' To be a light
to the dark places of the earth ; to rule inferior races mercifully
and justly ; to infuse into them a higher life ; to give them ' the
good news ' that makes men blessed and free, believing that as
the race is one, reason one, and conscience one, there is one Gospel
for and unto all ; nothing less than this was the thought—deeply
felt if sometimes inarticulately expressed—of our great ancestors
in the brave days of Old. And it is ours' also. By the possession
of British Columbia and Vancouver's Island we look across
into the very eyes of four hundred millions of heathen, a people
eager to learn, acute to investigate, and whom the struggle for
existence in thronged centres has made tolerant, patient, and
hardy.   Can we do nothing but trade with them ?

October 14th.—To-day we left Esquimalt by the "Prince
Alfred" on "the home stretch," friends on the wharf giving us
kindly parting cheers.   A delightful voyage of four days down
the coast brought us to San Francisco ; a wonderful city ' for its
age,' though not equal to Melbourne, the only other city in the
world it ought to be compared with.   Doubtless it is a fine thing
to escape frost and snow; but some people would endure all the
snow-storms of Quebec or Winnipeg rather than one sand-storm
in Frisco.

On Saturday morning Oct. 19th we breakfasted at the Lick
House, San Francisco.   On Saturday the 26th we breakfasted
at home in Ottawa.

———

And how does the country crossed by the Union and Central
Pacific Railways compare with our own north-west, has been
asked us since our return?   Comparisons are odious and therefore
the answer shall be as brief as possible.   The Pacific slope
excepted, for there is nothing in British Columbia to compare
with the fertile valleys of California, everything is so completely

in our favour that there is really no comparison except the old racing one of "Eclipse first and the rest nowhere." California itself, though its yield of wheat in favourable years is marvellous, is not a country to rear a healthy and hardy race. There is no summer or autumn rain-fall; the air is without its due proportion of moisture; and the lack of moisture is supplied by dust. The people look enervated, weary, and used up. In the course of a generation or two, unless a constant infusion of fresh blood renews their strength, the influences of climate must tell disastrously not only on their physique but on their whole spirit and life. Are Anglo-Saxons secure from falling into the same sleepy and unprogressive state, that the energetic Spaniards, who first settled the country, soon sank into?

But when we leave California and travel from twelve to fifteen hundred miles, through Utah, Nevada, Wyoming, and Eastern Nebraska, the contrast with our North-west is startling. Certainly population has been attracted to various points over this vast region. The Mormons with infinite toil and patience, have made the deserts of Utah bring forth food for man and beast, but they are deserts notwithstanding and yield nothing unless carefully irrigated; and the mean houses of logs or adobé—as sun dried clay bricks are called,—and the unintelligent careworn countenances of the people do not testify very eloquently in favour of Utah. The State of Nevada is rich in minerals, especially in silver; and the railway has been the means of developing these to a great extent, while the export of the bullion supplies to the railway a considerable local trafic. Along the Humboldt, and in side valleys, large herds of stock are fed ; and in parts of Wyoming, and Eastern Nebraska also, stock raising is carried on with profit. But what a country to live in ! Every where it has a uniform dry, dusty, or what an Australian writer would call "God-forsaken" look. For more than a thousand miles not a tree or shrub except sage-brush or grease-

wood, relieves the desolation.   And yet this is the country that
guide books describe as if it were the garden of the Lord, and to
which they summon the millions of Europe.   As we sat in the
railway train and read the description of the land we were passing
through ; read of boundless tracts of the finest pasturage in the
world ; of free soil on which anything and everything could be
raised, of slopes that would yet be clad with vines and bear the
rarest fruits ; and then looked out of the window and saw
limitless stretches of desert or semi-desert, high, arid, alkaline
plateaus, dotted scantily with miserable sage-brush, hundreds of
miles withont a blade of grass, a soil composed of disintegrated
lava and hard clay, or disintegrated granite or sandstone, or a
conglomerate of the two, we could hardly believe our eyes.   The
American desert is a great reality.   It is utterly unfit for the
growth of cereals or to support in any way a farming population,
because of its elevation, its lack of rain, and the miserable quality, or to speak more correctly, the absence, of soil.   The enterprise that ran "the pony express," that constructed telegraphs
and a line of Railway across such a country is wonderful ; but
not half so wonderful as the faith that sees in such a desert an
earthly paradise, or the assurance that publishes its visions of
what ought to be, for pictures of what is, or the courage that
volunteers the sacrifice of any number of foreigners to prove the
sincerity of its faith.

In a word, after reaching the summit of the first range of
mountains, from the Pacific, the railway in the United States
has to cross more than a thousand miles of desert or semi-desert.
According to the evidence of our senses, whatever guide-books
may say to the contrary, we discovered on "the home stretch"
that the great west of the United States, practically ceases with
the valley of the Missouri and of its tributary the Platte.

CHAPTER XIII.

CONCLUSION.

Crossing and re-crossing the Continent.—Writers on the North-west.—Mineral wealth behind Lake Superior.—The "Fertile-belt."—Our fellow travellers.—The "Rainbow" of the North-west.—Peace River.—Climate compared with Ontario.—Natural riches of the Country. — The Russia of America. — Its army of construction. — The pioneers.—Esprit de corps. — Hardships and hazards. — Mournful death-roll. — The work of construction — Vast breadth of the Dominion. — Its varied features.—Its exhaustless resources.—Its constitution.—Its Queen.

The preceding chapters are transcribed —almost verbally— from a Diary that was written from day to day on our journey from Ocean, Ocean-ward. The Diary was kept under many difficulties. Notes had to be taken, sometimes in the bottom of a canoe and sometimes leaning against a stump or a tree; on horseback in fine weather, under a cart when it was raining or when the sun's rays were fierce; at night, in the tent, by the light of the camp-fire in front; in a crowded wayside inn, or on the deck of a steamer in motion. And they were written out in the first few weeks after our return, as it was desirable,—if published at all—that they should be in the printer's hands at once.

As may be seen by a reference to the Itinerary in the Appendix, our Diary commenced at Halifax on the Atlantic coast on July 1st the sixth anniversary of the birth-day of the Dominion, and closed at Victoria on the Pacific coast on October 11th. The aggregate distance travelled by one mode of locomotion or another was more than five thousand miles, a great part of it over comparatively unknown, and therefore supposed to be dangerous country. We recrossed the Continent to our starting point by rail, the Secretary arriving at Halifax on November 2nd, having thus accomplished the round trip of nine or ten thousand miles in four months. None of us suffered from Indians, wild

(351)

beasts, the weather, or any of the hardships incidental to travel in a new and lone land. Every one looked, and was, physically better on his return than when he had set out. And yet there had been no playing on the road. We cannot charge ourselves with having lost an hour on the way; and Manitobans, Hudson's Bay Officers, and British Columbians all informed us that we made better time between Lake Superior and the Pacific than ever had been made before in these latitudes.

It is only fair to the public to add that the writer of the Diary knew little or nothing of our North-west before accompanying the expedition. To find out something about the real extent and resources of our Dominion; to know whether we had room and verge for an Empire or were doomed to be merely a cluster of Atlantic Provinces, ending to the west in a fertile but comparatively insignificant peninsula in Lake Huron, was the object that attracted a busy man from his ordinary work, on what friends called an absurd and perilous enterprise. All that is claimed for the preceding chapters is, that they record truthfully what we saw and heard. And having read since the works of Professor Hind, Archbishop Taché, Captain Palliser and others, we find, that though these contain the results of much more minute and extended enquiries and scientific information which renders them permanently valuable, they bring forward nothing to make us modify our own conclusions, or to lessen the impression as to the value of our North-west, that the sight of it produced in our own minds.

We are satisfied that the rugged and hitherto unknown country extending from the upper Ottawa to the Red River of the north, is not, as it has always been represented on maps executed by our neighbours, and copied by ourselves, impracticable for a Railway; but entirely the reverse; that those vast regions of Laurentian and Huronian rocks once pronounced worthless, are rich in minerals beyond conception, rich in gold, silver, copper, iron, tin, phosphates of lime, and—strange as the assertion may appear—probably coal; that in the iron back-ground to the basin of the St. Lawrence, hitherto considered valuable only for its lumber, great centres of mining and manufacturing industry, shall in the near future, spring into existence; and that for the development of all this wealth, only the construction of a Railway is necessary.

Beyond those apparently wilderness regions we came upon the fertile belt, an immense tract of the finest land in the world, bounded on the west by coal formations so extensive that all other coal fields are small in comparison. Concerning this central part of the Continent, we have testified that which we have seen, and as a summary it is sufficient to quote Hind's emphatic words, Vol. II, p. 234:

" It is a physical reality of the highest importance to the interests of " British North America that a continuous belt, rich in water, woods and " pasturage can be settled and cultivated from a few miles west of the lake " of the Woods, to the passes of the Rocky Mountains; and any line of " communication, whether by waggon road or railroad, passing through it, " will eventually enjoy the great advantage of being fed by an agricultural " population, from one extremity to the other."

Concerning the country from the Mountains to the sea, it is unnecessary to add anything here. The mountains in British Columbia certainly offer obstructions to Railway construction; but these obstacles are not insuperable, and, once overcome, we reach the Canadian Islands in the Pacific, Vancouver and Queen Charlotte,—in many respects the counter parts of Great Britain and Ireland, the western out posts of Europe,—our western islands are rich in coal, bitumenous and anthracite, and almost every variety of mineral wealth, in lumber, fish, and soil, and blessed with one of the most delightful climates in the world.

And now we might take farewell of the reader who has accompanied us on our long journey, but before doing so, it seems not

W

unfitting to add a few words concerning the routes of our fellow-travellers who parted from us at Forts Garry and Edmonton ; concerning those men whom we found engaged on the survey, and the general impressions left on our minds by all that we saw and experienced.

The Colonel spent ten days in Manitoba inspecting the military force on duty at Fort Garry, the Stone Fort and Pembina. Leaving Fort Garry, he travelled rapidly to Edmonton by the same trail that we had taken, in the hope of overtaking us before we had left for the mountains. Finding on his arrival that we had started seven days previously, he wisely decided to proceed 145 miles south-west to the Rocky Mountain House ; thence, through the country of the Blackfeet, to cross the mountains by North Kootenay Pass ; and thence into Washington Territory, U. S., and viâ Olympia to Victoria. He accomplished the journey successfully, though detained for two or three days by a snow-storm at the foot of the mountains ; but as the delay enabled him to shoot a large grizzley bear that approached within a few yards of his camp, he had no reason to regret it much. His southerly march from Edmonton gave him the opportunity of seeing the western curve of the fertile belt—"the rainbow of the North-west"—and he speaks of it, especially of that portion through the Blackfeet country, extending for about 300 miles along the eastern bases of the Rocky Mountains towards the international boundary line, with a varying breadth of from 60 to 80 miles, as the future garden of the Dominion ; magnificent in regard to scenery, with soil of surpassing richness ; and in respect of climate, with an average temperature during the winter months, 15 ° higher than that of the western portion of the Province of Ontario.

But we are now able to speak concerning a northwestern curve of the fertile belt as positively as of the district to the south which the Colonel traversed. At Edmonton, the Chief sent the

PEACE RIVER AT FORT DUNVEGAN *(looking Easterly.)*

Botanist and Horetzky northwards, with instructions to proceed by Forts Assiniboine and Dunvegan and across the Rocky Mountains by Peace River, the one to make then for the Upper Fraser, and the other to go still farther north and reach the sea by the Skeena or Nasse River. They also succeeded in their journey; and their reports more than confirm the statements of previous writers with regard to the extraordinary fertility of immense prairies along the Peace River, the salubrity, and the comparative mildness of the climate. It is quite clear that exceptional climatic causes are at work along the eastern flank of the Rocky Mountains, north as well as south of Edmonton. Whether the chief cause be warm moist winds from the Pacific or a steady current of warm air under the lee of the mountains, analogous in the atmosphere, to the Gulf stream in the ocean, or whatever the cause, our knowledge is too imperfect to enable us to say. But the great salient facts are undoubted. At Fort Dunvegan, six degrees north of Fort Garry, and nearly thirteen north of Toronto, the winters are milder than at Fort Garry ; and as for the seven months, from April to October, the period of cultivation, according to tables that have been carefully compiled, Dunvegan and Toronto do not vary more than about half a degree in mean temperature, while as compared with Halifax N. S., the difference is 1 ° 69' in favour of Dunvegan. Our two fellow-travellers assured us also that they had seen nothing between the Red River and Edmonton to compare with the fertility of soil and the beauty of the country about Peace River. They struck the mighty stream below Dunvegan and sailed on it up into the very heart of the Rocky Mountains, through a charming country, rich in soil, wood, water, and coal, in salt that can be gathered fit for the table, from the sides of springs with as much ease as sand from the sea-shore; in bitumenous fountains into which Sir Alexander McKenzie and Harmon both say that "a pole of twenty feet in length may be plunged, without the least resistance, and without finding bottom," and in every other production that is essential to the material prosperity of a country.

The following extract from the Journal of our Botanist gives a graphic description of what Peace River itself is ;—" This " afternoon we passed through the most enchanting and sublime " scenery. The right bank of the River was clothed with wood- " spruce, birch and aspen, except where two steep, or where " there had been landslides. In many places the bank rose " from the shore to the height of from 300 to 600 feet. Sand- " stone cliffs, 300 feet high, often showed, especially above " Green Island. The left bank was as high as the right, but " instead of wood, grassy slopes met the view ; but landslides " always revealed sandstone. In places, the river had cut a " passage through the sandstone to the depth of 300 feet and " yet the current indicated little increase. The river was full " from bank to bank, was fully 600 yards wide, and looked " like a mighty canal cut by giants through a mountain. Up " this we sped at the rate of four miles an hour, against the " current, in a large boat belonging to the Hudson's Bay Co'y.; " propelled by a north-east gale."

When we remember that the latitude of this river and the richest part of the country it waters is nearly a thousand miles north of the Lake Ontario, the language we have used about it may sound exaggerated because the facts seem unaccountable. But the facts have been long on record. The only difficulty was the inaccessibility of the country. In *Harmon's Journal* are such entries as the following :—

" Peace River, April 18, 1809.—This morning the ice in the " river broke up."

April 30th is shown by the public records, to be the mean time of opening of navigation at Ottawa, between 1832 and 1870. During that period, 38 years, April 17th was the earliest and May 29th the latest days of opening.

"May 6.—The surrounding plains are all on fire. We have "planted our potatoes, and sowed most of our garden seeds."

"July 21.—We have cut down our barley ; and I think it is "the finest that I ever saw in any country."

"October 6.—As the weather begins to be cold, we have taken "our vegetables out of the ground, which we find to be very "productive."

Another year we have the following entry :—

"October 3.—We have taken our vegetables out of the ground. "We have 41 bushels of potatoes, the produce of one bushel "planted the last spring. Our turnips, barley, etc., have produced "well."

In the journal of a Hudson's Bay Chief-factor published last year by Malcolm McLeod, Ottawa, is the following extract concerning the climate of Dunvegan, from the records of the celebrated traveller and astronomer—Mr. David Thompson :—

"Only twice in the month of May 1803,—on the 2nd and 14th, "did the thermometer fall to 30°. Frost did not occur in the "fall till the 27th September."

"It freezes," says Mr. Russell, "much later in May in Canada ; "and at Montreal, for seven years out of the last nine, the first "frost occurred between 24th August and 16th September."

In Halifax, N. S., the writer has seen a lively snow-storm on the Queen's birth-day ; and almost every year there is frost early in June.

Similar quotations could be given from other writers, but they are unnecessary. We know that we have a great North-west, a country like old Canada—not suited for lotus-eaters to live in, but fitted to rear a healthy and hardy race. The late Hon. W. H. Seward understood this when he declared that "vigorous, perennial, ever-growing Canada would be a Russia behind the United States." Our future is grander than even that conceived by Mr. Seward, because the elements that determine it are other than those considered by him. We shall be more than an American Russia, because the separation from Great Britain to which he invites us is not involved in our manifest destiny. We believe that union is better than disunion, that loyalty is a better guarantee for true growth than restlessness or rebellion, that building up is worthier work than pulling down. The ties that bind us to the Fatherland must be multiplied, the connection made closer and politically complete. Her traditions, her forms, her moral elevation, her historic grandeur shall be ours forever. And if we share her glory, we shall not shrink even at the outset from sharing her responsibilities.

———

A great future beckons us as a people onward. To reach it, God grant to us purity and faith, deliverance from the lust of personal aggrandizement, unity, and invincible steadfastness of purpose. The battles we have to fight are those of peace, but they are not the less serious and they are surely nobler than those of war. The victories we require to gain are over all forms of political corruption, the selfish spirit of separation, and those great material obstacles in the conquest of which the spirit of patriotism is strengthened. It is a standing army of engineers, axemen and brawny labourers that we require, men who will not only give "a fair day's work for a fair day's wage," but whose work shall be ennobled by the thought that they are in the service of their country and labouring for its consolidation. Why should there not be a high *esprit de corps* among men who are doing the country's work as well as among those who do its warfare? And why should the country grudge its honours to servants on whose faithfulness so much depends? "There is many a red-coat who is no soldier," said the Duke of Wellington. Conversely, there are true soldiers who wear only a red shirt.

PL. 69.

FORKS OF SKEENA RIVER *(January* 1873).

This thought leads us to make mention of the men who have been engaged for the last two years in connection with the Canadian Pacific Railway Survey, the pioneers of the great army that must be engaged on the construction of the work and on whom has devolved the heavy labour that commonly falls to the lot of an advance-guard. On our journey we met several of the surveying parties, and could form some estimate of the work they had to do. We could see that continuous labour for one or two years in solitary wilderness or mountain gorges as surveyor, transit-man, leveller, rodman, commissary, or even packer, is a totally different thing from taking a trip across the continent for the first time, when the perpetual novelty, the spice of romance, the risks and pleasures atone for all discomforts. Here are one or two instances of the spirit that animates the body.

The gentleman now at the head of party X had commenced work in charge of another party between Lake Superior and the Upper Ottawa. He remained out during the whole summer and winter in that trackless rugged region, previously untrodden by white men and rarely visited by Indians. After a severe winter campaign, he completed the difficult and hazardous service entrusted to him. On his return in the spring, he was told that it was desirable that he should go to British Columbia without delay; and, though he had not spent two weeks with his family in as many years, he started at once.

Near the end of the year just closed, the Chief was called upon to send a party to explore the section of country between the North Saskatchewan, above Edmonton, and the Jasper valley. It was deemed advisable to examine this wild and wooded district in the winter season, on account of the numerous morasses and muskegs which rendered it next to impassable at any other season. The party most available for this service had been engaged during the summer and winter of 1871 and the whole of 1872 in the lake region east of Manitoba, and had returned to Fort Garry after completing satisfactorily their arduous work. The Chief asked, by telegraph, the Engineer in charge if he was prepared to start at short notice for the Rocky Mountains on a prolonged service. Almost immediately after sending this message, the following telegram was received from the gentleman referred to. " May I have leave of absence to return home for a few weeks on urgent private business ?" This was at once followed by another; "Your message received. I withdraw my application for leave. I am prepared to start for the Rocky Mountains with my party. Please send instructions." It was evident that the first two telegrams had crossed. The members of party M, notwithstanding what they had gone through, away from friends and the comforts of society, were ready to undertake a march of a thousand miles still farther away, in the dead of a Canadian winter.

And what was the journey ? They knew that it implied hardships such as Captain Butler encountered, and which he so graphically describes in " The Great Lone Land." They knew that it meant a great deal more. The journey over, they were only at the beginning of their work, and the work would be infinitely more trying than the journey itself.

These are only two instances out of many of that 'Ready, aye Ready' spirit, which the British people rightly honour as the highest quality in their soldiers, from the lowest to the highest grades. With respect to the ordinary everyday work that has to be done, our own little experience gave us some idea of its discomforts. Among the mountains, there is hardly a day without rain, except when it snows. Leather gives way under the alternate rotting and grinding processes that swamps and rocks subject it to. Mocassins keep out the wet about as well as an extra pair of socks. Clothes are patched and re-patched until lock-stock-and-barrell are changed. At night you lie down wet, lucky if the blanket is dry. In the morning you rise to a rough breakfast of tea, pork and beans. When relations at home are just enjoying the sweet half-hour's sleep before getting up, you are off into the dark silent woods, or clambering up precipices to which the mists ever cling, or on the rocky banks of some roaring river, the sound of which has become positively hateful ; getting back to camp at night tired and hungry, but still thankful if a good day's work has been accomplished. And this same thing goes on from week to week,—working, eating, sleeping. Books are scarce for they are too bulky to carry ; no newspapers and no news—unless fragments from three to six months old, strangely metamorphosed by Packers and Indians, can be dignified by the name of news. Nothing occurs to break the monotony save rheumatism, festered hands or feet, or a touch of sickness, perhaps scurvy if the campaign has been long : the arrival of a pack-train with supplies, or some such interesting event as the following, which we found duly chronicled on a blazed tree, between Moose Lake and Tête Jaune Cache :—

" BIRTH,

" Monday, 5th August 1872.

" This morning at about 5 o'clock. ' Aunt Polly,' bell-mare to
" the Nth. Thompson-trail parties pack-train, was safely delivered
" of a Bay Colt, with three white legs and white star on forehead.
   " This wonderful progeny of a C. P. R. Survey's pack-train, is
" in future to be known, to the racing community of the Pacific
" slope, as Rocky Mountain Ned."

The Sunday rest and the next meal, are almost the only pleasures looked forward to ; and the enjoyment of eating arises, generally, not from the delicacies or variety of the fare, but from the appetite brought to it ; for luxuries, as we had considered fat pork, porridge, good bread, and coffee, after three weeks on pemmican, they need all the zest that hard work and mountain air can supply, in order to be thoroughly enjoyed three times a day, week in and week out.

In addition to all the—not ordinary but—extraordinary discomforts attending this class of work there are the dangers to
life, inseparable from the great extent of the work undertaken ;
the rapidity with which it was begun and pushed forward ;
extensives fires in the forest ; drowning, while endeavouring to
make the passage of some lake or river in a frail canoe or on a
raft ; to say nothing of starvation, which, notwithstanding the
utmost care and forethought, might, nay in some instances did
very nearly, occur, in consequence of accidents, like the two last
named, befalling some of the Commissariat department.

But this survey work implies more than hardships and
hazards. Already it has connected with its history a mournful
death-roll. At the outset, some tribes of Indians were expected
to give trouble. On the contrary, they have for the most part
been friendly and helpful. When nearly a thousand men were
engaged directly or indirectly on the work, and scattered over
pathless regions over a whole,continent, it would not have been
wonderful had supplies failed to reach some parties, and death
by starvation occurred. In no case has such a disaster yet happened. But there are forces that can neither be organized nor
bribed. Fourteen men have been destroyed by the elements ;
seven by fire, and seven by water ; destroyed so completely that
no trace has been found of the bodies of ten.

One party,—seven in number,—engaged in carrying provisions
north of Lake Superior, was surprised by the wide-spread forest
fires that raged over the west in the autumn of 1871. The body
of only one of its number could be discovered.

In the spring of 1872, a party that had finished its work well,
after an arduous winter campaign far up the Ottawa beyond
Lake Temiscamang, prepared to return home. The gentleman in
charge and one of his assistants separated from the rest, to take
on board their canoe two others who had been previously left at
a side post prostrated with scurvy. The four were known to

have then started down the river. That was the last seen of them, though the upturned canoe was found, and it told its own tale of an upset by rock or rapid or awkward movement of the sick men into ice-cold lake or river.

In the autumn of 1872, three others, on their way to begin their winter's work, were shipwrecked and drowned in the Georgian Bay.

All those men died in the service of their country as truly as if they had been killed in battle. Some of them have left behind wives and little children, aged parents, young brothers or sisters, who were dependent on them for support. Have not those a claim on the country that ought not to be disregarded?

That this work is too seldom looked at from any other save the "wages" point of view, is our excuse for putting the real state of the case warmly. Who are the men whose disciplined enthusiasm enables them to manifest the self-sacrifice we have alluded to? Many of them are men of good birth and education, who have chosen the profession of Engineering as one in which their talents can be made in a marked degree subservient to the material prosperity of mankind. Others have chosen it because of its supposed freedom from routine, and the prospect it is thought to offer of novelty, adventure, and such a roving life as every young Briton or Canadian, with any of the old blood in his veins, longs for.

And what 'wages' do these men, who deserve so well of their country, receive? Simply their pay by the month! They do not know whether they will have the satisfaction—that every man interested in his work has the right to look forward to—of seeing their work finished by themselves. Even after the preliminary surveys are completed, and the work placed under contract, the tenure of office is insecure. Sometimes a clamour is raised, against the presumed extravagance of the Government, when the newspapers have nothing more stirring to write about, or when some reporter fancies he has not received due attention. At other times, some unfeeling and unprincipled contractors conspire to effect the removal of men, whose only fault is that they have performed their duty faithfully. From these or other similar causes, engineers in the public service are sometimes most unjustly sacrificed. And, if remonstrance is made, the answer is ready.—'They received their pay for the time they were employed, and others, quite as competent, are ready and willing to take their places.'—Yes, and the same might be said of the officers and men of the British army, but they are treated very differently. The work performed on one of the military expeditions, such as the Abyssinian or Red River, about which so much has been written, and which are said to have shed such lustre on the British name, is really not more arduous than theirs The heaviest part of a soldier's duty on such expeditions it is well known is the long laborious marching. The work of engineers on the survey is a constant march ; their shelter, even in the depth of winter, often only canvass; they have sometimes to carry their food for long distances, through swamps and over fallen trees, on their backs; and run all the risks incidental to such a life, without medical assistance, without notice from the press, without the prospect of plunder or promotion, ribands or pensions. To be sure theirs is the work of *construction* only, and the world has always given greater prominence to the work of *destruction.*

To *construct* is "the duty that lies nearest us." "We therefore will rise up and build." Our young Dominion in grappling with so great a work has resolutely considered it from a national and not a strictly financial point of view; knowing that whether it 'pays' directly or not, it is sure to pay indirectly. Other young countries have had to spend, through long years, their strength and substance to purchase freedom or the right to exist. Our lot is a happier one. Protected "against infection and the hand

Pl. 60.

GREAT VALLEY OF PEACE RIVER (through the Rocky Mountains.)

of war" by the might of Britain, we have but to go forward, to open up for our children and the world what God has given into our possession, bind it together, consolidate it, and lay the foundations of an enduring future.

Looking back over the vast breadth of the Dominion when our journeyings were ended, it rolled out before us like a panorama, varied and magnificent enough to stir the dullest spirit into patriotic emotion. For nearly 1,000 miles by railway between different points east of Lake Huron; 2,185 miles by horses, including coaches, waggons, pack, and saddle-horses; 1,687 miles in steamers in the basin of the St. Lawrence and on Pacific waters. and 485 miles in canoes or row-boats; we had travelled in all 5,300 miles between Halifax and Victoria, over a country with features and resources more varied than even our modes of locomotion.

From the sea-pastures and coal-fields of Nova Scotia and the forests of New Brunswick, almost from historic Louisburg up the St. Lawrence to historic Quebec; through the great Province of Ontario, and on lakes that are really seas; by copper and silver mines so rich as to recall stories of the Arabian Nights, though only the rim of the land has been explored; on the chain of lakes, where the Ojibbeway is at home in his canoe, to the great plains, where the Cree is equally at home on his horse; through the prairie Province of Manitoba, and rolling meadows and park-like country, equally fertile, out of which a dozen Manitobas shall be carved in the next quarter of a century; along the banks of

A full-fed river winding slow
By herds upon an endless plain,

full-fed from the exhaustless glaciers of the Rocky Mountains, and watering 'the great lone land;' over illimitable coal measures and deep woods; on to the mountains, which open their gates, more widely than to our wealthier neighbours, to lead

us to the Pacific ; down deep gorges filled with mighty timber,
and rivers whose ancient deposits are gold beds, sands like those
of Pactolus and channels choked with fish ; on to the many
harbours of mainland and island, that look right across to the
old Eastern Thule 'with its rosy pearls and golden-roofed
palaces,' and open their arms to welcome the swarming millions
of Cathay ; over all this we had travelled, and it was all our
own.

> " Where's the coward that would not dare
> To fight for such a land?"

Thank God, we have a country. It is not our poverty of land,
or sea, of wood or mine that shall ever urge us to be traitors.
But the destiny of a country depends not on its material
resources. It depends on the character of its people. Here, too,
is full ground for confidence. We in everything " are sprung,
of earth's first blood, have titles manifold." We come of a
race that never counted the number of its foes, nor the
number of its friends, when freedom, loyalty, or God was concerned.

Two courses are possible, though it is almost an insult to say
there are two, for the one requires us to be false to our traditions and history, to our future. and to ourselves. A third course
has been hinted at ; but only dreamers or emasculated intellects
would seriously propose " Independence " to four millions of
people, face to face with thirty-eight millions. Some one may have
even a fourth to propose. The Abbe Sieyes had a cabinet filled
with pigeon-holes, in each of which was a cut-and-dried Constitution for France. *Doctrinaires* fancy that at any time they can
say, ' go to, let us make a Constitution,' and that they can fit it
on a nation as readily as new coats on their backs. There never
was a profounder mistake. A nation grows, and its Constitution
must grow with it. The nation cannot be pulled up by the
roots,—cannot be dissociated from its past, without danger to its

highest interests. Loyalty is essential to its fulfilment of a distinctive mission,—essential to its true glory. Only one course therefore is possible for us, consistent with the self-respect that alone gains the respect of others; to seek, in the consolidation of the Empire, a common Imperial citizenship, with common responsibilities, and a common inheritance.

With childish impatience and intolerance of thought on the subject, we are sometimes told that a Republican form of Government and Republican institutions, are the same as our own. But they are not ours. Besides, they are not the same in themselves; they are not the same in their effects on character. And, as we are the children even more than we are the fathers and framers of our national institutions, our first duty is to hold fast these political forms, the influences of which on national character have been proved by the tests of time and comparison to be the most ennobling. Republicanism is one-sided. Despotism is other-sided. The true form should combine and harmonize both sides.

The favourite principle of Robertson, of Brighton, that the whole truth in the realm of the moral and spiritual consists in the union of two truths that are contrary but not contradictory, applies also to the social and political. What two contrary truths then lie at the basis of a complete National Constitution? First, that the will of the people is the will of God. Secondly, that the will of God must be the will of the people. That the people are the ultimate fountain of all power is one truth. That Government is of God, and should be strong, stable, and above the people is another. In other words, the elements of liberty and of authority should both be represented. A republic is professedly based only on the first. In consequence, all popular appeals are made to that which is lowest in our nature, for such appeals are made to the greatest number and are most likely to be immediately successful. The character of public men and

the national character deteriorate. Neither dignity, elevation
of sentiment, nor refinement of manners is cultivated. Still more
fatal consequences, the very ark of the nation is carried period-
ically into heady fights; for the time being, the citizen has no
country; he has only his party, and the unity of the country is
constantly imperilled. On the other hand, a despotism is based
entirely on the element of authority.

To unite those elements, in due proportions, has been and is
the aim of every true statesman. Let the history of liberty and
progress, of the development of human character to all its rightful issues, testify where they have been more wisely blended
than in the British Constitution.

We have a fixed centre of authority and government, a fountain of honour above us that all reverence, from which a thousand
gracious influences come down to every rank; and, along with
that fixity, representative institutions, so elastic that they respond
within their own sphere to every breath of popular sentiment,
instead of a cast-iron yoke for four years. In harmony with
this central part of our constitution, we have an independent
judiciary instead of judges—too often the creatures of wealth,
adventurers on the mere echoes of passing popular sentiment.—
And, more valuable than even the direct advantages, are the
subtle, indirect influences that flow from our living in unbroken
connection with the old land, and the dynamical if imponderable
forces that determine the tone and mould the character of a
people.

"In our halls is hung armoury of the invincible knights of old."
Ours' are the old history, the misty past, the graves of forefathers.
Ours the names 'to which a thousand memories call.' Ours is
the flag; ours the Queen whose virtues transmute the sacred
principle of loyalty into a personal affection.

OCEAN TO OCEAN.

SANDFORD FLEMING'S OVERLAND EXPEDITION.

....

ITINERARY.

....

Journey from Halifax, on the North Atlantic, to Victoria, on the North Pacific, between July 1st and October 11th 1872.

DATE.	DESIGNATION OF PLACES BY THE WAY.		ESTIMATED MILES TRAVELLED.				
			LAND		WATER		TOTAL
			Rail	Horses	Stea'r	Canoe	
1872							
July 1.	From Halifax, along the route of the Intercolonial Railway, under construction and partly in operation, to Riviere du Loup.	To Truro	61				
		" Moncton.............	50	76			
		" Miramichi	19	......	115		
		" Bathurst	......	45			
		" Metapedia............	......	80			
		" Rimouski.............	......	110			
		" Riv. du Loup......	......	66			622
July 9.	From Riviere du Loup along the Grand Trunk, St. Lawrence & Ottawa and Northern Railways to Collingwood.	" Quebec.............	126				
		" Montreal............	166				
		" Ottawa.............	166				
		" Toronto.............	275				
		" Collingwood........	94				827
July 16.	From Collingwood by steamer through the Georgian Bay, Lake Huron and Lake Superior to Thunder Bay.	" Owen Sound	......	......	45		
		" Killarney...........	......	......	100		
		" Bruce mines........	......	......	135		
		" Sault Ste. Marie....	......	......	50		
		" Michipicoten Island	......	......	115		
		" Nepigon	......	......	150		
		" Thunder Bay......	......	......	100		695
July 22.	From Thunder Bay along the Dawson route to						
23.	Fort Garry.* Camp No.1.	" Shebandowan......	......	45			
24.	" 2.	" Brulé Portage......	......	......	......	60	
25.	" 3.	" Camp Ignace.......	......	......	......	55	
26.	" 4.	" American Portage..	......	......	......	61	
27.	" 5.	" Rainy Lake.......	......	......	......	60	
28.	" 6.	" Hungry Hall.......	......	......	......	90	
29.	" 7.	" Island Camp........	......	......	......	8	
29.	" 8.	" Northwest Angle....	......	......	......	70	
30.	" 9.	" Oak Point.....	......	80			
31.	" 10.	" Government House.	......	30			539
				Carried Forward.....			2,683

* Camps numbered from Lake Superior.

ITINERARY,—Continued.

DATE.	DESIGNATION OF PLACES BY THE WAY.		ESTIMATED MILES TRAVELLED.				
			LAND		WATER		TOTAL
1872			Rail	Horses	Stea'r	Canoe	
							2,683
Aug. 1.	From Fort Garry to Stone Fort and back.	Brought forward					
		To Government House.		40			
							40
		Camp.					
2.	From Fort Garry	No. 11.	" White Horse Plains.		33			
3.	to Fort Ellice.*	" 12.	" Rat Creek		37			
4.		" 13.	" Three Creeks		24			
5		" 14.	" Camp Assiniboine		40			
6.		" 15.	" Salt Lake		41			
7.		" 16.	" Qu'Appelle		45			
							220
8.	From Fort Ellice	" 17.	" Broken Arm River.		31			
9.	to Fort Carlton.	" 18.	" Lonely Tree		43			
10.		" 19.	" Little Touchwood		41			
11.		" "	" " "		"			
12.		" 20.	" Touchwood		43			
13.		" 21.	" Quill Lake Plain		42			
14.		" 22.	" Round Hill		43			
15.		" 23.	" S. Saskatchewan		46			
16.		" 24.	" Fort Carlton		18			
							307
17.	From Fort Carlton	" 25.	" Bears Paddling La.		38			
18.	to Fort Pitt.	" "	" " "		"			
19.		" 26.	" Jack-fish River		48			
20.		" 27.	" English River		41			
21.		" 28.	" Fort Pitt Guard		40			
							167
22.	From Fort Pitt to	" 29.	" Moose Creek		40			
23.	Fort Edmonton.	" 30.	" Snake Lake		42			
24.		" 31.	" Victoria Mission		40			
25.		" "	" " "		"			
26.		" 32.	" Deep Creek		44			
27.		" 33.	" Fort Edmonton		27			
							193
28.	From Ft. Edmon-	" 34.	" St. Albert		11			
29.	ton to Jasper	" 35.	" St. Anns'		39			
30.	House.	" 36.	" Round Lake		12			
31.		" 37.	" Lobstick Creek		29			
Sept. 1.		" "	" " "		"			
2.		" 38.	" Valad's Camp		26			
3.		" 39.	" Camp Minnie		23			
4.		" 40.	" McLeod River Camp		17			
5.		" 41.	" Indian Camp		12			
6.		" 42.	" Muskeg Camp		20			
7.		" 43.	" Plum Pudding Camp		21			
8.		" "	" " "		"			
9.		" 44.	" Bayonette Camp		25			
10.		" 45.	" Beaver Camp		17			
11.		" 46.	" Island Camp		26			
							278
		Carried Forward					3,883

* Distances between Fort Garry and Edmonton were measured by "Odometer."

ITINERARY,—Continued.

DATE.	DESIGNATION OF PLACES BY THE WAY.		LAND		WATER		TOTAL
			Rail	Horses	Stea'r	Canoe	
1872							
	Camp	Brought Forward.					3,888
Sept 12.	From Jasper No. 47.	To Jasper Lake.		4			
13.	House to Yellow " 48.	" Athabasca Camp...		15			
14.	Head Pass. " 49.	" Caledonian Valley.		17			
15.	" 50.	" Yellow Head Camp.		4			
							50
16.	From Yellow Head " 51.	" Moose Lake Camp..		40			
17.	Pass to Kam- " 52.	" Herd Camp.		4			
18.	loops. " 53.	" Camp Fraser.		13			
19.	" 54.	" Canoe River.		31			
20.	" 55.	" Albreda Camp.		25			
21.	" 56.	" Camp Cheadle.		26			
22.	" "	" "					
23.	" 57.	" Headless Indian..		13			
24.	" 58.	" Camp V.		14			
25.	" 59.	" Round Prairie.		14			
26.	" 60.	" Bunch Grass Camp		26			
27.	" 61.	" Camp Thompson..		12		25	
28.	" 62.	" Kamloops.				10	
							533
29.	From Kamloops to New	" Kamloops.					
30.	Westminster.	" Cornwalls.		58		16	
Oct 1.		"					
2.		" Lytton		48			
3.		" Yale.		56			
4.		" New Westminster..			95		
							253
5.	From New Westminster	" Burrard Inlet.		8	32		
6.	to Victoria. On board	" Waddington Harb'r			100		
7.	the steamer "Sir James	" Seymour Narrows..			80		
8.	Douglas."	" Nanaimo.			100		
9.		" Victoria.			80		
							400
10.	From Victoria to Alberni.	" Pacific Ocean.			150		
11.	Barclay Sound and back	" " "			150		
	Str. Sir James Douglas.						
							500
		Total Mileage..	957	2,185	1,687	485	5,314

SUMMARY.

	Miles.
Distance travelled by Railway	957
" " Horses, including waggon, pack and saddle horses	2,185
" " Steamers—on St. Lawrence and Pacific waters	1,687
" " Canoes or row-boats	485

From Halifax to Victoria   }.................................. Total miles.... 5,314
between July 1st and Oct. 11th. }